Flights of Imagination

Flights of Imagination

AVIATION | LANDSCAPE | DESIGN

Sonja Dümpelmann

UNIVERSITY OF VIRGINIA PRESS | CHARLOTTESVILLE AND LONDON

University of Virginia Press
© 2014 by the Rector and Visitors of the University of Virginia
Printed in the United States of America on acid-free paper
First published 2014

9 8 7 6 5 4 3 2 1

Library of Congress Cataloging-in-Publication Data
Dümpelmann, Sonja.
Flights of imagination : aviation, landscape, design /
Sonja Dümpelmann.
pages cm
Includes bibliographical references and index.
ISBN 978-0-8139-3581-2 (cloth : alk. paper)
ISBN 978-0-8139-3584-3 (ebook)
1. Airports — Location. 2. Airports — Landscape architecture.
3. Land use — Planning. 4. Aerial photography in landscape
design. I. Title.
TL725.3.L6D86 2014
711'.78 — dc23   2014003955

To my parents

Contents

Acknowledgments

In the course of writing this book, I received the help and support of many institutions and individuals to whom I am very grateful. The Graham Foundation for Advanced Studies in the Fine Arts provided generous funding to support this publication. The Foundation for Landscape Studies also facilitated this book's publication through their David R. Coffin Publication Grant. The Department of Plant Science and Landscape Architecture and the Graduate School at the University of Maryland (UMD) offered institutional and financial support. In 2010, I was awarded a Research and Scholarship Award by the UMD Graduate School in support of this project, and a nine-month fellowship at the Dumbarton Oaks Research Library and Collection of Harvard University gave me the precious time, peace, and quiet to work on some of the chapters of this book.

Archivists and librarians at the University of Maryland, Dumbarton Oaks, University of Illinois Urbana-Champaign, University of Miami, University of Nebraska–Lincoln, Harvard University, Harvard Graduate School of Design, Hoover Institution at Stanford University, U.S. National Air and Space Museum, Library of Congress, U.S. National Archives and Records Administration, Rockefeller Center Archives, Rockefeller Archive Center, Museum of the City of New York, Nebraska State Historical Society, Kansas Historical Society, Connecticut State Archives in Hartford, Imperial War Museum London, Landscape Institute London, the National Archives UK, British Airways Heritage Center, Department of Geography at Bonn University, State Archives of the City of Hamburg, Bundesarchiv Berlin-Lichterfelde, Landesarchiv Berlin, South African Airways Museum Society, Royal Academy of Fine Arts School of Architecture Copenhagen, and the Danish Art Library Copenhagen helpfully answered questions and made materials accessible. I am also thankful to Steven N. Handel; the staff of the Great Park Design Studio–Ken Smith Landscape Architect; Eelco Hooftman and staff at Gross.Max.; Gabriele Kiefer and staff at Büro Kiefer Landschaftsarchitektur Berlin; David Anselmi, Vice President of Operations and Planning at Parc Downsview Park Inc.; Maarten Buijs and the staff of West 8 Urban Design & Landscape Architecture; Michael Krebs of Grün Berlin

GmbH; and Richard Turner of the Metropolitan Washington Airports Authority for offering insights into their work and making materials available. Mary Daniels, Adam Kellie, and Inés Zalduendo at the Frances Loeb Library of the Harvard Graduate School of Design provided assistance with some last-minute queries and photographs.

Richard Etlin, Keith Morgan, Marc Treib, and Jack Williams supported this project all along, and John Beardsley, John Dixon Hunt, Keith Morgan, Joshua Shannon, and Terence Young read parts of the manuscript and provided valuable feedback. All shortcomings remain my own. I would like to thank Harold Platt and Marc Treib for the illustrations and references they sent, Gert Gröning and Kenneth Helphand for the inspiring conversations, Susan Herrington for her support, David Lazar for the initial choice of title, Toshihiro Higuchi and Eva Clymans for their help in translating Japanese and Dutch texts, and Terence Young for driving and joining me on my excursion to the Orange County Great Park. Shortly after concluding this book manuscript, I cotaught a seminar class at the Harvard Graduate School of Design together with Charles Waldheim. I am truly grateful to Charles for this opportunity and for the enthusiasm in airport landscape and airport-related topics we share.

During the time I was working on the project, I presented papers on selected parts at a variety of conferences including the 2008 meeting of the Society of Architectural Historians, the 2009 conference of the Society of American City and Regional Planning History, and the 2011 meeting of the European Society of Environmental Historians, receiving valuable questions and feedback. A first overview of parts of the project was published in *Landscape Journal* in 2010, and portions of chapter 4 were published in *Kunst Garten Kultur,* edited by Gert Gröning and Stefanie Hennecke (2010), and in *Ordnance: War + Architecture and Space,* edited by Gary Boyd and Denis Linehan (2012). First ideas for chapter 6 appeared in *Stadt und Grün* (October 2009). I thank the publishers and editors of these publications for their permission to incorporate materials into this book.

Boyd Zenner at the University of Virginia Press was most generous with her time and expertise and supported this project from its beginning. Mark Mones, Angie Hogan, and Susan Murray provided crucial assistance in transforming the manuscript and images into this printed book. I am very thankful to all of them.

I am grateful to my parents, who have always been encouraging and supportive of my flights of fancy and imagination even if they took me far from home. My father taught me how to take a hurdle in more ways than one. My mother has been the unwavering reader of all my texts and papers. She overcame her fear of flight for the first time in 2005 to visit me in the United States.

Flights of Imagination

Introduction

Flight, in particular powered flight, which first developed in the early twentieth century, has changed our perspectives on the world, has transformed our perceptions and imaginations of the world, and has changed the landscape itself and the ways we design and inhabit it. This book is about the new horizons that powered flight has provided to professionals designing and planning the built environment, including architects, landscape architects, and urban planners and designers. It deals with those moments during the twentieth and early twenty-first centuries when these professionals developed an aerial imagination and an epistemology based upon aerial vision, and when they realized the opportunities that the new technology offered them in shaping the land. It is about their various efforts in both utilizing and forming the new technology, and in turning the interface between earth and sky into a place where the earth meets the sky.

Altitude and verticality are often associated with knowledge, authority, power, virility, duty, and activity, whereas horizontality can symbolize submission and passivity. Flying meant conquering a new vertical, or, air space. However, perhaps aware of our vulnerability in the sky and of our human destiny, we have only desired flight when we know we can depart from and return to earth safely. After all, as human beings we are bound to earth through death, and only after death—as many religious cultures believe—may we ascend. As Kazimir Malevich, whose work was inspired by airplanes and the aerial view, observed in the 1920s: "His entire life [man] fights for his upright, conscious active position—for the vertical—. . . and he inevitably succumbs—to sleep and finally death."[1] How did landscape architects, architects, and urban planners involved in shaping the built environment work in this field characterized by the tension between the allure of the sky and the new and seemingly limitless opportunities offered by flight and aerial vision, and the gravitational pull back toward the earth necessitated by their own work and the limiting constraints of the conditions on the ground?

Dealing with both the airport landscape and the aerial view, this book presents the twentieth-century and twenty-first-century landscape as a motor and a product of increased aerial mobility. Examining the relationship between powered flight and the landscape, the book reveals a variety of ambiguities that are also characteristic of modernity in general. Airports were conceived both as cities and as landscapes, and they both instigated and resulted from conceiving of and planning air space on regional, national, and international scales. Planning and designing airports on the ground required that attention be paid to the space above ground. While early powered flight was dependent on nature in the sense that it required certain ground and climatic conditions, the technological development of faster, bigger, and more maneuverable airplanes soon demanded that these natural conditions be adapted to the new technologies as far as possible. Tracing the evolution and conceptualization of the airport as landscape, it appears as both a catalyst and a product of globalization. At the same time, the manufactured airport landscape offers features that act as vernacular counterpoints within an increasingly standardized technological environment. Many designers from the 1920s onward conceived of the airport landscape as a hybrid landscape with contrasting modernist and vernacular character traits and as an expression of what more recently has been called "glocalism." In operation and closed, airports have always been positioned at the nexus between the local and the global, and between nature and technology.

While the airport landscape had to be designed to be experienced on the ground, it also had to accommodate the vertical view. Design professionals in the early twentieth century began to understand the aerial view as a way of knowing that was both disembodied and embodied, abstract and experiential, rational and imaginary, factual and aesthetic, microscopic and macroscopic, detailed and contextual, harmful and essential. Francesco Petrarch's frequently cited self-conscious notation of the land from the elevated perspective of Mont Ventoux near Avignon in the late Middle Ages foreshadowed this dialectic, and the ambivalence, ambiguity, and fluidity of scales that characterized the aerial view in the twentieth century. In the context of this book, therefore, Petrarch's relatively meager portrayal of the actual prospect from the "Windy Mountain" over the Italian Alps, the Province of Lyon, the Rhône, and the bay of Marseilles is less important than the inner conflict in which he found himself. He was torn between the admiration of the bird's-eye view on the one hand, and his devotion to God, his religious duties, and his own soul, past feelings, and motivations on the other.[2] While it is the subjective account and the allegories used in the letter that have led scholars to characterize Petrarch as one of the first humanists, the account's setting also makes him a figure of transition between the Middle Ages and the modern world, in which it became common to seek out landscape prospects for both the pleasurable experience and the scientific revelations they offered.

The contrasting qualities of the aerial view, and the fact that it has repeatedly and in various contexts been used to draw attention back to the ground, are recurring themes in this book. For twentieth-century landscape architects, architects, and urban planners, the view from above was both affective and objective, contextual and detailed. It provided control and surveillance, as well as inspiration and freedom for the imagination. It became clear that aerial vision was necessary for both attack and defense in warfare, and that it could support plans for conservation and destruction in urban and environmental planning. In addition, powered flight and progress in aerial photography enabled shifting relatively flexibly, smoothly, and effortlessly between scales.

Before they were first confronted with powered flight and the opportunities it offered, landscape architects' and architects' experience in designing and planning for machine-powered transportation had been limited to the train and the automobile. In the nineteenth century, gardens had been laid out at railroad stations to advertise a town or suburban development. The gardens often exhibited the latest horticultural fads and provided fresh flowers for dining cars and for purchase by passengers.[3] In 1902, the American City Beautiful advocate Charles Mulford Robinson promoted "the railroad beautiful," a network of station gardens and plantings along railroads that he hoped could "have an even national importance, changing the face of the country 'as seen from the car window,' and carrying its influence very far."[4] The railroad also inspired landscape architects to consider how train passengers and observers perceived landscape. The experience of European station gardens, and the fascination with the new means of transportation and its velocity, induced the American railroad garden advocate Donald G. Mitchell to argue in 1867 for openings in screen plantings on embankments so that the train's movement and speed seemed enhanced, thereby heightening the onlooker's experience. At the same time, these "windows" would enable train passengers to view the scenery through which they were passing.[5] The railroad and its increased speed of passenger travel may also have influenced the design of nineteenth-century public urban parks, where scenes abruptly alternated between sublime, picturesque, and beautiful effects; in eighteenth-century landscape gardens, scenes were designed to unfold slowly to the walking or carriage-driven visitor.[6] With the development of the mass-produced automobile at the beginning of the twentieth century, opportunities for landscape architects multiplied. In the United States, they were involved in laying out tree-lined parkways to connect urban public parks and in designing scenic drives and roads along the Blue Ridge Mountains and in numerous other locations to provide for pleasurable drives between cities, in the country, and to state parks.

In 1922, Charles W. Eliot noted that the automobile also required designs for simple and broad views rather than "intimate and confined views" that could not "be appreciated from a fast moving vehicle." Adopting the eighteenth- and nineteenth-century scopic regime of the landscape garden to the conditions of early-twentieth-century automobile culture meant that openings and vistas through woods or shrubbery had to be wider and farther apart, and "every accent of the prospect and planting" had to be "stronger because of the brief time in which it [was] seen."[7] Comparing the visual experience of automobile travel to that of a movie film and its rapidly moving images, Eliot noted that designs needed to exaggerate details. Skeptical of the effects of "this rush of life and its accompanying slurring of attention to the perfection of details," he asked whether "automobiles and the other concomitants of the rush of life" were ultimately "to govern and control" the art of landscape architecture.[8]

As soon as aviation took off, therefore, the question was how far this new technological accomplishment would influence the practice of landscape architecture and lead to new designs that responded to the aerial view and the technological requirements of flight. In 1910, when airplanes were still taking off and landing on open fields, the balloonist Charles C. Turner mused that in contrast to the automobile, the "flying-machine" would not "necessitate any modification of the landscape". However, by the late 1920s, a new type of transportation hub was developing that comprised an ordered open landing field, hangars, and a terminal building housing a waiting room, a ticket sales desk, and offices.[9] The aerial perspective offered by the airplane was also considered a novelty, especially when compared to the visual experience offered by other means of transportation. A 1920s advertising brochure by the German Lufthansa AG addressed to Americans visiting Europe stressed that air passengers travelling between 1,000 and 5,000 feet (305 and 1,524 meters) above the ground could "observe in one moment from ten to twenty times as much of Old Mother Earth as from the slowly moving train." Furthermore, they would not miss the smallest detail.[10] Writing in the 1930s, Gertrude Stein commented that "the earth seen from an airplane is more splendid than the earth seen from an automobile." For her the automobile was "the end of progress on the earth" since, although it enabled greater speeds, the views it offered were "the same as the landscapes seen from a carriage, a train, a wagon, or in walking": they were horizontal.[11] The earth seen from an airplane was something else: it was vertical.

The development of powered aviation provided landscape architects, architects, and urban planners and designers with a new type of landscape to work on: the airport. It also offered them aerial views to work with, captured in aerial photographs. Observant, critical designers noted these two developments in the postwar years. In 1948, the influential pioneering British landscape architect Brenda Colvin pointed out not only that airports would become an increasingly important landscape feature, but also that "the new viewpoint" at high altitude and speed could affect the ground plan. She drew her readers' attention to the fact that urban open space, public parks, gardens, and the surroundings of important buildings and airports would "be seen from a new angle and from far greater distances than were planned for in the past."[12] From the aerial viewpoint, verticality on earth mattered less while ground pattern became more significant. Colvin suggested that broad color effects achieved by particular ground plantings and different types of turf, crops, and trees be used to treat airport surroundings.[13] The German-born architect Erwin Gutkind was less specific but equally clear when he proposed only a few years later that the architects' focus of the future would "be airports—not railway stations" and that "the aeroplane has given us a new view, a new vision and a synoptic eye." Echoing Le Corbusier, Gutkind urged his colleagues to act as "self-disciplined rebels . . . worthy of the powers which reason and instinct have placed at the disposal of humanity." He explained: "An entirely new element is introduced into the building of our cities and the re-shaping of our environment. We have the choice whether the aeroplane of the future shall be the unerring instrument, the incorruptible recorder, of INDICTMENT or FULFILLMENT."[14]

This book follows the two developments explicitly noted by Colvin and Gutkind and implicitly present in the work of many of their colleagues during the twentieth and early twenty-first centuries. It consists of three parts that parallel a flight, with takeoff (chapter 1), flight (chapters 2 through 5), and landing (chapter 6). Chapters 1 and 6 deal with the airport landscape and selected developments on the land that have occurred as a direct result of the development of powered aviation. These two chapters frame a middle part consisting of four chapters that explore how the aerial view has influenced our perception of the land and what impact it has had on design and planning, and vice versa.

Takeoff

At the beginning of the air age, the layout and design of airports quickly became a concern of airport managers, cities, and pilots, and it attracted the attention not only of engineers but also of landscape architects, architects, and urban planners. They were gripped by the general enthusiasm for aviation that swept the United States and Europe, especially after Lindbergh's 1927 flight across the Atlantic.[15] Although the American architect John

Walter Wood complained in 1940 that "the well-groomed appearance and efficiency of the modern air liners and of air-line personnel is in marked contrast to the confusion and unkempt appearance of many of our airports,"[16] many design professionals had by that time become "air-minded" and strove to take advantage of the new business opportunities the new technological accomplishment offered. The question that confronted them was how to lay out the threshold between earth and sky, and how to design the spaces of transition. They needed to accommodate both modern mobile and immobile standardized technological equipment including aircraft, runways, and radio towers for an increasingly global passenger transfer and make a place that was comfortable, calming, accommodating, and capable of rooting, or "grounding," passengers. As facilities that accommodated the new global culture of flight, airports were the quintessential modern built environment and nodes in increasingly global networks. They were organizing paradigms of a modernity that built upon a new space-time relationship enabled by powered flight.

The cartographic European flight schedules published by Lufthansa in the late 1920s and 1930s that located airports and indicated flight routes and schedules appear as adept representations of this new time-space relationship (fig. 1). Although they were not to scale, they combined a spatial cartographic representation of air routes connecting most of the major cities in Europe with the representation of scheduled flight times along these air routes. The numbers on the lines indicating the air routes were route numbers that could also be found on independent timetables that often also included price lists.[17]

By traveling at higher speeds in the air, the airplane had shrunk space and had fundamentally changed the time-space relationship. A journey from Berlin to London that in 1905 took at least twenty-four hours by rail and ship, in 1932 took only seven hours by airplane.[18] Thus, by the 1930s it had become possible to wake up in Berlin and go to sleep in London on the same day. While mail delivery in the United States from New York to San Francisco had taken four days by train in 1900, it took only twenty-six hours by plane in 1924.[19] The awareness of this new time-space relationship, a part of what was generally described at the time as air-mindedness, led the Los Angeles city planner Carol Aronovici to surmise in 1930 that city planners faced "a new phase of community building which might be called 'time-space' or fourth dimensional planning,"[20] an idea that has recently gained attention again in the form of temporary urbanism and flexible master planning.

Globalization, the new time-space relationship, and the aerial perspective influenced the design of early airport landscapes and continue today to provide landscape architects with inspiration and objectives for their airport

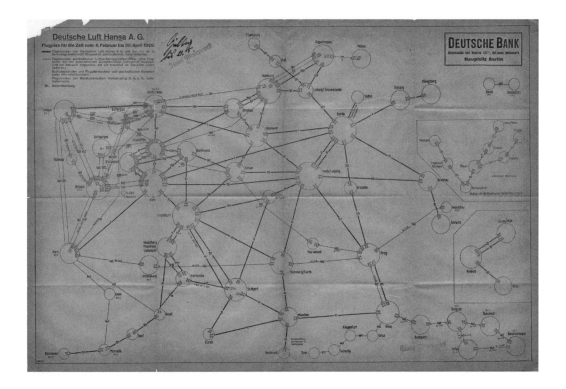

landscape designs. Chapter 1 explores early airport ideas, the conceptualization of airports as cities and landscapes, and the role that the vernacular has played in the design of these modern built environments. The universalizing classicist and modernist aesthetics used in the design of many early terminal buildings was often paired with vernacular modernist garden and open space designs. Early airports as a whole, therefore, often gave formal expression to what has been called the ambivalence of modernity: its internationalism and uprootedness on the one hand and its vernacular idioms and rootedness on the other. The airport is an example of an environment where the vernacular functioned (and still functions) as both "an agent of modernization" and "a product of globalization."[21] This becomes particularly clear in the open space laid out at Rand Airport near Johannesburg, a South African airport that in the early 1930s was serviced by the British Imperial Airways (fig. 2). The centerpiece of the airport's airside open space design was a gigantic "airman's clock" that displayed Johannesburg time (fig. 3). As Bernd Hüppauf and Maiken Umbach have observed, "the condition of modernity required a life independent of place and experienced time, the seasons, movements of sun and moon, or the individual's inner psychological sense of time,"[22] in short, a life that resembled that of a frequent air traveler. Airport environments like the one at Rand Airport were thus designed to "ground" the traveler by providing neatly laid-out parterres framing a large

FIG. 1. The 1929 spring schedule and air route plan of German Lufthansa AG. (Lufthansa via National Air and Space Museum [NASM 9A08797], Smithsonian Institution)

FIG. 2. (*Above*) Rand Airport near Johannesburg, South Africa, 1930s. (South African Airways Museum Society)

FIG. 3. (*Right*) The airman's clock at Rand Airport near Johannesburg, viewed from the control tower balcony, 1930s. (South African Airways Museum Society)

clock that displayed local time. Chapter 1 illustrates how the attempt to define a sense of place, promote cultural memory, and forge local and regional identities through the celebration of vernacular cultures has continued and can be found in a number of modern airport environments today.

Flight

Early discussions about airport design included the concern for the view from the air. Humankind has had a fascination with flight and the aerial view from time immemorial, and it has innate faculties that enable it to understand and imagine this perspective from an early age. The earliest discovered plan drawings—even if, strictly speaking, they are in most cases hybrid representations that combine plan projections with elevations—date back to about 3000 BC. Researchers have shown that young children are able to orientate themselves in aerial photographs without instruction and that Australian Aborigines could identify landscape features and locations in aerial photographs without ever before having seen any similar views of the world from above.[23] However, despite their innate and learned familiarity with plan and bird's-eye views, the new technologies that enabled powered flight and further developed aerial photography at the beginning of the twentieth century refocused design professionals' attention on the aerial view and sparked their imagination, in addition to providing them with a new tool.

The aerial view and its meaning for and utilization in landscape architecture, architecture, and urban planning at particular moments in the twentieth century form the topic of chapters 2 through 5. Powered flight has excited and inspired inventors, scientists, pilots, engineers, and the general public for about one hundred years. In the 1920s, it inspired, provided new business for, and became a helpful tool in the work of not only archaeologists, geographers, and foresters but also of professionals designing and planning the built environment. By 1930, even students in city planning were taken on aerial field trips.[24] Although initially the pursuit of a group of elitist, gifted, adventurous men and pioneering, emancipated, boundary-breaking women, flight has become democratized, and the aerial view it offers has become ubiquitous, not least because of the development of aerial photography.

As for many other professionals in the 1920s and 1930s, aerial vision became a modern way of seeing and knowing the land for designers of the built environment. The aerial view represented and constructed the world. Chapter 2 focuses on this new epistemology and on the ideas and conceptions of space and of the natural and built environment that the aerial view induced and facilitated. The aerial view flattened the earth, revealing landscape and settlement patterns, and it dissolved boundaries. The aerial view supported the conception of the city as organism and finally of the metropolitan region. In more general terms, this widening of the view also became apparent figuratively in the increasingly established understanding of landscape architecture and planning as dealing with the scale of gardens, regions, and entire nations. On the occasion of the 1937 San Francisco exhibition on contemporary landscape architecture, the architectural historian Henry-Russell Hitchcock noted that the current understanding of "modern gardening" as connecting buildings to the land and preserving "all the values of the existing natural environment" brought regional and national planning and urbanism "within the field of gardening."[25]

In the first half of the twentieth century, many designers thought that the aerial view could facilitate a new spatial understanding in landscape, architecture, and urban planning and design. When Walter Gropius described his Bauhaus buildings in Dessau, aerial views offered context and an overview of the architecture before the reader was taken on a virtual tour of the building by means of a photo-essay consisting of horizontal views. Gropius noted that the two-dimensional photograph was inadequate to portray space, or the experience of space. The aerial views, however, facilitated positioning the Bauhaus building in abstract space, and the photo-essay that guided the reader through the building's interior was meant to provide the best possible experience of tangible space, which Gropius considered the container and backdrop of movement and life itself.[26] Although axonometric plan projections resembling aerial views were a common representational tool in the 1920s and 1930s, the Bauhaus teachers also acknowledged that space could not be dealt with only on an abstract level. After all, as László Moholy-Nagy noted, space "is a reality of our sensory experience," dependent on physical movement, touch, and hearing.[27] Therefore, as much as the aerial view established a distance from the ground, it also redirected attention to the experience on the ground. The aerial view was used to explore how spaces were and could be inhabited.

Both the detailed indexical view that seemed to be "objective," to convey the truth, and that could best be captured in photographs, and the synoptic and contextual vision from airplanes were used by design professionals as critical-analytical tools. The English-born city planner Guy Wilfried Hayler estimated that "there would be fewer opponents of city planning, could they see the average city as it actually is, from the cockpit of an aeroplane."[28] Chapter 3 explains how, in the late 1920s, oblique and vertical aerial photographs were used to foster regional and national identities and how they were employed by both regionalist and avant-garde architects to both legitimize and confirm accepted opinions. Aerial photographs bolstered their urban critique of dense and dark tenement districts built in the late nineteenth century as a result of city expansion and land speculation in cities like Berlin and Vienna.

The examination of the ideology and rhetoric underlying design professionals' use of aerial imagery in the early twentieth century places some of today's developments into perspective. In the last two decades, during which the deregulation of the air carrier industry has led to the proliferation of cheap flights, the number of films and illustrated books that present aerial photographs of cities and other landscapes has greatly increased. These do not include only contemporary aerial photographs, nor do they focus only on major urban centers or renowned natural beauties and landscapes. Many new books consist of assemblages of aerial photographs taken in the early years of powered flight and portraying the historical development of small towns, cities, and entire regions.[29] In addition, since 2005 computer programs like Google Earth, Bing Maps, and Maps Live have enabled computer users to virtually fly across the world and view the earth from above in the different scales of regularly updated satellite and aerial images. This recent revival of interest in the aerial view as captured in photographs and on film has both contributed to and resulted from the recent "resurgence of local and regional 'identity politics' in the West."[30]

A case in point is a 2010 three-part television film series entitled *Germany from Above* (*Deutschland von oben*) that was advertised as "lofty television of the homeland" (Heimatfernsehen der erhabenen Art) on the German program website.[31] The success of its aerial cinematography led to a second three-part episode in 2011, and finally to the production of a movie of the same title that was shown in German theaters in June 2012. The questions posed and the statements made in the films addressed issues very similar to those that the architects Erich Ewald and Karl Heinrich Brunner explored in their illustrated books written in the 1920s and discussed in chapter 3. Despite the technological progress in aviation, aerial photography, and surveillance technology since the 1920s, the aerial view is praised now, as it was then, as a new and insightful experience and as a tool to identify good and unsuccessful city planning schemes.[32] The aerial view is seen as revealing both the wonders and the problems and challenges of the world. Like the writers of the 1920s, authors almost a century later describe how landscape features have shaped the people and their settlements and where Germany is its most authentic. Now, as in the 1920s, the broad and contextual aerial views are implicitly intended to bring the reader, or viewer, nearer to earth and nearer to the homeland.

Aerial photographs have been characterized as having the ability to forge local, regional, and even national identities and to inspire landscape architects and architects like Roberto Burle Marx and Alvar Aalto to develop design forms that have contributed to shaping their nation's cultural identity. Focusing on the use of the aerial view and the aerial imagination in landscape architecture and urban planning and design in the early twentieth century, chapter 3 shows that contemporary aerial representations in films like *Germany from Above* have precedents and that the uses assigned to the aerial view and the ideology implicit in the views from above have hardly changed despite, or rather because of, the progress in related technologies.

Flight and the views it afforded and that were captured in aerial photography became the tools Le Corbusier described as "the direct and immediate expression of progress."[33] Following developments in architecture, aerial views and axonometric projections were used in the landscape architecture of the 1930s as a visual rhetoric to signify modernity. Only in a few cases, however, did the distanced aerial view actually provide the distance necessary for the development of modernist designs based on new spatial and formal arrangements as well as on a new social order.

Closely connected with these attempts on the ground were the first roof gardens built in the European capitals and especially on skyscrapers in New York. Roof gardens were products of the aerial imagination whose construction was enabled by new building materials and styles. They were designed both as living space and as a perch from which to look down upon and out across the city, and for being looked down on from offices and apartments located on higher floors. Besides the roof gardens' immediate experiential quality, therefore, the ground patterning of these exterior spaces above ground was of importance.

World events soon required a revision of this design practice. Whereas before World War II it had often been the designers' intention to provide for gardens and open space whose artful patterns made them landmarks from above, during the war such landmarks needed to be disguised. In the countries at war, landscape architects along with architects and individuals from a number of other design professions enlisted as camouflage officers. With their skills in site analysis and design and their knowledge of plants, they were especially well trained to provide large-scale camouflage work to protect industry, airfields, and cities against the aerial view and air raids. As shown in chapter 4, landscape architecture in and of itself was to a large extent considered camouflage work. If it could be used to "cultivate beautiful air views," it could likewise be used to disguise the land. As camoufleurs, landscape architects and other design professionals acted as scenographers in the theaters of war. Guided by some of the design principles relevant in eighteenth-century landscape gardening and by the principles of Gestalt psychology, they developed site and planting designs using artificial and live materials to blend buildings unobtrusively into the landscape, camouflaging them in particular against the view from above. This vertical camouflage, or design for the "anti-aerial view," blurred the notion that aerial photography portrayed a truthful image of the land. In fact, it now became the photo interpreter's feat to decipher and decide where the truth lay. Landscape architects and other design professionals working as camouflage officers bridged art and science. Working predominantly for the aerial view, they were especially preoccupied with two-dimensional patterns on the earth. Using natural and artificial materials and employing the scientific principles of perception, they were "breaking the division between subject and background and equalizing the picture's surface."[34] As the Gestalt psychologist Rudolf Arnheim noted years later when writing about the "order and complexity in landscape design," most landscapes and gardens seen from an airplane assumed "the character of a texture" created by vegetation and contrasting with "man-made architecture." According to Arnheim, "depending on the taste of the times, the architect and designer will emphasize this difference of textures by giving the buildings shapes and colors contrasting with those of nature; or play down the difference, either by adapting the buildings to the texture of nature (ivy-covered walls; artificial ruins) or, vice versa, by applying architectural geometry to the garden."[35] Arnheim was expressing a principle fundamental in camouflage design. In the postwar years, landscape architects used selected methods of camouflage to blend new infrastructure like transformer and nuclear power stations into the landscape. While a big concern was the creation of even, uncluttered, and pleasurable horizontal views, the aerial view also continued to inspire designers and guide their decisions.

The use of aerial photography for military reconnaissance purposes and for the development of camouflage schemes resembled the use early landscape ecologists made of it in pattern recognition and in the identification of different ecotopes. In both landscape ecology and landscape planning, aerial photographs have provided a cognitive and intellectual method and an analytical tool, thereby drawing the two fields closer together. Aerial photographs have also offered a conceptual tool and a representational means for the philosophical holism underlying the fields' scientific epistemology. As social scientists pointed out in 1960, aerial photographs "enforce[d] intellectual generalization, by which man is able to comprehend entities and relationships which may not be evident on direct view of the landscape."[36] The ability to use aerial photographs to zoom in and out, providing both macro and micro views, detail, and context, made them fitting instruments for urban and landscape planning besides providing an inspirational tool. As chapter 5 shows, aerial photographs continued to support the common metaphor of the city as organism in the postwar years. Aerial photographs were considered an efficient tool to identify rundown urban areas for urban renewal schemes. However, while city centers were renewed with the help of aerial photography, it was also used to protect and conserve landscapes and natural resources. Aerial photography contributed to what was thought to be a scientific method in regional landscape planning, in which form, in the shape of land-use designations, followed the prevalent function assigned to a particular area. Aesthetic concerns regarding horizontal views always played a role in landscape planning, to larger and lesser degrees depending on the country and its planning frameworks and legislation. More recently, the development of Google Earth has led to the first landscape-planning schemes that take the aerial, vertical view into consideration as well.

The exploration of the moments throughout the twentieth century when flight and the aerial view excited the imaginations of landscape architects, architects, and urban planners shows that it always also led to a heightened attention to matters of the ground, to the ground view, and to humankind's relationship with nonhuman nature on earth. Consciously or unconsciously, design professionals followed Maurice Merleau-Ponty's 1961 advice to "return to the 'there is' which underlies" scientific thinking, "a thinking which looks on from above, and thinks of the object-in-general."[37] According to Merleau-Ponty, attention needed to be paid to the site and the soil, and to the body moving through and on them. Influenced by these phenomenological concerns and by the early earth art of the 1960s, landscape architects paid renewed attention to movement and the visual horizons in their park projects by modulating the ground and designing the ground plane. As Malevich mentioned at the beginning of the twentieth century, humankind must always return to the ground and to horizontality.

Landing

As a prime characteristic of airfields and airports, horizontality has in these past years been a dominant theme in the conversion of former airfields and airports into parks and new neighborhoods. Abandoned airports have provided landscape architects with new opportunities and new horizons for the design of new large parks. The ideas and designs for these areas offer insight into the current understanding of the relationship between humankind and its environment. The designs for Tempelhofer Freiheit and Nature and Landscape Park Johannisthal in Berlin, and for Orange County Great Park in Southern California that are analyzed and interpreted in chapter 6 show that former airfields have a large potential for urban redevelopment. While they are global phenomena resulting from capitalist urban development, these parks on former airfields are both mirrors and motors of local social and environmental politics and policies. Both informing and informed by these, the park designs seek to accommodate human visitors and wildlife, turning "nature" into a commodity for consumption and into a means for the respective city's place-marketing. Whereas the airfields were once points of physical departure for travelers to other cities, countries, and continents, when turned into parks, they become sites that transport visitors into different mental worlds.

Larger than many other postindustrial grounds occupied by steel- and gasworks and railway switchyards, decommissioned airfields offer many cities unforeseen opportunities and enough space to include areas for wildlife conservation. As exceptionally large urban and suburban parks, designed landscapes on former airfields often include "conflicting habitats and uses [that] call for a long-term, bird's-eye view of the whole system . . . by a multidisciplinary team . . . working in collaboration."[38] The interdisciplinary bird's-eye view used in the designs discussed in this book is based upon an understanding of nature that includes humans but at times is also considered to need protection from humans. In diverse forms, the designs are informed by ecocentric restoration—itself "a technology just about as old as the airplane"[39]—and they showcase postmodern ecological science and approaches to park planning and design. With different planning approaches and designs the park designers have tried to return the airfields back to nature. The transformation of former airfields into park landscapes that in some cases have also acted as environmental compensation measures may become even more important in the future. While on the one hand, aviation is among the fastest-growing sources of human-induced carbon-dioxide emissions, on the other hand, surges in fuel prices and decreased federal subsidies have caused some air carriers in the United States to cut their services to small airports, which now lie unused. Although the details of these events would have been hard to predict in the 1920s, when there were up to eight thousand aircraft in active service in America,[40] some planners at the time did foresee that parkland turned into an airfield might be transformed back into parkland, thus coming full circle and becoming part of a metropolitan and regional park system.

WHILE THIS BOOK deals with some events and developments during the twentieth century and into the twenty-first that turned the interface between earth and sky into a place where the earth meets the sky, it omits many others. Written from the perspective of landscape architectural history in the Western world, this book concentrates on selected projects and moments throughout the twentieth century when aviation and the aerial view assumed special importance for landscape architecture and the related disciplines of architecture, urban planning, and design. Since its professional beginnings in the 1880s in the European countries and its professionalization in the United States in 1899,[41] landscape architecture has expanded and diversified its field of activity. From private gardens and public parks to urban, regional, and environmental planning, landscape architects have come to design and plan an increasingly broad range of landscapes. Because of the obvious relationship between built structures and the open spaces and nature surrounding them, and due to the close connection between landscape architecture, nonhuman nature, architecture, and urban planning (landscape architects were among the first urban planners), this book bridges landscape architectural, environmental, architectural, and planning history. It oscillates between science and art, art and nature, technology and landscape. Landscape architecture's inherent interdisciplinarity and "fuzziness" warrant excursions into the histories and events in related fields.[42] By examining how, at particular moments in some countries, the professions of the built environment used, influenced, and were influenced by powered aviation and the aerial view, this book also shows how this influence transcends countries and continents. Like flight, which knows almost no geographical boundaries, it is not limited to just one particular region or country.

As products of modernity, aviation and landscape architecture with its affiliated professions developed alongside each other. Flight lifted landscape architects and their colleagues into the air. The aerial view transformed the way the landscape was studied, analyzed, planned, designed, and managed, and it eventually forced the professionals dealing with the built environment to pay renewed attention to life, movement, and views on the ground. Both the construction of aviation infrastructure on the ground and the aerial perspective have furthered the artistic and scientific development of landscape architecture, architecture, and urban planning and design through the twentieth and into the twenty-first centuries.

One | *Plans in the Air*

THE EVOLUTION OF THE AIRPORT LANDSCAPE

Huffman Prairie, a meadow located about eight miles (12.87 kilometers) east of Dayton, Ohio, was the site of Wilbur and Orville Wright's first powered flights in 1904 and 1905 (fig. 4). The flat, open terrain provided them with a suitable experimentation ground near their hometown after their first success at powered flight at Kitty Hawk, North Carolina, in 1903. The Wright brothers had moved in 1900 to Kitty Hawk, where steady winds to carry their craft and soft, sandy soils to cushion crashes had provided them with an ideal testing ground for their early experiments. As soon as technological progress allowed for the first air meets to be held in Issy-les-Moulineaux in Paris, France, in 1908, and near Reims, France; Brescia, Italy; and Johannisthal, southeast of Berlin, Germany, in 1909, however, it became clear that not only the airplanes themselves needed to be improved but that the takeoff and landing grounds also needed further development if flying was to become more than a popular pastime of a few daring, adventure-seeking, or scientifically and technically minded individuals.

The conquest of the air was therefore also always a matter of the conquest, or at least the availability, of the ground. Aviation required more than unobstructed airspace; it also required land. The provision of large, unobstructed stretches of open land in or near cities had already posed a challenge for the early balloonists of the late eighteenth and the nineteenth centuries. Pleasure gardens, public urban parks, and open spaces such as parade and military training grounds therefore quickly became favored locations for balloon ascents, regardless of whether their purpose was public spectacle or scientific research. These open spaces also provided the first aviators with worthy, dignified settings. A late-eighteenth-century etching (fig. 5) representing the first manned balloon flight by Jean-François Pilâtre de Rozier and the Marquis d'Arlandes, which was directed by Joseph and Étienne Montgolfier from

the gardens of the Château de la Muette near Paris on November 21, 1783, showed the balloon as if it was a central feature in the symmetrically laid-out palace gardens. The balloon appears in the foreground, ascending from an octagonal brick holding station where, in baroque gardens, a water basin, fountain, or the platform for fireworks typically would have been located. The balloon is flanked on either side in the middle ground of the engraving by long, rectangular lawns and flowerbeds, by ordered rows of people and clean-cut tree arches, and by regularly planted groves of trees. Beyond the garden enclosed in the back by a grotto with three exedras, the engraving shows a hilly landscape with small, scattered villages.

Only a few months after Pilâtre de Rozier and the Marquis d'Arlandes had flown across this landscape of suburban Paris, the physicist Jacques Charles and one of his collaborators, Nicolas Robert, ascended in a balloon from an even more famous garden, the Jardin de Tuileries. Popular locations provided the starting points for the first balloon ascent in Scotland, undertaken by James Tytler from Comely Gardens, Edinburgh's pleasure garden, in 1784.[1] A few months later, Vincent Lunardi's first flight was intended to take off from the Hospital Gardens at Bedlam near London. After John Jeffries had ascended with the French entrepreneur and balloonist Jean-Pierre Blanchard over London from the Rhedarium Gardens near Grosvenor Square in November 1784, he noted that "an open place, such as Hyde-Park,

FLIGHTS OF IMAGINATION

or Kensington-Gardens, may be chosen, where any number of people may be gratuitously indulged with a view, without crouding [*sic*] on the workmen, and impending the operation of filling the Ballon, which must ever be the case in small inclosures."[2] In Britain, where ballooning received less attention from the scientific community than in France, "balloonmania" in the late eighteenth and early nineteenth centuries led to organized balloon ascensions for entertainment purposes from pleasure gardens and public urban parks. London's Cremorne Gardens was home to one of the most impressive balloons, the *Royal Cremorne*, and at Vauxhall Jean-Pierre Blanchard opened a Balloon and Parachute Academy. In the 1840s and 1850s, balloons ascended from the Derby Arboretum on the anniversary of the public park's opening.

Although balloon ascents were new and challenging at the time, their requirements were limited to the provision of a large and accessible open space. Powered flight in the twentieth century, on the other hand, required even more space and also began to pose higher demands on other qualities of the site. Airfields were added to the existing infrastructural nodes of railway stations and shipping ports. Although the land of some early airfields, like Johannisthal, southeast of Berlin, had to be cleared of trees, these sites were

FIG. 5. The first manned flight of the Mongolfier brothers' balloon by Pilâtre de Rozier and Marquis d'Arlandes, November 21, 1783. Ca. 1783. Colored engraving. (bpk, Berlin / Art Resource, NY)

chosen because they seemed naturally prone to allow for the easy takeoff and landing of aircraft. The desirable "natural" conditions that early airport builders sought were, as the engineer Archibald Black reported in 1929 in the United States, level terrain on open ground, naturally draining soil, "close growth of tough all-year grass," low or evenly distributed precipitation, and freedom from fog and gusty winds.[3] Thus, the first airfields were flat and grassy, measured approximately 850 by 1,100 yards (approx. 750 by 1000 meters), and were outfitted on their periphery with simple lightweight buildings. They were marked by a white circle 150 feet (approx. 45 meters) in diameter and by the place-name in giant letters. Often a centrally located smoke pot indicated the wind direction. By the end of World War II, however, these "pleasant pastoral scenes," as another author, Sydney E. Veale, called them, were outdated (fig. 6). "Sheep that once grazed placidly on the aerodrome's grassy acres," he asserted,

> can no longer share the pasturage with the wheels of the aeroplane, and the gentle undulations that often relieved the flatness of the scene can no more be tolerated. Men must bring to the chosen site machines and materials to rectify the frugalities of Nature, and scar the surface with broad, straight deep-laid runways, fell trees and other obstructions that might endanger the fast-moving vehicles of the air. Where Nature has been sparing in her gifts, they must hue and cut and excavate and level, blast and drill to make a site. They must decapitate mountains, fill swamps, hack a way through virgin forests, and drive avenues through dense jungles. They cannot—they dare not—rely only upon the bounty of Nature to serve the aeroplane as they did so largely in the first twenty-five years of flying. Modern airports must be man-made.[4]

Airports had become manufactured sites, and the only thing left to be determined by nature was the orientation, length, and strength of the main runway, which had to parallel the prevailing wind; the runway's elevation above sea level was also a factor since that affected the atmospheric density. Airport design had become a new profession and "airport building a new branch of civil engineering."[5] In the following decades, airport construction led to the creation of artificial lakes for drainage, as in the case of Chicago's Lake O'Hare, the largest body of water in the region. It also caused the flattening of mountains as in Charleston, West Virginia, and Branson, Missouri; the filling of water bodies as in the cases of Kansai Airport in Japan and National Airport in Washington, D.C.; and the drainage of wetlands.

By the time Veale described this shift in airfield requirements, a variety of professionals had become involved in the planning and design of airfields and airports, including engineers and architects, city planners, and landscape architects. In Europe, Friedrich Andreas Fischer von Poturzyn noted

in 1925 that the "grounding" of aviation was an enormous task in and of itself, and one 1929 American aviation brochure was fittingly entitled *The Future of Aviation Is on the Ground*.[6] The layout of the airfield; the architecture of the terminal and hangar buildings; the design of airport gardens and of the overall landscape; and determining the airport's relationship to the city, to other airfields, and to other means of transportation were important tasks these professionals had to tackle, and not only out of functional necessity. Improving aviation's image on the ground could help to increase public support and air-mindedness, a state of mind that many nations at the time considered important for social and economic progress.

Building an airport landscape consisting of airports and their network became a challenge in the early twentieth century that is reflected in the tension between modernist and vernacular expressions of airport design. Not only did the construction of airfields and airports involve the use of large stretches of land, but powered aviation also meant that land use became dependent on air space and vice versa. High obstacles surrounding the airport, whether buildings or trees, had to be prevented, and architects and planners who in the 1920s and 1930s argued for or against decentralized settlement patterns could use the development of powered flight to variously bolster their arguments. Overall, aviation in the early twentieth century

FIG. 6. The newest attraction at Tempelhof: Nine hundred sheep graze on the airfield, 1932. Photograph. (bpk, Berlin / Art Resource, NY)

still appeared as a rather exceptional modern technology that was inserted into architectural, urban planning, and land development frameworks and paradigms developed in the nineteenth century. Airfields, and later airports, were added to the metropolitan environment as modern landscape infrastructures. Architects, landscape architects, and planners attempted to merge the new technology with the urban landscape that had been developing since the nineteenth century. Majestic and monumental terminal buildings modeled upon railway stations and embedded into naturalistic parkland reflected the optimism and faith in the new technology while at the same time domesticating it so that it would no longer appear fearsome and threatening to the general public, but instead as a technology that both improved mobility and offered a sublime and pleasurable experience. As the takeoff locations of the first manned balloons show, aviation was from its beginning connected to designed landscapes like gardens, plazas, and urban parks. The development of powered flight required engineers, planners, architects, and landscape architects to design new landscapes adapted to the new technology.

The Airport and the City

Similar to the construction of railway stations on what was in the nineteenth century the periphery of the city, the first airfields and airports were located just outside the urbanized areas. In 1912, Charles C. Reade, the New Zealand–born town planner and advocate of the garden city movement, envisioned that big cities like London would become surrounded by airfields, much as railway stations had been established in the big industrializing cities of the nineteenth century.[7] Many cities converted their former parade grounds into airfields as they had for the first balloon ascents. This was the case in Berlin, where the Tempelhofer Feld, which had been used as a parade ground by the Prussian army since the eighteenth century, began to be used for the first balloon ascents in 1885. Almost a half century later, in 1933, the British poet Stephen Spender aptly described the heterogeneous landscape surrounding what had by then become Tempelhof Airport from the aerial point of view of an approaching air passenger as a "landscape of hysteria." In "The Landscape near an Aerodrome," written only a few years before Tempelhof was enlarged and the old terminal building was replaced by the monumental new architecture designed by Ernst Sagebiel, Spender evoked the melancholic picture of a dull suburban industrial landscape whose black chimneys and "squat buildings" enclosed the airport and formed a "fraying edge" around the city. Regardless of the poem's symbolism, Spender's description captured characteristics typical of airport environments at the time. Tempelhof's immediate surroundings were made up of public parkland, allotment gardens, residential neighborhoods of varying urban and suburban character, rail lines, and cemeteries. The location of airports on the urban periphery was the logical consequence of the land availability and relatively low property prices in these areas that often also accommodated other unseemly and potentially hazardous, polluting, and unwanted land uses. The U.S. Air Force General William Mitchell observed in 1930 that "nearly all airports near cities are alongside cemeteries." He doubted that this could have "a particularly cheering effect on passengers or pilots," especially since "on rising or landing, they see the cemetery conveniently near, usually with a funeral taking place."[8]

To prevent any false associations and convince the hesitant public of aviation's security, on the one hand, and to minimize the time involved in air transportation on the other, airports had to be designed in an appealing, orderly fashion that welcomed air travelers and "grounded" them by representing the respective city, region, or nation, and they had to be located in or near the city center. Planners agreed that the time saved by air travel as compared to rail or automobile transportation must not be lost by the time spent getting to the airport of departure, embarking and disembarking the plane, and traveling from the arrival airport to the final destination. As one later observer commented, "The invisible merchandise of an airline is time."[9] Therefore, if air travel in the United States was to be viable for distances of less than five hundred miles (804.67 kilometers), William Mitchell contended in 1930, airports had to be "constructed in centers of population."[10] Due to the lack of space and the multitude of vertical obstructions in city centers, the ideas developed at the time for city-center airports were more visionary than realistic, in most cases disregarding aviation's basic requirements. Because cities were already congested and space was scarce, Mitchell proposed that different means of transportation could be layered, or stacked above the same area, and he imagined that airports would be built on platforms or roofs.[11]

Mitchell's idea was not new but built upon more than twenty years of more or less visionary designs drawn up by architects in the countries that were experimenting with flight. In many cases, their designs were part of utopian city concepts inspired by new building technologies and inventions like the elevator that enabled the construction of skyscrapers and would one day, some architects envisioned, lead to the construction of vertical cities in which life would require more vertical and less horizontal movement. Already in 1910, Eugène Hénard had presented a sectional drawing of a city street including a house with a rooftop landing terrace for airplanes. In 1914, Antonio Sant'Elia had drawn up his futuristic plan for a hybrid airplane and train station in a city center, and in the 1920s, Le Corbusier had fantasized about an airport surrounded by four skyscrapers in the heart of his Contemporary City. Resembling Sant'Elia's vision, Le Corbusier's plan prescribed a hybrid station located "in the midst of skyscrapers" where "the airplanes . . . would land . . . on the roof of the station" above roads for automobiles.[12] The American architect Francis Keally sketched his vision of an airport on a deck that stretched across New York's Pennsylvania Station, the Post Office building, and an adjacent lot, a location that together with the roof of Grand Central Station was considered at the time the only potential area in the heart of Manhattan for such a use besides Central Park (fig. 7).[13] In London, several ideas were developed for a central airport above part of one of the parks and above Waterloo, King's Cross, and Paddington Stations. Although the English engineer and inventor Archibald M. Low provokingly contended that using London parks as landing grounds was a more democratic use for them than their use as "circular walks for aimless couples" and grounds where horsemen could "display themselves to their admirers," most aviation enthusiasts strove for visionary solutions that saved as much park land as possible. One plan suggested that part of a park be covered by a glass winter garden whose roof would provide a landing ground.[14] Several proposals were made for different types of landing towers, for example, a tower that held a single pivoted runway that could be turned into the direction of the wind for landing and takeoff and a tower that would accommodate autogiros, a short-takeoff-and-landing craft and precursor to the helicopter invented by the Spanish engineer Juan de la Cierva.[15] Another inner-city space that offered itself to utopian airport proposals was the airspace above rivers, river islands, and bridges. Jos H. Wenneman predicted a comeback of the covered bridge as commuter airport and inner-city landing station for auxiliary planes that picked up and dropped off passengers from the main airport.[16] While proposals were made in New York City to build on the Hudson River and in London to cover part of the Thames, the architect André Lurçat offered a spectacular design for Aéroparis, an auxiliary airport on a platform above the Île de Cygnes in the Seine River with metro access, hangars, and auto garages on lower levels. Lurçat considered the island—984 yards (900 meters) long, flat, and located in the immediate vicinity of the city center—as ideal terrain for a new airport for the French capital, which was at the time searching for alternatives to Le Bourget.[17]

Besides these visionary scenarios that involved existing cities, a number of planners and architects in the 1930s envisioned cities growing up around airports on the one hand and the dispersion of settlements as a result of increasing private aircraft on the other. When the first air meets were held at the beginning of the twentieth century, it was already a common belief that aviation would lead to decentralization and to the new ordering of town and country.[18] This belief persisted and gained strength in the postwar years, when many planners envisioned that private flying, in addition to commer-

FIG. 7.
Robert Keally's vision
for an airport above
Pennsylvania Station
in New York City.
(Robert L. Davison,
"Airport Design
and Construction,"
Architectural Record 65
[May 1929], 494)

cial aviation, would increase and change social and urban patterns. Many planners believed that airports would result in the formation of new cities. In the wake of the futurists' *architettura aerea* and *aeropittura* and in reference to Frank Lloyd Wright's settlement schemes, the Italian urban planner Domenico Andriello in 1947 even used the term "air urbanism" (*aerourbanistica*) to suggest the influence that he thought aviation would have on architecture and planning. The new city of Guidonia, constructed in the 1930s in response to plans for a military air base, offered an example from his own country.[19] While some of the first dense utopian urban schemes that conceptualized the "vertical city" had envisioned the existence of aircraft capable of vertical takeoff and landing, Frank Lloyd Wright likewise assumed that citizens of his spread-out Broadacre City would use private airplanes, autogiros, and helicopter taxis in addition to automobiles. In Broadacre City, aerial transportation facilitated urban decentralization rather than urban centralization.

The belief that private aircraft and helicopters in particular would contribute to changing lifestyles and settlement patterns continued to be strong in the United States in the aftermath of World War II, when the 1944 Servicemen's Readjustment Act, also known as the GI Bill, helped many of the 16 million soldiers and sailors of World War II purchase homes in predominantly suburban areas. In a 1943 University of Chicago round-table discussion of "the airplane and the future" between the sociologist Louis Wirth, the *New York Times* science editor Waldemar Kaempffert, and the United Air Lines president William Patterson, that was broadcast by the National Broadcasting Company, the discussants assumed that air transportation would lead people to live more dispersed over the countryside.[20] In 1946, the sociologist William Fielding Ogburn also predicted the increase of private flying and as a consequence the distribution of urban homes over larger areas. Even more than the automobile, the airplane would contribute to creating a metropolitan community covering a large geographical area and to what Andriello in Italy called the "regional city."[21] In denser areas, use would be made of building rooftops as helicopter landing pads.[22] Wright's visionary 1930s settlement patterns adapted to air and automobile transportation, and the expectations of an increase in private air transportation provided frameworks and parameters within which many American architects chose to work in the postwar years. Thus, when in 1945 the American architect and architecture professor Ralph Rapson designed the *Greenbelt House* for a suburban neighborhood within the "Case Study" House Program sponsored by *Arts & Architecture* magazine, he added a helicopter in his aerial perspective. While the *Greenbelt House,* named for its greenbelt of interior planting that divided the pavilion-like structure into two parts, was one of the most unconventional designs in the program, Rapson's aerial perspective drawing encapsulated what was then considered the conventional American dream. The breadwinning (white) husband, taking off in his private helicopter for his daily commute to the city, is waving good-bye to his (white house-) wife, who is in the yard hanging up laundry to dry. Once in the city, the air commuter's helicopter required landing pads that by the 1950s had become common components of urban and regional land-use plans.

These visionary scenarios were based on the principle that what mattered most in the provision of airports was the travel time they could save if they were either centrally located or well connected to other transportation networks. While some planners—influenced by the paradigm of the separation of functions so prevalent in city planning at the time—had early on envisioned separate airports for cargo in the industrial zone and for passengers and recreation near the residential areas of the city,[23] in the 1930s some avant-garde architects like Norman Bel Geddes and Richard Neutra began conceptualizing the airport as a transfer point rather than a terminal. As Richard Neutra's 1930 airport project *Rush City Air Transfer* implied, this projected airport for his visionary American *Rush City Reformed* not only catered to "speed and fluidity in the transition from air to ground vehicle" but was also intended to give an architectural expression to this flowing transition and to the continuity of space and time. Neutra's project relinquished the static monumental entry plaza so typical of the front side of many early airports and was based instead on the objective of a "smooth, rapid and inexpensive" transfer of goods and people between different means of transportation.[24]

The Airport as Part of the Park System

In his design for *Rush City*, Richard Neutra envisioned the greenbelt area surrounding a central urban core that would have looked much like the urban visions of Antonio Sant'Elia and his contemporaries Ludwig Hilberseimer and Le Corbusier as a desirable location for his airport. Due to their spatial requirements, the open space they offered, and their recreational and entertainment value, airports were associated from their beginning with greenbelts and parks. On occasion they were conceptualized and even designed as parks, and some professionals argued that airports could also become a part of the city's open space network. Airport planners faced questions similar to those that had been posed by park planners in preceding decades. Like the establishment of public urban parks, airport building required the provision of a large open space. As park planners had done at the turn of the century, airport planning professionals demanded that municipal authorities plan ahead and acquire suitable grounds to prevent their development for other purposes. The American engineer E. P. Goodrich suggested that if they were not used immediately, the large open spaces could be equipped with athletic fields and used for recreational purposes, turned into parks, or used as wildlife preserves.[25] While there was some disagreement about whether airports, like parks, would increase real estate prices in their vicinity, it was just as vital for airports as for parks to be integrated into the city's transportation network.

As early as 1913, the German landscape architect Leberecht Migge proposed that airfields could become an integral part of a city's open space system. Migge, who had observed that the green, open space of allotment gardens was the first thing one perceived when riding into a city by train, probably aimed to create a similar perception for air travelers. Not only would visitors to a city perceive it as a healthy, green, urban environment, but its own citizens would benefit from the hitherto unknown excitement and diversion that the incorporation of airfields into parkland could offer. Like open-air museums, amusement parks, and race courses, Migge argued, airfields could be assigned to a city's open space management.[26]

As soon as the first commercial airlines had been established, landscape architects and city planners in a number of countries began to perceive airports more widely as "open spaces," "green gaps," and "refreshing lungs" that could offer public playing fields and other recreational facilities. Influenced by the developments in Europe and the United States, in 1928 Masashi

Onosaki, a researcher at the Tokyo High School of Landscape Architecture and captain of the Japanese Army Air Reserve, wrote that due to the general lack of public open space in Japanese rural and urban areas, airports could fulfill a valuable social function, providing fresh air and grounds for recreational activities.[27] In Britain in 1933, the landscape architect Richard Sudell argued that "an airport near a town constitutes a 'lung,' which, if suitably equipped with restaurants, terraces and adequate means of access, should become popular as a resort on fine days for those interested in watching flying." Sudell also considered it possible that "parks, playing fields and golf courses could be laid out in conjunction with airports, if only for that reason that such areas, under the control of the airports authorities, could be kept free from tall obstruction that would detract from the efficiency of the airport."[28] A year later, the engineer and Royal Air Force officer Nigel Norman, who served on the Aviation Committee of the London Chamber of Commerce and on the Council of the Air Registration Board, also found it important to consider "airport sites in conjunction with the provision of open spaces for other purposes."[29] While he observed that London's planned greenbelts did not sufficiently cater to future aviation requirements because they were too narrow, he speculated that, conversely, airport locations might influence the position of what Raymond Unwin had described as the "green girdle", the corset of parkland containing London's growth. Due to London's extreme urban growth and its regional planning schemes of the 1920s and 1930s, Norman warned, sites for airport use needed to be secured in a timely fashion.

An extensive discussion about the siting and function of airports that built upon the common association of airports with parks occurred in the United States, where the park movement had been particularly strong and had led a number of small and large cities to draw up park system plans to order their future development. After the 1926 U.S. Air Commerce Act had determined that airport planning and design was a municipal function controlled by the federal Department of Commerce, numerous municipal governments and some private individuals drew up plans to establish, operate, and maintain new civil airports. The question of the siting of airports was linked to discussions about professional responsibilities. Since airports were understood conceptually as open space, some landscape architects employed as park superintendents and directors chimed into the discussions led by different professional groups and municipal agencies that each wanted to claim airport planning and design for themselves.[30] Interestingly, but possibly due to the lack of an official American city planning journal at the time, one of the first articles on airport building, by the influential airport engineering expert Archibald Black, was published in *Landscape Architecture* in 1923. In his article, Black attempted to characterize airport building as a "new phase of engineering",[31] only to concede that because of this, airport planning and design was also related to landscape architecture and city planning. Although the U.S. Department of Commerce assumed, like Black, that the airport designer would have a basic engineering education, it contended more generally in 1928 that the "airport designer . . . should possess a thorough knowledge of flying in order to see proposed airport sites as with the eyes of a pilot."[32]

While they did not always agree with their colleagues from other fields, landscape architects hardly agreed among each other, either. In 1928, Theodore Wirth, superintendent of parks in Minneapolis, Minnesota, considered the parks department to be the agency appropriate for administering and managing airports. He encouraged all park superintendents to "be 'airminded' and provide an efficient and well-managed airport for [their] city."[33] Wirth considered his opinion to be supported by a Kansas Supreme Court ruling that stated that municipal airports served recreational as well as commercial purposes. He also claimed that park departments often possessed or could easily acquire grounds suitable as airports and that the park administration was the best-equipped department to landscape airports. He believed that "to serve its purpose well and be a credit to the municipality, [the airport] must be landscaped and made otherwise attractive, sanitary, and serviceable to a high degree, just as with any other part of the park system."[34] The following year, Ulysses S. Grant III seconded Wirth's ideas at the Municipal Airport Conference sponsored by the American Road Builders Association. Grant, who at the time headed the Office of Public Buildings and Public Parks of the National Capital, considered the park departments the best equipped to purchase, develop, and operate airport sites. He argued that until they were used as airports, they could be used as parks for recreation. In Grant's mind, airports, like parks, should fulfill recreational purposes. To provide for future airports, he suggested, cities merely needed to enlarge their park systems and eventually employ airport superintendents as part of their park department staff.[35]

In contrast to Wirth and Grant, the landscape architects L. H. Weir and Gilmore D. Clarke and the landscape architect–turned–city planner John Nolen did not favor an affiliation of parks and airports. Weir's position, representing something of a compromise, was that terminal facilities and airlines should be administered separately from parks, but that landing fields could be usefully connected to "large parks and outlying reservations, golf centers, [and] large bathing beaches," an idea that was promoted by the U.S. Army Air Corps and illustrated repeatedly in the 1920s. Reckoning with an increase in the use of private planes, Weir drew attention to the impact that the private automobile had had on park landscapes, where many carriage driveways had consequently been turned into "automobile pleasure driveways."[36] While Nolen also proposed the establishment of a separate administrative unit for airport matters, Clarke countered Wirth's and Grant's views more directly by emphasizing the differences between parks ("works of art out-of-doors") and airports (industrial and "primarily business enterprises") that would be difficult to accommodate in the same department due to their opposing objectives. Clarke feared that if airports were to come under the jurisdiction of park departments, the threat of development would mean that no park would be safe for the public's enjoyment. "Already," he pointed out, "Central Park, in the City of New York, has been suggested by several aviation enthusiasts as a suitable place for an airport."[37]

The editor of *City Planning*, the journal founded in 1925 as the official organ of the American City Planning Institute in which much of this exchange of opinion took place, likewise disagreed with Grant, arguing that aviation needed a separate management run by engineering specialists independent from the park department. He maintained that park professionals could offer their services to the airport authorities regardless of whether their department was officially responsible for airport matters.[38] The opinion voiced by *City Planning* was sanctioned only a short time later by an airport study carried out by the Harvard School of City Planning under the direction of Henry V. Hubbard, Miller McClintock, and Frank B. Williams. In the report, Hubbard and his assistant Howard K. Menhinick made clear that "an existing park in the heart of a city or indeed anywhere else should not be considered as an opportunity for the location of an airport." Although they drew several parallels between parks and airports,—for example, it was considered beneficial for cities to procure land for both parks and airports in advance while land prices were still low, and parks and airports were to be developed as continuous areas uninterrupted by roads—the Harvard airport study also made it clear that airports were not to be regarded primarily as recreational facilities. They were parts of a transportation system that could, in the best-case scenario, be connected to the city centers by parkways. McClintock and his assistant Paul Mahoney therefore concluded that the airport, "if it is to be placed in an existing department, . . . belongs in the department of public works." While ten of the eighty-one investigated airports were at the time already administered by the department of public works, the study found that the same number of airports was managed by park departments. This was the case in Atlantic City, Boston, Buffalo, Cleveland, Des Moines, Minneapolis, St. Louis, Spartanburg, Syracuse, and Wichita. In some of these cities, the land used for airports was even designated as parkland.[39] Occasionally airports were also planned in conjunction with parks. Toledo, Ohio, disregarded the skeptical voices that warned against the security hazard that airplanes would pose to park visitors, and included an airport in its park system plan. The city's Bay View Park, located north of the mouth of the Maumee River, was to be enlarged to incorporate an athletic field and the airport, including a lagoon that could serve as an emergency landing area for seaplanes when Lake Michigan was too rough.[40] Such attempts to fit airports into nineteenth-century urban planning frameworks were prevalent in the 1920s and 1930s. It was therefore only logical that airports themselves would be conceived as both a city and a landscape, corresponding to the ideals of the City Beautiful movement.

"The Airport Beautiful"

Although planners in Europe and the United States—then considered the main territories of air transportation—had by the 1930s determined that airports were to be regarded first and foremost as transportation rather than as recreation features, the question of whether they were assets, nuisances, or both, remained a matter of interpretation. While the negative effects of noise and other types of pollution were hardly considered in the early years of powered flight, the visual appearance of airports preoccupied designers and critics. In 1928, the *New York Times* writer H. I. Brock described the American airport as "a blot on the landscape—a bigger eyesore than the old railway station used to be in the urban scene."[41] In Britain as well, airports were considered to be poorly designed, equipped, and managed, and although individual airports were pointed out for single successful features, in general, as one American observer pointed out in 1930, there were "no airports existing either in America or abroad which represent ideal solutions of the program."[42] Consequently the American city planner Carol Aronovici demanded in 1930 that "the land habitat of these great devices of human progress [i.e., airplanes]" had to be designed in a way "that they may keep our esthetic sense in tune with our mechanical achievement." It was time, he declared, that "the architect, the engineer, the landscape designer, the expert on light and color, should correlate their knowledge and experience and impress air transportation with the imaginative genius that a combination of the arts and the sciences are capable of producing."[43] Similarly, in Germany the prominent airport architect Ernst Sagebiel not only conceived of all airport buildings as one "total building" (*Gesamtbauwerk*), but implied that he considered the airport a total work of art. Back in the United States in 1931, H. Vandervoort Walsh, an assistant professor of architecture at Columbia University, warned that flying would "never become generally popular until airports become more than merely practical and safe." Walsh argued that airports had to be designed in a way to "affect the human emotions" and to establish "a mental state of ease through a feeling of comfort, safety and other emotions producing pleasure."[44]

Architecture's aim to satisfy not only bodily functions but also the human mind and spirit became a topic among early airport builders. They believed that beauty and comfort could affect the psychology of air passengers. As Le Corbusier announced in his *Towards a New Architecture*, architecture determined "the various movements of our heart" and influenced the senses. It was "a phenomenon of the emotions."[45] An ordered and beautifully laid-out airport was therefore not only an asset and advertisement for its city, but it also had the potential to soothe and calm passengers, convincing them of the security of flight. This was a relevant topic at a time when in the United States over 50 percent of all accidents occurred in the airport zone.[46] Already in the nineteenth century, gardens and designed landscapes had been characterized as having the capacity to soothe and heal, and they had consequently been laid out surrounding some of the first asylums for the mentally ill. Although this belief was not new, nineteenth-century medical science provided an increasing body of research supporting the theory that the qualities of the environment influenced character, well-being, and health. As a consequence, morals and mental and physical health were considered directly dependent on environmental conditions and aesthetics, a belief that was carried into the twentieth century and was implicit in architects' deliberations on airport design and architecture. It was also obvious that what the air passengers saw of the airport—regardless of whether it was from above or from the ground—would shape their experience and impressions of the city they were visiting. When the British landscape architect Richard Sudell included a chapter entitled "Airport Development" in his 1933 manual on landscape gardening, he anticipated that "in the future visitors will receive their first impressions of a country as much from its airports as from its harbours."

To improve airport design, various institutions in different countries in the 1920s began to organize design competitions for architects. In France, students of the Parisian École des Beaux-Arts were required to design an "airway terminus" near a big capital city. In Britain in 1928, the Royal Institute of British Architects invited young architects to participate in a design competition for "the design of an aerodrome" of a metropolis like London for the year 1943.[47] British planners hoped to catch up with airport development in the United States, Canada, France, and Germany, where domestic flights were more useful due to greater distances between cities and where aviation was more heavily subsidized by the government.[48] In Germany, individual cities like Berlin, Munich, and Hamburg had carried out airport design competitions in 1925 and 1926. In 1931, although possibly inspired by the need for a new airport in Breslau, the renowned Schinkel Competition announced annually by the Berlin Society of Architects and Engineers sought architectural ideas for a fictitious airport for a mid-sized east

German city. After a first student competition had been held in the United States in 1926, three years later the Lehigh Portland Cement Company of Allentown, Pennsylvania, sponsored a competition in anticipation of a new market in runway construction.[49] The need to design the airport as a beautiful asset led some American authors and professionals to imagine it as both a city or civic center on the one hand, and as a landscape or garden on the other. In both cases, the formal language of classical and modernist French gardens provided the airport designers with inspiration for their plans.

In the wake of the American City Beautiful movement, architects involved in airport building strove to pair utility with beauty, thereby tackling the airport as a miniature city in itself. The authors of the Harvard airport study contended in 1930 that the airport "should be beautiful as well as practical,"[50] and many early designs conceptualized the airport as a civic center, attributing to it an important social function. The airport was "a complex organism," as John Walter Wood explained some years later in 1940, using the organism metaphor that had by then become so common among urban professionals to describe the city.[51] Like city planning, airport planning, design, and construction had by the 1930s finally come to be seen as a comprehensive planning task that required the knowledge and collaboration of different experts. Wood therefore concluded that while city planners needed to be consulted on the location and site selection of airports, engineers were necessary for dealing with grading, drainage, runway construction, and lighting. Architects, according to Wood, were indispensible when it came to the comprehensive planning of airport layout and the design of buildings.[52]

The results of the American Lehigh Airports Competition that attracted 257 design submissions and also caught the architects' attention abroad stressed the observations and suggestions common in the United States at the time. Terminal architecture was to appear solid, stable, permanent, and dignified, portraying aerial transportation as secure and safe and providing a representative gateway to a city. Airports were to be connected to other means of transportation and to be easily accessible from the community they served. The jury also contended that the competitors who were asked to indicate the "treatment of marginal areas" on the site plan, and provide "an airplane view of the whole airport with its complete layout,"[53] perceived airports as providing open spaces for public health and enjoyment. More specifically, they saw the airport's marginal areas as potential public recreation grounds, playgrounds, and amusement parks.[54] Apart from the hangars, architects were typically considered less responsible for the facilities on the airside; runways, lighting, and drainage were seen as falling in the engineers' domain. However, the competition guidelines asked for the provision of an effective landing area of 3,500 linear feet (1,067 meters) in all directions and for concrete runways, not least to boost the sponsor's business. The jury later considered the use of taxi strips and parallel runways separating incoming and outgoing traffic, new ideas at a time when not all experts thought that runways were necessary under all circumstances.[55] While many participating architects employed standardized landing-strip designs, they used them in ways that could enhance the overall ornamental Beaux-Arts appearance of the airport when viewed from the air. Even though the proposed terminal architecture varied, exhibiting elements of art deco, different regionalist, and Georgian colonial styles, most projected airports were based on the Beaux-Arts model of baroque urban design. They used ceremonial axes and bilateral symmetry as their main ordering devices. The terminal building typically marked the end of a straight central approach road and was flanked on either side by hangars. On the landside, geometrically shaped forecourts, plazas, and rond points often anteceded the building. Many designers used obelisks and fountains, typical features of baroque urban plans, as vertical markers along a central axis and in the center of plazas and forecourts, and in some cases replaced them with more functional, modern features like radio towers and light beacons. The architectural conventions at the time were so strong that the City Beautiful character traits of enclosure and boundedness were applied to airfields despite their horizontality and necessity of future expansion, and despite the allegedly boundless means of transportation they were serving. As a previously invented means of mass transportation, the railroad and its stations were often referred to in discussions of airport and terminal design.[56]

While the landside area in the design by the city planners Odd Nansen and Latham C. Squire, who won third prize, resembled parts of the urban plan of Washington, D.C. (fig. 8), many designs similarly used geometrical and axial street and path patterns at the sides and in front of the terminal building to order open spaces for different aviation-related and recreational uses. Some designs—like the winning entry by A. C. Zimmerman and William H. Harrison, and Edward C. Remson's layout, which received an honorable mention (fig. 9)—combined picturesque park areas with geometrical open space designs, thereby turning the airport into a miniature City Beautiful where the rigid monumental forms of the public buildings were offset by the picturesque scenery of parks and park systems. As in some of the other design proposals, the park areas in Zimmermann and Harrison's design contained a small hotel, playgrounds, a swimming pool, shops, and stores.

Planners and designers believed that turning an airport into a meaningful, pleasurable, beautiful asset and a comfortable amenity entailed providing recreational facilities like observation decks, restaurants, swimming pools, as well as parks and gardens. It involved creating garden and park designs and landscape frameworks that were attractive both from a ground

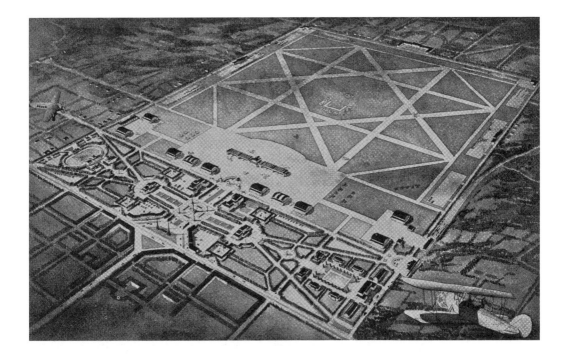

and an aerial perspective. Authors repeatedly envisioned the future airport as having "the appearance of a park or a country club and command[ing] the pride and respect of the public."[57] In the United States, the care taken in the landscaping and in the provision of recreational facilities at airports in Europe was viewed with admiration and as a model to be emulated. In Germany, in addition to railway stations, stadium and restaurant architecture provided models for airport architecture. In fact, flat-roofed European airport buildings were often terraced toward the field to provide space for viewing, and for restaurants and café terraces. Thus, the American press paid attention to the park, athletic field, cafés, and balconies provided at Rome's airport, to the summer garden and restaurant near Tempelhof's runway and on top of the terminal building, and to Croyden's hotel and roof terrace.[58] The financial benefits that these recreational facilities could offer to the airport and the entire city as whose gateway and figurehead it was serving led American airport builders to argue in favor of capitalizing on aviation's spectacle. After all, powered aviation had begun as a recreational activity for many aviation enthusiasts, whether they were involved actively as inventors, pilots, or investors, or passively as pleasure- and thrill-seeking spectators. Following the Lehigh Airports Competition, in 1930 Stratton Coyner argued that there was "no reason why airports should not have many of the features of an amusement park, as the visitors to a flying field are there principally for amusement." A year later Sterling R. Wagner predicted

FIG. 8. Airport design by city planners Odd Nansen and Latham C. Squire for the Lehigh Airports Competition, 1929. (Lehigh Portland Cement Co., *American Airport Designs* [New York and Chicago: Taylor, Rogers and Bliss, 1930]; reproduced with permission of The American Institute of Architects, 1735 New York Avenue, NW, Washington, DC 20006)

FIG. 9. Winning entry at the Lehigh Airports Competition, 1929, by A. C. Zimmerman and William H. Harrison. (Lehigh Portland Cement Co., *American Airport Designs* [New York and Chicago: Taylor, Rogers & Bliss, 1930]; reproduced with permission of The American Institute of Architects, 1735 New York Avenue, NW, Washington, DC 20006)

in his master's thesis in landscape engineering submitted to the New York State College of Forestry at Syracuse University that children's playgrounds, tennis courts, and swimming pools would become parts of future airports serving the airport personnel, passengers, and residents in the region.[59] But there were psychological reasons for outfitting airports as recreational facilities as well. As some airport architects and builders argued, like aesthetically pleasing environments, recreational facilities at airports could also enhance public confidence in flying. Francis Keally noted that "by going to the airport for dancing, dining and athletic recreation, the public has grown accustomed to the idea of flying and overcome its fears; has begun to accept it as a definite part of the routine of modern life instead of thinking about it as a dangerous adventure."[60]

In Washington, the first privately owned airport provided an open-air swimming pool. Thoughts about how to extend the amenity-value of the new airport, which was built on reclaimed land in the Potomac River in the late 1930s, led to planning a bridle path circumscribing the landing field. Small cities like Enterprise, Alabama, went to extremes, planning their airports as country clubs, or "airparks." In the 1934 plan, three runways were supposed to cut through the heart of a nine-hole golf course, and the terminal building was designed to resemble a country club (fig. 10). The airpark in Enterprise was built under the New Deal Relief and Public Works Program. While many small towns throughout the United States built landing fields with the help of relief programs, in Alabama these projects inspired the establishment of airparks, which were understood as airfields combined with recreational facilities like baseball fields, athletic fields, playgrounds, picnic grounds, swimming pools, and golf courses, thus becoming community centers. The airpark was considered a "new deal" and a distinct contribution to public life by the Works Progress Administration. As a communication of the Civil Works Administration pointed out, the airpark met the requirements for the relief program, since it did not compete with private enterprise, was likely to be built voluntarily, and did not entail any maintenance costs for towns, cities, or the federal government. The airpark program in Alabama that contributed to a network of landing facilities was also considered a means to support national defense, and it was seen as a symbol "of the Central Government." In fact, no program seemed better designed than the airpark program to achieve domestic New Deal politics on both a local and national scale: while work on the airpark could act as a relief program for the unemployed, the airpark itself could offer recreational facilities for the increased leisure time. The landscape architects Garrett Eckbo, Daniel U. Kiley, and James C. Rose seconded this idea, arguing in 1939 that rural airports could be interpreted as nodes of recreational planning in the rural environment, where they would literally and figuratively elevate the population's horizons. Conversely, government officials also believed that airparks could bolster regionalist planning politics, attracting "urban visitors to the country" by providing small towns with a park, "one of the city's most attractive assets." The Public Works Administration of Alabama distributed model plans for airparks that included golf courses and athletic fields, and landscape architects worked alongside the supervising architect for the Civil Works Administration to design the park and recreational features.[61]

In the United States in the 1940s, it was generally assumed that growth in private aviation would necessitate the provision of many small airports

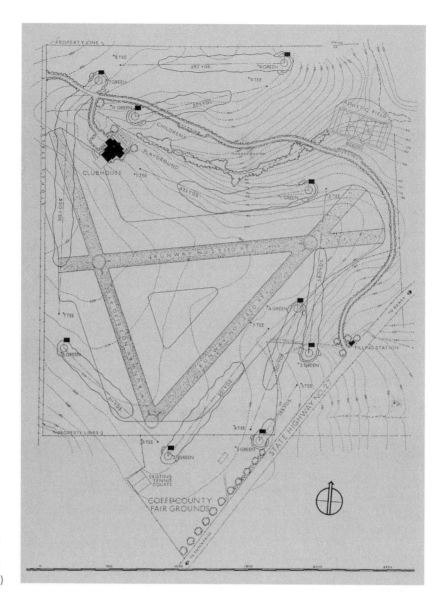

throughout the country. The Civil Aeronautics Administration in the U.S. Department of Commerce therefore produced a number of prototypical plans for class I airports with 1,800 to 2,500–foot- (549 to 762–meter-) long landing strips and class II airports with 2,500 to 3,500–foot- (762 to 1,067–meter-) long landing strips that took into account the rural setting of small towns. Many prototype plans included the provision of adjacent park areas and other recreational facilities like golf. Related to the idea of merging or combining aviation with recreational land uses was the establishment of exclusive aviation country clubs that often included tennis courts and swimming pools and that first became popular among wealthy private flyers in the United States in the 1930s. They were seen by their patrons as comparable to yacht and golf clubs.[62] As early as the late 1920s Richard Neutra was commissioned to plan an airport-resort complex for the Falcon Flyers Country Club near Bakersfield, California, a secluded retreat that, like many other planned airport country clubs, was never built. More successful were the aviation country clubs built on Long Island and in Miami on Biscayne Bay. There, a twenty-two-unit apartment court provided accommodations for nonresident visiting members and a permanent residential area with homes and private hangars was planned for club members.[63] While many planned early aviation country clubs were not built, some residential communities for private plane owners, called airparks to evoke scenic beauty and spaciousness, have been constructed throughout the United States since the postwar years as the result of initiatives by individual private flyers and private developers. Although they were initially envisioned as decentralized residential neighborhoods from which the private pilot would commute daily to his downtown job and to recreation areas, sports events, and family and friends' homes from 200 to 500 miles (321.87 to 804.67 kilometers) away, airparks have increasingly been planned as resort villages, retirement communities, and residential neighborhoods of second homes.[64] To increase their business and economic growth in the postwar years, the aviation, oil, and gas industries were intent on seeing this new settlement form develop and proliferate. According to a brochure issued by Esso Aviation Products, airparks and small airports would attract "a desirable, progressive class of citizen," and the private airplane would increase the "50-mile trading radius of the automobile . . . to 150 miles or more" and position "communities . . . in the mainstream of commerce and prosperity." The airparks envisioned by private flyers and private industry in the postwar years were not only recreational facilities in and of themselves, but, similar to the WPA airparks before World War II, they also provided recreational facilities like tennis courts and swimming pools and functioned as community centers.[65]

Of course, no airport today has golf greens integrated into its grounds on the airside like the example from Enterprise, Alabama, discussed above. However, golf courses have been built adjacent to airports as planners had suggested in the 1930s and 1940s. More recently, golf courses have been built south of the Salt Lake City International Airport, west of the airport in Oakland, and south of Suvarnabhumi International Airport in Bangkok. Besides various recreational facilities, many contemporary airports have the amenities typically found in cities: shopping malls, hotels, restaurants, hospitals, and chapels. In fact, throughout the twentieth century and into the twenty-first, the airport has continuously been conceptualized as a city, an idea that received a special boost once the first jetliners began to fly across continents and oceans in the late 1960s. In the early 1960s, Idlewild International Airport in New York City was referred to as "Terminal City." It was, according to one commentator, "a great place to go for a shoeshine, or a meal, or to see a pretty girl, or see a giraffe, or get a haircut, or pray, or purchase a gift, or spend a night." "You can even catch a plane there," he added.[66] Scholars and economists began to talk of airports as "the city of the future," the "airport city," and, more recently, the "aerotropolis."[67] In 1969, the Italian utopian architect Paolo Soleri proposed that the airport should be assimilated or transformed into a city. He criticized the fact that airports were never the actual departure and arrival points of passengers, calling them a "parasite appendix whose reason resides outside of itself . . . because the aim of the traveler is nowhere to be found inside of it."[68] Recently some scholars have argued that airports can be likened to cities because of the surveillance, monitoring, and regulatory systems that have come to order these complexes, especially since the terrorist attacks of 9/11. In contrast, others have pointed to the fact that urban culture has throughout history been a product of mobilities,[69] implying that urban, suburban, and exurban growth in the vicinity of airports is a logical consequence of their construction. Early airport builders knew this and therefore implicitly and partly unwittingly worked with similar conceptions when they were developing the first airport designs.

The Airport as Landscape

In addition to urban culture with its social functions, the designed landscape and its visual effects also have to be understood as both a product and a motor of mobilities. It is understandable, then, that some architects, landscape architects, city planners, and critics conceived of the airport not only as city, but also as landscape. Besides the airport's social functions, its overall visual effect played an important role in the schemes and concepts of early airport designers. Other professionals assumed a less conceptual point of view but were still preoccupied with the improvement of the airport landscape as a whole or with designing specific gardens and open spaces for airports and embedding the buildings and runways in designed landscapes.

Like many designs submitted to the Lehigh Airports Competition, the airport layout published in the *American City* in 1928 designed by John Nolen to meet all necessary requirements for a class "A" airport appears to have been inspired by baroque town and garden plans, and especially by the designs for Versailles (fig. 11).[70] The advocates of the City Beautiful movement had considered garden art as civic art, using renaissance and baroque garden designs based on geometrical layout and bilateral symmetry as models for park and urban designs. In Nolen's plan, the terminal buildings head one of the corners of the quadrangular field, and the hangars flank the field on

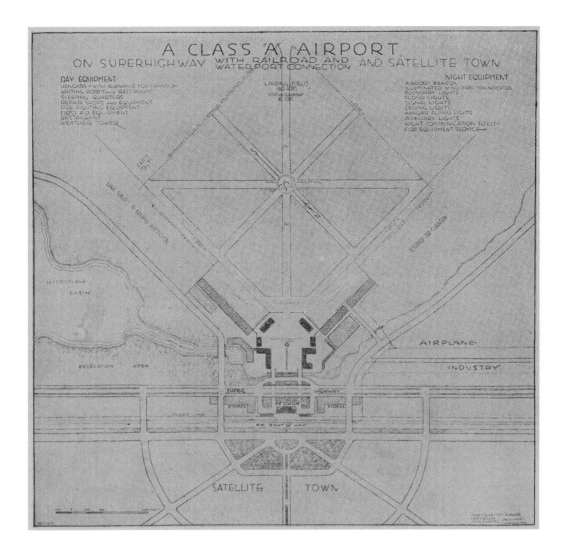

A CLASS "A" AIRPORT
ON SUPERHIGHWAY WITH RAILROAD AND WATERPORT CONNECTION AND SATELLITE TOWN

either side. From the terminal, there is direct access to a superhighway and a railroad. On the landside, Nolen plotted a satellite town whose street plan was based on a patte d'oie, similar to the layout of the town of Versailles in front of the palace. What at Versailles were the gardens, in Nolen's design is the landing field.

The gardens of Versailles provided a favorite model and inspiration for architects involved in airport planning, not least because of their expanse and what the landscape architect Fletcher Steele described in 1936 as their "two-dimensional effect."[71] Steele noted that "their area is so great compared with the utmost practicable height of walls and verdure that enclosures have been little more than low frames."[72] Not only were seventeenth-century palace gardens often laid out on what to many seemed to be flat terrain, but they

FIG. 11. John Nolen, design for a class A airport, 1928. (H. M. Olmsted, "The Airport and the Municipality," *American City* 38, no. 1 [1928], 118)

were to be first experienced visually from an elevated viewpoint on the top floors of the palace, reinforcing the notion of an unbounded two-dimensional pattern and plan. In her comprehensive early-twentieth-century volumes on the history of garden art, Marie Luise Gothein also stressed how Le Nôtre's gardens were based upon the attainment of overview and clarity to provide a representative frame for courtly entertainment and politics.[73] A few years later, in 1917, the Harvard assistant professor Henry Vincent Hubbard and the Harvard librarian Theodora Kimball used a similar interpretation in their formative textbook *An Introduction to the Study of Landscape Design*. They posited that the intended effect of grandeur in gardens like Versailles was achieved through their unlimited extent stressed by the design of a system of allées running through woodlands and structuring the bosquets and parterres. On flat terrain, the authors surmised, no other system could unite open parterres and other design features and produce an effect of "enormous simplicity and spaciousness."[74] To illustrate these points and highlight their two-dimensional geometry, Georges Gromort used a number of aerial photographs and aerial views drawn by the garden architect Achille Duchêne in the section on French seventeenth-century gardens of his 1934 treatise on garden history.[75] Many architects and landscape architects at the beginning of the twentieth century rediscovered the evocations and generative force of the architectural and urban plan in general and the plan of Versailles in particular.[76] Le Corbusier among others saw Versailles as a model for the comprehensive planning process that he envisioned for early-twentieth-century town planning.[77] The seventeenth-century project of Versailles stood at the center of urban, regional, and even national planning initiatives, and André Le Nôtre's axes running through the garden into the surrounding forests, woodlands, and countryside were in the early twentieth century believed to express the French Sun King's dominance over his territory and the larger rational organization and mastery of space. Whereas in the seventeenth century this space was limited to the ground, in the case of the first airports built at the beginning of the twentieth century, it included air space. On the ground, the runways recalled the broad path and water axes in seventeenth-century French gardens. While the runways were visually extended on the ground by lighting and height regulations along the aircraft approach paths, they also extended into the air, thus creating air space. The linear horizontal conquest of space begun at Versailles that has so often been read as symbolizing the scientific revolution gained new heights with the advent of powered aviation in the early twentieth century.

It becomes understandable, then, that in 1928 the *New York Times* writer H. I. Brock would compare airport design to André Le Nôtre's garden designs, arguing: "There is excellent reason why Versailles should furnish useful hints toward the ornamentation arrangement of an airport. The indispensable nucleus of an airport is a park—or, if you choose, a lawn on a vast scale. About the lawn must be buildings duly related to it as the buildings of a palace are related to its park and courts."[78] Due to "the great scale of the plan and the enormous part played in the scheme by the landscape effects," Brock contended, "the primary problem is one of landscape, which you must in the end treat as one of landscape gardening." The writer envisioned the airport as "a sort of park centre" that appeared "from the air . . . as a chief ornament of the Persian carpet of the map—the air-traveler's new landscape on the flat." Besides drawing a morphological comparison between the airport and the baroque gardens of Versailles, Brock stressed the ornamental value that geometrical patterns seen in Persian carpets and seventeenth-century French gardens had for airport landscapes: "Formal garden patterns on a generous scale look very well from the air—are, indeed, more effective than they are on the level."[79] The ornamental garden patterns to which Brock referred also resembled the landing-strip designs that architects and engineers developed in the late 1920s once the higher velocities and weight of airplanes and the increased use of fields required firm runways (fig. 12). Their abstract designs and modular concepts could be adjusted to the respective field requirements and extended to cater to the expected future growth of air transportation.[80] While efficiency principles regarding spatial requirements, construction costs, and maximum load were the guiding factors in their deliberations, they produced symmetrical, ornamental schemes. Designers were excited about the aerial view and the "new idea in landscape composition" it offered, and anticipated that it would "become of considerable importance in the future."[81] Formal, abstract, and symmetrical planting designs enclosing airports and runways were also considered appropriate for enhancing the airport's visibility from the air and for the economic benefit of the airlines. At some airports, plantings and landscaping were used to further accentuate the buildings that were designed to appear as easily recognizable landmarks, or, as in the case of Heston Airport in England, as visual metonyms in the form of an arrow or an aeroplane. At Heston, even the central approach road was laid out to help orientate pilots by pointing to magnetic north.[82]

The concern for airports' pleasurable aesthetics and functionality reflected the ongoing discussion at the time about the relationship between form and function in architecture and society in general. In fact, the question of whether form followed function or function followed form in a more or less literal sense appeared in a variety of discourses surrounding aviation. With regard to airport design, John Nolen had demanded in 1928 that "there must be skillful, liberal and far-sighted designing and planning *for* aircraft, as well as the designing and construction *of* aircraft, and such planning must be coordinated."[83] The German architect K. Wittmann seconded

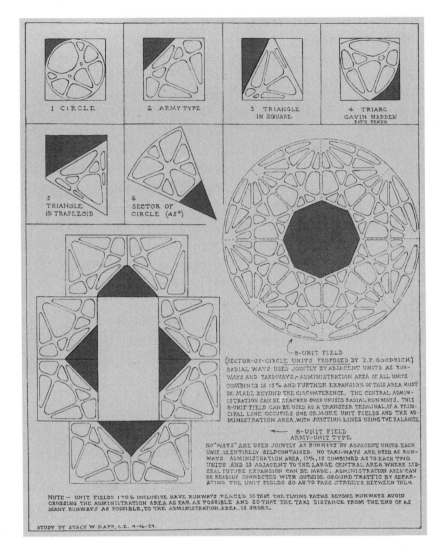

FIG. 12. Landing
strip designs, 1929.
(Robert L. Davison,
"Airport Design
and Construction,"
Architectural Record
65 [May 1929], 509)

these thoughts in 1931, when he claimed that there was an interdependency between the development of airplanes and air stations.[84] However, functionality continued to dominate airport design, and in 1943 the American architect Francis Meisch argued that airport designers should challenge aircraft designers with a new airport type consisting of a parallel runway system that required aircraft little affected by crosswinds and equipped with landing gear that was capable of maximum directional control at ground speeds.[85]

Proposals such as this one led even William F. Ogburn, who speculated on the social implications of aviation in 1946, to question the general assumption that technology determined social and cultural developments. Years before, authors had already begun to complicate and challenge the technologically determinist assumption that social, cultural, economic, and political developments would follow or be sparked by aviation. In 1925, the Austrian author Friedrich Andreas Fischer von Poturzyn, writing for the German Lufthansa AG, had pointed out that to "shrink" the contemporary "three-week-world" to a "three-day-world" did not depend on technological progress as much as on a progressive mind and spirit. In the United States, Waldemar Kaempffert, the science editor of the *New York Times,* stated during World War II that social and economic developments were not the "result[s] of a natural development of technology" but depended on "more factors than aerial transportation." Considerations about airport planning and design in the 1920s and 1930s therefore also involved aesthetics and landscape architecture.[86]

As example of an airport landscape that appeared to have been inspired by Versailles or baroque city plans, Brock presented a visionary design by architect Francis Keally (fig. 13). Keally was considered an architecture expert on airport design issues and served as a professional advisor to the Lehigh Airports Competition program committee shortly thereafter. His airport for air- and seaplanes appeared as a two-dimensional pattern made up of monumental geometrical figures. The circular landing field was part of an extensive and elaborate symmetrical garden that included a large rectangular entrance court, a hippodrome-shaped plaza, and another large rectangular plaza with a central obelisk along the main central axis, as well as elongated water basins and an intricate pattern of straight intersecting streets. Keally proposed to turn the building roofs into gardens "in keeping with the general pattern of the landscape rug," thereby camouflaging much of the architecture as landscape. He anticipated the more recent practice of establishing green roofs on airport buildings. Whereas Keally's ideas at the beginning of the twentieth century were largely guided by aesthetic concerns, by the beginning of the twenty-first century, when impermeable surface areas of airports have reached the extension of twice the size of Central Park, arguments for green roofs in the airport environment have been based foremost on their functional ability to offset temperature increases and contribute to storm-water management. Keally suggested, in keeping with the ideas discussed by many of his city planning and landscape architecture colleagues at the time, that the airport be connected to park areas and thereby offer "an agreeable area of greenery" to the surrounding suburban community that included shrubberies, flower beds, hedges and "all sorts of formal gardening devices."[87] In fact, the architect encouraged his colleagues to take into consideration the surroundings in which they were constructing airports, claiming that airports should blend into the surrounding landscape through their color scheme and become an integral part of the city plan.[88] In a similar vein, Brock had stressed that airports had to fit into "a suburban lay-out

FIG. 13.
Francis Keally,
visionary airport
design, 1920s.
(Robert L. Davison,
"Airport Design
and Construction,"
Architectural Record
65 [May 1929], 494)

so as to beautify the suburb instead of leaving a cruel scar across its eventual inevitable checkerboard."[89]

In addition to the Beaux-Arts influence that was apparent in early airport design through the adherence to the City Beautiful paradigm and classical garden layouts like Versailles, modernist design languages also inspired early airport designers. In the United States, airports displayed some of the first realized modernist landscape designs. While architects experimented freely with the use of art deco and vernacular styles like Spanish colonial revival in terminal architecture, landscape architects similarly used the first commercial airports as experimentation grounds for new formal expressions. The new means of transportation provided these professionals with new design opportunities challenging accustomed forms and perspectives. In 1930, Jacob John Spoon, who ran a landscape practice in White Plains, New York, argued for turning airports into "airparks" using "formal landscape design . . . of the familiar or more modernistic type." According to Spoon, mass plantings of trees and shrubs in geometric shapes, wide grass and flower strips, and broad walks of bluestone, gravel, and white sand would appear attractive from the air. To save costs he proposed that the extensive plantings for expansive airfields be carried out with native shrubs and trees. His vision included terminal forecourts that were bracketed by rows of clipped trees and structured by parterres enclosed by clipped hedges (fig. 14 and fig. 15).[90]

FLIGHTS OF IMAGINATION

FIG. 14. Jacob John Spoon, watercolor sketch showing the landscape design in front of an airport terminal building. (Jacob John Spoon, "Why Not Artistic Design in Airports?" *American Landscape Architect* 3, no. 2 [August 1930], 33)

FIG. 15. Jacob John Spoon, watercolor sketch showing a bird's-eye view of an airport landscape design. (Jacob John Spoon, "Landscape Design for Airports," *American Landscape Architect* 3, no. 2 [August 1930], 32)

Spoon's colleague, the Nebraska landscape architect Ernst Herminghaus, promoted a similar design vocabulary. In a 1930 article entitled "Landscape Art in Airport Design," he observed that "all aviators will tell us that it is the geometrical gardens that stand out, even to the untrained eye." Herminghaus attributed beauty to geometrical layouts and believed that with the exception of Washington, D.C., European cities were more beautiful than American cities because they had "more formal gardens, plazas, and squares." The excitement about powered flight and its novelty led landscape architects like Herminghaus to oscillate between the banal realization that "looking down upon a garden from the air is the same as looking at its plan" and emphatic exclamations about the new possibilities and requirements of "'aerial' landscape architecture."[91] In fact, the architect Francis Keally stated that making the airport appear orderly, harmonious, and beautiful from the air would not be difficult since architects had always planned "with the bird's eye view in mind."[92] Despite the familiarity of architects and landscape architects with the plan, and therefore with the aerial view, Herminghaus considered it worthwhile to point out that due to the distance from the ground, the view from the air could require "balances that are a mile or more apart."[93] Because yellow and orange were the colors most easily detected from the air, and details were not perceptible to the aerial viewer at high speeds, he proposed planting brightly colored masses of plants. Due to the novelty of airport design and the functional necessities that could be better handled by engineers, he considered it wise for landscape architects to limit themselves to the decoration of terminal buildings and the landside design of airports. Landscape architects indeed tended to play a subservient role, often adapting their design vocabulary to the airport architecture.

Herminghaus's own chance for practicing the principles he had elaborated on came when he was commissioned to design the grounds in front of the terminal and the landside areas of the hangars at Fairfax Airport in Kansas City (fig. 16 and fig. 17). As was common for many early airports in the United States, the buildings were located along the boundary roads and enclosed a corner of the field. By setting back the administration and passenger building 400 feet (122 meters) from the intersection and positioning the hangars so that they flanked the terminal building on either side along the roads with a setback of 100 feet (30.48 meters), ample space for gardens was provided. Herminghaus's design centered on the terminal building and reflected the bilateral symmetrical layout of the buildings. In line with the monumental axes used in the City Beautiful design of civic centers, Herminghaus's design was anchored on a central axis that ran toward the main entrance of the terminal building. He laid out the axis as a 15-foot-wide by 150-foot-long (4.57 by 45.72 meters) reflecting pool planted with water lilies and marked at its end points with circular water basins including central

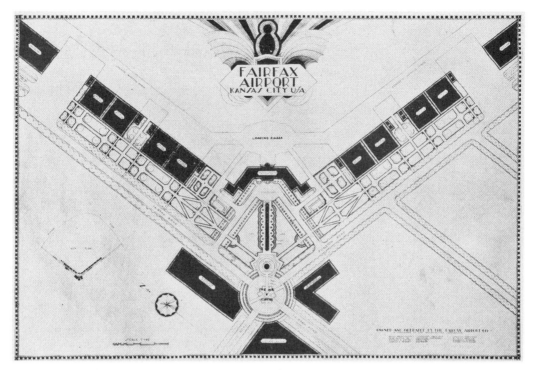

FIG. 16. Ernst Herminghaus, plan for Fairfax Airport, Kansas City. (Ernst Herminghaus, "Landscape Art in Airport Design," *American Landscape Architect* 3, no. 1 [July 1930], 17)

FIG. 17. Fairfax Airport, Kansas City. Landscape design by Ernst Herminghaus. (Ernst Herminghaus, "Landscape Art in Airport Design," *American Landscape Architect* 3, no. 1 [July 1930], 15)

fountains. The pool was flanked by cones of arborvitae planted at regular intervals and by bow-shaped planting beds set into lawn and filled with masses of brightly colored tulips and petunias. The lawns in front of the hangars were "decorated or paneled with low hedges of privet . . . [i]nterposed at accents and centers [with] trimmed arbor vitae and elms." Probably more engaged with the cost of the extensive plantings than with the design opportunities, Herminghaus nevertheless expounded: "Since the vertical dimension is not important, very little height is needed."[94]

Herminghaus was hired for Fairfax Airport by the Woods Brothers Corporation from Lincoln, Nebraska, for which he had already successfully worked on subdivision planning and design in Lincoln. Built between 1928 and 1930 and located on a big bend of the Missouri River about three miles north of the city center, Fairfax Airport was at the time of its official opening in October 1930 considered one of the "finest airports in America" and one of the most beautiful in the world.[95] The August 17, 1930, *Kansas City Star* attributed the airport's successful design to the fact that "the scheme for development of the setting for the terminal building was carried through . . . before the building itself was finished and has resulted in the mirror pool, flower gardens, lawns and walks."[96] Indeed, on August 25, 1929, the *Topeka Daily Capital* reported that the Woods Brothers' "landscaping and nursery department . . . came into such use that it put Fairfax in a class all by itself. No other airport in the United States has been so beautifully landscaped and made attractive to the eye and the aerial traveler as at Fairfax."[97] The effort undertaken at Fairfax Airport reflected the high hopes of city officials and of the Woods Brothers Corporation in this project. They deemed Kansas, specifically the Kansas City area, advantageous terrain for the fledgling aviation industry due to its location, topography, climate, and demographics.[98] As the largest city located in the geographical center of the United States and as the second-largest rail terminal with twelve transcontinental railways radiating in all directions, Kansas City was expected to become an important center of air transportation and hailed as the "Nearest by Air to Everywhere."[99]

From its opening after restructuring in 1930 and through the 1950s, Fairfax Airport acted as model for airport landscaping and "beautification" schemes in the United States. During this time, articles, pamphlets, federal publications, and technical manuals began to draw attention to airport landscaping and planting design and to the role that the aerial view should play in it, although at the beginning the limited experience allowed for only rudimentary comments. Airport landscaping was considered both a means to "beautify" the airport for the ground and aerial view, and a structural device that could order the airport landscape and that, especially when seen from above, could also "produce unity of appearance in the completed plan."[100] To prevent vertical obstacles in the flight paths, planting had to be limited to shrubs, flowers, and grass. Both utilitarian and aesthetic considerations had to be taken into account, leading the landscape architect Glenn L. Hall to comment at the Annual Convention of the American Institute of Park Executives that "low shrubs, bright-colored flowers in masses and grass may be used to help the aviator distinguish the outlines and location of the field as well as to beautify the area for those seeing it from the ground."[101]

In Europe and Japan, similar ideas about airport landscapes prevailed. By the postwar years, the airport had become "two-dimensional architecture" for Le Corbusier, its splendor being its wide, open space. In his eyes, the sleek, magnificent forms of the airplanes could best be highlighted against a "naked" airport characterized by "sky, grass, and concrete runways." However, while he proposed a minimalist low terminal structure, passengers were to disembark into "the neatest, prettiest flower bed or other such adornment," thus creating a marked tension between welcoming vivid ornament and color, and minimal, cool, clean, and clear-cut geometry. He exclaimed: "Rather disembark into flowers than rocks from Burgundy! . . . Let Holland furnish fields of tulips and Versailles the flowerbeds!"[102]

In Stuttgart, the landscape architect Hermann Mattern tightened the airport buildings' connection to the ground by designing an appropriate landscape framework (fig. 18). While the terminal buildings designed by Ernst Sagebiel's office in 1936–37 were given a distinct modernist industrial touch through the choice of flat roofs, the airport hangars were outfitted with pitched roofs constructed of dark-brown tiles, thus adapting to the vernacular architectural character of the region. Although it is likely that functional considerations like air-raid protection, camouflage, and the scarcity of building materials inspired these decisions, Sagebiel's declared design objective was to fit the airport's architecture into the landscape and to design a silhouette that would dissolve into the surrounding scenery. The 1,041-yard- (952 meter-) long visitor terrace designed for 50,000 people, which began in front of a restaurant seating 2,500 people, curved around the northwestern edge of the landing field.[103] The terrace adhered to Sagebiel's design principle of blending the airport into the landscape by providing an architectural element that emphasized the horizontality of the building complex, tapering down to the ground level and blending with earthen slopes. Mattern's planting design further stressed this design intent. The clean-cut, monumental ledges of the long terrace were broken up and thereby "softened" by interspersed shrub plantings. The selection and irregular planting of tree and shrub species adhered to the rural character of the region, blending the building complex and landing field into the surrounding agricultural land. Irregularly spaced low-growing dog roses, hazels, blackthorns, and brambles inconspicuously marked the boundary of the landing field. Besides these species, the plantings along the approach road included walnut, apple, and

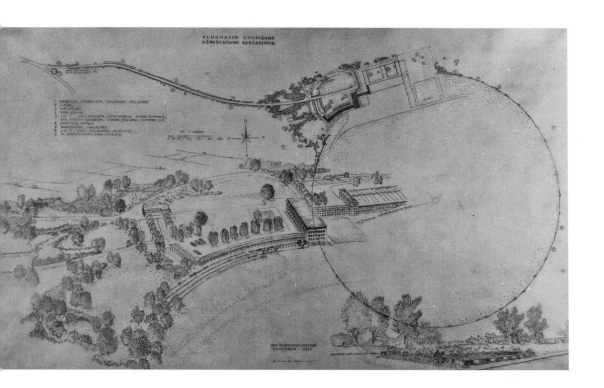

FIG. 18.
Hermann Mattern,
landscape design
for Stuttgart airport
designed by Ernst
Sagebiel's office,
November 1937.
(Architektur-
museum TU Berlin,
Inv. Nr. F2648,
Nachlass Hermann
Mattern)

linden trees, elderberry, lilac, hawthorn, laburnum, cornel cherry, snow-ball bushes, and Canadian poplars. The open space and planting designs by landscape architects in Germany took on many character traits used in that nation's public urban parks and reflected the two predominant design approaches, the "architectural" and the "naturalistic." Thus, the open spaces surrounding airport restaurants were often characterized by architectural lines marked by cut hedges and colorful flowerbeds. At the same time, both regionalist ideas and air-raid protection measures led to landscape designs that attempted to blend the airport into the surrounding landscape.[104]

The Japanese air force pilot and landscape architectural researcher Masashi Onosaki expressed similar ideas about airports in his country, where up until the 1920s airports had been considered only as military establishments. He proposed that Japanese airports should be covered by soft, refreshing, bouncing green lawns "like carpets." In contrast to hard, bare gravel surfaces that evoked anxiety, lawns could comfort passengers and pilots and provide a welcome, soothing open space to nearby residents. Mixing in clusters of clover could further improve the lawn as a ground for pasturage and as an aesthetically pleasing asset. For Onosaki, the airport was not a delicate garden but a wild landscape that portrayed an entire continent by evoking associations and romantic sensations like "twilight with remote mountains glowing in purple; misty dawn; heat haze in spring;

stars and the moon in summer; the nighttime song of insects in autumn; and . . . snow in winter." His planting proposals for airports included bands of dwarf white vegetation to mark and offset the airport boundaries. The height of the plantings in these areas should be staggered, with the taller plantings farthest from the landing strips.[105] Influenced more by the trends in Western landscape design that at the time were particularly engaged in discussions about architectural and "naturalistic," or "wild," garden designs, than by the Japanese garden tradition, Onosaki proposed that circular or square-shaped Western-style flower gardens should be planted near airport buildings and along approach roads. Flower displays could also be used to spell out the airport's name or to form aeronautical signals. Onosaki suggested naturalistic plantings of Japanese plants for other airport areas, and that the woods surrounding the airfield should be outfitted with sinuous paths and roadways.[106]

The use of landscaping and plants for enhancing the aesthetic appearance of airports continued to be discussed after World War II and has held some relevance ever since. In the United States, Florence Bell Robinson, a professor of landscape architecture at the University of Illinois in Urbana-Champaign and an expert in planting design, stressed the latter's importance in the overall planning and design of airports in a small publication entitled *Landscape Planting for Airports*, issued as Aeronautics Bulletin no. 2 by her university's Institute of Aeronautics. Her manual was an attempt to establish a theoretical foundation for the first experiences with airport planting design. However, more than producing new knowledge or design inspiration, Robinson's manual was an adaptation of existing knowledge and design principles to the new task at hand. She considered plant choice and arrangement crucial for developing a scheme that was attractive from both the aerial and the ground perspectives. To achieve this, particular attention needed to be paid to "the balance between the open, sunny area of the field and the heavier, darker masses of buildings and plants with their shadows." She noted that the "balance of masses and tones is more evident from the air, less so from the ground." Thus, while the planting design needed to contribute to an interesting aerial view, it was also a helpful tool in establishing attractive approaches on the ground. Robinson identified the transfer point between the modes of transportation—typically the terminal building and its surroundings—as "the center of interest about which everything else revolves."[107] The air- and the landside of this node should be treated differently. The large open space of the field should contrast with large, "formally" arranged plantings in front of the terminal entrance that directed traffic and provided a dignified entry from the airport to the city and vice versa. Robinson considered "hedges bordering ample paths" and "specimen shrubs or small trees" as appropriate materials that would "add needed shadows for interest" and "enhance the architectural design with harmonizing textures and colors." The views for waiting passengers would be enhanced by a foreground created with a mass of dense plantings with coarse texture that contrasted with the glaring light of the vast open space of the landing field. This way, Robinson explained, the passengers' view would be directed toward the point of departure.[108]

In a more carefully edited publication issued a year later, in 1950, by the Civil Aeronautics Administration and the Department of Commerce entitled *Airport Landscape Planting,* some of Robinson's recommendations were taken up. Once again attention was paid to the aerial view. This time, however, greater importance was attributed to the cost factor of plantings and their maintenance, and as a result irregular rather than geometric planting patterns were proposed. The manual argued that plant loss and replacements would be less conspicuous and less costly in informal schemes.[109] It did not mention the hazard that certain tree and shrub species posed by attracting birds that could cause bird strike and "ingestion." Not until the 1960s would this danger begin to be addressed systematically with the plantings and choice of species in the airport environment. The two design approaches proposed in the 1950 manual were illustrated by prototypes based on Herminghaus's Fairfax Airport design (fig. 19 and fig. 20).

GROUNDING THE AIRPORT

From the beginning of airport construction in the late 1920s, forging a specific identity to help orientate passengers and advertise the respective city, region, and nation played an important role in airport design. Airport names were typically marked in big letters on the landing field or on the roofs of prominent buildings. Furthermore, during the 1920s, when contact flying was still prevalent, town and city names were air-marked on rooftops along airways to facilitate the pilots' orientation. After the first experiments with painting the names of cities and towns on building roofs had been made in the United States by the Army Air Service along its Model Airway between Dayton, Ohio, and Washington, D.C., a committee appointed by the Department of Commerce tested and made recommendations for air marks that would be illuminated at night.[110] In many cases, airport air marks were complemented by iconic designs of airport structures and open space. A symbolic and iconic landscape could facilitate passenger orientation. Few people at the time had the geographical knowledge to be able to "read" the landscape from the air and orientate themselves on account of the topographical features and the signs of human habitation visible when looking down on the land from the air (see chapter 2). Whereas train passengers in the nineteenth century could recognize city panoramas and skylines aided by landmarks such as cathedrals and church steeples, the aerial view

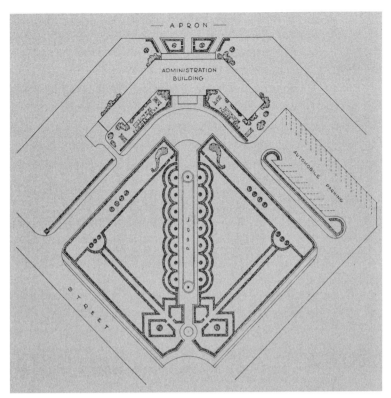

FIG. 19. Design prototype for "elaborate" airport planting developed by the U.S. Department of Commerce, 1950. (U.S. Department of Commerce, *Airport Landscape Planting* [Washington D.C.: U.S. Government Printing Office, 1950], 4)

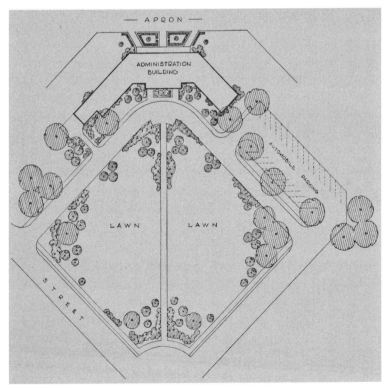

FIG. 20. Design prototype for "simple" airport planting developed by the U.S. Department of Commerce, 1950. (U.S. Department of Commerce, *Airport Landscape Planting* [Washington D.C.: U.S. Government Printing Office, 1950], 5)

provided new patterns unfamiliar to most air passengers. As one aviator put it in 1910: "Every aeronaut knows how difficult it sometimes is to recognize even familiar country from above. . . . Seen from above, hills and towers which serve as landmarks on the ground are scarcely visible."[111]

While the aim for airport gardens and landscapes was to be recognizable from the air, they likewise were intended to forge identities from and on the ground. In many cases, the gardens and landscapes clothed the modern airport facility including its machinelike hangars, the often modernist terminal buildings and control towers, and its airplanes—the "machine[s] for flying"—in a vernacular garb.[112] As a quintessentially modern means of transportation and land use, aviation in both a figurative and literal sense was and took people up into the air, thereby disrupting and dissolving conventional connections with place. To (re-)connect air passengers to place, to the ground, and to particular locations, gardens and landscapes that embodied the vernacular or that built upon classical formal vocabulary thought to establish ties with history, were designed and built at airports. Although attempts were undertaken in the United States to standardize airport facilities and landscaping, this latter part of airport design was most easily dissociated from the modern process of standardization that occurred with regard to runways, terminal buildings, and overall airport size and layout. Airport gardens and landscapes were literal examples of how "local and regional identities [were] constructed within—rather than against—the context of the modern."[113] In airport construction, the vernacular of integrated gardens and surrounding landscapes often acted as a "civilizing force in modernity."[114]

To create place, forge identity, and welcome air passengers sometimes only small vernacular gardens were laid out that resembled the first railroad gardens, or, as in the case of the 1925 design for Tempelhof Airport, an existing boulevard flanked by rows of majestic poplars was integrated into the overall design.[115] In more prominent locations, designers and planners expended considerable effort to provide attractive landscape designs. An attempt to forge a specific locational identity was undertaken in the United States at El Paso Airport, where a small cactus garden on the otherwise barren ground greeted air travelers (fig. 21).

In contrast to this small Texan vernacular garden, at the Seaplane Station of the Santos Dumont Airport in Rio de Janeiro, a more elaborate tropical garden, including a water basin holding "rare and typical Brazilian plants" such as Victoria water lilies, was laid out in front of the passenger entrance to the terminal building, which had been inaugurated in June 1937.[116] The water basin was sunken slightly below the level of the entrance plaza and could be accessed from three sides by narrow pathways marked by rows of paving stones set into the lawn. The same differently sized and loosely

FIG. 21.
Cactus garden in
front of the El Paso
Airport, Texas, ca.
1930s. (American
Airlines via
National Air
and Space Museum
[2008-1202], Smith-
sonian Institution)

spaced stones framed the basin. Broader paths laid out with quadrangular
white paving stones led to the terminal building and facilities. Along the
edges of the pathways, white concrete benches provided seating opportunities. This vernacular modernist garden led up to the modernist terminal
building that featured art deco interiors.

When the airport plans for a municipal airport in the U.S. capital took
shape in the late 1930s, planners determined that its grounds should evoke
an eighteenth-century landscape in keeping with the late-eighteenth-
century urban plan. Henry N. Boucher and S. E. Sanders, landscape architects in the landscape unit of the Public Buildings Administration who were
in charge of the airport landscape design, advised that all airport structures
should "adhere to the colonial atmosphere of the site."[117] The latter was
thought to be evoked by, among other things, the remains of Abingdon, the
home of Martha Washington's son John Parke Custis. The terminal building's architecture was consequently designed to invoke the nearby colonial
home of George Washington at Mount Vernon (fig. 22). The building was
elevated above the landing field so that "splendid view[s] of the National
Capital" could be obtained from the interior observation terrace.[118] Several
rows of "observation parking" were provided outside on elevated ground
along the northwestern edge of the field, catering to the increasing number of motorists. In 1941, shortly after its opening, the airport was proudly
advertised as one of the scenic areas and a "beauty spot" of the capital.

FIG. 22. Drawing
illustrating the
Washington
National Airport
terminal building
and its model,
Mount Vernon.
(Interdepartmental
Engineering Com-
mission, *Washington
International Airport*
[Washington D.C.:
U.S. Government
Printing Office,
1941])

A brochure suggested that Washingtonians would "flock to the field as to one of their favorite parks." The romance of flight, it was assumed then, could also be captured on and from the ground. The 1941 airport publication offered this romantic vision: "When the sun sinks beyond the range of hills to the west, the scenic areas of the airport will be among the most comfortable and interesting places about Washington." To accomplish this effect, "the rising ground within the airport" was landscaped so that it provided a "background of greenery for the airport itself and . . . a pleasant foreground to the view over the airport, the river, and the city from a series of parking terraces."[119] Promoted as a national model of airport operation and design, the planners took care to include generous upper-level dining facilities and observation decks in the new terminal building. In Washington, a visit to the airport was as much about watching planes taking off and landing as it was about enjoying the scenery that provided the backdrop to these movements: a stretch of green interspersed with the monumental white markers of the capital city: the Capitol, the Jefferson Memorial opened in 1943, and the Washington Monument.

These early attempts to use airport garden and landscape design to forge local, regional, and national identities and ground travelers through creating a sense of place became widespread practices. Since the 1960s, this interest has paralleled environmental concerns, efforts to protect and conserve the landscape, and noise-abatement measures that have played an important role in the siting of new airports.

Seen today as one of the spaces most emblematic of the globalized world, airports have become subject to different readings. One of the best-known descriptions is by Marc Augé, who has criticized the airport as a nonplace, "a space which cannot be defined as relational, historical and concerned with identity."[120] Other critics, however, have evaluated airports positively as miniaturized, self-contained cities that are more active and culturally diverse than most American downtowns and that encapsulate the *pleasures* of postmodern existence including feelings of placelessness, nonbelonging, and detachment.[121] Like the airport as a whole that connects "'spaces of globalization' with 'spaces of territoriality,'"[122] its gardens and landscapes have become manifestations of "glocalization." Regardless of their formal design and aesthetics within what is generally assumed to be the quintessentially modern world of the airport, the designed gardens and landscape incorporate the idea of the vernacular, relating the airport to its surroundings in more or less imaginary ways. Airport gardens and landscapes are both a result of globalization (as parts of the airport) and an attempt to counter the airport's inherent placelessness by bringing local landscape qualities and character traits to the foreground. After all, the vernacular has typically been understood as a denial of mobility, internationalism, and multiculturalism. Airport gardens and landscapes play an important role in the airport's function as a transmitter "for shifting from global to local and vice versa."[123] Many airport gardens and landscapes stress the individual locations and geography, attempting to create a sense of place, slow down the flow, and ground, or root, the travelers. They seek to counteract the isolation of the airport environment and reconnect passengers to the rhythms of the natural world. As airports are being turned into cities replete with shopping malls, hotels, restaurants, hospitals, and chapels, and as they are increasingly being privatized as in the cases of Frankfurt (Fraport), Amsterdam (Amsterdam Schiphol Group), and Heathrow (BAA Ltd.) and run as global air transport businesses,[124] their gardens and landscapes have more than ever before also assumed profit-generating functions. No longer are aiports seen only as amenities that can provide stressed and sleep-deprived travelers with a sense of place and a relaxing environment; airport managers also see the possibility of increased revenue through the creation of both a more attractive ambience and a more distinctive and instantly recognizable environment.

What landscape architects have come to deal with in airport environments is what Tim Cresswell has described as, on the one hand, "a largely ahistorical and non-placebound space of flows," and on the other, "the rooted and historical space of place."[125] One may argue that the parks and landscapes are what remains of the romance of air travel. The French classical and modernist garden models and the idea of unobtrusively blending airports into the surrounding countryside have continued to play a role in airport design. Although landscape architecture still plays only a subservient role in airport design, the conceptual idea of airports as city and as landscape and the importance of landscape perception from the air has reverberated in designs for new and expanded airports since the postwar years.

When the new Idlewild jet airport was built on a former golf course and reclaimed marshland in Jamaica Bay, Queens, New York City, in the 1950s, an expansive central open space formed the heart of the airport complex. The idea to enclose an open space with terminal buildings and airplane docking stations had been born in the 1940s, when City of New York planners first developed a design that might have caused Reyner Banham to describe the postwar airport as "demented amoeba" characterized by "amorphous disintegration, blurred boundaries."[126] The 1946 airport master plan prepared by Downer, Green and Carillo; the architects Delano and Aldrich, later replaced by Harrison and Abramovitz; and the landscape architects Gilmore Clarke and Rapuano and Holleran presented an amoeba-shaped complex whose central open space was given over to parking. While much of the central area would indeed finally be reverted to this use, the design that was realized in the 1950s included a central park, also referred to as the mall (fig. 23). The 220-acre International Park was surrounded by the International Arrival Building, the central heating plant, and seven airline terminals. A brochure published for the dedication of the International Arrival and Airline Wing Buildings promoted the park as being "planned to make Terminal City beautiful from the air as well as from the ground" and as the "major attraction for visitors in the metropolitan area." The park design included elements similar to the design features at Versailles. Four circular fountains flanked with beds of tulips were positioned along an axis between the International Arrivals Building and the Heating and Refrigerating Plant, a transparent structure that faced the International Park with a curtain of glass.[127] The fountains diminished in diameter, creating a forced perspective when viewed from the terminal and a telescoping effect from the other end. The biggest, 60-foot- (18.28-meter-) high Fountain of Liberty located in front of the terminal building was illuminated by colored lights at night (fig. 24). The 1,000-foot- (304.8-meter-) long axis of fountains (fig. 25) was intersected halfway by a long water basin that resembled the transverse axis of the canal in Versailles and also enforced the perspective if viewed from the center of the park. Instead of woods as in the case of Versailles, these design features were surrounded by parking areas, which, however—as one of the promotional brochures illustrated very colorfully—were embedded in

FIG. 23. (*Top*) Aerial view of New York International Airport, December 17, 1957. (The Port Authority of New York & New Jersey)

FIG. 24. (*Middle*) Simulated night view of a model of Terminal City, New York International Airport, showing the 1,000-foot-long (305-meter-long) landscaped Liberty Plaza in front of the International Arrival Building. Immediately adjacent to the Control Tower is the 60-foot-high (18-meter-high) Fountain of Liberty, with three smaller fountains and large reflecting pools extending along the length of the plaza. (National Air and Space Museum [NASM 00136484], Smithsonian Institution)

FIG. 25. (*Bottom*) Fountains and grounds in front of the International Arrivals Building at New York International Airport. Photograph by Joseph W. Molitor, Ossining, NY. (The Port Authority of New York & New Jersey)

areas covered by grass and tree-covered road embankments. The *Architectural Forum* announced the landscape design in 1958 as setting "the scene for a new kind of permanent world's fair." Nighttime views showing the illuminated transparent terminal structures and the colored fountains of the International Park were among those most often used to illustrate articles about the new airport. In fact, the airport's lighting system was highlighted as covering "the entire area with a blanket of never-ending daylight."[128]

Less representational, more subtle, but likewise inspired in some details by French patterns while connecting to the local landscape was Daniel U. Kiley's landscape design for Dulles International Airport, 20 miles (32.1 kilometers) west of Washington, D.C., at Chantilly, Virginia. Built in 1958–62 on approximately 10,000 acres (4,047 hectares) of farmland with three hundred homes, Dulles opened shortly after New York International Airport. Expanded several times since then, the heart of the airport is Eero Saarinen's terminal building (fig. 26). Working within the greenbelt of trees that had partly been left standing and in part was newly planted surrounding the entire airport grounds to provide a screen and noise buffer, Kiley sought to embed Saarinen's sculptural terminal building into the surrounding Virginia countryside. Using red cedar, hawthorn, tulip poplar, quaking aspen, and London plane trees, he designed planting patterns that responded to the geometrical volumes of the terminal building and the geometry of the landing strips and at the same time connected to the flowing hedgerows of

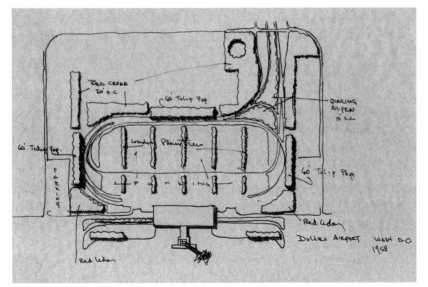

FIG. 27. Daniel Urban Kiley, sketch for the landscape design surrounding the terminal building at Dulles International Airport, 1958. (Courtesy of the Frances Loeb Library, Harvard Graduate School of Design)

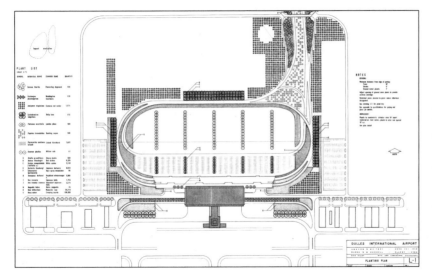

FIG. 28. Daniel Urban Kiley, planting plan for Dulles International Airport highlighting the scale and structure of the plantings, undated. (Courtesy of the Frances Loeb Library, Harvard Graduate School of Design)

the local surroundings (fig. 27 and fig. 28). He wanted the designed landscape to stand out from the natural patterns in its details while at the same time connecting the terminal building and its infrastructure with the larger landscape. Kiley intended framing the hippodrome-shaped parking space in front of the terminal building with double rows of tulip poplars. The species was later changed to the stiffer-appearing red oak and in the north finally replaced by a parking garage. The trees formed rectangular blocks that acted as counterweights to the terminal building and unified the entire terminal landscape. Beneath the trees, evergreen red and white azaleas, and hollies were to form a checkerboard pattern that changed colors throughout

FIG. 29. Firethorn along the slopes of the parking bowl, Dulles International Airport, 1960s. (General Photographic File, 1986–1995, folder 42, box 6, RG 237-G, Records of the Federal Aviation Administration, U.S. National Archives and Records Administration)

FIG. 30. Rows of red azalea flanking the terminal building, Dulles International Airport, 1960s. (General Photographic File, 1986–1995, folder 42, box 6, RG 237-G, Records of the Federal Aviation Administration, U.S. National Archives and Records Administration)

the seasons—from green and white, to green and red, to green and green. These planting blocks were to be bordered on the outside with dark evergreen Japanese holly. As if heeding the advice of the first landscape architects involved in airport design, Kiley designed these "horizontal mural[s] beyond human scale" to be viewed from landing and departing airplanes.[129] Kiley's plan proposed groves of eastern red cedars planted at 20 feet (approx. 6 meters) on center between the circulation routes and parking lots. The cedars were meant to conceal service buildings and function as a connecting and unifying element between the surrounding landscape and the landscape of the terminal. They provided a dark evergreen foil for the blocks of tulip poplars and other flowering trees and shrubs. Rows of London plane trees di-

FLIGHTS OF IMAGINATION

vided the parking lot into five sections. The rows nearest the terminal were highlighted by underplantings of red azalea. Grids of firethorn underplanted with creeping myrtle covered the gently sloping edges of the parking lot (fig. 29), and Wicherian rose and Japanese holly lined the approach ramp to the departure drop-off. Rows of red azalea flanked the terminal building (fig. 30). Kiley's terminal landscape consisted of gridded mass plantings of a variety of tree and shrub species and evergreen ground-covering plants. Mass plantings of azaleas, firethorn, and abelias in particular provided brightly colored surfaces throughout the seasons, and through the use of evergreen ground cover, the airport could always appear neatly grounded in the larger landscape. Eastern red cedar planted in grids along the approach roads and at the corners formed a permanent dark evergreen frame and a link to the mixed forests and woods beyond the airport boundary. The tree plantings on the medians of the access road and the dogwoods along its outer slopes that were never realized were intended to "compress space" for the approaching car drivers and to channel views, thus highlighting the effect of the iconic terminal building and its control tower once passengers and visitors entered the spacious open area surrounding the terminal. Kiley intended the grid tree plantings to provide for both easy maintenance and visual interest, especially when viewed from a moving car.[130]

The use of colorful shrubs on the slopes of the sunken parking lot (parking bowl) and on the grounds bracketing the terminal building meant that deplaning visitors and enplaning travelers were greeted by a welcoming explosion of color. While the vegetation's color drew attention to the terminal area, the plants' low height ensured the prominence of the iconic architecture. Kiley's planting plan also turned the parking lot into a monumental entrance court to the terminal. Besides the jet, the car was celebrated in the airport's overall design, and the terminal became a transfer station between automobile and air traffic. Whereas at Idlewild and other airports located near or on preexisting bodies of water, no additional retention basins for water runoff were needed, at Dulles International, Kiley had to work with a lake as retention basin for the water runoff from the terminal building. In contrast to the rest of his airport landscape, the lake north of the parking lot that collects water runoff from the terminal roof, and the creek that connects it with the Potomac River, are embedded into forest plantings. These include willows, maple, ash, and other deciduous trees common in the area in addition to coniferous plantings. While the terminal sits in geometrical planting beds in which plants are situated with engineered precision, the lake is located within irregular loose forest plantings that tie the airport into Virginia's countryside, which has since been engulfed by suburban sprawl.

Landscape design also received a lot of attention in a visionary project sponsored by the Graham Foundation for Chicago O'Hare International

Airport. In 1964, a group of sixteen architecture, urban planning, and landscape architecture students at the University of Illinois at Urbana-Champaign under the direction of various Chicago planning officials, professional architects, engineers, and the university professors Jack S. Baker and Robert D. Katz prepared a study for the conversion of O'Hare into an airport for vertical takeoff and landing (VTOL) aircraft. Because these aircraft required relatively little space for landing and takeoff, fourteen circular flight pads were designed consisting of stars of six 1,500-foot- (457.2-meter-) long runways each and distributed at regular intervals across the airport area (fig. 31). The new technology would, according to the planners, decrease the destruction of the natural landscape and safeguard open space. They proclaimed the "VTOL landscape" at O'Hare to be a sculpted topography formed by mounds and lakes that would appear from the air as an "impressive pattern in the landscape fabric," serving as a "visual symbol of Chicago's importance as an international activity center." The designers envisioned the marginal airport zones as a buffer between the airport and the adjacent communities that would be used for agricultural, nursery, and forestry production and educational purposes "by displaying the vanishing Illinois prairie vegetation which once covered the region."[131] Plantings and excavated swales surrounding the circular landing pads were to alleviate the effects of extreme climatic conditions on-site through soil protection and repository for winter snow and surface drainage. The landscape design proposed that low plants with various colors, textures, and growth habits would cover the swales in concentric bands, making the landing pads appear as targets from the air (fig. 32). Vegetated earth mounds near the highway exchanges were to provide elevations for visual interest that contrasted with the "subtle prairie topography," whereas water bodies near the gateways to the airport not only visually emphasized the architecture but would also be used in the airport's air-conditioning system and provide recreational amenities. For a short period in the 1960s and 1970s, designers considered VTOL passenger aircraft an opportunity to provide a more environmentally sensitive landscape infrastructure. In 1970, the British landscape architect Brenda Colvin thought that VTOL aircraft offered an incentive to "tidy up and re-arrange the clutter that now collects in the hinterland of runway and airport buildings." She considered "the dreary look of British passenger airports" to ruin the "surrounding scene for many miles"—not a welcoming sight for tourists or those returning home.[132]

The landscape architects Peter Walker, Adriaan Geuze, and Shlomo Aronson have more recently used ideas expressed at the beginning of the air age in their designs for airports in Munich, Bangkok, Amsterdam, and Tel Aviv. Peter Walker's 1990s design for the garden of the Kempinski Hotel on top of an underground parking garage at the Munich Airport, which opened in

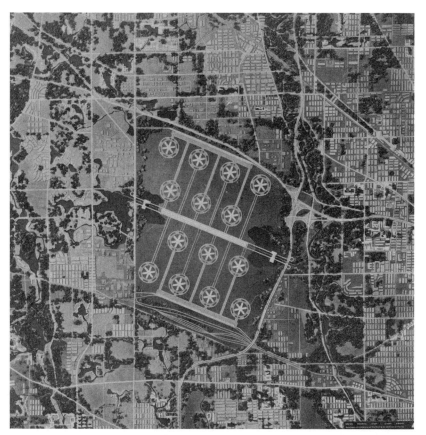

FIG. 31. (*Left*)
Plan showing VTOL
flight pads envisioned
for O'Hare Airport,
Illinois, 1965. (*O'Hare
Airport: A Design Po-
tential Study* [Urbana-
Champaign: College of
Fine and Applied Arts,
1965]; Courtesy of the
College of Fine and
Applied Arts, University
of Illinois at Urbana-
Champaign)

FIG. 32. (*Below*)
Planting plan for
one flight pad at the
envisioned O'Hare
Airport for VTOL aircraft.
(*O'Hare Airport: A Design
Potential Study* [Urbana-
Champaign: College of
Fine and Applied Arts,
1965]; Courtesy of the
College of Fine and
Applied Arts, University
of Illinois at Urbana-
Champaign)

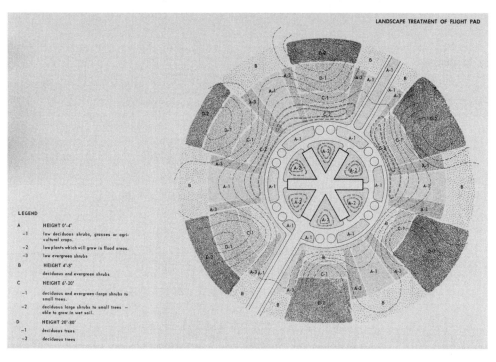

1992, was based on a strong graphical pattern that is best viewed from the air, from the top floors of the hotel, and the above-ground parking garage across the street. Like the landscape architects involved in the first airport landscapes, Walker used elements typical of seventeenth- and eighteenth-century French parterre gardens: rows of sculptural trees, cut hedges, lawn, and colored gravel. In contrast to early airport landscape designs that were focused on the terminal building and based on bilateral symmetry and 90-degree grids and axes, however, Walker's garden is structured by a more complex order based on two overlapping grids, and does not center on the hotel building, although it does take into account the building lines and skin. Influenced by Walker's predilection for minimal art, the garden design for Murphy/Jahn Architects' Munich hotel building appears as an abstract serial pattern. It is embedded in an overall airport landscape planned by Grünplan GmbH under the direction of the landscape architects Günther Grzimek, Winfried Jerney, Lore Kellinghaus, and Eberhard Krauss and the architect Eberhard Stauss. To minimize the impact that the construction would have on the ecosystems and to integrate the airport structures into the landscape in a visually appealing way, the landscape plan built upon the analysis of the different landscape types and patterns found in the Erdinger Moos. The plan used the color scheme and the geometry and horizontality of the flat land-scape, consisting of open fields and meadows, canals, and allées to structure the airport landscape and provide it with a visual identity. This site geometry, which follows a northeast–southwest orientation, and the north–south- and east–west-oriented airport structures were overlaid to create both continuity throughout the larger landscape and an airport-specific landscape. A central allée leading to the main terminal building forms the backbone of the entire airport, and other tree lines and gridded groves structure the open spaces in the terminal area. To facilitate orientation, only tall-growing trees that provided porous "barriers" were planted in rows and as forested swaths along the transportation routes and as buffer zone surrounding the airport. The tree pattern and selection were inspired by the straight lines and existing species of the surrounding agricultural landscape. Water-retention areas were planned as a wetland, and care was taken to protect a system of interconnected ecotopes and to connect the airport to the regional open space network.[133] Three viewing platforms in the form of sculpted pyramidal earth mounds were positioned at various locations on the airport's periphery to allow the public an overview of the runways and access to the spectacle of flight.

A more explicit example of identity politics shaping the airport landscape can be found at Tel Aviv's Ben Gurion International Airport in Israel. In the early 2000s, the office of Shlomo Aronson designed a rectangular 4.9-acre (2-hectare) central garden flanked by two parking structures and enclosed

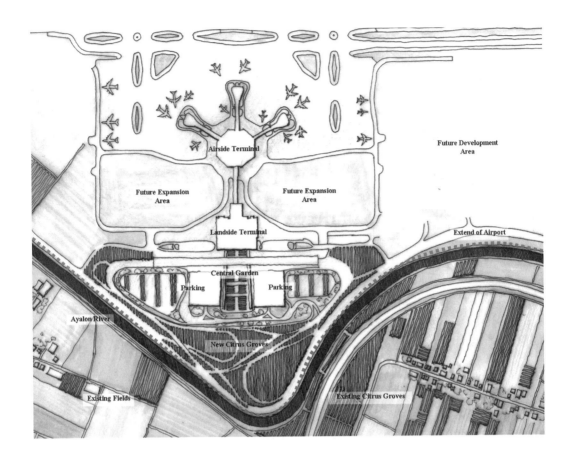

Airside Terminal

Future Development
Area

Future Expansion
Area

Future Expansion
Area

Landside Terminal

Extend of Airport

Central Garden

Parking

Parking

Ayalon River

New Citrus Groves

Existing Fields

Existing Citrus Groves

by the terminal building on one side and bordered by approach roads on the other (fig. 33). The designers wanted the central terraced garden to appear as an entrance to Israel that conveyed an abstract and "condensed impression" of the country's landscape that could transmit a "deeper feeling of place."[134] A succession of terraces imitates the gradual terrain elevation that occurs from the coastal plain around Tel Aviv to the mountains of Jerusalem. The terraces are designed in a variety of abstract patterns using plant species typical of the different landscape zones that visitors to the country would traverse when moving from Tel Aviv to Jerusalem. Thus, from a paved area that represents the sea, beach, and a coastal promenade with different surface patterns and materials, the visitor steps up to a palm and water garden formed by a grid of palm trees, narrow water channels, and quadrangular lawns. A wheat terrace follows, representing agricultural fields and leading up to three more terraces that are planted with an orange grove, grasses, and finally an olive grove representing the Judean Hills. The garden can be perceived from a variety of viewpoints in the garden itself and from the parking structures on either side. From elevated viewpoints, the central garden appears as a collage of abstract images. The landscape architects' work

FIG. 33.
Shlomo Aronson
Architects, design
for the garden
and landscape
at Ben Gurion
International
Airport, Tel Aviv.
(Courtesy of Shlomo
Aronson Architects)

extended to the areas surrounding the new interchange and approach roads to the airport, where they took care to carefully sculpt the land and blend it into the surrounding agricultural land by designing a productive landscape. Newly planted citrus groves integrate the airport into the surrounding field pattern and are leased to nearby farmers, who maintain the crops in exchange for the fruit.

At Schiphol Airport outside of Amsterdam, the landscape architecture firm West 8 proposed in the 1990s to merge the airport with the surrounding agricultural landscape by planting grids of 25,000 inexpensive native birch trees (*Betula pubescens*) that would be thinned out over time and turned into more or less densely wooded areas. The birch tree plantations require little maintenance, are resistant to high water and salt content in the soil, and do not attract birds, potential hazards for aircraft. Since the jet age, and in particular, since a bird-strike accident at Boston's Logan Airport in October 1960 caused the death of all but eleven passengers onboard a Lockheed Electra, potential collisions between birds and aircraft have been addressed through the development of less-sensitive aircraft engines and through wildlife management at airports. The wildlife management measures range from killing by poisoning and shooting, to the use of sonic devices and trained falcons to deter birds from feeding, roosting, and nesting to specific landscape designs. For example, to minimize the bird-strike hazard, West 8 stipulated that all water bodies comply with specified measurements so that they would not become overly attractive to birds. At the same time, all water bodies designed as canals and ponds to drain, retain, and store rainwater were to function as an additional element to visually integrate the airport into the polder landscape of the nearby Haarlemmermeer.[135] The designers had to strike a delicate balance between providing for the safety of the flight and ground operations and establishing healthy and functioning ecosystems and a visually pleasing environment.

West 8's planting and management concept for a "green airport" differentiated between three different areas (fig. 34). For the central area crossed by runways and taxiways, the firm proposed rough grassland along the runways and manicured lawn along the taxiways. The core of the airport was surrounded by a ring of elms—reminiscent of the elm avenues typical of the Dutch countryside—connecting green nodes planted with London plane trees. Remaining spaces outside of the runways were also planted, thereby creating a transparent vegetative veil, or "green haze"—as the designers termed it in their design manual—that unified the buildings and grounds of the expanded airport area. Passengers and people working and visiting the airport were intended to perceive it as a park, or as part of the larger landscape surrounding Amsterdam. Situated in a drained and dried shallow lakebed almost immediately adjacent to Amsterdamse Bos—

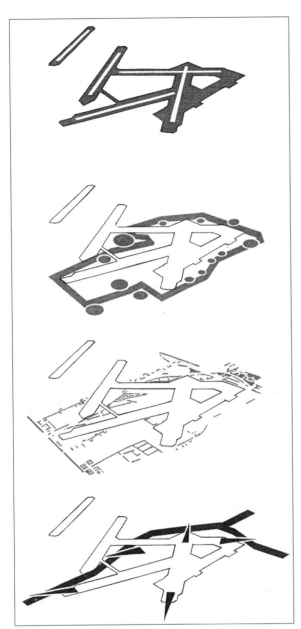

FIG. 34. West 8 urban design & landscape architecture, diagram illustrating the conceptual idea and strategy for the landscape design and management plan for Schiphol Airport, Amsterdam. The diagram distinguishes between the grass areas near the runways, a greenbelt and green cores, fragmented green areas throughout the airport zone that are treated comprehensively, and sight lines. (© WEST 8 urban design & landscape architecture B.V.)

Amsterdam's big urban forest built between 1929 and the 1950s under the direction of the urban planner Cornelis van Eesteren and the landscape architect Jacopa Mulder—the airport landscape connects to this icon of early-twentieth-century functionalist park design through bike paths and plantings. Whereas the former landscape treatment of the airport had tried to hide the runways and airport operations on the airside from the view of passing motorists to prevent their distraction, West 8's treatment explicitly integrates these parts into a comprehensive landscape plan. The landscape design had to take into account the view sheds that are essential for the safe and smooth functioning of the airport. For example, the terminal building, the radar station, and lights had to be clearly visible from all runways. In the springtime, daffodils, planted underneath the trees to form geometrically shaped fields, add color, and clover was used as initial ground cover to fertilize soils. Beehives placed in the birch groves allow the clover to be naturally propagated until it is replaced in the natural succession by grass species. The management plan, including the mowing cycles, determines whether the ground cover during summertime appears as lawn or blooming meadow. West 8 proposed that planters in front of the terminal building should represent a "typically Dutch picture"[136] with plantings of festuca, tulip, lilies, helianthus, and chrysanthemum. While the firm was in charge of the overall design guidelines, it also designed several open spaces at the airport including the garden of the central office building, the square in front of the terminal, courtyards, car parks, and public observation areas. Not only is West 8's Schiphol project an example of the use of landscape architecture in creating a national and regional identity, but it also shows how both aesthetic and functional-technological concerns have come to influence the design of the contemporary airport landscape. Whereas environmental concerns regarding noise, pollution, and land consumption played a relatively small role at the beginning of the air age and designers were more concerned with the aesthetics and the engineering of the airport landscape than with its ecology, with the beginning of the jet age this began to change. As many landscape architects were assuming the role of regional landscape planners, the airport and its environment began to be considered in ecological terms as well. Thus, the landscape planner Ian McHarg, known for his "ecological method" (see chapter 5), was invited to submit a chapter to the 1969 volume entitled *Master Planning the Aviation Environment*. In the same year, an environmental impact report prepared by the hydrologist Luna Leopold for the U.S. Department of the Interior prevented the completion of the construction of what at the time was projected to become the largest jetport in the world in south Florida, 36 miles (57.94 kilometers) west of Miami. Leopold argued that the jetport construction in the Big Cypress Swamp would lead to the loss of the Everglades National Park and the destruction of the south Florida ecosystem.[137] Unsurprisingly perhaps, the evolution of airport landscape designs has paralleled, if not contributed to, the general shifts that have characterized the development of landscape architecture in the last fifty years. Professionals involved in the planning and design of airport landscape today try to accommodate technological functions, natural processes, and aesthetics. They also always seek to create a landscape that establishes a unique identity.

Although the attempt to use landscape architecture to firmly ground the airport in its respective region and country has produced more pronounced expressions in the last decades, it is not new. Besides the airport and terminal buildings that in many cases by 1930 included homey waiting areas that resembled private living rooms, the design of the outdoors also attracted some attention, even though airport literature beginning in the 1920s tended to treat the matter, if at all, only secondarily after the functional engineering and architectural details. While some American landscape architects employed by municipal governments were still arguing for the inclusion of airports into urban park systems, others were already working on landscape designs for airports. After the railroads had provided them with work in the late nineteenth century, and parkways and roads had been offering design opportunities since the 1910s, by the late 1920s landscape architects considered aviation another source of work. While the romantic vision of flight has in the meantime largely been obliterated, the attempt to fuse technology, nature, and landscape in airport environments has continued. Throughout the twentieth century and into the twenty-first, airports have been perceived and conceptualized as cities, and they have been designed as landscapes.

Two | *Air-Minded Visions*

THE AERIAL VIEW IN EARLY-TWENTIETH-CENTURY
LANDSCAPE DESIGN AND URBAN PLANNING

When powered flight took off in the early twentieth century, design professionals discovered more than the new opportunities that the planning, design, and construction of airfields and airports offered them. The aerial view from the airplane captured on photographic film also provoked many excited responses and musings among designers and their critics. The aerial view sustained a new epistemology and new and existing ideas and theories, and it enabled new methodologies in design and planning practice.

In 1929, the artist and Bauhaus professor László Moholy-Nagy argued that the "new vision" the airplane enabled from the air—the new space of human experience—promoted the creation of flowing space that integrated the interior and exterior living environment on the ground.[1] Space as understood by modern architects flowed through rooms, buildings, sites, entire cities, and the surrounding landscape to the horizon and beyond it. Space was continuous and infinite. Moholy-Nagy illustrated his argument with aerial photographs of city streets, roofs, and industrial buildings in his book *The New Vision*. Indeed, the aerial view not only provided a new factual knowledge of the land, but it also provided context and insights into spatial and even temporal relationships on the ground that before the proliferation of aerial photographs had been accessible only to balloonists and early pilots, or through the imagination.

As Moholy-Nagy noted in the caption of an aerial photograph of a mountainous landscape, the view from above revealed the overall context.[2] Along with the concept of regional, national, and global space being facilitated by new airways spanning continents and the globe came the idea, observed later, in 1974, by Henri Lefebvre that "things [can] not be created independently of each other in space . . . without taking into account their interrelationships and their relationship to the whole."[3] The aerial view therefore supported a new epistemology that was not exclusively based on facts, but on the recognition that—as the gestalt psychologist Max Wertheimer explained in 1934—"truth .... is a question of the relationship between the proposition on the one hand and the object on the other."[4] Thus, Wertheimer believed that "facts about the world were necessary, but they were not in themselves sufficient guarantors of Truth."[5] Based on the holistic belief that "the world was constructed of wholes and patterns of relation," Wertheimer argued that truth was "a matter of grasping the significance of different facts in terms of their relationship to one another and to a larger whole."[6] Truth and objectivity were not to be found in the facts themselves but in their relationships. Both a materialist appreciation of the aerial view and the holistic understanding of the world it supported influenced its use by the design and planning disciplines preoccupied with shaping our living environment throughout the twentieth century and until today.

The aerial view appeared as an implicit and explicit trope in architectural, design, and planning discourse in the 1920s and 1930s. While it influenced the way landscapes and cities were designed and represented, it was also used to validate and legitimize these same designs. Designers of the built environment realized the opportunities the embodied and disembodied aerial view could offer both for their design and artistic production, and for its reception. They began to understand the aerial view as a way of knowing that is both abstract and experiential, rational and imaginary, factual and aesthetic, microscopic and macroscopic, detailed and contextual, harmful and essential. This dialectic and its inherent ambivalence and ambiguity so typical of modernity characterized the designers' use and reception of the aerial view.

While this chapter distinguishes the different tropes of the aerial view that to some degree already existed before the invention of powered flight, it lays out how these became particularly relevant for design professionals in the early twentieth century and helped form and support their ideas and conceptions of space and the natural and built environment. Many themes introduced in this chapter reappear in the following three chapters that address design professionals' use of the aerial view at particular moments in the twentieth and early twenty-first centuries.

Aerial Views and the Airplane Vantage

As soon as the first scheduled commercial flights had taken off in Europe and the Americas and aerial photographs began to proliferate in the daily and specialist press, architects, landscape architects, and planners in Europe and the Americas excitedly anticipated the new opportunities and inspiration that the view from above at high speeds would offer them in their work. Looking from above and from a distance seemed to literally and figuratively offer the space for imagining and designing new futures. The fascination with the new spectacle of powered flight seems almost to have made these professionals, and people in general, forget that aerial views had already been imagined, constructed, painted, photographed, and described long before the first powered and piloted flight by Orville Wright on December 17, 1903. Before the airplane vantage, balloons had provided aerial views, and towers, church steeples, and mountaintops had offered a bird's-eye perspective of landscapes, cities, castles, and gardens. Writers and artists had captured such bird's-eye views in letters, poetry, paintings, and engravings, engaging for centuries with the main ideas and themes related to the aerial view that became influential in the design and planning disciplines during the early years of commercial powered flight.

Imagined bird's-eye views of towns and gardens depicted in mural paintings, drawings, and engravings from the fifteenth-century onward portrayed their subject in its full glory, extent, and context. Although based in part on surveys, these early bird's-eye representations were subjective renderings expressive of contemporary power relations. Such subjectivity is also evident in the meanings that twentieth-century architects and urbanists would later attribute to oblique and vertical aerial photographs. Early balloonists were fascinated with the new two-dimensional, map- and relief-like scenery afforded by the aerial view. Similarly, as the first pilots and plane travelers became enamored with the landscape patterns seen from above, professionals dealing with the built environment also realized both the beauty of the abstract patterns and their usefulness in design practice. The patterns discovered from above and photographed from balloons and subsequently from airplanes also facilitated the reading of the landscape as a palimpsest, first by archaeologists like the Italian Giacomo Boni, the American-born Henry S. Wellcome, the Englishmen G. A. Beazeley and O. G. G. Crawford, the German Theodor Wiegand, and finally by design professionals. It also supported their understanding of the landscape as an ecosystem. The aerial view as perceived by balloonists, pilots, and design professionals provided context and a new conception of boundless space.

While the actual aerial views obtained from an airplane were not very different from those obtained from a balloon, the early-twentieth-century invention of powered flight by the Wright brothers in the United States and by Alberto Santos-Dumont, Louis Blériot, and Henri Farman in Europe did provide more flexible opportunities for aerial observation. A first shift toward a more flexible and kinetic aerial observation had occurred with the first manned balloon flights in France in 1783. In contrast to the stable and fixed viewpoint from hillsides and mountaintops that artists and writers had used from the late fourteenth century onward in support of their bird's-eye view paintings and descriptions, the balloon offered a more flexible means of aerial observation of land and settlement forms. The first aeronauts saw what artists and writers before them could only imagine and deduce through rational analysis and comparison. Experiencing the aerial view, as the early British balloonist Thomas Baldwin exclaimed, could even overwhelm the imagination.[7]

A second shift toward increasingly flexible and controllable aerial observation came with the development of the airplane, which allowed passengers to extend the duration and area of their kinetic aerial observation. Airplanes could fly more easily than balloons along directed flight paths and at different elevations and speeds. Powered flight increased the sense of empowerment that artists' patrons in the fourteenth to eighteenth centuries could express only in poems and more or less imaginary paintings and engravings that depicted the bird's-eye view. The development of powered flight and the almost parallel evolution of aerial photography therefore promoted the rediscovery of vertical scenery in the early twentieth century, leading to the evolution of its epistemology and its application in twentieth-century architecture, landscape architecture, and urban design and planning.

Two essential observations that had been used to characterize the aerial view of the earth since the beginning of manned flight were important in this development: First, the earth from above seemed more or less flat, resembling a map, or on occasion a relief. Second, this two-dimensional rendering of the earth's surface made it appear as an abstract pattern that also seemed boundless, without frame or edges. Overall, this meant that landscape, described in its pictorial tradition since the sixteenth century as horizontal scenery, could now also be understood as vertical scenery. This dramatic shift in perspective meant that people had to learn how to read the view from above. Surprisingly, it was not only the general public that was unfamiliar with the aerial view: even design professionals trained to read plans and maps needed to get used to it.

FLATNESS AND RELIEF

Given that the actual views of the earth experienced by balloonists and the early aviators were similar, it is only logical that early descriptions of the appearance of the earth seen from airplanes resembled reports by the early balloonists. The seeming suspension of time and movement and the new view—the god's-eye view—onto what now appeared to be an ordered, flat, spherical world in two dimensions caused both excitement and bewilderment among eighteenth- and nineteenth-century balloonists and twentieth-century pilots alike. The balloonists' and pilots' comments on the flat appearance of the earth's surface and on its appearance as a map, carpet, relief, and a miniature world were particularly common and anticipated the use of aerial photographs in mapmaking and model building.

When the American physician John Jeffries ascended over London in a balloon with Jean-Pierre Blanchard in 1784, he described the earth as "a beautiful coloured map or carpet, not having the least appearance of hill, elevation of buildings, or inequality of surface whatever."[8] At lesser heights and at times when the sun cast long shadows after dawn and before dusk, the earth could appear as a miniature relief, as Prince Pückler-Muskau noted after his 1817 balloon ascent above Berlin:

> One can think of nothing more beautiful than the sight of how the crowds, streets, houses and finally the towers gradually became smaller and smaller, how the former noise became a quiet murmur and then a soundless silence, and then finally how the whole of the earth we had left was spread out below us like a relief by Pfyffer: the splendid linden trees were merely a green furrow, the Spree appeared like a thin thread whereas the poplars of the Potsdamer Allee threw huge, many-miles-long shadows over the immense plain. . . . I never before witnessed anything comparable to this scene even from the summit of the highest mountains.[9]

Pückler had probably recently seen the world-famous relief built by the Swiss officer Franz Ludwig Pfyffer in the years preceding 1786 in Berlin's Royal Palace, where it had been on show in the early years of the nineteenth century. The relief that measured 19.69 by 13.12 feet (6 by 4 meters) was one of the first of its kind and offered the public a realistic overview of all of Switzerland and its Alpine landscape.

Like Jeffries, Baldwin, and Pückler before them, pilots in the early twentieth century pointed out how the earth could appear as a flat surface, map, or relief. The U.S. Army Major Herbert E. Ives noted in 1920 that the earth seen from an altitude of 1.24 miles (2,000 meters) and above appeared flat, almost without relief, and that it lacked extremes of light and shade. As a result of this and the layer of atmospheric haze, "the earth below presents the appearance of a delicate pastel."[10] Pückler and Ives acknowledged that light created a three-dimensional effect, that it articulated objects or solids and thereby provided information on the surface structure of the earth. The American World War I Air Force Commander William Mitchell noted the relationship between increased abstraction of forms and shapes on the ground and increased height. In 1930, he wrote that from above 1.24 miles (2,000 meters) the earth began "to melt into an apparently flat surface, and the country takes on the appearance of a map." He observed that on clear days at higher altitudes of up to 3.72 miles (6,000 meters) cities, rivers, lakes, and forests were still very easily distinguished, and great mountains and volcanoes looked "like little hillocks on a relief map."[11]

The abstract patterns recognized from the air fascinated early aviators, air passengers, and design professionals. Flyers also noted the boundlessness of these patterns. In contrast to the conventional perception and representation of the landscape from a traditional horizontal viewpoint, the vertical aerial view was two-dimensional and did not appear framed. The earth appeared as "a boundless plain," as the twenty-two-year-old balloonist Vincent Lunardi, Tuscan secretary to the Neapolitan ambassador in England, noted in 1784.[12] As the early aeronaut Gaspard-Félix Tournachon, called Nadar, realized in the second half of the nineteenth century, no longer was the landscape a framed scenic picture with fore-, middle-, and background based upon linear perspective, but it appeared as an infinite two-dimensional plane of abstract lines and forms. In 1858, Nadar described the earth seen from above as a children's miniature world and as a neat infinite patchwork pattern:

> Below us . . . the earth unrolls into an immense carpet without edges, without beginning and end, in variable colors of which green dominates in all shades. . . . The irregularly checkered fields have the air of those multicolored but harmonious patchworks produced by the patient needle of the housewife. It seems as if an un-exhaustible box of toys has been opened across the earth, the earth that Swift describes to us as Lilliput, as if all the buildings of Karlsruhe had left their stock there. . . . It looks like a map because there is no perception of changes in land elevation. Everything is to the point. The river runs at the height of the mountain summit; there is no perceptible difference between the evenly mowed fields of lucern and the high forests of secular oak. And this purity of lines, this extraordinary clarity of this small microcosm where everything appears with the exquisite impression of a marvelous, delightful neatness! No waste, no scruffy seams.[13]

High oblique views of the earth likewise showed that the earth was continuous and that life had lost its frame since the horizon that was visible in these views "traveled" with the viewer.[14] In the air as on the ground, the horizon invited the viewer to move on and on. As David Leatherbarrow has observed, the horizon "always recedes or keeps itself remote," it "is always somewhere else, . . . resisting all efforts toward it," and it "drifts away to the exact degree that I move toward it, both horizontally and vertically."[15] Furthermore, in the words of Edward S. Casey, the horizon is "in principle open—to new content, new structure, new possibilities. It does not act as an edge that would impede my moving or looking," and it is therefore indeterminate.[16] In fact, in the eighteenth century, the age of the Grand Tour and balloon travel, it became common to describe travel as "broadening our horizons."[17] The aerial view therefore did both: it literally and figuratively broadened the view by eliminating edges and frames, while at the same time it made certain edges, borders, and limits between different surface textures and objects on the ground visible for the first time. While oppressive and restrictive in some contexts, these edges, borders, and limits could provide orientation, comfort, visual pleasure, and inspiration in others. As Hegel suggested, becoming aware of a limit meant to overcome and pass beyond it.[18] When seen from the air, the ground patterns created by edges, borders, and limits provide abstract images that have attracted many writers, artists, and design and planning professionals throughout the twentieth and twenty-first centuries.

Like Nadar's description of the aerial view, portrayals by twentieth-century architects and artists were often more inventive and metaphorical than factual. To Le Corbusier, flying across Argentina, Uruguay, and Paraguay in 1929, mountain ranges like the Andes appeared as wrinkles on the skin of the earth. The delta of the Parana reminded him "on a bigger scale of French or Italian Renaissance engravings in books on the art of gardens."[19] Whereas the earth as a whole appeared to him as a "poached egg," Gertrude Stein compared the earth she saw on her flights across North America in the 1930s to cubist paintings: "The wandering line of Masson was there the mixed line of Picasso coming and coming again and following itself into a beginning was there, the simple solution of Braque was there and I suppose Leger might be there."[20] Writing on aerial archaeology, Stein's contemporary John Piper, the painter, printmaker, and founder of the contemporary art journal *Axis,* observed that the cubists painted "elevations of wineglasses, gardens and windows at Nice" with an "added richness and meaning of plan-patterns."[21] Although by the early twentieth century, landscape had become an abstract pattern in the eyes of many artists regardless of whether it was represented from a horizontal, oblique, or vertical view, the latter gained attention. Photographers like Alvin Langdon Coburn and later László Moholy-Nagy experimented with aerial perspectives, climbing onto the tower of New York's Metropolitan Life Building and Berlin's radio tower to capture in their photographs the patterns created by the abstract lines and forms of the urban spaces below.

A NEW SCENERY

Seeing landscape from above was also a sublime experience. Whereas in the mid-eighteenth century British authors and painters had begun to record horizontal landscape views as sublime—awe-provoking, beautiful, and pleasurably threatening—the vertical aerial view also provided a sublime experience, in particular for the first aeronauts. Vast stretches of land unfolded beneath them, revealing the beauty of theretofore unseen landscape patterns. Viewing the land from above in a balloon was an unpredictable, yet pleasurable adventure. Even from a shaky balloon still largely at the mercy of nature's forces, the landscape and its nature no longer appeared as a threatening wilderness. On the contrary, the conquest of the air made the conquest of the land seem more possible. Although many of the first balloon flights were undertaken for scientific purposes and were geared toward the collection of climate and atmospheric data, the new view of the earth overwhelmed and awed many early aeronauts, moving them to write about what they saw. In September 1784, Vincent Lunardi recorded his balloon flight from London's Artillery Ground to a meadow in Stondon, near Ware in Hertfordshire, as a sublime experience:

> The stillness, extent, and magnificence of the scene, rendered it highly awful. My horizon seemed a perfect circle; the terminating line several hundred miles in circumference. This I conjectured from the view of London; the extreme points of which, formed an angle of only a few degrees. It was so reduced on the great scale before me, that I can find no simile to convey an idea of it. I could distinguish Saint Paul's, and other churches, from the houses. I saw the streets as lines, all animated with beings, whom I knew to be men and women, but which I should otherwise have had a difficulty in describing. It was an enormous beehive, but the industry of it was suspended. All the moving mass seemed to have no object but myself, and the transition from the suspicion, and perhaps contempt of the preceding hour, to the affectionate transport, admiration and glory of the present moment, was not without its effect on my mind. . . . [H]ow shall I describe to you a view, such as the ancients supposed Jupiter to have of the earth, and to copy which there are no terms in any language. The gradual diminution of objects and the masses of light and shade are intelligible in oblique and common prospects. But here every thing wore a new appearance, and had a new effect. The face of the country had a mild and permanent verdure, to which Italy is a stranger. The variety of cultivation, and the accuracy with which property is divided, give the idea ever present to a stranger in England, of good civil laws and an equitable administration: the rivulets meandering; the sea glistening with the rays of the sun; the immense district beneath me spotted with cities, towns, villages and houses, pouring out their inhabitants to hail my appearance.[22]

Although Lunardi, like most balloonists, focused his account on the visual experience, the auditory impression also contributed to the overall sublime and awe-provoking effect of early manned balloon flights. Lunardi noted the stillness in the air, Baldwin commented that there was no echo, Pückler observed a "soundless silence," and when Garrick Mattery, associate editor of the *Philadelphia Inquirer,* described his flight with Thaddeus S. C. Lowe over Philadelphia on a summer evening in 1860, he noted how the city and its life seemed to lie asleep below, with only a "vague murmur . . . like the distant hum of invisible insects" audible from above.[23] The sounds of life receded into the distance, or even disappeared entirely, creating a detached, unworldly atmosphere in air space.

Sublime visual experiences like Lunardi's were turned into public spectacle when panoramas—large, circular paintings displayed in specially constructed buildings—portrayed bird's-eye views of cities. The first panorama paintings were urban bird's-eye views from elevated positions like the roof of a modern factory in London, the roof of the Tuileries in Paris, and the Aventine Hill in Rome, offering imaginary aerial perspectives either of the city in which they were shown, as in the cases of London and Paris, or of faraway cities, as in the case of the Roman panorama that was shown in Berlin.[24] Through their unframed 360-degree presentation, bird's-eye panoramas and similar visionary devices like dioramas and cycloramas that imitated travelers' views from elevated positions like church steeples, rooftops, and hilltops paralleled the first aeronauts' perception of what seemed to be an endless, unbounded landscape. The panoramas eventually also offered a kinetic experience, when the observers were positioned on a slowly moving circular platform. Among the moving panoramas developed for theater stages at the time could be found the so-called balloon panorama, which was used as an additional attraction in pantomime productions in the 1820s and 1830s. The moving balloon panoramas were inspired by early-nineteenth-century balloon flights, such as the 1836 balloon flight from London to Weilburg, Nassau, undertaken by the aeronaut Charles Green, along with Thomas Monck Mason and Robert Holland. As a scenery painting that showed the earth from above along a particular route of flight, the balloon panorama was held and positioned on the stage by horizontal rollers. When actors went on a balloon flight, the vertical or oblique aerial panorama unrolled vertically from the top to the bottom of the stage, thereby simulating the unfolding of scenery below a balloon car.[25]

By the early twentieth century, critics had begun to argue that the aerial view could give rise to a new artistic paradigm and a new understanding of landscape. As a consequence of the aerial view and the perceived flatness of the earth, the *New York Times* writer H. I. Brock wrote in 1926, "what 'scenery' is will have to be revised." Attesting to the scenic value of the flat North American plains when seen from above, he asserted that "the seeming monotony of a flat country is now transformed into a pattern of colors." Brock claimed that the earth seen from an airplane not only created a map effect but also a "Persian rug effect."[26] The aerial view asked for attention to surface and surface pattern. According to Brock, cultivating beautiful air views on the plains required farmers to "take more care of the plane geometry of agricultural operations." This "rug-pattern scenery" and "cubistic beauty" of aerial vision would, according to Brock, "become a most important factor in art and advertising—and in conversation."

Indeed, it would only be a couple of years before planners began to warn of the nuisance of air advertising in the form of signs painted on roofs along air routes. It became clear that, just as advertising billboards had proliferated along roads and highways, similar developments were to be expected from aviation.[27] The authors of the 1930 Harvard airport study therefore cautioned that "misuse of the scenery visible from the air is sure to begin soon,—indeed it is already beginning."[28] In Britain, the Aerodromes Committee of the Royal Institute of British Architects warned in 1931 that air advertising was "rapidly becoming a major nuisance in the United States." The committee considered it a "large-scale interference" in landscape amenities for both air and ground travelers and cautioned that advertisement could also be confused with deliberate air-markings of towns, routes, etc., thereby endangering air navigation.[29] Brock, however, was more concerned with the new aerial scenery's affective and lyrical capacities. Like his nineteenth-century colleague George Washington Peck before him, who had argued that the bird's-eye view would lead to a new "Poetry of our Cities," Brock anticipated that the new vertical scenery would inspire a new type of poetry.[30]

READING THE LANDSCAPE FROM ABOVE

The new vertical perspective from balloons and airplanes caused consternation among balloonists, early aviators, and design professionals alike, despite the training the latter had in site analysis, mapping, and plan drawing. The seeming suspension of time and movement did nothing to facilitate orientation from the air. Pilots and their passengers found the amount of information the aerial view provided overwhelming and the new perspective it afforded difficult to interpret. As László Moholy-Nagy and many of his contemporaries noted in the 1920s and 1930s, people needed to become accustomed to and learn how to read views from above.[31] At the beginning of powered flight in 1910, Charles C. Turner had commented on how difficult it was for aeronauts "to recognize even familiar country from above" since hills and towers that served as landmarks on the ground were hardly visible from the air, and from an altitude of 5,000 feet (1.52 kilometers), 1,000-foot- (304.8-meter-) high hills with gentle contours could easily be missed.[32] Ten years later, in 1920 during her first flight as a passenger at an air meet near Long Beach, Los Angeles, Amelia Earhart realized that "one of the senses which must be developed in flying is an acuteness in recognizing characteristics of the terrain, a sense seldom possessed by a novice."[33]

In the 1920s, American aviation strip charts, modeled on European examples, assisted pilots in this visual navigation (fig. 35). Air guides consisting of simplified strip charts and a verbal commentary on the principal visible landscape features fulfilled this purpose for passengers. Aviation strip charts showed a single air route, mostly between two cities, and represented only the landmarks that were visible from the sky, including waterways and lakes, main and secondary highways, transmission lines, railroads with one, two, and three tracks, race tracks, polo fields, golf courses, mountain ranges, mountain plateaus, and clearings. To enhance clarity, the use of colors was limited to green (woods), blue (water), black (railroads, prominent buildings, monuments), brown (prominent ridges, hills, mountains), and red (roads in the early charts, cities, and towns). To further improve on the clarity of the graphical representation, from the 1920s onward roads were depicted as white lines. When an air route lacked landmarks that could aid in visual navigation, they were on occasion created artificially. In 1922, the Royal Air Force used a tractor to plow a 390-mile ditch that could guide airmail pilots across the Syrian Desert between Egypt and Baghdad. This "modern technique of Desert communications . . . gave the impression of a pencil having been drawn across the desert" and on occasion also included marking landing fields with numerals inscribed into the earth.[34]

From 1930 onward, the backsides of many aviation strip charts showed a map for night flying. These black-and-white maps representing the nighttime environmental conditions prominently indicated the beacon lights that had been constructed approximately ten to fifteen miles apart along the flight routes to guide pilots during night flying. Thus, the early aeronautical strip charts sought a balance between a relatively "realistic" and an abstract representation of the land to aid the pilots' orientation.

The Aerial View Captured on Photographic Film

Aviation strip charts provided pilots with a necessary aid for orientating themselves above ground at high speeds. For this purpose it was sufficient—even necessary—that these maps displayed only selected landscape features and elements visible on the earth's surface from high altitudes. But the aerial view offered pilots more information about the land than what was conveyed on strip maps, and the photographic camera turned out to be ideal for capturing that information. Confronted with the difficulty of recognizing and identifying landscape features from above, William Mitchell remarked in 1930 that the pilot's "mind is not capable of recording everything at once, but a photographic plate in a camera can do this."[35] In fact, it was the camera's capability of fixing an aerial view and providing what Charles

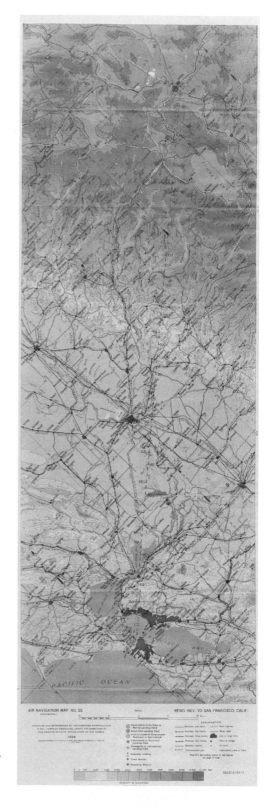

FIG. 35. Aeronautical strip chart
for the route from Reno, Nevada,
to San Francisco, 1924. (Donald G.
Duke, *Airports and Airways* [New
York: Ronald Press, 1927])

Sanders Peirce at the end of the nineteenth century called an "index" and what Susan Sontag has more recently called the "anthology of images"[36]—an act the eye is not capable of and the mind is overwhelmed with—that provided many advantages in times of both war and peace. Aerial photography offered a new tool and method to a variety of disciplines, including architecture, landscape architecture, and planning. It could record all the visible details of the earth's surface and subsurface, as archaeologists were quick to realize. Aerial photographs could offer an indexical view. Thus, although many design and planning professionals took to flying as both pilots and passengers, in most cases it was not the direct aerial view that they used in their work but the mediated photographic image of the earth from above.

Aerial photography was largely a result of the progress in aviation and warfare, in particular during World War I. Its beginnings, however, go back to the second half of the nineteenth century, when balloons provided platforms for the first attempts at aerial photography and cinematography. In 1858, Nadar took the first aerial photographs from a balloon near Paris. Only a couple of years later, in October 1860, the American photographer James Wallace Black accompanied the balloonist Samuel A. King on a flight above Boston (fig. 36). Interestingly, neither the subject nor the presentation of his photograph showing a view over a central part of Boston corresponded with the new perception of the "endless" landscape, which was described in early aeronautical texts as an "immense carpet without edges" (Nadar) and that implied a loosening of boundaries and a breaking up of borders. Not only did this early aerial photograph focus on Boston's business district, Brattle Street, and the harbor, but it was framed by an oval passe-partout, thereby assigning it the function of a city portrait and containing it safely within eighteenth- and nineteenth-century pictorial conventions.

Nadar's and Black's early urban aerial photographs built upon a long tradition of painted city portraits and bird's-eye views. Painted bird's-eye views of cities adorned some Renaissance palaces as in the early example of Pinturicchio's paintings of Rome, Milan, Genoa, Florence, Venice, and Naples in the loggia of Innocent VIII's Belvedere in the Vatican. The late-fifteenth-century representation of Florence known as the *Map with the Chain (Carta della catena,* 1490)—considered to be the first printed comprehensive city view from an elevated viewpoint of the modern era—combined the knowledge gleaned from various selected viewpoints to make the representation both as informative and recognizable, and as "true to nature," or "lifelike," as possible. Similar to some of the first urban aerial photographs, therefore, the early city portraits resulted from the search for total knowledge about the respective towns. They also reflected the prevalent Renaissance conception of the city as a microcosm that was clearly distinguishable from its surrounding countryside and therefore could be grasped easily from an elevated vantage point in the distance.[37] Like later nineteenth- and twentieth-century photographers, painters in the fifteenth and sixteenth centuries were intent on depicting a city's context and relationship to its hinterland, celebrating the city's importance and influence. However, in contrast to the mechanical representation on photographic film that fixed one individual viewpoint at a time and therefore often also tended to focus on a building ensemble, or one particular building, artists in the fifteenth and sixteenth centuries often combined a variety of viewpoints in one painting. At the end of the fifteenth century, Italian artists began to use the cities' ground plans to paint imaginary "perspective plans" from viewpoints that were "physically impossible at the time," and that, as Lucia Nuti and other authors have shown, were nonexistent.[38] One of the first was Jacopo de' Barbari's famous six-sheet woodcut of Venice (ca. 1500), "an all-embracing view from above as only God could attain."[39] Venice is spread out, of course, on the flat terrain of islands in a lagoon, which is why—with the exception of the city's campaniles—there were no elevated vantage points from which to view the city. Although research has shown that Barbari's woodcut, whose purpose was probably to celebrate the city, was likely based on detailed surveys conducted from campaniles and then systematically adjusted to serve the plan's pictorial and iconographical purposes, artists at the time still required a certain amount of invention and imagination to produce an illusionary aerial view. Imagination and political intent continued to inform the representation of cities in painted bird's-eye views. In the nineteenth century, resident and itinerant artists produced imaginary bird's-eye views of rapidly growing hamlets, towns, and cities in the New World as lithographic prints for an early mass market to attract people and industry to these places. Offering general overviews, these pictorial bird's-eye views portrayed ideal visions and often did not correspond to the exact conditions on the ground, although they were increasingly based on cartographic knowledge as the nineteenth century progressed.[40] If, in fifteenth-century Italy, many painted and etched bird's-eye views were still based on the dream of attaining a godly view, by the nineteenth century in the United States this dream had given way to more pragmatic fantasies that involved the growth and wealth of the represented newly founded cities. Aerial photography finally provided a means that could increase pictorial accuracy with relative ease. In contrast to earlier bird's-eye views, aerial photographs could offer real evidence and images of authentic circumstances, even if they were, of course, directed and positioned by the photographer.

After Nadar and Black, scientists in England, France, Austria, and Russia continued experiments with aerial photography from balloons through the last decades of the nineteenth century. In Germany, in 1893, Hans Gross was able to take some of the first aerial photographs of Berlin from a balloon, just a few years before the German film pioneer Oskar Messter made the first aerial film in 1897 from the balloon *Kondor,* part of the airship battalion in Tempelhof. In the United States, George R. Lawrence, a Chicago studio photographer, documented the devastation of the 1906 San Francisco earthquake in a panoramic aerial photograph measuring 48 by 18¾ inches with the help of unmanned aerial kites.[41] With this he anticipated the function that satellite imagery fulfills today when portraying the expansion of disaster zones resulting from earthquakes, floods, fires, storms, and wars. Before Lawrence, several late-nineteenth-century photographers in the United States had taken single- or multiple-plate panoramic photographs of cities from towers and hilltops. Though often similar in their viewpoint and scope to the lithographic bird's-eye views, these photographs lacked the latter's boosterism. Late-nineteenth-century panoramic photographers who tried to capture cities in their completeness were attempting to portray them as civilized, comprehensible, and therefore controllable places. The panoramic visions often affirmed the views of the privileged upper classes predominantly inhabiting elevated locations.[42]

In 1909, the German town geometer P. Kahle commented on the theretofore unimaginable advantages that dirigible zeppelins offered to aerial photography, mapmaking, and the exploration of new lands. But even locations close to home could appear novel in aerial photographs. In 1913, the German garden magazine *Die Gartenwelt* proudly presented its readers with a first aerial photograph of the Botanic Garden Berlin-Dahlem taken from the zeppelin *Hansa*.[43] Until that time, most of the early aerial photographs and films had been taken from either tethered or dirigible balloons, airships, and kites. Further improvement and advances in aerial photography required not only the development of photographic equipment—that is, improved and new types of cameras with rapid plate-changing mechanisms, and new types of lenses, filters and film; it also required progress in the control, steering, and speed of airships, qualities that were finally much improved by powered flight.

While airplanes provide more stable stations for cameras, their controlled movement also enabled more flexible flight paths offering a variety of aerial viewpoints. Piloted and powered flight provided suitable conditions for the development of vertical aerial photography along with photography from oblique angles that, as Herbert E. Ives explained, was comparable to the "heretofore fictitious 'bird's-eye view'" and the most satisfying from a pictorial point of view.[44] Oblique aerial photographs looked downward and sideways across a landscape, providing panoramic views. They were taken at an angle to the ground with the optical axis of the camera directed between the horizontal and the vertical. Oblique aerial photographs, in particular, could show how sites fit into a landscape. Vertical aerial photographs, on the other hand, could more readily reveal landscape patterns. Taken from airplanes since 1908 with the camera axis perpendicular to the land, vertical aerial photographs do not display a one-point perspective, a vanishing point, or a horizon and sky. They were considered to provide "the most complete and uniform picture of the landscape that is possible."[45] In 1930, William Mitchell therefore noted: "Never in our history have we been able to see as much or learn as much of the earth's surface as we do from aircraft."[46]

Besides the military, many professions dealing with the land realized the potential of aerial photography from airplanes for their purposes and development. Before design and planning professionals became aware of the opportunities aerial photography could offer them, geographers and British, German, and Italian archaeologists saw the advantages of aerial photography. The latter soon developed what has become known as aerial archaeology, the use of aerial photographs for site discovery and surface mapping. The British, German, and Italian interest in colonial power and in forging a national identity and conscience was a motivating force in these endeavors. Surveying and inventorying ancient sites during the late-nineteenth- and early-twentieth-century colonial wars in Africa were acts of colonization and the basis of Western "power-knowledge." However, aerial archaeology was also used closer to home. When the Venetian architect Giacomo Boni directed the excavations of the Roman Forum, he used photographs taken between 1899 and 1906 from a captive balloon to document the progress of the excavations and celebrate the Roman past as the foundation of the new modern Italian state. Aerial photography could unveil layers of history and facilitated the understanding of the landscape as a palimpsest.

The use of aerial photography in detecting and unveiling the past was especially promoted in Britain by Osbert Guy S. Crawford, who had served as an observer in the British Royal Flying Corps during World War I. As a result of his successful first attempts at aerial archaeology in Britain in 1919 he was appointed the first archaeology officer of the Ordnance Survey one year later. Crawford observed how the detection of prehistoric sites was made possible by the character traits of plant cover, which was sensitive to differences of soil and moisture. The different moisture content of filled-in ditches, for example, promoted plant growth in these locations. "Thus," Crawford concluded, "from above one sees and can photograph, a belt of darker green corn following the line of the vanished ditch." He noted that especially when detecting larger sites, "the distant view [was] necessary to convert chaos into order."[47] To illustrate what has since become known among archaeologists as the "Persian carpet effect," Crawford, who liked cats, used an analogy that compared the low viewpoint of a cat with the higher viewpoint of a human being. When looking at a carpet pattern, the cat would see only an unintelligible jumble of lines and colors whereas a human being would perceive the lines and colors as an ornamental pattern. Crawford used this analogy, which he illustrated in two photographs showing the cat and human perspective of the same carpet, to explain aerial archaeology in lectures.[48] Given that many early aeronauts and pilots had likened the earth's surface when seen from above to a flat carpet, Crawford's choice of analogy appears very fitting. What the analogy also showed was that the human viewpoint, if compared to that of most animals, can already be considered as "aerial," a character trait that is made use of in the design practice of model building that experienced a renaissance in the 1920s and 1930s.

Archaeologists had demonstrated how aerial photographs showed the landscape as a palimpsest, and how they could be used as evidence to both uncover facts and reveal context and relationships of and between artifacts and sites. Inadvertently archaeologists had also shown that aerial views and photographs literally and figuratively presented spaces in between to imagine, reconstruct, and represent history.

By the time that aerial archaeology had finally also taken off in the United States in the 1920s, a number of other disciplines had also begun to make more serious use of the new technology that had undergone further development during World War I. In addition to scholars in disciplines of the earth sciences like geography, ecology, geology, and soil science, in the interwar years various professionals who dealt with shaping the land realized the potential of the aerial view captured in vertical and oblique aerial photographs from airplanes. Architects, landscape architects, and city planners were attracted by the analytic and synoptic quality of the aerial view, and they were drawn toward both the expressive and critical-analytical qualities of aerial photographs. They appreciated aerial photography's immediacy; the velocity of its relatively inexpensive mechanical production and reproduction; the precise, factual, and realistic images of the earth it could provide; and the contextual, holistic view it offered. Aerial photographs resulted from, and enabled, both disembodied and embodied views. Design and planning professionals appreciated this dialectic: the factual evidence, assurance of reality, and realistic spatial relationships that aerial photographs offered on the one hand, and their affective and expressive qualities on the other.

AN OBJECTIVE VIEW:
MAPPING THE EARTH VIEWED FROM NOWHERE

In 1888, the U.S. Army Lieutenant Henry A. Reed had already pointed out that "the naturalness of the photographic representation might convey some information not afforded . . . by a topographical map."[49] Design professionals considered all types of aerial photographs a valuable functional visualization tool because of their factual precision. This precision played an important role in the provision of basic mapping material and in land design and development as will be seen here and in the following chapters. Aerial photography meant "focusing on facts," as a mid-twentieth-century brochure of the aerial photographic mapping company Fairchild Aerial Surveys was entitled.[50] Even today, Pictometry, a company founded in 2000 that offers vertical and oblique aerial photography and related software to state, federal, and private agencies in the United States and abroad, advertises its images to municipal planners and developers as "presenting a real world view."[51] The widespread assumption that *vertical* aerial photographs are particularly truthful and objective also reflects a common epistemological belief of the late nineteenth and early twentieth centuries. It is telling that even today the "view from nowhere" and the "god's-eye perspective" are used as metaphors for objectivity. In the 1950s, Maurice Merleau-Ponty criticized contemporary scientific thinking as "high-altitude thinking" and a "thinking which looks on from above, and thinks of the object-in-general."[52]

Besides their arguably flawless imagery, the mechanical means of production of aerial photographs made them appear to be unmediated objective representations of the earth's surface, "true to nature,"[53] and "representing things as they really are."[54] The medium—aerial photographs—was believed to be the message. In this sense, they were expressions of what Daston and Galison have called "mechanical objectivity," an "epistemic virtue" that developed in the second half of the nineteenth century among scientists who considered image production by machines like photographic cameras rather than by the human hand and intellect the most "objective" representational means. Aerial photographs were seen as representations of objective knowledge and of what Daston and Galison have described as "blind sight, seeing without inference, interpretation or intelligence."[55] As the fine art photographer Edward Steichen noted when reporting on his duties as an aerial photographer in World War I, aerial photographs "represent[ed] neither opinions nor prejudice, but indisputable facts."[56] Design professionals believed that aerial photographs never lied. In contrast to maps that displayed only selected information depending on the objectives and the whim of the respective cartographer, aerial photographs were seen as a more reliable source of information and were thought to give "a truer view of the world."[57] Their use for surveillance and the detection of enemy positions during World War I emphasized this belief. The view from above captured in vertical aerial photographs did not allow for any secrets. It was believed to convey "the unvarnished truth."[58] "The airman," as William Mitchell stated in 1930, "can see everything that lies on the surface of the ground or water. Nothing that floats on the water can be hidden because there is no such thing as a tree or ditch or overhanging cliff by which it might be concealed."[59] Instead, by both providing and representing a means of knowing and understanding the earth's surface (and subsurface), the view from above allowed for the sensation of "conscious mastery,"[60] control, and power. Aviators, so it seemed, were able to assume a godly point of view, thus increasing the distance between subject and object, spectator and spectacle, man and the world, and mind and matter that underlay Petrarch's portrayal of his ascent of Mont Ventoux.

In the first decades of the twentieth century, architects, landscape architects, and city planners therefore saw the "aerial picture" as "a speedy and accurate means of . . . showing exact conditions,"[61] which was a valuable quality for surveying and mapping cities, regions, and other project areas. The idea that aerial photographs provided an objective view of the earth's surface lay at the basis of the first aerial mapping endeavors. Like a single vertical aerial photograph, photo mosaics—composites of vertical aerial photographs that covered adjacent land areas (also called aerial photographic maps or photomaps)—were to present an aerial view from nowhere, that is, from no fixed viewpoint. To the casual observer, the elimination of the fixed viewpoint objectified the aerial view. As with single vertical aerial photographs, it was believed that in mosaic maps made from aerial photographs "everything is shown in true proportion and in its proper location."[62] The viewer's attention was not directed to a particular feature as in many more interpretative oblique photographs, and the land appeared clearly visible in all its details, determined by different forms, shapes, textures, and color tones. In turn, it was exactly this "objective" quality of vertical aerial photographs and mosaics that provided the basis for specific subjective purposes, as will be briefly noted below and further elaborated on in chapters 3, 4, and 5. Thus, while the viewpoint and therewith the observer in aerial photos and mosaics were "nonexistent," "non-identifiable," or "hidden," the land was exposed and subject to the aerial gaze.

By the 1920s, aerial photographs had become essential to any activity that had to do with the use of the land. In the United States and Canada, where large stretches of land had yet to be surveyed—in 1930 more than half of the United States had never been mapped[63]—vertical aerial photographs in particular provided the basis for a variety of map types including planimetric and contour maps and photo mosaics. To obtain as little distortion as possible, the flight altitude of airplanes had to be the same along their entire course, the tilt of the airplane and camera had to be as small as possible, and only in the case of flat terrain was parallactic displacement minimal. Parallactic displacement in vertical aerial photographs describes the tendency of vertical structures or terrain features located far from the photo center point to appear to lean outward, with the bottom of the structure or feature appearing closer to the center point than its top. Aerial photographs that were to be used as the basis of planimetric and contour maps, and photo mosaics in most cases therefore required substantial corrections through various elaborate instrumental measures. If exact measurements were not required because maps were merely needed as illustrations or for plotting other information, the two fastest methods typically used to produce maps from aerial photographs were the direct tracing of lines on frosted celluloid that was laid over the aerial photographs, and the waterproof inking of relevant lines directly on the photograph. The latter procedure would be followed by the bleaching of the photograph so that inked lines would remain on a white background.

Aerial mapping, or aerial photogrammetry—the use of aerial photographs in the surveying of land—was not only comparatively inexpensive, but also very fast and accurate.[64] It was therefore especially valuable in expansive countries like the United States, where the Department of Agriculture, the Forest Service, and the Soil Conservation Service were the principal public sources of aerial photos. In addition, a number of private companies were founded that offered their services for aerial surveying and mapping, among them Brock & Weymouth in Philadelphia, the Fairchild Aerial Camera Corporation in New York City, Spence Air Photos in Los Angeles, and Edgar Tobin Aerial Surveys in San Antonio. The Airmap Corporation of America advertised itself as "An Engineering Service for Engineers by Engineers," calling the value of aerial photographs to the attention of "municipal, railroad, electrical, highway, hydraulic and valuation engineers and foresters."[65] Aerial photographs proved particularly helpful in the mapping of terrain that was difficult to access on the ground, like marshes and coastal areas. However, aerial maps were also used for many other purposes: for the assessment of land uses, including surveys of forest and mineral resources and for soil preservation studies; for irrigation and water supply projects; for river and harbor development; and for the layout of power lines, highways, and railroads.

They also provided a new means of surveillance that could be used to control land and property taxation as well as to arrest lawbreakers. One of the first municipalities revalued by an aerial survey was Middletown, Connecticut. During the process, almost 1,900 buildings were discovered that had previously escaped taxation. As early as 1922, the police in U.S. cities had realized that aerial mosaic maps provided information on the location and details of roof exits, scuttle holes, and skylights that could help in "directing a raid or surrounding a burglar."[66]

Many authors, like S. S. Steinberg, contended that mapping from the air would never fully replace ground surveying. However, the temptation to base planning work exclusively on the aerial view was great for a number of reasons, not least because it saved time and money. Aerial surveys enabled planning to be carried out clandestinely. The power-knowledge that aerial surveying provided was subject to abuse in times of both war and peace. For example, in the 1920s surveyors in the United States had already noted that with the airplane and the respective photographic equipment, large areas could be mapped for determining the location of power transmission lines "without . . . arousing the suspicion of landowners who are thus kept in ignorance of the fact that a corporation is about to seek a right of way."[67] It was pointed out that aerial mapping gave power companies an advantage over unsuspecting farmers, who would be confronted with development plans that appeared literally out of thin air.[68] City planners considered aerial mapping advantageous because, among other things, it prevented surveyors from annoying people by "roam[ing] round their garden treading on their favorite flowers!"[69] This, however, may have been a self-serving argument from a group with an interest in minimizing citizen opposition to city planning schemes. In fact, in 1944, Russell Van Nest Black recognized that "not the least value of air photographs in planning is in what they show of things in the interiors of blocks and large properties—things not ordinarily shown on maps and not visible from the street or road."[70] As will be shown in chapter 5, this argument would recur in the postwar years, when systematic research was undertaken into the use of aerial photographs for quantitative and qualitative surveys regarding urban buildings and socio-economic patterns.

"THE IMAGE LIVES!": THE AFFECTIVE AND SYNTHETIC QUALITY OF AERIAL PHOTOGRAPHS

Whereas the disembodied, objectifying, distanced, and detached view captured in aerial photographs could facilitate mapping and planning endeavors, as well as different types of surveillance and control, some planning and design professionals saw more in aerial photographs than two-dimensional patterns, recognizing that they also had affective, synthetic, and expressive qualities. In fact, planners believed that aerial photographs offered more "realistic" views that were less abstract than diagrammatic maps and therefore more easily grasped by an untrained public. In other words, the landscapes of aerial photographs could more easily be "inhabited" than the same landscapes presented as cartographic maps. In addition, design and planning professionals saw in aerial photographs materials that could be used in the design process and in design representation. They came to recognize that aerial photographs had affective qualities and that they enabled phenomenal embodiment. The aerial camera thus had "twin capacities, to subjectivise reality and to objectify it,"[71] as John Berger pointed out for the camera in general in his 1978 response to Susan Sontag's *On Photography*. Aerial photographs could both reproduce an image representing facts, and produce an image thereby appealing to the creative imagination. Despite this arguably new perspective, aerial photographs could evoke memories of actual bodily experience, suggesting what a particular place or space felt like on the ground.

The French-born American architect Paul Philippe Cret also considered the artistic merit of vertical aerial photographs for the study of gardens, landscapes, and urban form.[72] In 1921, Cret argued that since their color values and shadows made the aerial photographs appear livelier than simple plans, they could also portray some of the ephemeral atmospheric and emotional character traits of a place. This represented a very different view of the uses of aerial photographs from the one prevalent in World War I, when vertical photographic surveying on a large scale was first practiced. The reconnaissance photographs taken from airplanes during World War I showed distanced, emotionally detached views of devastated landscapes and barren battlegrounds with trenches, dugouts, and embattlements appearing as abstract geometrical lines and forms. Human bodies were often not visible in these photographs because of the altitude at which they were taken. And yet, the potential sensuous quality of aerial photographs in general had been noticed as early as 1909. In Germany, the town geometer P. Kahle excitedly commented on aerial photographs taken from dirigible airships, proclaiming: "The image lives!"[73] Depending on the weather and light conditions and the height at which they were taken, many vertical aerial photographs exhibited an ambiguous character that oscillated between a two- and three-dimensional representation of the earth's surface. Through the production of overlapping aerial photographs that could be viewed through a stereoscope, the same photograph could be seen either as a two-dimensional pattern (without stereoscope) or a three-dimensional living space (through the stereoscope). Stereoscopes, which despite their arguable simulation of tangible, vivid, three-dimensional environments had gone out of fashion by the late nineteenth century due to the unconcealed mechanical production of the stereoscopic effect and their waning entertainment value, underwent a renaissance through their use in military air intelligence during World War I.[74]

Even without a stereoscope, some architects and planners, like Cret, acknowledged the lively qualities and the visual sensuousness of aerial photographs, whether vertical or oblique. In fact, they attributed to these photographs some of the qualities of what Arnold Berleant has called the "participatory landscape,"[75] a depiction of landscape that engages viewers, drawing them into the picture and inviting them to inhabit the depicted landscape. These vivid qualities of aerial photographs also caught the attention of the German surveyor Alfred Abendroth, who shortly after World War I explained how architects, city planners, and "landscape picture-makers" (*Landschaftsbildner*), or landscape gardeners could use these as well as the cartographic qualities of aerial photos in the design process. In fact, for all designs concerning "the earth's surface, its construction and planting," vertical and oblique aerial views would provide the best basis because they alone offered the "correct spatial imagination of nature." According to Abendroth, no other means of representation had the powerful spatial effect of aerial photographs, which conveyed a "lively image of the locality in its smallest detail."[76]

Like Cret and Abendroth, the painter John Piper some years later highlighted the affective quality of vertical aerial photographs. Basing his argument on aerial photographs used in archaeology, he posited that although they were "completely un-art-conscious," they were "beautiful" and could evoke feelings for a space and for the spatial relationships between physical features.[77] Thus, Piper attributed to aerial photographs both a functional and aesthetic quality that made them both tool and artwork. Despite their detailed representation, Abendroth argued, vertical aerial photographs and their mosaics were much easier to read than maps. They could be produced faster than a survey plan and provided a more vivid image. In the design process, aerial photographs could reveal where sightlines should be established, which natural features should be highlighted, where human habitation should be sited, and which location would be appropriate for what land use. As Abendroth pointed out, the aerial view could also show "ugliness that needed to be veiled."[78] The understanding was that the aerial perspective could be used to create pictorialized scenery in which certain landscape features would be framed, centered, or elevated. In 1909, P. Kahle had already pointed out that aerial photography from dirigible airships could lead urban planners to take into account the "landscape aspect" (*landschaftliche Anblick*) of the urban realm, that is, the landscape of open space, when laying out new neighborhoods.[79]

It would have been clear to these commentators that drafted architectural and landscape architectural plans were similar to vertical aerial photographs—at least with regard to the overhead view they offered. However, in contrast to a plan that Le Corbusier described as "an austere abstraction" and "nothing more than an algebrization and a dry-looking thing," vertical aerial photographs had a lively quality. Cret's and Abendroth's insistence on this character trait stressed their belief that, in contrast to the plan that, as Le Corbusier noted, called "for the most active imagination,"[80] aerial photographs were as near to reality as any vertical representation of the terrain could be. In fact, Cret, Kahle, Abendroth, and Piper were aware of the difference between surface and plane, and edge and line. Whereas an edge that appears as a relatively straight line in an aerial photograph is formed by two surfaces, drafted straight lines in an abstract plan drawing depict an edge between two planes. As the psychologist James J. Gibson has pointed out, the geometric plane is "a very thin sheet in space" that lacks texture and substance.[81] In contrast, edges appearing in vertical aerial photographs convey the textural qualities and substance of the different adjoining surfaces. As a consequence, they can never appear as sharp as ruled lines in a plan drawing, resulting in a livelier representation of the surface qualities.

Aerial photography provided a new tool not only for the design process, but also for the representation of designs. If design drawings were inserted into aerial photographs, the design context could be shown more clearly and vividly. Exemplifying the use of both vertical and oblique aerial photographs in the design process, the American landscape architect F. A. Cushing Smith argued that vertical air maps of university campuses gave landscape architects a better idea of the relationship between the campus and its surroundings and better enabled "the landscape architect to apply his design to existing conditions."[82] Oblique photographs in particular could illustrate the way existing and projected buildings were inserted into the existing topography. Cushing Smith proposed to test designs through photomontage by inserting oblique photographs of models into oblique aerial photographs of the larger site, a standard practice today, when computer programs like Photoshop have come to facilitate this process. These representational techniques were the result of empirical embodiment, or inhabitation, of the respective land-scape in the aerial photographs. By placing a sketch or model photograph of a new landscape feature or building into an aerial photograph, spatial relationships could be tested. This representational technique simulated the projected environment, and by facilitating mental engagement with it, the viewer could gauge what it would be like to inhabit the new landscape.

Oblique aerial photographs were also used for collages that were intended to give an impression of what areas of a particular city would look like after a new plan was carried out. In the case of *The Regional Plan of New York* de-veloped in the 1920s, collages consisting of aerial photographs and perspec-tival drawings illustrated proposed inner-city developments (fig. 37). These collage representations included aerial views of what was considered the "ultimate development of Glenn Curtiss Airport," of the proposed apart-ment and park development along the waterfront of Brooklyn Heights, and of the proposed new Brooklyn downtown.[83] Besides supporting a heavy-handed approach to design and planning, the use of collage by inserting design drawings or model photographs into aerial photographs, as noted by Abendroth and Cushing Smith and as practiced in *The Regional Plan of New York,* enabled synthetic and contextual vision. It facilitated creating "realistic" three-dimensional images of proposed landscape and urban de-signs and establishing both mental and ultimately physical connections to their surroundings. Although the collages suggested here for use in design representation, of course differed significantly in design and intent from the mixed-media art first developed by cubist artists like Picasso, Bracque, and Gris, they shared an "engagement with modernity."[84] While the cubists had a liking for materials like wallpaper and newspaper that were artifacts of popular culture and mechanical production, design and planning pro-fessionals discovered the use of reproducible aerial photographs and of the aerial perspective for design representation and the testing of designs and plans. Despite the difference in intent, design, and media, what Gertrude Stein observed for cubism—the fact that "the framing of life, the need that a picture exist in its frame, remain in its frame was over"[85]—seems also to have been applicable to parts of design representation in the early twentieth century. The aerial view captured in photographs directed attention to the relationship between different parts of a design and its context. It acknowl-edged that a design was always part of a larger landscape.

Synoptic and Contextual Visions

Besides revealing the minutest facts, details, and elements, aerial photo-graphs also offered beautiful synthetic views that showed the relationship between these elements. Vertical aerial photographs in particular showed

FIG. 37.
Aerial photograph
and collage of an
aerial photograph
and a perspectival
drawing used
to illustrate the
proposed apart-
ment and park
development along
the waterfront of
Brooklyn Heights.
(Committee on
Regional Plan of
New York and Its
Environs, *Regional
Plan of New York and
Its Environs,* vol. 2,
*The Building of the
City* [Philadelphia:
Wm. F. Fell Co.
Printers, 1929],
486, 489)

patterns and a landscape continuum, a landscape without boundaries. They could illustrate the continuity and connections between the city and its surrounding areas, and between different landscape formations characterized by various types of plant cover. The mapping techniques developed for military and civilian purposes produced sequences of photographs that, placed together as a mosaic, covered extensive land areas and could be extended as required. Aerial photo mosaics were "a carpet without edges" (Nadar). Taking photographs while moving above the earth's surface in an airplane, literally providing an endless sequence of both vertical and oblique aerial views, offered a view of continuous space and time, or—to apply Gertrude Stein's observations on cubist paintings to this context—of life without a frame. In photo mosaics, edges and frames were therefore also transcended in a very practical sense: The vertical photographs were taken along parallel lines of flight in such a way that they significantly overlapped on all sides. Thus, there were no edges and limits, and photo mosaics throughout their production process and as final products gave expression to an edgeless world. Because the photos assembled into one mosaic were not taken simultaneously but froze sequential moments in time, photo mosaics expressed both the compression and the continuity of time. They were a construct of synchrony and contemporaneity.

Vertical and oblique aerial photographs could therefore literally offer a holistic perspective, a view that many early-twentieth-century scholars supported in its figurative sense, hoping that it could tie together the arts and sciences and support scientific endeavors that were based on both reason and intuition. The aerial view supported and sustained holism and the principle of totality, epistemological beliefs developed at the end of the nineteenth century that played an important role in ecology, in reinforcing the idea of the city as organism, and in the conception of regional space. These ideas, concepts, and the development of ecology and its subfield landscape ecology contributed to shaping the theory and practice of the design disciplines concerned with the built environment in the twentieth century.

Holism's foundational idea that "the whole is greater than the sum of its parts," famously expressed by the Austrian philosopher and eugenicist Christian von Ehrenfels in 1890, was introduced into ecology by Frederic Edward Clements (1905, 1916) and more explicitly by John Phillips (1931). Ehrenfels had pointed out that we perceive phenomena as patterned wholes, rather than as individual elements that form these wholes. Using a melody as example, Ehrenfels noted that its essence did not consist in its notes, but in the meaningful order created by those notes together. For this reason, Ehrenfels argued, a melody could be transposed to a variety of keys and still be recognized. More widely read and cited by ecologists than Ehrenfels, however, was the 1926 book *Holism and Evolution* by the South African statesman Jan Christiaan Smuts, who has been quoted by ecologists and environmental planners ever since.[86] Smuts argued for creative evolution, an understanding of the evolution of life on earth as a dynamic process in which life forces within living organisms, rather than outside them, were driving them onward and making them develop into new forms.[87] As opposed to a mere mechanical system that lacked inwardness, Smuts contended that the "whole" that was "*more* than the sum of its parts" had "something internal, some inwardness of structure and function, some specific inner relations, some internality of character or nature, which constitutes that *more*."[88] However, the whole seen as such was not something additional to the parts. Smuts contended that the whole "*is* the parts in a definite structural arrangement and with mutual activities that constitute the whole."[89] Thus, it was the specific combination and relationship of parts that made up and defined the whole. Holism as defined by Smuts was a belief in life shaped by entities that consisted of both material and spiritual qualities, "matter" and "mind."[90]

With regard to visual phenomena, gestalt psychologists like Max Wertheimer proposed that analytical and empirical approaches be complemented by efforts of synthesis to "see the gestalt," that is, to identify the organizing pattern of the whole. The gestalt psychologists around Wertheimer posed and tried to prove that visual perception was not a learned skill but that the brain intuitively and spontaneously organized sense data into simple patterns, so that people grasped and saw "the whole," or, in the terms of the gestalt psychologists, the figure against its ground. This phenomenologically oriented proposition was based on the qualitative analysis of the experience of visual phenomena, in particular, and showed in Wertheimer's first experiments of flat, abstract dot patterns. As he explained, certain scientific situations required an interpretation "from above" because the whole could determine the behavior of its parts, or "its parts exhibit[ed] characteristics which they owe to their position within the larger entity."[91] Besides this fundamental belief in holism, the four gestalt principles laid out by Wertheimer that were particularly relevant for designers and ecologists were the laws of good form (*Prägnanz*), closure, proximity, and similarity.[92] Good form described the understanding that perceived wholes tended toward maximum regularity, clarity, and simplicity. Applied to visual phenomena, closure was understood as the tendency to see segregated or imperfect wholes as complete or closed forms. The principle of proximity meant that objects that appeared close to each other were perceived as a unity. Similarity implied that objects that appeared in the same form or color were perceived as a grouped formation.

The visual identification of patterns and wholes on the basis of these principles lay at the basis of much ecological research and later landscape and urban planning, and of contemporary design education. Aerial photographs that captured the view from above provided the contextual and synoptic vision required to reveal the visual patterns of the earth's surface, and details of these patterns in their context. Designers, ecologists, and other scientists were interested in identifying, codifying, and using these patterns, thereby consciously and unconsciously applying the theories of their colleagues in gestalt psychology. As an important part of German intellectual culture at the time with roots in eighteenth- and nineteenth-century German philosophical ideas, gestalt thinking and holism were also important in the creative production and education at the Bauhaus. László Moholy-Nagy envisioned a new understanding of architectural space based on holism as it was being applied in biology and ecology at the time. Future architecture, he contended in 1929, had to conceive of and realize a "total constellation" (*Gesamtkonstellation*) that understood the individual as part of a biological whole. This meant that housing, or any other architectural type, should, according to Moholy-Nagy, be developed on the basis of a general understanding of human needs as they related to the "biological whole," that is, of human life in the world and humankind's relationship to its environment, rather than merely on the basis of the specific needs of the individual. Architects were to position the human being in space, thus concentrating on the relationship between humans and their environment. As he mentioned in his book *Von Material zu Architektur,* architecture needed to take into account the new findings in biology.[93]

HOLISTIC VISION AND THE PATTERNS
OF THE "AERO-LANDSCAPE"

As part of biology, ecology had first been described by the German scientist Erich Haeckel in 1866 as the scientific study of the relationships between living organisms and their environment. Studying the relationships between organisms rather than the individual organisms themselves tied into ideas that a couple of decades later were summed up as holism. Although at first not all ecologists shared a belief in holism and the principle of totality,[94] these ideas facilitated the development of ecology and the use it quickly came to make of aerial photography. By the 1920s, when aerial photographs had begun to play an increasingly important role in landscape architecture and urban planning, professionals in these fields were also looking toward ecology as a scientific foundation of their practice.

Before the development of powered flight, ecological researchers had already been using photography on the ground and from elevated viewpoints for some time. Despite pointing out "the misleading definiteness which a photograph seems to give a bit of vegetation," Frederic Clements had in 1905 considered it an "indispensable instrument for the ecologist . . . important for recording the structure of vegetation . . . [and] the study of the habitat."[95] Photographic mapmaking was considered an adequate and helpful tool for drawing vegetation maps. Clements advised that for this purpose panoramic photographs be taken from a hill or mountain. As aerial photographs were more easily available, therefore, their use in ecology became obvious. The use of aerial photographs taken from a tethered balloon in Germany in 1887 for the identification of tree species had been an early exception to survey-ing vegetation from the ground, and its objective was the drawing up of a vegetation map for use in forestry.[96] With the advent of powered flight, foresters were among the first to systematically use aerial photographs, em-ploying them for the identification and mapping of forest areas, especially in the remote regions of Canada and other British colonies. The stereoscopic analysis of vertical and oblique aerial photographs was used to identify tree species, observe their growth rate and stand density, and plan the extraction of timber and control deforestation. Whereas the use of aerial photography in forestry primarily catered toward economic interests, its use for predom-inantly scientific purposes quickly followed suit.

In the 1920s, the use of aerial photographs to identify land and vegetative patterns was already recognized as a tool for understanding natural pro-cesses, especially in regions of the world that were still relatively unknown and difficult to access on the ground. One of the first uses of aerial photo-graphs in the name of ecology was undertaken as part of a British colonial mission in Northern Rhodesia in 1931, and the military was also more or less directly involved in facilitating the use of aerial photography in ecological research in a number of subsequent cases, as discussed in chapter 3. After all, the exploration and study of landscapes from the air could also provide valuable knowledge for colonial expansion and military reconnaissance. In Northern Rhodesia, the British Aircraft Operating Company was carrying out surveys to locate copper and potential farm sites when the British for-est officer Charles Robinson Robbins seized the opportunity to experiment with the use of aerial photographs for ecological land classification.[97]

This experiment inspired the German geographer Carl Troll to pioneer landscape ecology, a field from which later landscape planners would draw. Throughout his career, Troll maintained that aerial photography had led him to develop the concept of landscape ecology. In 1968, he wrote that "aerial photo research is to a great extent landscape ecology," and a few years later, he claimed that aerial photography had "begun a new epoch in scientific geography."[98] Troll, who in the 1920s had already realized the potential of aerial photography to help establish holistic viewpoints from which to study landforms and their ecological processes in their totality, coined the term "landscape ecology" (*Landschaftsökologie*) in 1938, the same year he accepted a position as director of the Department of Geography at

Bonn University. Based on Erich Haeckel's definition of ecology and Arthur Tansley's portrayal of ecosystem, Troll described landscape ecology as the "analysis of a physico-biological complex of interrelations, which govern the different areal units of a region."[99] He considered landscape ecology not "a new science, but a specific outlook of integrated research"[100] that had "accrued from the task of air foto [sic] interpretation for different purposes" like vegetation mapping, forestry taxation, oil prospecting, soil mapping, archaeology, and hydrology and that demanded "the comprehension of the complete landscape pattern and of the mutual interrelations of landscape elements." In Troll's concept of integrated research, landscape was "the total spatial and visual entity" of human living space consisting of the geosphere and the biosphere, including humankind and man-made artifacts.[101] Thus, Troll considered landscape as a fully integrated holistic entity, a viewpoint strengthened by the undiscriminating representations of aerial photography.

In addition, the use of aerial photography in the formation of landscape ecology applied the ideas of physiognomics—the hermeneutic construction of the internal character of human beings based on their outer bodily appearance—to the earth sciences. Physiognomics, a popular and scientific practice that went back to the eighteenth-century theories of the Swiss poet and pastor Johann Kaspar Lavater, became particularly popular and prominent in Weimar Germany and later informed racist Nazi ideologies. Many of its proponents in Weimar and Nazi Germany, and in the preceding periods, embraced the fusion of "intuitive, imaginative insight and empirical evidence,"[102] a position also held by many exponents of holism. Troll and landscape ecologists after him used the visual appearance of the earth's (sur)face in aerial photographs to gain knowledge about the respective landscape's ecology. While physiognomics was implicit, if not explicit, in the discussions of aerial views by the first landscape ecologists, it also informed the views of many contemporary garden architects on the ground. Basing their design ideas on both ecology and the physiognomy of plant communities and individual plants, planted as single specimens or in masses, German garden architects like Willy Lange had already proposed, in the first decade of the twentieth century, garden designs that imitated natural landscape formations. Lange saw "plant physiognomy as the artistic parallel of scientific plant ecology," explaining that the physiognomic impression of plants should guide their use by the designer to create the desired artistic effect.[103]

As a geographer with a Ph.D. in botany, Troll understood that the interpretation of "the visible phenomena, particularly . . . the plant cover,"[104] led to new knowledge about other landscape elements like soil and geology. "The pattern of vegetation, landforms or soils, as seen from a bird's eye view," Troll argued, "is the key to the understanding of the areal arrangement of landscape elements in general and of their ecosystems in particular."[105]

Vertical aerial photographs produced "an outline of the regional ordering and distribution of landscape elements."[106] They provided a "pictorial reproduction of the landscape pattern" that helped the geographer and ecologist to "conclude from one or two visible elements[,] e.g. plant cover and landforms, the general character and the areas of certain ecosystems."[107] Early on in his work, Troll found a parallel in the research of Russian geographers who used the term "aero-landscape" to describe the landscape units identifiable in aerial photographs.[108] Landscape ecology therefore studied the spatial configurations of certain ecosystems rather than the material cycles and energy flows within an ecosystem. Troll's "ecotope"—the smallest homogeneous spatial landscape unit—was considered a "spatial-temporal manifestation of a specific ecosystem in a natural or cultural landscape."[109] Thus, landscapes could be interpreted and visualized as being composed of ecotopes. The analysis of plant associations of the different ecotopes was of particular importance for landscape ecological research.[110]

Besides coining new terms to describe their theories, Troll and his later landscape ecologist colleagues used metaphors that were identical or similar to those used by the early balloonists and pilots to describe the earth's surface. Landscape ecologists characterized the landscape as a textured carpet or patchwork pattern, as a mosaic, and as consisting of *tessera*, a term applied to ecology by the Swiss-born soil scientist Hans Jenny in 1958 to describe ecotopes or "small landscape elements" that could be compared to the "elaborate mosaic designs on the walls of Byzantine churches, which are made up of little cubes, dice or prisms called tesseras."[111] Important for landscape ecologists was the recognition of the texture and pattern of the land so that it could be classified and evaluated. Implying the existence of a landscape physiognomy, the landscape ecologist Zonneveld later observed that "the [aerial] photograph presents only the visual image, but just as the total impression of a man's face reveals much of his character, so the photograph reveals much of the total character of the land."[112]

Troll's experience working for the Colombian-German Air Transport Society (Sociedad Colombo Alemana de Transportes Aéreos, or SCADTA)—one of South America's first airlines, formed in 1919 by Austro-German entrepreneurs—and traveling in Ecuador, Colombia, and Panama in the late 1920s likely played a decisive role in the use of aerial photography for landscape ecology. In addition to the flights that offered him insights into and new perspectives on South American terrain, Troll's enthusiasm for SCADTA was based on the fact that the air carrier combined its practical concerns and commercial business with scientific goals. As early as 1921, SCADTA had founded a scientific department to undertake topographical and meteorological research. During his time with SCADTA, Troll photographed many South American landscapes and continued the study of their flora that he had begun in 1926 while flying over Bolivia on a research trip. "From the air you just see much that is concealed from you on the ground," he enthusiastically wrote to his mother in 1928.[113]

In the 1930s and during the war years, after having returned to Germany, Troll sought to advance the practical application of his science. Motivated by his ambition to exhibit geography's potential and secure for it a leading position among the sciences considered relevant for warfare, he was eager to see the results of his geographical photo research used by the state, especially in the context of the developing field of spatial planning. However, Troll's landscape ecological research would be used for more than warfare, as related in chapter 4. After the war, it would also play an important role in the development of regional landscape planning.

AERIAL PHOTOGRAPHY AND THE REGION

The region as a spatial unit played an important role in early ecology in general and in landscape ecology in particular. Although Carl Troll's initial research in and development of landscape ecology were based upon aerial photo analyses and field studies that focused on the plant cover in more or less inhabited rural regions, one of his objectives was to overcome physical-morphological landscape studies by exploring what role plant geography could play in human geography. As geographers, ecologists, planners, and designers realized, the aerial view could facilitate and enhance both the study and planning of human habitation on the earth. The use of the region as a spatial unit also became increasingly important in urban planning and design. Its definition in these fields was sustained by aerial photography. In the 1920s, design and planning professionals realized that the aerial view provided context and facilitated contextual vision and sweeping views while at the same time providing detailed information about cities and their hinterland. As urban scientists continued to observe into the second half of the twentieth century, photographs allowed urban areas to "be described with valid generalization but with little or no loss of detail."[114] A useful tool for surveying cities within their regions, aerial photography enabled observation of the relationship between the city and its environment, and contributed significantly to the city being imagined as a metropolis within a region. Aerial photography played a role in the development of a regional consciousness and regionalist planning approaches. In fact, the development of aerial photography paralleled urban growth in the second half of the nineteenth century and in the early twentieth century. By the time the first metropolitan planning agencies had been founded with the *Regional Plan of New York*, the Plans for Greater Berlin and London, and for the German Ruhr region, aerial photography was technologically advanced enough to become an adequate tool and means of illustration for these wide-reaching planning initiatives. While the military use of aerial photography had been the primary motor in its early development, by the 1920s, metropolitan and regional planning initiatives provided an adequate testing ground for further improvement. In turn, the production of oblique and vertical aerial photographs facilitated and legitimized comprehensive planning initiatives.

The aerial imagination had already played an important role in the late-nineteenth- and early-twentieth-century work of Patrick Geddes, the early proponent of regionalism and regional planning whose work would become an inspirational force for the American historian Lewis Mumford, and in the projects undertaken in the second half of the twentieth century by landscape architects and environmental planners like Ian McHarg and Philip Lewis (see chapter 5). In his work at the beginning of the twentieth century, the Scotsman Geddes stressed the importance of an elevated viewpoint for the survey and conceptualization of regional space. Born in 1854, Geddes, who had been trained in biology and held a part-time professorship in botany at Dundee University, was committed to a humanistic education that combined the arts and sciences as well as to the improvement of society and its welfare through planning and his idea of regionalism. His idea of the Outlook Tower and the related concept of the Valley Section have attracted particular attention from his followers interested in regional planning. Both the Outlook Tower and the Valley Section depended on an "overviewing practice"[115] that at the time of their ideation was possible only from hillsides, mountaintops, and balloons. However, the invention of powered flight did not pass Geddes unnoticed. In fact, he and his collaborator, the sociologist Victor Branford, argued that powered flight promoted regionalism. They thought that it might be able to "reverse the railway tendency towards the de-regionalizing and de-spiritualizing of travel" and anticipated that the air traveler would once again see "the natural regions of the world, and these more than ever of old, in broad and synoptic vision, which again is intensified by the ecstasy of flight, to inner clarity and unity."[116] As will also become apparent at later moments throughout the twentieth century, the contextual aerial view enabled refocusing attention on local conditions and circumstances. David Matless has observed that an "educated detachment" was considered "necessary to revive local attachment,"[117] to appreciate local life and how it related to the world, an idea practiced by Geddes that many later environmentalists shared.

In 1892, Geddes bought a six-story building at the upper end of Edinburgh's Royal Mile. He envisioned this Outlook Tower to be a museum and educational institution, "an Index-Museum to the World," as he called it. The building had already been used as a public observatory and for that purpose hosted a camera obscura underneath the domed roof of the top floor. As visitors moved through the Outlook Tower redeveloped by Geddes, their attention was first focused onto Edinburgh and its hinterland through the camera obscura in the top of the tower. The advantage of the camera obscura was, as Geddes's American colleague Charles Zueblin noted, that it "combine[d] . . . the advantages of the astronomical observatory and the microscopical laboratory."[118] It enabled a focus on details of the city and its inhabitants' social life and customs while at the same time offering a wider field of vision than did the naked eye. Indeed, the camera obscura epitomized Geddes's deductive way of exploration and reasoning, and it made Edinburgh and its region appear as a microcosm. Geddes looked at Edinburgh "as a biologist, seeking a solution for the general question by studying a single cell through a microscope."[119] Descending the tower's floors, the visitor was confronted with exhibits about ever-larger spatial units, from Scotland to the English-speaking world, then to Europe and finally to the world. The world was presented on the ground floor, from which the visitor then exited into the real Edinburgh, thus coming full circle.[120] With this framework, Geddes tied together local, regional, national, supranational, and universal space, expressing his synoptic vision. He wanted to draw the visitors' attention to local geographical, social, and cultural qualities and character traits and how they related to the universe. The kinetic and phenomenological experience of the Outlook Tower took the visitor on a journey from the real city and its region out into the world and back again. Similar to the 1968 film *The Powers of Ten* discussed in chapter 5, a visit to the Outlook Tower consisted of a virtual zoom into and out of a particular location. It dealt with different scales, and in this way attempted to place humanity into a universal order, although the order in the case of Geddes's Outlook Tower was still the imperial one of the nineteenth century.[121] It offered views onto the city and its region, thus also stressing the interrelationships between the city and its hinterland.

The idea of the region as the fundamental spatial unit for scientific research and planning also lay at the heart of Geddes's Valley Section. The Valley Section was an analysis and idealist vision of the different settlers and their occupations and settlement types in the various landscapes in what would today be called a river watershed. Geddes described the Valley Section in bird's-eye views, section drawings, and in the following words:

> Beneath vast hunting desolations lie the pastoral hillsides. Below these again, scattered arable crofts and sparsely dotted hamlets lead us to the small upland village of the main glen. From this again one descends to the large and prosperous village of the foothills and its railway terminus, where lowland and highland meet. East or west each mountain valley has its analogous terminal and initial village upon its fertile fan shaped slope, and with its corresponding minor market; while central to the broad agri-

cultural strath with its slow meandering river, stands the prosperous market town, the road and railway junction upon which all the various glen villages converge. A day's march further down and at the convergence of several such valleys stands the larger county town. Finally at the mouth of its estuary rises the smoke of a great manufacturing city, a central world market in its way. Such a river system is . . . the essential unit for the student of cities and civilizations. . . . By descending from source to sea we follow the development of civilization from its simple origins to its complex resultants.[122]

The Valley Section lay at the heart of Geddes's idea of regionalism, which built upon the teachings of the French sociologists Auguste Comte and Frederick Le Play, and which may also have drawn from the botanical survey work of his friend the French biologist Charles Flahault. Like Carl Troll after him, Flahault identified the region as a spatial unit in his botanical surveys. The region's boundaries were defined on the basis of plant associations and their "social species" (indicator species) that pointed to specific environmental conditions that in turn could lead to conclusions about the economic opportunities of a particular region.[123] Similarly, Geddes theorized that the human occupations hunter, shepherd, agriculturalist, and fisherman in his conceptual valley region depended on the respective environmental conditions. Following Comte, he further believed that the well-being of families, their work, and the location of their homes were interdependent. To understand a region, one had to study the interrelationships between "folk, work and place." Critical of the impact of mechanized and standardized technology and intellectualism on the modern world, Geddes promoted experiential, empirical learning and a world order that was "inter-regional rather than super-national or super-imperial."[124] His Valley Section stressed the importance of folk life and culture, and it illustrated the relationships and interdependence between the different settlers in a region and their environment. Despite his seemingly environmentally determinist bent, Geddes saw the relationship between people and the environment as dialectical: the environment determined the people's occupation and life as much as they in turn shaped the environment.[125] He summed up his idea by remarking that "it takes the whole region to make the city."[126] He perceived the city and the region as an integrated whole and argued that the city should be studied in the context of the region, ideas that were taken up decades later by various architects, planners, and landscape architects, including Ludwig Hilberseimer and Ian McHarg.

While powered aviation and aerial photography were not yet available to support Geddes's concept of the Valley Section and his idea of regionalism, by the 1920s, some years before his death in 1932, urban planners began using aerial photographs in their studies of the relationship between cities and their suburban hinterland. The aerial view revealed that the city no longer had a clear boundary and that it was connected to its environs in multiple ways. In fact, later in the century, aerial views became a means to uncover sprawl and the increasing urbanization of the planet.

Looking at and understanding context and transcending boundaries meant that the scales urban professionals were handling in their work became smaller as the areas under their supervision became more extensive. The altitude of the flight path and the type of camera lens used determined the size and scale of the survey maps. The Fairchild Aerial Camera Corporation considered a scale of 1"–400' appropriate for city surveys. Because of the greater detail that was depicted and more easily legible in air photographs at scales ranging from 1"–400' to 1"–200', these were deemed especially appropriate when traffic needed to be counted or when new streets and other new physical features needed to be explained to citizens who had difficulty reading line maps.[127] A smaller scale of 1"–800' was suggested to be most useful for regional planning studies and could be achieved by photographs taken with a 20-inch lens camera when flying at an altitude of 16,000 feet (approx. 4,877 meters). In the United States in the early 1920s, Kansas City, Newark, and New York were among the first cities to use aerial maps for taxation purposes, for the formulation of zoning determinations, and for the landscaping of parks and parkways. The Fairchild Aerial Camera Corporation, which had been incorporated in 1918 and had assembled its first aerial camera one year later, produced the first mosaic map of Manhattan in 1921 for testing and advertising purposes. It was quickly put to use by officers of the New York City Board of Estimate and Apportionment in their selection of park sites. After Fairchild provided the New York City Board of Estimate and Apportionment with further maps for city planning in 1922, the need for information in extended areas led the board to commission Fairchild to undertake the 1923–24 aerial mapping of the five boroughs of New York City. Covering a territory of approximately 625 square miles (1618.74 square kilometers), Fairchild produced a large mosaic map that pictured the entire city in its minutest details (fig. 38).[128]

The new aerial photographic techniques produced a popular image of the city as a metropolis within a region, that is, a metropolitan region, and therefore contributed to regional planning in more than just a practical way, as will be shown in chapter 5. By 1926, the Fairchild Aerial Camera Corporation had produced aerial mosaic maps for several counties, testifying to the need for regional planning and leading Sherman Fairchild to anticipate that entire states would soon be mapped from the air.[129] Aerial photography encouraged thinking and envisioning the city as a metropolis that both depended upon and influenced entire regions. It supported in particular

FIG. 38. Sherman Fairchild (*left*) presenting the aerial mosaic map of the five boroughs of New York City to the Board of Estimate and Apportionment. (Folder "FAAC, 1920–1925: Brochures, Company," box 85, Sherman Fairchild Papers, Manuscript Division, Library of Congress)

what Robert Fishman has called the "metropolitanist tradition" in regional planning, an approach taken by the elite establishment. It was based on the belief that despite its growth into a metropolitan area, the future city would still be focused around its historic center.[130]

Already before aerial photographs became more easily available to city planners in the 1920s, aerial views had been used to illustrate these ideas that underlay the first American initiatives in metropolitan planning. Both the reports of the 1901–2 *McMillan Plan* for Washington, D.C., and of the 1909 *Plan of Chicago* used panoramic bird's-eye views painted in watercolor by Jules Guerin to show the proposed growth of these cities into metropoles. Following these examples, *The Regional Plan of New York and Its Environs* developed in the 1920s also opened with a watercolor painting by Jules Guerin depicting New York City in a panoramic view "looking southwest across the center of the region." In 1908, the popular picture volume *King's Views of New York* had already provided, spread across two pages, a painted bird's-eye view of "Greater New York" that roughly corresponded with the area of *The Regional Plan*.[131] Many previous editions of *King's Views* also included bird's-eye views painted by the illustrator Henry M. Pettit. By the time *The Regional Plan* was drawn up, aerial photographs had become more readily available, so that both panoramic paintings and aerial photographs could be used.

In 1923, Nelson Peter Lewis, who served as chief engineer of the Board of Estimate and Apportionment of New York City from 1902 to 1920 and directed the physical survey for *The Regional Plan,* observed that city planners in the United States had in the past thought "in too small units" and that they had been "too prone to regard the corporate limits of the city or town as [the] horizon."[132] Broadening the horizon to encompass the *"wide area"* of an entire region,[133] "regional planning"—a term Lewis set off with quotation marks[134]—was encouraged by the availability of aerial photographs. It is therefore not surprising that the Fairchild Aerial Camera Corporation undertook its first experimental mosaic mapping of Manhattan in 1922, the same year that the Russell Sage Foundation formed a Committee for the Development of a Regional Plan of New York and Its Environs, encompassing the area within 50 miles of Manhattan with almost 9 million inhabitants. By the early 1920s, city planners, officials, businessmen, and philanthropic reformers had realized that the city's problems, including subway crowding, street congestion, disease, crime, and overcrowded tenement districts, could be solved only if they were dealt with comprehensively in a regional context. In his 1930 account of the committee's regional planning work, the writer Robert L. Duffus included an oblique aerial photograph by Fairchild Aerial Surveys that showed Manhattan Island looking north and identified its position and function as "The Heart of the Region." The photograph was also meant to show how congested Manhattan was and that it was "surrounded by others [areas] only slightly less crowded."[135] *The Regional Plan* focused on an area of 100 miles in diameter, an area that could be viewed out of an airplane on a clear day at the height of a half mile (approx. 805 meters). The first two volumes describing the *Regional Plan* included several oblique aerial photographs mostly taken by Fairchild Aerial Surveys that were overlaid with white lines and outlines. These indicated planning proposals for parks, a suburban rapid-transit system, new bridge locations, and new expressway, highway, and parkway routes.

Planning experts like John Nolen and informed observers like the Harvard librarian Theodora Kimball attested to the value of aerial photography for regional planning. Nolen stated in an address that the planning of the New York region required aerial photographs and that "this art is one of the highest contributions in the field of regional planning."[136] For Kimball, "the large mental view" needed for planning was facilitated by aerial photographs "essential to [the] study of the broad relations of city and region."[137] Nelson P. Lewis argued that aerial photographs provided planners with "new" information. Underdeveloped urban areas could be easily identified and slotted for development. "From a vantage point a mile above ground," Lewis pointed out, "we can see where [traffic] conditions can be improved by cutting through a short connection which would establish a new thoroughfare."[138] Furthermore, Lewis wrote, aerial photographs of Manhattan Island showed "how great an obstruction Central Park offers to traffic up and down the island, testifying to the need of "additional north and south traffic capacity."[139]

THE CITY AS ORGANISM

Following the view Geddes illustrated in his Valley Section and Outlook Tower, many subsequent planners considered the region to be anchored by the city. Similarly, Robert Duffus noted in his book on New York City's *Regional Plan* that the city formed the "heart" of the region. The new perspective enabled by flight and captured in aerial photographs changed both humankind's image of the city and its relationship to the city. Planners thought that this perspective permitted the "study [of] conditions in their proper relation one to another,"[140] offering a complete view of the city and its functioning. In the December 1920 issue of the *American City,* the English-born city planner Guy Wilfried Hayler seconded the idea expressed in an 1831 romantic fantasy by Victor Hugo that visitors from a strange town should ascend the highest tower to grasp the place as a whole.[141] From the 1920s onward, aerial photography facilitated this holistic vision of the city, thereby promoting the perception of the city as a comprehensive whole. The synoptic vision enabled by aerial photography also reinforced the centuries-old analogy drawn between city and organism, and the city and nature in general. The early balloonist Vincent Lunardi had described the city of London as a beehive, and in 1888 the British balloonist John MacKenzie Bacon described the anatomy of London as follows: "Every detail of the great capital lay mapped out below us. . . . [O]ne could grasp as never before what were the lungs of London and what her arteries. . . . The Northern tramways were the ways towards York and Cambridge, and Piccadilly was the Bath Road. And there were those greater arteries that carry England's life-blood to and from her heart."[142] In Europe and the United States, beginning in the 1920s, architects, sociologists, and geographers regarded cities as organisms with a life cycle. Viewing the city from the air was thought of as viewing a microorganism through a microscope. The aerial view facilitated the perception of the city as an organic, natural phenomenon outside of human control, a belief that in recent decades has again gained currency among designers and urban professionals.

Explaining the ideas underlying the Bauhaus, Walter Gropius laid out his conception of the city as an organism made up of various cellular units understood to be the buildings and roads. With an aerial view of cities before his mind's eye, he explained that a clear, successful "city image" (*Stadtbild*) depended upon both the overarching unity of its parts, and the variety of their types and sizes.[143] Gropius shared this idea with other Bauhaus architects, such as Ludwig Hilberseimer, who later extended the idea of the "city organism" to the region, which, with a nod to Geddes, he described as an "organic entity, an organism in which the whole is related to the parts, as the parts are related to the whole."[144] Gropius, like many of his colleagues at the time, was building upon two traditions of intellectual thought that gained strength in Germany in the early twentieth century and tied into each other: the holistic, as opposed to the mechanistic, interpretation of the world; and studies in physiognomy and gestalt, that is, the visible form and shape of people, things, and figures, and their perception.

Scholars in the new field of human ecology tried to identify the processes and laws underlying the formation and decline of neighborhoods and the changes in land uses and values. Their use of analogies with processes in plant and animal ecology and their use of the organism metaphor to describe cities were based on the same holistic philosophy mentioned above that also influenced Gropius and his Bauhaus colleagues, and that could be readily supported visually by the aerial view. It also enabled the observation of the relationship between the city—the "organism"—and its context—the "environment," or region. The city-as-organism analogy continued to be employed throughout the twentieth century and even shone through Roland Barthes's 1964 observation that the view from the Eiffel Tower added a romantic, harmonious quality to the "frequently grim urban myth" and thereby turned the city into "a kind of Nature" that could be compared to "the ocean, the storm, the mountains, the snow, the rivers."[145] Barthes's structuralist interpretation and naturalization of the city recalled an argument consciously or unconsciously made by early-twentieth-century American skyscraper architects like Louis Sullivan, who considered their buildings to be in harmony with nature. In the mid-nineteenth-century United States, the bird's-eye view from the balloon inspired writing about "the physiognomy of cities" as a parallel to American nature writing. In 1847, the journalist George Washington Peck, writing in the New York–based monthly periodical the *American Review*, noted that the bird's-eye view could inspire not only philosophical contemplation about cities but also a new genre of American writing, "the Poetry of our Cities." After all, he observed, "the noise of Broadway . . . is somewhat like the sound of Niagara heard from the Cataract Hotel," and "when, from repaving, or any other cause, the current [on Broadway] is turned into a bye street for a few days, it seems as dangerous an operation as tying the great aorta."[146]

This analogy between the city and the human body and its physiognomy was already common among enlightened planners in the eighteenth century and in particular in the nineteenth century, when such open spaces as parks and gardens were described as the lungs of a city and streets were likened to arteries.[147] These spaces between buildings appeared particularly clearly in the comprehensive and synoptic views of the urban fabric offered by aerial photographs. In fact, aerial photography facilitated a perception of the city as consisting of architectural volumes standing in a context of differently characterized open spaces, an observation that was analogous to one of the aims of the painted and etched city portraits of the fifteenth and sixteenth centuries. While aerial views offered insight into areas of potential urban development that were difficult to access from the ground, like marshland, they also facilitated the preservation of such natural features and open space. Hayler remarked in 1920 that "from the air, the value of space, fresh air and light are realized much more than on the ground, where one is too near the picture to comprehend it properly." The aerial view revealed how much a city's identity depended on parks, open spaces and trees that from above were "seen as distinguishing landmarks."[148]

Like Hayler in 1920, Barthes in 1964 also commented on Hugo's account, pointing out that "the bird's-eye view . . . gives us the world to read and not only to perceive." Barthes noted Hugo's insight that the bird's-eye view "permits us to transcend sensation and to see things *in their structure.*"[149] Thus, no matter which ideas and concepts the aerial city view could readily promote and support and how awe-inspiring and sublime it could be, it also transcended these sensations. It provided hard data, facts, and a broader outlook.

After World War I, city planners recognized aerial photographs to be "as essential to town-planning as a contour map or a geological survey."[150] Aerial photographs became a visual aid of planners, designers, and city officials, professions that became increasingly powerful. The idea of the aerial view captured in photographs as displaying the absolute truth was tantamount. Discussions, articles, and books that displayed and promoted the use of aerial photographs in city planning and landscape architecture proliferated in Europe and the United States. In June 1919, the use of aerial photography in city planning was a subject of discussion at the sessions of the First Inter-allied Town Planning Conference held in Paris under the auspices of the Société Française des Urbanistes. There, Captain Bouché of the French Army Aerial Photographic Service presented a paper on the topic. Aerial photographs were considered to be particularly useful if the area under study covered several miles, or if knowledge about details such as housing block interiors was required. Vertical aerial photographs supplemented by oblique photographs were seen as excellent tools for the improvement of building ensembles, for the reparceling of property, for the verification of maps, and for the rendering of "bird's-eye perspectives of proposed improvements."[151]

In 1920, the British *Garden Cities & Town Planning Magazine* dedicated its April issue to the use of aerial photography in town planning, and the German journal *Der Städtebau* published several articles about the subject in its 1919 and 1920s issues. In France, *L'Architecture* published "L'Aviation au travail" based on a talk that the engineer (Ingénieur des Manufactures de l'État) and administrator of the Compagnie Aérienne Française Henry Balleyguier had given at the city planning congress in Lyon in March 1920. Like his colleagues in other countries, Balleyguier stressed the time-saving aspect of vertical aerial photographs for mapping and surveying, and the artistic merit of photographed bird's-eye views.[152]

Given both the extensive development and use of aerial photography during World War I and the war's devastation of towns and cities, it was only logical that aerial photography would be used to survey war-damaged and devastated regions in postwar reconstruction work. Pictures taken by photographers of the United States Air Service included aerial images of the destroyed French towns Vaux and Montfaucon. These aerial photographs portrayed the villages in a way that echoed their description by Kurt Lewin, the later gestalt and social psychologist: They appeared as "'war islands' in a land of peace either lying on and covering the land or surrounded by land, superseding it."[153] However, aerial photography was seen not only as a tool to rebuild and reconstruct cities, but also as an instrument to indict, "attack," correct, and "heal" what were considered the mistakes of city building in previous centuries. Gropius demanded that "physicians" come to the rescue of the "old sick bodies" of the cities and fight the "symptoms of disease of the old city organisms" by way of the new architecture.[154] Aerial photography was therefore considered, as had been noted in 1919 by George B. Ford, member of the Executive Committee of the American City Planning Institute, as an instrument that could suggest "new possibilities in the esthetic aspect of towns as they will be seen by the aerial traveller."[155]

Three | *"Cultivating Beautiful Air Views"*

DESIGNING AND PLANNING WITH AND FOR THE AERIAL VIEW

In 1928, when commercial air transport was assuming a greater importance, the American landscape architect–turned–city planner John Nolen pointed toward the new jobs that aviation provided for architects. In addition to the design of airport buildings, the design and layout of buildings, open spaces, and cities as a whole would provide new work. According to Nolen, architects could be employed to create "beautiful air views" for the "air sight-seer," a new type of pleasure-seeking individual for whom aerial sightseeing trips were offered at the airports of many major European cities. Like Nolen, the American writer H. I. Brock anticipated that the view from airplanes would inspire architects and require them to envision how cities would look from the air. Would the buildings built by people who had imagined them as being looked up at also be satisfying when looked down upon? he asked when recording his flight above New York City.[1] Nolen and Brock echoed a concern that in 1909 had already inspired the German art critic Fritz Wichert to describe house roofs as the new façades, and that had led the Italian-born aviation enthusiast and publisher Henry Woodhouse to state in 1916 that aerial transportation would lead to the beautification of cities.[2] At the time, airplanes were not yet traveling at altitudes of 6.2 miles (10,000 meters) or more as they do today, and at the more common altitude of 0.6 to 1.2 miles (1,000 to 2,000 meters), architectural details could still be easily observed.

With the aerial view from airplanes gradually becoming a more accessible experience and increasingly influencing diverse fields of cultural production like the fine arts and literature,[3] professionals like Wichert and Nolen considered it a logical consequence that the new perspective would also affect the way buildings, gardens, and parks were designed and cities were imagined and built.

For the design and planning disciplines, the aerial view of the earth captured with the clarity and precision of aerial photographs provided a functional and technical aid, a critical-analytical tool, and artistic inspiration. As discussed in chapter 2, aerial photographs sustained and supported a variety of interconnected philosophical beliefs, concepts, and ideas important to the design and planning of the built environment. On a pragmatic level, they were used as functional and technical devices, providing the basis for maps and for the supervision of construction work. In the realm of design and planning practice, aerial photographs were soon also used as critical-analytical tools, as they could offer relevant contextual information for site analyses and for the detection of weak spots in designs. In addition, the aerial view and aerial photography promised architects, city planners, and landscape architects inspiring new perspectives for their creative work, encouraging them to design for the aerial view on and above the ground.

The Aerial View as a Critical–Analytical Tool in Urban Design

Aerial photographs offered a critical instrument for the study, design, and planning of urban form and land use. They enabled designers and planners to see new possibilities. Many architects and city planners also considered the aerial view from airplanes a constructive critical-analytical tool to identify and rectify flaws in city planning and urban development. Le Corbusier fittingly captured this use of the aerial view in his oft-cited 1935 exclamation "L'avion accuse" (The airplane indicts). He noted: "We now have a record, aero-photographic plates, which proves that at all costs we must save our cities. . . . The plane exposes the fact that men have built cities not for the satisfaction of mankind, not to engender happiness, *but solely to make money at mankind's expense.*"[4] According to Le Corbusier, the airplane "gets to the heart of the cruel reality—with its eagle eye it penetrates the misery of towns."[5] In the 1929 English translation of his book *Urbanisme* (1924), oblique aerial photographs of the monotonous rows of townhouses in a London suburb were positioned facing the title page and the foreword to illustrate the "vice of planning." In this publication, Le Corbusier also presented his *Plan Voisin* for Paris by juxtaposing its grid of high-rise buildings sitting in vast green open space with the existing dense medieval quarters of Paris shown in vertical aerial photographs (fig. 39). According to the Swiss-born architect, the airplane revealed the "jumbled city . . . terrifying in its confusion" for the first time.[6] Unlike in World War I, when airplanes were first used to attack cities and destroy entire villages, in peacetime they could be used to "attack" what were considered cities' architectural and social ills.

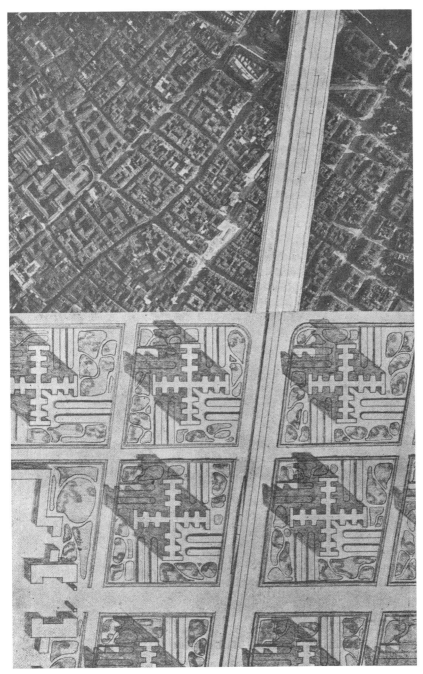

FIG. 39. Le Corbusier's *Plan Voisin* for Paris juxtaposed with the existing dense medieval quarters of Paris shown in vertical aerial photographs. (Le Corbusier, Paris, Plan Voisin, 1925, Extrait de *Urbanisme* 1925. © 2012 Artists Rights Society [ARS], New York / /ADAGP, Paris / F.L.C.)

An article in the *American City* pointed out in 1922 that the same method of aerial photographic surveying used during the war "will disclose the logical points of attack for those who are bent, not upon destructive but upon important constructive work, upon the better utilization of natural conditions for commerce, for homes or for wholesome recreation."[7]

However, the aerial view from airplanes did not ubiquitously lead to a modernist outlook and aesthetic. Unlike the progressive modernist architects and planners who, like Le Corbusier, saw in the airplane a vehicle to view the earth from above and criticize humankind's creations and capitalist development, and who were also fascinated with the new aesthetics that this vision and the new technical accomplishments offered, some architects and planners were more interested in the use of aerial photographs for cultivating a sense of place and forms of belonging. They could be used, for example, to foster a new national identity and a deeply felt appreciation of the native land (*Heimatliebe*). This was the case in Germany, whose aerial supremacy and ambition were severely curtailed by the Treaty of Versailles and whose nationalism many saw as having suffered both from the loss of World War I and from the foundation of the Weimar Republic. The Treaty of Versailles prohibited the establishment of a German air force and considerably restricted civil aviation. In Germany, initiatives in aviation therefore focused instead on aerial photography and photogrammetry, the science of mapping based on aerial photography. The public benefited from this development in the form of several books by architects featuring aerial photographs of different landscapes and cities.

The Austrian architect Karl Heinrich Brunner considered Germany's advancement and supremacy in the field of aerial photography a path to "peaceful international cultural work."[8] The aerial vision used by the deadly bombers in World War I was now, in the interwar years, used as a visual rhetoric to foster universalism and intercultural understanding. Having served in the aeronautical division charged with aerial reconnaissance during World War I, in 1928 Brunner published a book, *Weisungen der Vogelschau: Flugbilder aus Deutschland und Österreich und ihre Lehren für Kultur, Siedlung und Städtebau* (Lessons of the bird's-eye view: Aerial photographs of Germany and Austria and their lessons for culture, settlement and town planning), that was lavishly illustrated with aerial photographs of settlements, villages, and towns across Germany and Austria. He argued that aerial photography provided the basis for comprehensive city and regional planning schemes that would improve the living environment. The view from the airplane afforded a new "spirit of totality" and offered insight into the evolution of settlement patterns that from the distance, according to Brunner, looked like an "almost natural creation of centuries."[9] Brunner stated that cities should be seen as a whole made up of the living and working community of all its citizens. The aerial view and aerial photographs, he believed, could help resolve the dichotomy between city and country, technological progress and nature. On the one hand, the views from above promoted the appreciation of the native landscape by illustrating the beauty of towns and their surroundings. On the other hand, aerial views relentlessly uncovered defects. While Brunner saw such defects in the dense tenement districts at the edges of Vienna and Berlin that had been built in the late nineteenth and early twentieth centuries, he acknowledged that modern urban planning since then had made some progress in the provision of open space.[10] His rather elusive "lessons," or suggestions, included the implementation of building codes imposing height and density restrictions on the periphery of cities, the collaboration between municipalities in planning matters involving metropolitan regions, and traffic planning that prevented congestion. He saw the architect's work as "comprehensive design" (Gesamtgestaltung).[11] Brunner's technological romanticism was fully revealed in his appeal to readers not to "understand landscape in completely analytical terms," but, like a poet, "to see the godly in nature," a feat most easily accomplished by viewing the landscape from above.[12]

This double vision—based at once on a belief in modernity and grounded in a conservative ideology—and Brunner's tone were shared by the German architect and ministerial official Erich Ewald, who published several picture books featuring aerial photographs in the 1920s. In his 1922 dissertation at the Technical University Berlin, Ewald tackled the question of how aerial photography could facilitate work in city planning. Like his German colleague Abendroth, he pointed out the use of aerial photography—"the vivid representation of reality"—in the design process. Thus, the landscape pattern seen in aerial photographs could provide the skeletal structure for new settlement patterns. The country road could form the backbone and main road of the new settlement, dirt roads could become residential streets, and agricultural land parcels could form the basis for new properties. Ewald also considered aerial photographs a suitable means for the site analysis and design of parks, gardens, and cemeteries.[13]

In his lavishly illustrated volume Im Flugzeug über Berlin (In the Aircraft above Berlin), he used aerial photographs to illustrate the city's history and to reveal flaws in its urban plan, open space designs, and recent development. For example, he pointed out how the construction of the cathedral had destroyed the ensemble of Palace, Lustgarten, and Altes Museum, not least by creating an ill-defined leftover open space north of the cathedral and east of Altes Museum. Furthermore, the layout of the Lustgarten, dominated with paths that Ewald called "much too broad," also contributed to the loss of spatial definition in this part of the city (fig. 40). Ewald criticized other plazas and garden squares like Alsenplatz north of the Reichstag, whose

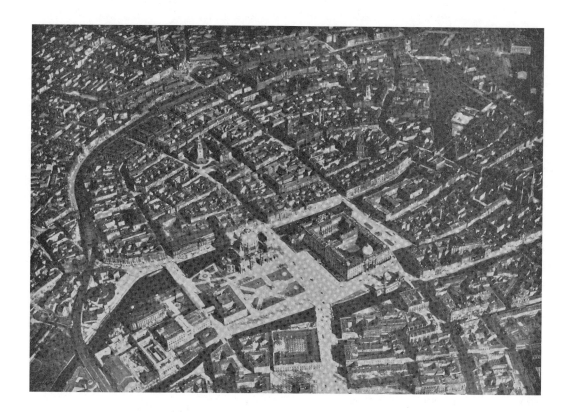

FIG. 40. Aerial pho-
tograph of Berlin's
city center used by
Erich Ewald in *In the
Aircraft above Berlin*
(*Im Flugzeug über
Berlin*) to show that
aerial photography
could not only illus-
trate the city's his-
tory but also indis-
criminately reveal
flaws in its urban
plan, open space
designs, and recent
development. (Erich
Ewald, *Im Flugzeug
über Berlin* [Marburg:
Elwert'sche Verlags-
buchhandlung,
1928])

unity was destroyed by the "fussy distribution of garden ornamentation and
paths" that were "too numerous and broad." According to him, the biggest
mistake readily revealed by aerial photographs was the rapid and "mechanical" development of tenement blocks, "an expression of the materialistic
and capitalist bent of our times."[14] In various other publications, Ewald
presented aerial photographs of different landscapes and settlement types
as testimony to the German's extraordinary bond with and dependence on
nature. Ewald's reactionary modernist attitude was revealed particularly
clearly in his volume *Deutschland aus der Vogelschau* (Germany from the
bird's-eye view), in which he used 249 aerial photographs to illustrate a text
on German history. He attempted to show that throughout history German
settlements had been integrated into the topography and tied so closely to
the soil that they appeared as organic creations naturally growing out of
the land rather than as "mechanical artwork." Implying that "the Roman"
had produced "mechanical," albeit artful, settlement patterns, Ewald used
aerial photographs to support a national subtext based on psychological and
anthropological models that juxtaposed "the Roman" and "the German."
According to Ewald, the German had gained a deep appreciation of and
connection to his homeland and people through his virtuous toil and work
in nature.[15]

Paradoxically, both Ewald and Brunner used technology, or mechanical records—aerial photographs—of the detached aerial view to try to increase people's emotional attachment to their roots and their investment in their native land. They presented incrementally grown settlement structures and medieval urban forms through a modern visual framework that could legitimize their architectural and urban design preferences. Responding to Camillo Sitte's 1889 *City Planning According to Artistic Principles,* Ewald promoted urban design principles that were based more on the picturesque urban structures of the Middle Ages than on the contemporary ideas of urban form promoted by the avant-garde. Both his and Brunner's works offered sentimental, lofty views of the condition of German and Austrian towns that stood in contrast to Le Corbusier's aggressive and provocative urban critique facilitated by the view from above and published in his oft-cited 1930s volumes *Précisions* (1930), *The Radiant City* (1933), and *Aircraft* (1935).[16]

Le Corbusier criticized the same developments that Brunner and Ewald disliked—the monotonous, dense, dark, and overcrowded tenement districts of the late nineteenth century—and the Swiss-born Frenchman's aerial view has been described similarly as a "double vision of reason and poetry, analysis and revelation."[17] According to him, the aerial view from the airplane revealed the pathologies of the nineteenth-century industrialized capitalist cities: "immense sites encrusted with row after row of houses without hearts, furrowed with their canyons of soulless streets."[18] However, instead of using the aerial view to elevate historic town patterns, as did Brunner and Ewald, Le Corbusier was more intent on employing the bird's-eye view for looking and planning ahead and for developing settlement patterns that suited modern man. In fact, in contrast to his German colleague Ewald, who endorsed Sitte, Le Corbusier condemned medieval town plans that had grown incrementally around zigzag meandering pathways. In his view, it was unfortunate that "the Pack-Donkey's Way is responsible for the plan of every continental city; including Paris."[19] Airplanes and aerial photography offered an analytical tool, in particular for those who did not want to experience the cities as pedestrians, and the aerial view could therefore offer a starting point for rescuing the cities "from disaster." Le Corbusier wrote in 1941 that the cities' "rotten sections must be destroyed; new cities must be built." His fantasies of future cities were built on the hope that "dignity, strength and a proper sense of values will become apparent in the aspect of our new cities." It was the elevated viewpoint from the air that he thought could lead the eye to see clearly and the mind to make wise decisions in future city building.[20]

The avant-garde shared Le Corbusier's views. In 1924, Hans Schmidt, the architect, city planner, and leader of Neues Bauen in Switzerland, had argued that every city should have its Eiffel Tower from which architects could observe the "chaos" of the nineteenth-century city and learn about their professional responsibilities. Views from elevations like the Eiffel Tower—itself a symbol of modernity—and the airplane, he argued, would teach architects that the quality of cities depended not so much on their picturesque or monumental aesthetic qualities as on the organization and "regulated form" of building volumes that catered to human movement in space. Against the "chaos" and "endless mush of houses" seen in nineteenth-century cities like Paris, Schmidt posed the vision of an urban fabric with the "rhythm of an organic ensemble." In a similar vein, the catalogue of the British 1937 exhibition *Airports and Airways*, which tellingly also included a section on aerial photography, declared that the "new angle of vision" offered by airplanes was necessary to understand the "chaotic planning," the "muddle," and the "disadvantages" of London's medieval plan.[21]

Aerial Urban Visions

As much as the aerial view could lead professionals dealing with the shaping of the land to assume a detached position and to objectify what they saw, the patterns of the earth also provided strong aesthetic images that produced pleasurable and emotional responses in the viewer and inspired creative production. Le Corbusier used his first flights across South America to capture on paper what he saw from the air. He believed that the aerial view would reveal, as Charles Jencks has noted, "principles of organization which have previously remained hidden, just as the microscope had done."[22] Using the aerial views as inspiration, he therefore also sketched what he imagined and envisioned. A few years later he gave the following advice on the basis of this experience: "Take a plane and you will see, and you will understand, and you will decide."[23] On an airplane above Rio de Janeiro and São Paulo in 1929, Le Corbusier famously conceived of his ideas for reforming these Brazilian cities. He was one of a number of European architect-planners who visited South America in the 1920s and 1930s to lecture and consult on urban planning and who was able to observe cities and landscapes from an airplane. As he pointed out, the South American continent was "dimensioned for the plane." He predicted that "airline networks will become its efficient nervous system."[24] When he arrived in Buenos Aires, a group of French Aéropostale pilots including Antoine de Saint-Exupéry were competing with the Germans and Americans to develop and establish the first airmail routes in South America. Commercial air transport had begun there, as in most other parts of the world, in the 1920s. But airplanes also provided the visiting European architect-planners with a valuable observatory and sometimes, as in the case of Le Corbusier, with a "studio." Gliding across the South American continent gave these professionals an overview of the

FIG. 41. Le Corbusier, sketch for a gigantic curvilinear expressway connecting the plateaus of Rio de Janeiro's mountainous hinterlands with the promontories along the coast. (Le Corbusier, Rio, Urbanisme, 1929, Plan FLC 32091. © 2012 Artists Rights Society [ARS], New York / /ADAGP, Paris / F.L.C.)

sprawling cities that testified to the newfound economic prosperity and the population growth in this part of the world.

In Rio de Janeiro, the aerial view enabled and inspired Le Corbusier to imagine a gigantic curvilinear expressway that connected the plateaus of the city's mountainous hinterlands with the promontories along the coast. His design idea was to resolve the problems of traffic congestion and lack of space to allow for the city's expansion. The expressway would be built at a height of up to 328 feet (100 meters) on top of a belt of immeuble-villas with hanging gardens that offered views of the bay, sea, and mountains (fig. 41). In his idiosyncratic prose, Le Corbusier described the housing as the "nest of a gliding bird."[25] It seems as if by offering the inhabitants and motorists of his utopian construction awe-inspiring bird's-eye views, Le Corbusier hoped to democratize the aerial view that elated and fascinated him but at the time was available only to a privileged few. In a procedure similar to the one he used at Rio, Le Corbusier's analysis of São Paulo began with his flight into the city. This aerial overview provided him with an impression of the city's outline, its location within the region, and its skyline. Supplemented by auto rides that revealed the city's problem with traffic congestion, Le Corbusier's aerial investigation led him to again suggest the construction of elevated

FIG. 42.
Le Corbusier,
sketch for elevated
expressways for
São Paulo. (Le
Corbusier, São Paulo,
Urbanisme, 1929,
Plan FLC 30301. ©
2012 Artists Rights
Society [ARS], New
York / /ADAGP,
Paris / F.L.C.)

expressways as viaducts. Two of the expressways were to cross at right angles in the city center. "You won't fly over the city with your autos but you
will drive over it," he explained. Similar to Rio, the expressways in São
Paulo would be located on "earthscrapers," continuous horizontal blocks
that accommodated offices in the city center and housing toward the edges
(fig. 42).[26]

The excitement of flight produced a tension in Le Corbusier's attitude
toward the relationship between architecture and its environment. He was
awed by the landscape that unfolded below him when flying, but he wanted
to "play a match for two, a match of the 'affirmation of mankind' against or
with the 'presence of nature.'" Adnan Morshed has pointed out that Le Corbusier's flight over Rio and its landscape "instilled in him a megalomaniac
desire to compete with that very landscape."[27] The tension between leaving
an iconic imprint on the land on the one hand, and adapting to the existing patterns of the environment on the other became particularly apparent
in Le Corbusier's visionary and utopian ideas for the urban design of Rio
de Janeiro and São Paulo. Although it can be described as a monumental
iconic structure, the curves of the Rio viaduct were adapted to the landscape. It functioned as an artificial promontory connecting natural hillsides,
mountains, plateaus, and beaches. When seen from the sea, the horizon-

tal structure provided an even datum topped by mountain peaks. "The eye saw . . . two things: nature and the product of the work of men. The city announced itself by the only line that can harmonize with the vehement caprice of the mountains: the horizontal."[28] In contrast to the curving lines in Rio and the structure's embeddedness in the mountain skyline, Le Corbusier's design idea for São Paulo merged less with the topographic contours of the undulating site and instead involved viaducts running along two straight "pure" lines that formed a cross. Although the viaducts formed a superstructure imposed onto the landscape, they left the valleys "free for sports and for local parking."[29] Both design ideas were based on traffic arteries and the premise that they connected the cities to each other as well as to other cities and landscapes in the region and on the continent.

Le Corbusier's flights during his stay in South America had sensitized the architect to regional matters, and to the different landscape patterns and the ecological processes they were based upon that defied political boundaries. He noted, for example, the water cycle: "the clouds that will sadden a home, or assure abundant crops, or rot grapevines; . . . The water vapor in suspension in the atmosphere is precipitated and suddenly the whole earth is covered with water: dew."[30] He observed that "the shades of grass indicate the degree of humidity in the soil. All biology, all fundamental organic life is evident from above."[31] As a result of the airplane, he contended, "the various regions of the world have . . . been made suddenly and overwhelmingly evident."[32]

Le Corbusier's approach to urban design in these South American cities was monumental, experimental, daring, provocative, and utopian. As Adnan Morshed has shown, the snaking structure of Le Corbusier's viaduct for Rio can also be read as the "literal trace of a twentieth-century neocolonizer's aerial odyssey towards the 'uncolonized' interior." The aerial view facilitated a design idea that was based not only on the connectivity between cities, but in particular on that between cities and the country's hinterland. In this way it also supported the 1920s Brazilian avant-garde movements that promoted the assimilation of the hinterland into Brazil's nationalist consciousness.[33]

In contrast to Le Corbusier's uncompromising, hardhanded, and artistic conceptual design gestures that he mythically attributed to his sweeping aerial views, some of his colleagues used aerial views for theoretical, scientific approaches that were more closely related to the architectural and social history of the respective sites. The same Karl H. Brunner who had studied German and Austrian towns from his airplane during World War I traveled to Chile in the same year Le Corbusier went on his trip to Argentina, Uruguay, Paraguay, and Brazil. As a result of his acquaintance with the Chilean architect Rodulfo Oyarzun Phillipi during the latter's studies in Europe, Brunner was appointed advisor for urban development in the

Chilean Ministry of Public Works in Santiago in 1929. The aerial view and aerial photography turned out to be an invaluable tool for Brunner, in particular when dealing with urban areas for which plans and statistical data did not exist. He also promoted the use of aerial photographs and air maps in his 1939 *Manual de urbanismo* (Manual of urbanism), the first work of its kind published in South America, which itself was lavishly illustrated with many aerial photographs. In the late 1920s and 1930s, Argentina, Brazil, Chile, and Columbia proved to be fertile grounds for the development of new air routes because of their expansion, rural character, and topography. For example, in 1925, Colombia's capital, Bogotá, could still only be reached from the Pacific coast by a combination of train and automobile rides and from the Atlantic coast by riverboat up the Magdalena River and train rides. Depending on the weather conditions, the trip took from one to four weeks.[34]

When Brunner moved from Chile to Colombia and began work in Bogotá in 1934, he could capitalize on the aerial photographs taken by SCADTA.[35] Aerial photographs enabled a broader holistic outlook for Brunner's planning work. He did, in fact, apply one of the "lessons of the bird's-eye view" that he had pointed out in his 1928 book of aerial photographs: his urban development plan for Santiago included the surrounding municipalities, thereby supporting planning on a metropolitan and regional level. The plan also revealed Brunner's sensitivity to local conditions and traditions including social and economic facts—information that he believed could to a large extent also be gleaned from aerial photographs. His plan proposed a number of small interventions in the existing urban fabric, including opening streets, creating open spaces, and removing buildings that had been built in the courtyards of housing blocks. The planned new neighborhoods in the extension zones continued and creatively adapted the existing street grid and housing typologies.[36]

The provision of social housing and open space lay at the heart of much of Brunner's work in Chile, Colombia, and Panama between 1929 and 1948, when he returned to his native Vienna. The lack of open space in the fast-growing South American cities was revealed particularly well in aerial photographs, as Brunner's German colleague Werner Hegemann was able to demonstrate in articles he published on his visits to Buenos Aires in 1931.[37] Like Le Corbusier before him, Hegemann, who had begun to publish Brunner's journal *Die Baupolitik* as a supplement of *Der Städtebau* in 1929, explored the city from an airplane. His recommendations for Buenos Aires were more in tune with Brunner's ideas than with the 1929 avant-garde scheme that Le Corbusier had proposed for the city and that was reminiscent of his Parisian *Plan Voisin*. Like Brunner, Hegemann did not dismiss the street grid. He supported pragmatic solutions to local problems, and he promoted regional planning and the adaptation of regional architectural styles and traditions. Brunner's and Hegemann's planning ideas for South American cities relied heavily on the systematic scientific paradigm.[38]

Because of their radical and utopian character, it does not surprise that Le Corbusier's schemes for the South American cities he visited remained on paper while many of Brunner's plans were carried out. The architects' plans and suggestions revealed the two predominant architectural movements at the time. In contrast to Le Corbusier, the exponent of the international modern movement, Brunner (like Hegemann) was more preoccupied with developing a regionalist approach to the problems at hand. The aerial view from airplanes supported the arguments and qualifying character traits of both movements. It enabled Le Corbusier to develop his grand schemes, and it also facilitated the small-scale interventions proposed by Brunner. At the same time, however, the aerial view led Le Corbusier to recognize regional landscape characteristics, while it enabled Brunner to extend his plans to comprehensive regional schemes.

Air-Minded Garden and Landscape Designs

On smaller grounds, too, the aerial view engaged the imagination of landscape architects. As a result of the publication of aerial photographs and the occasional opportunity to experience flight themselves in civilian aircraft, or while serving the country in military aircraft during World War I, landscape architects in Europe and the United States became increasingly air-minded. They used aerial photographs as analytical tools, produced designs inspired by the aerial view, and in some cases even for the aerial view. In 1920, the American geologist Willis T. Lee pointed toward the new opportunities that aerial photography afforded landscape architects, although he was careful to comment that "observation from the air can never take the place of close examination of the ground." Assisted by the U.S. Army and Navy Air Services, Lee spent nine months taking pictures from airplanes to determine "the practical value" of aerial views and photography for geography and other professions that relied on the study of the earth's surface. In his 1922 book *The Face of the Earth as Seen from the Air*, he noted the advantages that aerial photographs would offer the "landscape gardener." Whereas in the past the latter had had to rely on maps and horizontal views, in the future, oblique and aerial photographs would enable studying landscape "features in their correct proportions and relationship." Furthermore, Lee proposed that photographs of completed projects and famous gardens and grounds from around the world could be used for study and inspiration.[39]

The architects Edmund Gensemer Krimmel and James Kellum Smith hoped to produce a pattern book of design ideas for this purpose, modeled on the 1909 album of balloon photography entitled *Paris vu en ballon* (Paris seen from a balloon) by André Schelcher and Albert Omer-Decugis from the French Aéro-Club. Both architects had gained experience with aerial photography during World War I, when Krimmel served in the Army Air Force Intelligence Service and Smith in the Aviation Section and the Signal Officers Reserve Corps as a reserve military intelligence aviator. As a Fellow of the American Academy in Rome in 1920, Smith prepared a list of gardens, civic improvements, and public squares to be photographed in Italy, France, and England.[40] Architects like Krimmel, Smith, and Paul Philippe Cret thought that aerial photographs provided an excellent means to compare actual conditions with proposed design and planning schemes. These attitudes reflected the contemporary American Beaux-Arts approach that was heavily based on studying classical design precedents in other countries and adapting them to the American context. Aerial photographs, like plans, seemed to be an ideal means of representation for expansive geometrical garden designs like the ones at Versailles and Vaux-le-Vicomte. However, although this was a new use for aerial photographs, it hardly expanded the ways and methodologies of (landscape) architectural production. In contrast, it reinforced the inflexibility of the Beaux-Art training with its focus on meticulously rendered measured plan (besides perspectival) drawings and studies of classical historic precedents.

But the aerial view also inspired attempts by landscape architects to renew their design practice. Like Le Corbusier, the American landscape architect Marjorie Cautley used her flight from Stockholm along the Baltic Coast to Finland to sketch while the horizon was tilting back and forth and while "existing forms [were] shap[ing] and reshap[ing] themselves in bewildering succession." This was no doubt a challenging endeavor for somebody trained in perspective drawing and used to searching for the vanishing point on the horizon. In 1930, Cautley enthusiastically reported on her flight in an article programmatically entitled "New Horizons from Aloft," provocatively asking her fellow landscape architects whether there was "no broader outlook, no bird's-eye view for the student of land, its use, and its thoughtless abuse?" Only a year before, her American colleague Fletcher Steele had anticipated change as a result of the new perspective that the view from airplanes offered, noting: "Suddenly, in our day, our point of view is changed. The former imaginary bird's-eye view has become a commonplace point of aeroplane vantage. . . . The master of height finds the world simplified. For form he sees a great flatness, and for line the horizon. All else is but pattern. We may safely expect new patterns." Having observed the European attempts to bring garden design up to par with the architectural and artistic avant-garde at the Exposition Internationale des Arts Décoratifs 1925 in Paris, Steele believed that new approaches in American landscape architecture would result not from "new designs so much as through a new perspective on things as they are."[41]

Steele was an astute observer of modern landscape architecture in France, and in articles published in 1929 and 1930 he sought to familiarize his American readership with the new formal expressions in landscape architecture exhibited there. He presented extravagant garden designs by the French contemporary designers Gabriel Guévrékian, the Vera brothers, Pierre Legrain, André Lurçat, Le Corbusier, Albert Laprade, and Robert Mallet-Stevens. Their designs on show at the Parisian 1925 exhibition and carried out in France thereafter were based on strong graphical patterns that had mostly been conceived to be viewed as pictures from elevated vantage points, such as the balconies and terraces of adjacent houses. As Dorothée Imbert has observed, the designers treated the ground plane in these gardens as a picture plane.[42] They used form as "surface covering," as Fletcher Steele remarked, which "affect[ed] fundamental matters of design no more and no less than "wallpaper affects the design of a room.""[43] As a characteristic of modernist landscape architecture, Steele cited the tendency to both relieve "the often monotonous stiffness of formal work," on the one hand, and to bring "order into nature" on the other. As if he were describing a cubist painting, he noted: "The old axis is retained in spirit, but changed almost beyond recognition. It is shattered and its fragments moved, duplicated and bent. . . . Formal objects are put thus in occult rather than symmetrical balance." At the same time, he observed that "natural forms such as trees, rocks and streams" were often distributed according to "architectural principles of axis, transverse axis, symmetrical balance, etc."[44] And yet, although a few American landscape architects like Jacob John Spoon, Ernst Herminghaus, and Steele himself experimented with what they considered modernist principles—namely a balanced, not necessarily symmetrical "formal design" and "blocks" of plants of the same "type, color and foliage"—landscape design in the United States at the time generally still lacked a "spirit of modern display," as Spoon noted in 1931.[45]

Given the French interest in modernist design and architecture and the fact that France had hosted the first groundbreaking attempts at aviation, it is unsurprising that French landscape architects were among the first to produce air-minded garden designs in the 1920s. French enthusiasm for aviation and flight had never abated since the first manned balloon ascents in the late eighteenth century. Another high point was reached at the beginning of the twentieth century, when the Brazilian Alberto Santos Dumont in 1906 achieved in Paris what has become known as the first official powered flight in Europe. This feat was followed in 1908 by the Frenchman Henri Farman winning the first Grand Prix of the air held at the first European aerodrome in Issy-les-Moulineaux outside of Paris. The flight covered

.62 miles (1 kilometer) and lasted one minute and twenty-eight seconds. Furthermore, the opening of the First Paris Aeronautical Salon at the Grand Palais in 1908 and the first international aviation meet held in Reims in August 1909 testified to the enthusiasm and progress in French aviation.

The French landscape architect André Vera paid particular attention to the new sport and seems to have taken aviation more seriously than many of his air-minded colleagues. A decade after Louis Blériot had been the first to fly across the Straits of Dover in July 1909, Vera published a fictitious garden for an aviator (fig. 43). In the bird's-eye view drawn by his brother Paul, he wanted to show that the aviator had "exerted his power . . . on a few acres and completely subdued them. His Daedalian tyranny being recent, his authority [was] still severe." He described the garden composition as "rigorous: the interlocking surfaces are indissoluble, the proportions are exact, and the oppositions clear."[46] Except for the airplane hangar to the left of the house and garden, the layout of the grounds was similar to Vera's other geometrical garden designs, based on the idea of the garden as an extension of the house, providing rooms for different outdoor activities. Like many of his other garden proposals, the aviator's garden had rectangular garden rooms, delineated by clipped evergreen hedges and straight lines of trees, parterres, and a tennis ground. The geometrical layout, however, supported the aerial view, as did the monochromatic plantings of red next to yellow and orange. As noted earlier, American landscape architects also used this device in their early designs for airports. Vera considered the aviator's garden seen from the air an expression of strong will and determination to provide the returning aviator with a "spectacle of certainty." Using prose akin to that of the Italian futurists, he described the creative forces at work in this garden. The garden design would, he asserted, make anybody seem superhuman, like a Titan.[47] Modern man had acquired the view previously considered the domain of God. Vera had already remarked in 1912 that gardens should "catch and retain the attention of the passerby" and "present him or her with a global and condensed picture." "The composition of a modern decorative work," he remarked, should no longer be "analytical as it was during the centuries of pleasure, but undoubtedly synthetic."[48]

The enthusiasm for aviation and the modernity it stood for also showed in the inclusion of helicopters and airplanes in design drawings. In fact, some landscape architects were more able to demonstrate their alleged modernity and air-mindedness by including airplanes and helicopters in their perspective drawings of gardens than by the designs themselves. For example, as if to stress his modernity, Vera's French colleague Achille Duchêne included a helicopter in his perspective drawing of a suburban rooftop garden for artists in the series "Gardens of Tomorrow" illustrated in his 1935 volume *Les jardins de l'avenir* (fig. 44). He favored the bird's-eye view in many of

FIG. 43. Paul Vera,
Garden for the Aviator,
1919. (André Vera,
Les jardins [Paris:
Émile-Paul, Frères,
Éditeurs, 1919])

his drawings and often mounted his camera on chateau rooftops to take photographs showing his garden projects as grand, unified wholes.[49] Duchêne used the aerial perspective as a representational device but employed traditional design elements and symmetrical compositions to shape the land. While criticizing the avant-garde artists and technological progress exemplified by the automobile, the telephone, and the airplane, he nevertheless took the liberty of adding a helicopter to his perspective drawing of the artists' garden.

More than his French colleagues, who were merely fascinated by the view from above, the Danish landscape architect Carl Theodor Sørensen used the

FIG. 44.
Achille Duchêne,
bird's-eye view
of the "garden
of tomorrow for
a family of two
artists." (Achille
Duchêne, *Les jardins
de l'avenir* [Paris:
Fréal & Cie, Éditeurs,
1935])

aerial perspective not only to test and illustrate his designs but also to loosen historic ties and experiment with abstract form. Throughout his career he was particularly interested in the aesthetic, functional, and social aspects of his profession. Gardens were to be practical, useful, and designed for people to live in and move through. For children, for example, the garden was a place to play. Due to his interest in visual art, he favored pure and overlapping geometric forms in many designs. His implicit reference to futurist, suprematist, and constructivist art seems plausible. In fact, Sørensen used geometric forms like those of the exponent of suprematism Kazimir Malevich, whose abstract and reductive art was inspired by aviation and the aerial view. Most of Sørensen's designs, when seen in plan view or from above, appeared as strong two-dimensional visual patterns.[50]

FLIGHTS OF IMAGINATION

FIG. 45.
C. Th. Sørensen,
axonometric draw-
ing 1:500 of the
garden for Jens J.
Jarl, Klampenborg,
Denmark, 1932. (*Have-
kunst* 15 [1934], 110)

In 1929, Sørensen designed the grounds surrounding the "House of the Future" at the Building and Housing Exhibition of the Academic Architects' Association in Copenhagen. Surrounding Arne Jacobsen and Flemming Lassen's futurist house with helicopter landing pad and underground port, Sørensen provided a paved terrace and rectangular planting beds arranged in a grass lawn, with the entire garden enclosed by an ivy-clad fence. Viewed from the roof terrace or from the helicopter that complemented the axonometric drawing, the planting beds appeared as the geometric forms of an abstract painting.

In his garden design for the engineer Jens J. Jarl in Klampenborg, Sørensen used a favored design motive: the circle overlapping a rectangular form (fig. 45). He included an airplane in the axonometric drawing of the garden. Whether Sørensen added the plane because of his client's interests is not clear, but the plane, which also acted as the north arrow, signified the modernity of the design. As with the "House of the Future," Sørensen collaborated on this project with Arne Jacobsen, who designed the functionalist house. Sørensen wanted the garden to be low-maintenance and to complement the simplicity of the modern white cube. A whitewashed concrete wall enclosed the garden's expanse of open lawn, kitchen garden, children's play area, drying area, and flower beds including plantings of sneezeweed, phlox, rhododendron, and roses.

Like his garden design for the "House of the Future," Sørensen's 1952 design for the triangular sloping church square in Kalundborg, Denmark, with its low, clipped barberry and privet hedges, was also meant for view from an elevated position. In fact, the geometrical pattern covers the inclined square like an unrolled carpet. The photograph representing Sørensen's work in Elizabeth Kassler's 1964 book *Modern Gardens and the Landscape* fittingly shows the view from the church steeple.[51]

Although Sørensen was concerned with how people would experience his gardens, he rarely produced perspective sketches. Instead, he used illustrations that described his gardens as seen from detached viewpoints outside. As if he were heeding Leon Battista Alberti's and Raphael's advice to renounce foreshortened views, he communicated his design ideas in isometric or axonometric plans proving exact measurements so as not to delude.[52] Sørensen considered these representations resembling the aerial view as a means to test his designs.

While axonometric representations are almost as old as humankind itself, their use in modern times surged after the 1923 De Stijl exhibition in the gallery L'Effort Moderne in Paris, in which axonometric drawings by the architect Cornelis van Eesteren and the artist Theo van Doesburg were exhibited. In addition, the work by the artists El Lissitzky and Kazimir Malevich—who likewise used axonometry, stressing its ability to both let the object project forward and backward into space as well as to lift it up and make it appear as if it hovered freely in infinite space—influenced the representational techniques used by architects and landscape architects affiliated with the avant-garde movements in the 1920s and 1930s.[53] These professionals considered axonometric and isometric representations to be analytical, rational, and conceptual, while at the same time offering objective information on the material quality of the respective design object, regardless of whether it was a building or garden. Axonometric and isometric projections hovering in infinite space also gave expression to many avant-garde architects' understanding of a metaphysical ontogenesis of space. According to Walter Gropius, humankind could experience infinite space as a result of its relationship with the universe. Although this was where the ideas and visions of space were born, humankind could ultimately only create space with the finite means of the material world.[54]

Axonometries and isonometries often also resembled model photographs despite the latters' inherent perspective, because models of specific buildings and gardens also often did not include context, were most often viewed and photographed from an elevated oblique viewpoint, and often were restrained, simple, and minimalist representations that concentrated on the essential volumes and lines. The black-and-white model photographs reproduced in books and journals in the 1920s and 1930s often resembled axonometric and isometric drawings due to the angle at which the photographs were taken, which reduced perspectival foreshortening to a minimum.[55] Like axonometries and isonometries, three-dimensional models could also give the beholder a total, or comprehensive, impression of the building or garden.

Although they showed the designed object mostly from above (rather than from below), axonometric and isometric drawings did not position the viewer, but would let him or her float in free space. Consequently these visual representations did not portray any perspective distortion, but produced an equalizing space. This stood in contrast to the bird's-eye-view garden paintings and engravings used by popes, cardinals, aristocrats, and landowners to depict their gardens since the sixteenth century. These representations also imparted a different political message. By consciously stressing certain elements while neglecting others, by adding nonexisting projected features, and by directing the viewer's gaze toward what were deemed the most important elements in the painting or engraving, they showed off their owner's personal wealth, prestige, power, control, pride, and aspirations. As was the case in the late-sixteenth-century lunettes by Giusto Utens that depicted several of the Medici villas, the principal view in bird's-eye perspectives was often directed along the main or central axis of the garden leading up to the villa or palace, which frequently assumed a central and sometimes even elevated position in these representations. The gardens literally appeared to lie at the feet of the respective villa, or estate owner. Furthermore, bird's-eye perspectives were also the best way to represent estates and gardens of the time in their full glory, extent, and context. From the fifteenth into the eighteenth centuries, many garden designs were dominated by intricate geometrical and symmetrical patterns developed for the horizontal ground plain. Elevated features like terraces and artificial hills, like the mount in the gardens of the Roman Villa Medici on the Pincio Hill, from which the splendor of the planted parterre patterns could be viewed at ease and in their full extent, therefore became integrated elements of the garden designs themselves. Bird's-eye-view paintings and engravings could elevate the viewpoint even farther and proved especially adapted to visualize ornamental garden designs in their full detail and extension. Furthermore, these representations could illustrate the relationship of the estate to the surrounding terrain, a function that in the case of sixteenth- and seventeenth-century Italian gardens became important as it could illustrate how nature had been turned into art by juxtaposing elaborate garden designs with the "wilderness" outside the garden walls. The representation of seventeenth-century French and Dutch gardens embedded in forests and wooded areas and in the agricultural field patterns became relevant because of the seemingly infinite straight pathways running from palaces into the countryside that established axial relationships between various palaces, thereby expressing the power relationships between them and the surrounding countryside.[56]

In contrast, in the 1920s and 1930s, Sørensen and other landscape architects interested in modernism often represented their designs without context, floating in infinite space. This made the abstract shapes and geometrical forms they used easily legible. Some designers like Vera in France and Ernst Herminghaus (see chapter 1) in the United States argued that geometrical patterns and mass plantings in bright colors that clearly identified the respective site designs catered best to the aerial view, an observation sustained by the number of aerial photographs taken of geometrical land patterns that were published in journals and books at the time. However, at the same time that Vera and Herminghaus were praising the advantages of geometrical and, to a certain extent, modernist designs, the aeroplane vantage was also used as an argument for nativist and regionalist garden designs that were not set apart from but merged with the surrounding countryside using "native" plants. To promote "more garden designs rooted in the soil," the German landscape architect Otto Valentien paralleled the convictions voiced by his architecture colleagues Ewald and Brunner with regard to city planning. According to Valentien, due to the possible bird's-eye view of gardens sited on slopes in mountainous territory, these gardens had always been perceived as being more closely tied to their environment than gardens on level ground into which people could not see. Because of the possible views onto and into gardens in mountainous terrain, Valentien considered it particularly important that their design merge with the surrounding countryside.[57]

ROBERTO BURLE MARX, ALVAR AALTO, AND THE AERIAL IMAGINATION

Creating both graphic and pictorial landscapes that appeared as abstract attractive patterns from above or from oblique angles, and that rose as volumes and on occasion merged with the surrounding countryside and scenery when seen from the ground was the intention of the Brazilian landscape architect Roberto Burle Marx. Although he only mentioned in passing that many of his gardens were explicitly designed for both the aerial and the ground view, it is largely the perception and reception of his designs from oblique angles and from above, documented in widely distributed aerial photographs, that has turned them into icons of twentieth-century landscape architecture. One may argue that his modernist designs required a modern elevated vantage point, or, conversely, one may assume with some of his contemporary critics that the modern aeroplane vantage induced bio-morphic forms as a response to the rapidly modernizing world. Because of their attractiveness when viewed from above, these forms that dominated many of Burle Marx's designs after 1938 lent themselves in particular to roof gardens and garden, plaza, and pavement designs that would be seen from above. This was the case in two of his early commissions in the 1930s and 1940s. Burle Marx used biomorphic shapes on the roof of the exhibition wing of the Ministry of Education and Health building in Rio that were intended to be seen from the connected sixteen-story block. Commenting on the flowing forms in this design at the Fifty-Fifth Annual Meeting of the American Society of Landscape Architects in Boston in 1954, Burle Marx allowed the audience a glance into his inspirational world, or rather, into the world he aspired to evoke in the viewer and visitor. The flowing forms, he said, brought "to mind the configuration of the Brazilian rivers, as seen from the windows of a plane." Furthermore, he drew attention to the fact that al-though the garden beds appeared from above as a two-dimensional picture, when seen from the roof level, they had "the same volume in proportion to the Ministry that the river beds have to the mountains of the landscape."[58]

Burle Marx also used amoebic shapes for laying out garden spaces on Plaza Salgado Filho in front of the modernist main terminal building of San-tos Dumont Airport in Rio, completed in 1947, as well as for the terminal's roof garden. Both gardens were visible from approaching airplanes and were intended to provide air passengers with a memorable arrival in what was then Brazil's national capital. In line with the Vargas government's intention to build a new national identity through a number of architectural works and through the promotion of Brazilian aviation, Burle Marx's garden designs fostered a Brazilian identity. Plaza Salgado Filho's lush tropical vegetation, its lake, biomorphic planting beds, and curving pathways accentuated by benches offered a microcosm of Brazil's plant life and geography. The small lake was designed as a haven for disappearing species of the regional flora. The plaza was the starting point of more extensive open space projects sur-rounding the Museum of Modern Art and along Guanabara and Botafogo Bays in the 1950s, which continued into the 1970s with the building of the famous Paseo de Copacabana. Although Le Corbusier's vision of the curved elevated highway in this location did not come to fruition, Burle Marx's project along the bays almost seems to have resolved the tension between "nature" and the man-made that had characterized the French architect's earlier design gestures and conceptual ideas for Rio's urban renaissance.

Santos Dumont Airport was also the first of the four Brazilian airport sites for which Burle Marx designed gardens throughout his career, which lasted until his death in 1994. In 1951 and 1978, he designed a garden for Rio's Galeão International Airport. His garden for Pampulha Airport in Belo

Horizonte dates back to 1953 and was followed by a design for Salgado Filho Square next to Guararapes Airport in Recife in 1957. Burle Marx used his characteristic amoebic forms in some of these airport gardens, thus providing that "beautiful airview" for the passengers of approaching planes that John Nolen had asked for in 1928.

In the context of Burle Marx's residential garden designs, the oblique view from elevated points played a more important role than the vertical aerial view. In his 1948 Odette Monteiro Garden (today Luiz Cezar Fernandes Garden) in Correias, the layout of curving walkways that wind their way up to the highest elevation in the garden provided views onto colorful biomorphic patterns of mass plantings of yellow and purple coleus on sloping terrain. In fact, from some viewpoints the swaths of monochrome plantings emphasized the slopes and shapes of the ground. A selection of indigenous trees blended the garden into the surrounding hillside and mountain scenery.

Over the past half century, a number of critics have—often only in passing—pointed out the relevance of the aerial view to Burle Marx's work.[59] Familiar with Burle Marx's 1954 talk in Boston, two years later, the British landscape architect Geoffrey Jellicoe attributed "the peculiar pleasure given by" the garden and landscape designs of his Brazilian colleague Roberto Burle Marx to "a new set of emotions and reactions arising primarily from air travel." Further, he pointed out, "his water curves are analogous to coastline curves seen from the air, rather than land-locked lakes seen from the ground; the imposition of one pattern upon another is like the passage of cloud shadows over the landscape."[60] Given the South American context of most of Burle Marx's work, Jellicoe could have been reminded consciously or unconsciously of Le Corbusier's imaginative descriptions of parts of South America seen from an airplane. Flying across Uruguay, the latter had experienced its plain as "an immense panther skin, green and yellow from its lit-up pastures spotted by an infinite number of circles of seemingly black shadows. How black and thick the shadows of clouds are on the earth and on cities," Le Corbusier had exclaimed.[61] Eight years after Jellicoe's remarks, the Italian art critic Pier Maria Bardi, who had emigrated to Brazil in 1946, used an aerial photograph of the vegetation on the banks of the Amazon River in his 1964 book *The Tropical Gardens of Burle Marx* to show that his garden designs were inspired by the geography of his native country and in particular by the undulating shorelines of the Amazon (fig. 46). More recently, the art historian Valerie Fraser followed this line of thought when she described Burle Marx's roof garden of the exhibition wing of the MES building in Rio de Janeiro as "a miniature landscape, like a physical map or aerial photograph of a segment of flat tropical wetland." Fraser pointed out further that the paved area suggested "a slow-moving river meandering back and forth and the planted areas, the banks and islands." Her interpretation

FIG. 46. High oblique aerial photograph of
the vegetation on the banks of the Amazon
River used by Pier Maria Bardi in his book
The Tropical Gardens of Burle Marx. (P. M. Bardi,
The Tropical Gardens of Burle Marx [New York:
Reinhold, 1964], 54)

built upon the idea that Burle Marx employed the forms of tropical wetlands
as part of a larger design strategy to reclaim "all things Brazilian."[62] Thus,
not only the use of indigenous plants—many of which Burle Marx himself
had discovered in the Brazilian rainforests and subsequently cultivated at
his own estate in Barra de Guaratiba—but also the use of forms that recalled the geography of his native country imbued Burle Marx's designs with
the nationalist flavor that was so common for the Brazilian avant-garde from
the 1920s onward. To distance themselves from their European forebearers
and to create their own national identity, members of the urban artistic and
intellectual avant-garde embraced everything that was perceived by Euro-
peans as the "exotic other," including the hinterland and "jungle," and the
traditions and cults of the rural non-Westernized population. Burle Marx
looked to the Brazilian hinterland, in particular to the tropical rainforests
and wetlands, for inspiration for original designs that reflected his country's
new cultural spirit. In fact, his profession allowed him to participate in a
more literal sense than many of his artist colleagues and friends in what
Fraser calls the "'Reclaim the Jungle' movement, an attempt to reclaim . . .
an idea traditionally associated with danger and to make it accessible to the
urban intellectual imagination."[63] Although Burle Marx was rather elusive

about the inspirational value of the aerial perspective and although he did not experience the rainforest firsthand until 1950,[64] it appears likely that the aerial views of his native Brazil and especially the Amazon played a role in the development of the abstract biomorphic forms in his designs. Scheduled passenger flights up the Amazon River from Belém to Manáos had begun by the time Burle Marx started his career, in 1934.

Parallel developments such as the use of aerial photographs by the Finnish architect Alvar Aalto—eleven years Burle Marx's senior and as inspired by biomorphic shapes and modernism as his Brazilian colleague—also testify to the importance of the aerial view as design inspiration and as an instrument to provide design with both national and international legitimacy. Both Burle Marx and Aalto grew up and began their careers in countries that were striving for independence from colonial empires (Brazil) and foreign occupation (Finland). The search for and construction of a common culture through a modern emblematic design and imagery that could foster a national identity while at the same time exhibiting modernity therefore played an important role in these countries. It is no coincidence that in the postwar years the architectural critic Sigfried Giedion programmatically singled out these two countries in the tropics and near the polar circle as modern architectural centers in which the "creative impulse" reigned.[65]

In contrast to Burle Marx, Aalto, the son of a government surveyor, had himself used aerial photographs of his native Finland in articles he wrote in the 1940s in an effort to define a national style.[66] Thus, it was only logical for Giedion to infer in the second, 1949, edition of his well-known work *Space, Time and Architecture* that Finland's nature and landscape character had inspired Aalto's architectural forms. The Finnish architect, Giedion argued, "found a direct incentive in the curved contours of the Finnish lakes, shaped with astonishing smoothness by nature itself and set in high relief by forest masses pressing on all sides down to the water's edge."[67] What Giedion captured here in words was visually portrayed in an accompanying oblique aerial photograph of Lusikkaniemi Point, a curved peninsula at Aulanko Park, a nature reserve 62 miles (100 kilometers) north of Helsinki. The scenic beauty of Lusikkaniemi Point began to attract Finnish and international tourists on a larger scale at the beginning of the twentieth century, and it has since become a fashionable spa resort. Because it was also the site of a medieval Viking hill fort, Aulanko Park combined natural beauty with cultural heritage, thus playing an important role in the construction of Finnish culture and identity.[68] In fact, the iconic peninsula seen from a bird's-eye perspective had already begun to play an important role in the Finnish national consciousness at the end of the nineteenth century, when it began to be perceived as symbolizing the quintessential Finnish landscape and was replicated in photographs that were first taken from Aulangonvuori

Hill and then from its granite lookout tower constructed in 1906 (fig. 47). The high viewpoint that lent itself to the construction of the national land-scape imagery was further elevated once the first flights had taken off in Aulanko in 1930. It is therefore not surprising that the 1945 picture book *Suomi kuvina* (Finland in pictures), published to promote the national spirit, used an aerial photograph of Lusikkaniemi Point as a two-page spread at the beginning of the book as the backdrop for the printed words of the Finnish national anthem. After all, the anthem's composer, Jean Sibelius, who was born in nearby Hämeenlinna, claimed to have had Aulanko's landscape in mind when he composed "Finlandia."[69] By the 1940s, the landscape imagery offered by the aerial view of Lusikkaniemi Point had come to do both: it presented Finland as pure nature and therefore as politically neutral, and it evoked nationalist sentiment. In 2011, picture postcards depicting oblique aerial views of Lusikkaniemi Point with titles like "The National Scenery Aulanko" and "The National Scenery in Winter" were still being sold in the café below the lookout tower. They included a postcard showing a Finnish woman posing in national costume on the platform below the lookout tower with the lake and peninsula as backdrop.

Giedion used the aerial photograph of Lusikkaniemi Point to illustrate the parallels between the natural shape of the iconic landscape feature and the curving walls and biomorphic forms in Alvar Aalto's designs. It appeared

FIG. 47.
Lusikkaniemi Point in Aulanko Park as seen from the lookout tower on Aulangonvuori Hill, Finland. (Photograph by the author)

on the same page as the ground plan of Aalto's Finnish Pavilion for the 1939 New York World's Fair and a photograph of his famous Savoy glass vases. The use of a ubiquitous modern technology—aerial photography—to portray a millennia-old landscape feature that was used to foster a Finnish national identity also seemed to capture what Giedion saw as one of the characteristic qualities of Aalto's architectural design: a combination of "worldwide orientation" and "regional roots," a quality that Kenneth Frampton would later describe as critical regionalism. In a similar way, the aesthetic of Burle Marx's garden and open space designs was universally appealing and successfully contrasted with the straight and austere lines of architecture typical of the international style. His garden designs appeared rooted in the respective regional landscape through the use of site-specific plants as well as patterns and materials connected to local and regional traditions. While it remains difficult to reconstruct the designers' aerial imagination, it is certain that at the beginning of the jet age in the 1950s and 1960s, the aerial view offered design critics a new perspective for interpretation.[70]

LOFTY VIEWS FROM LOFTY GARDENS

Burle Marx's roof gardens were examples of what by the end of the 1920s had already come to be called "roof life for town dwellers."[71] In fact, by the time Burle Marx began to design roof gardens, they were no longer a novelty. Although roof gardens had been planned and realized for centuries, the construction of the first skyscrapers in North American cities at the end of the nineteenth and the beginning of the twentieth centuries led to a surge of gardens on rooftops. In addition, the proliferation of flat roofs as a result of their iconic status in modernist architecture, new building materials, and Le Corbusier and Pierre Jeanneret's promotion of roof gardens in their 1926 essay The Five Points of a New Architecture (Les Cinq points d'une architecture nouvelle) increased their number in the big European and American cities in the 1930s. Walter Gropius pointed out that roof gardens could be used "to pull nature into the stone desert of the city" and to transform future cities into what from the air would "give the impression of a big park."[72] Roof gardens were an integral part of what the architectural avant-garde envisioned as the new "vertical city," in which, as Le Corbusier explained, "cells which have for so long been crushed on the ground" are piled up "high above the earth, bathed in light and air."[73] Roof gardens therefore were part of the early-twentieth-century urban imaginary of life in the air that connected aviation and skyscrapers and also led to the idea of establishing airports that bridged rooftops. As elevated platforms, many roof gardens were removed from the ground and the ground view while at the same time being visually accessible from surrounding skyscrapers and airplanes. Sandwiched in vertical space between the ground and views from above, and occupying a middle ground, roof gardens were a physical manifestation of modernity's ambiguity. A means to colonize air space and lift life off the ground, they at the same time often also suggested a firm grounding on the earth by simulating environments commonly found on the ground.

In 1933, the British landscape architect Richard Sudell reported that roof gardens were becoming popular in London, Berlin, and New York. While a combination of factors led to the construction and popularity of roof gardens at the time, architects and landscape architects promoted them as creating attractive air views for pilots and air passengers. Sudell anticipated that aviation would "very well affect the question of roof gardens" as flying became "more and more a personal or family undertaking."[74]

The American architect Benjamin Betts noted that attractive air views should be offered not only to airplane passengers—as John Nolen had proposed a few years before—but also to the users and inhabitants of high-rise buildings. Architects argued that because skyscraper views not only enabled looking across the city and onto the street life unfolding below, but also revealed the surrounding unseemly barren lower rooftops, these should be turned into lofty roof gardens. In addition, roof gardens were seen as a means to make good use of expensive ground and provide additional open space in dense inner cities, for example, as playgrounds and additional private open-air rooms. Their importance for public health caused the British landscape architect Lady Allen of Hurtwood to argue that roof gardens should "in the future, be considered as essential as a bathroom."[75]

In New York City, roof gardens had already begun to appear in the 1890s as public establishments on the roofs of theaters. As Meir Wigoder has noted, these gardens enabled people to see the city from above "as if it were a sublime, romantic view enjoyed from a mountain crag." Once New York City's first skyscrapers had been built by 1910, the privileged voyeuristic onlookers could ascend to even greater heights in their quest for excitement, awe, and inspiration on the one hand and for an exceptional position that enabled detachment from the world below on the other. David E. Nye has pointed out that the skyscraper view had become a part of the popular consciousness by the late 1920s and that businessmen consciously sought it out as a means to visualize their power. The higher their offices were located, the more empowerment and control over the world they could feel.[76]

A prominent skyscraper roof garden project with a highly representational function that set an example on an international scale was the roof garden landscape installed on the setbacks and roofs of the lower buildings of the Rockefeller Center in New York City (fig. 48). The architect Raymond Hood who had first conceived of the gardens, suggested in 1930 that besides offering beneficial environmental effects, roof gardens could attract tenants to the planned building complex.[77] Facilitated by the fact that Rockefeller

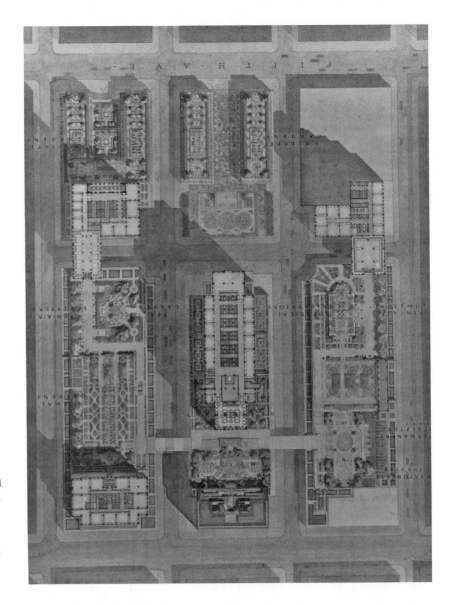

FIG. 48. Associated Architects, design for Rockefeller Center Gardens, 1932. (© 2012 Rockefeller Group Inc. / Rockefeller Center Archives)

Center was a comprehensive development, the roof garden idea was taken up in the subsequent architectural designs, and by 1937 gardens had been built on the roofs of La Maison Française, the British Empire Building, the Palazzo d'Italia, the International Building East, Radio City Music Hall, and on the eleventh-floor roof of the Radio Corporation of America (RCA) Building. Advertised as a "modern version of the hanging gardens of Babylon,"[78] the gardens were intended to provide visitors with respite and onlookers from the higher surrounding buildings with "beautiful air views."

The largest and most elaborate of Rockefeller Center's sky gardens was the Gardens of the Nations, located on the eleventh-floor terraces of the RCA

FIG. 49. Gardens
of the Nations on
the setbacks of
the RCA Building
of the Rockefeller
Center in Midtown
Manhattan. (© 2012
Rockefeller Group
Inc. / Rockefeller
Center Archives)

Building and conceived by the Welsh landscape architect Ralph Hancock (fig. 49).[79] Opened in April 1935, the Gardens of the Nations presented "authentic types of garden design and architecture representative of the best in ornamental horticulture from all over the globe," and provided visitors with information on gardens and horticulture.[80] Not only did the lofty roof gardens signify Rockefeller Center's modernity and technological prowess, but their elevated location and theme also symbolized the Rockefellers' global and international orientation, reach, and influence. The Gardens of the Nations brought together idealized expressions of garden cultures from different countries in the universal, or supranational, space of rooftops high above the ground.

Using design features derived from different garden cultures and periods in Europe and the United States, Hancock designed an "International Rock Garden," an "American Native Garden," "A Patio Garden from Ancient Spain," a "Japanese," an "English," an "Italian," a "French," a "Dutch," and a "Modern Garden." A bird sanctuary for nature lovers was also included in the scheme. Possibly as a reaction to the world financial crisis and the resulting interest in urban gardening at the time, the rooftop plantings also included fruit trees and a vegetable garden, complete with a beehive. Besides providing office workers and visitors in the surrounding buildings with pleasing vistas, the gardens were also intended to act as a didactic venue and an exhibition of garden cultures and "skyline horticulture" for Manhattan shoppers and businessmen. Thus, some of the photographs used to illustrate the gardens in a small brochure showed the vegetative features in the foreground of wide-angle shots of New York City's skyline. Others concentrated on the actual garden features to highlight the fact that elaborate plantings and designs could now be carried out at an elevation of one hundred feet above street level. Separated from one another by walls to protect them from wind, the Gardens of the Nations were designed as stage sets to transport the visitor into different worlds. Thus, the "American Native Garden" featured "native plants, ferns and mosses," a rail fence, and a rural postbox to transport the city or suburban dweller "to a woodsy spot in New England." An ancient well head from Granada was used in the "Patio Garden from Ancient Spain" to give the garden an air of authenticity. In contrast to this attempt to stereotype different garden cultures from a variety of historical periods, the rock garden, which was still considered a novelty in the United States at the time, was thought to be "international" because of the provenance of its plants. Another garden that was considered to transcend national boundaries was the "Modern Garden," probably modeled on Gabriel Guevrekian's design for the "Garden of Water and Light" at the 1925 Parisian Exposition Internationale des Arts Décoratifs.

In 1933, some years before the inception of the Gardens of the Nations, Fletcher Steele, one of the American landscape architects most interested in modernist expression, had been among the landscape architects consulted about proposed layouts for the roof gardens. His comments might also have been influential in the creation of the Gardens of the Nations since he deplored the "monotonous sameness" of the roof garden designs presented to him. To counter this effect, Steele suggested that each roof garden design should be based on a different motive. The roof gardens could, he argued, direct visitor's attention to the sky above, to views over the city, and "inward to the garden itself."[81] Stressing the middle ground provided by the roof gardens, Steele recognized the new visual opportunities they offered. Apart from providing visual delight and opportunities for bodily engagement and experience in the garden spaces themselves, they could frame views onto and into the city from above. They also provided a space not only open to the sky but nearer the sky, which could be drawn into the garden by means of reflecting pools or framing devices. Although most rooftop gardens since have been designed to be used and lived in, the idea to design elaborate roof gardens as objects of visual delight and patterns to be seen from above has continued.

In summary, the aerial view enabled the uncovering and discovery of city and landscape patterns, provided comprehensive oversight of large stretches of land, and, beginning in the 1920s, when the aerial view had become more common, provided new tools and inspiration for city planners and landscape architects. However, only a few decades after the landscape features and city forms had been discovered through powered aviation, they provided points of orientation for the deadly bombers of World War II. Ironically, therefore, only shortly after devising the first schemes and designs aimed at making airports, rooftops, and gardens visible and attractive from the air, landscape architects in the countries at war were involved in disguising human settlement and action and blending it into the landscape by designing camouflage plantings for airfields, air-raid shelters, and other military and civilian constructions. The German architect Fritz Wichert's early-twentieth-century vision of house roofs as the new façades was repeated more than thirty years later in the context of camouflage measures during World War II by Leopold Arnaud, dean of Columbia University's School of Architecture. Arnaud pointed out that "with the development of aviation, the fifth façade, the roof, is also of importance." He predicted that "the practical knowledge obtained from the study of camouflage as a war emergency will unquestionably give valuable experience to the designer, and will affect the appearance of architecture in the future."[82] During World War II and in the postwar years designers were employed to develop land camouflage schemes and create "invisible landscapes."

Four | Concealing the Land

CREATING INVISIBLE LANDSCAPES OF WAR AND PEACE

In 1945, Lee Miller photographed the nineteenth-century garden of Linderhof Palace near Oberammergau in Bavaria (fig. 50). The black-and-white photograph shows garden statues and pavilions covered with camouflage netting in front of a background of mountains in the distance. Miller captured the seemingly deserted and silent palace grounds with their mystical veiled structures on a sunny day from the shade underneath a tree. Her photograph conveys a surreal and eerie atmosphere not only because of the light contrast and the viewpoint, which suggests what a soldier on reconnaissance might see as he stumbled out of the undergrowth from the woods upon the seemingly peaceful Linderhof, but also as a result of the tension between the visible and clearly identifiable camouflage netting on the one hand and the invisible objects it hides on the other. Mystery, confusion, and irony result from this perspective on the ground, while disorientation of the bombers flying above was one of the initial goals of disrupting and disguising the axial neobaroque layout of the gardens with camouflage nets. In Munich, fifty-six miles northeast of Linderhof, the surfaces of the centrally located Königsplatz and the plaza east of Barer Strasse between Gabelsberger and Theresienstrasse were painted in a way to suggest city fabric and roads running across them (fig. 51). This way, German intelligence hoped, bombers would be disorientated and prevented from bombing the central railroad station, one of the vitally important lifelines of the city.[1]

Clearly identifiable landscape features like Linderhof's neobaroque gardens, Munich's city plazas and rail lines, and natural features like lakes were landmarks that provided pilots with easy orientation, enabling them to find their bombing targets. To save and protect lives, landmarks and conspicuous buildings had to be rendered invisible to the aerial view. They had to be camouflaged. As the American landscape architect Ralph Rodney Root

argued in 1942, "Landscape effects for the sake of pictorial pattern . . . completely lose importance in camouflage design."[2] Instead, "the problem of the camoufleur [was] to build the project so that it fits completely into the existing ground pattern . . . without the introduction of forms alien to its surroundings."[3] Besides concealing landmarks, all war-faring countries during World War II were concerned with disrupting the enemy pilot's vision and deceiving him through the building of decoys. Beginning in World War I and increasingly during World War II, camouflaging industry, infrastructures, and human habitation against the aerial view became one of the occupations of design professionals. Camouflage turned the land subject to military operations into landscapes of war. Given the scientific and artistic training of professionals in the design disciplines, these experts were especially suited for camouflage work. In turn, the new experiences gained in land camouflage during the war also proved useful in landscape and urban design after the war. Design culture built upon a variety of design principles, conceptual ideas, and measures that began or were further developed and

FLIGHTS OF IMAGINATION

promoted during the war. The preoccupation with patterns and gestalt, with the art of illusion, with the creation of scenery, and with the multiplicity of scales was common to both military camouflage and urban and landscape design.

Camouflage as "Art–Science"

Although camouflage at the beginning of World War I was considered an art and the domain of artists, a number of other experts were employed in the development of a variety of camouflage measures during World War I and World War II, including architects, landscape architects, set designers, film producers, engineers, and horticulturists. Artists and professionals from various fields were competing against each other either as civilians on the home front for public commissions in camouflage, or as officers in uniform for posts in the respective camouflage sections of the military. The theoretical question of whether camouflage should be considered an art or a science became a political one, as artists, design professionals, and scientists sought to offer their services to the military and apply for the competitive, highly sought-after posts in the camouflage units. Due to the increased complexity of warfare, however, it had become clear by World War II that camouflage

FIG. 51. In Munich, the surface of the centrally located Königsplatz (*A*, right of center) and the plaza (*B*, left of center) east of Barer Strasse between Gabelsberger and Theresienstrasse was painted in a way to suggest city fabric and roads running across them. (*Evidence in Camera* 1, no. 5 [November 16, 1942], 183)

needed to be a collaborative effort between disciplines. Camouflage, as the British architect and officer in the Air Ministry's Camouflage Branch Hugh Casson pointed out, could be called an "art-science."[4]

The idea to render the forms and colors of guns and machinery "invisible" to the enemy through the application of painted patterns and materials was developed in the early months of World War I by the French artist Lucien-Victor Guirand de Scévola, who was serving for an artillery unit at the Battle of the Marne.[5] De Scévola's idea took hold, and in February 1915, the French army put him in charge of the first camouflage section charged with developing techniques for concealing artillery and other equipment. The French term "camouflage" was subsequently adopted in the German and English languages and used to describe the concealment of troops, camps, vehicles, and other military equipment, as well as elaborate schemes of deception. Although De Scévola did not belong to the artistic avant-garde and was known instead for his true-to-life, pastel-colored portraits, in his wartime practice he used the techniques of deformation and deconstruction employed in cubist artworks.[6] For his camouflage section he hired some painters with leanings toward impressionism and cubism, although the latter art's great masters, Picasso and Bracque, only learned of camouflage indirectly. Gertrude Stein's frequently quoted report on her and Picasso's own first sighting of a camouflaged truck on the Parisian Boulevard Raspail stated that they "had heard of camouflage but . . . had not yet seen it and Picasso amazed looked at it and then cried out, yes it is we who made it, that is cubism."[7]

While artists like the French Claude Forain and Jacques Villon, the German Franz Marc, and the Americans Thomas Hart Benton, Grant Wood, and Charles Burchfield were soon signing up or being recruited as military camoufleurs, critics began to comment on the parallels between camouflage and abstract art.[8] Serving as the commanding officer of the first American Camouflage Section, the American theater director Homer Saint-Gaudens noted that camoufleurs were widely considered "the painters of a new brand of scenery,"[9] and he referred to the first American Camouflage Section, which ultimately became part of the Fortieth Engineers and supported the Allies in France, as the "Fantasy Forces."[10] Although Saint-Gaudens quickly widened the range of experts involved in the Camouflage Section, assembling a group of painters, sculptors, architects, carpenters, metal workers, scenic artists, paint manufacturers, electricians, and "65 men from Hollywood—assistant directors, property men, scenic painters,"[11] the first camouflage groups that organized themselves in the United States consisted mainly of artists.[12] The American artists Sherry E. Fry and Barry Faulkner founded the first civilian Camouflage Society in New York shortly after the United States entered World War I in 1917.

The parallel between camouflage patterns and techniques used in particular in horizontal camouflage on land and at sea, and abstract art was also noted by the writer Lida Rose McCabe. In 1918, she observed that the camouflaged navy station in New York Harbor was "a veritable floating salon of Cubist, Futurist and Vorticist color-feats significantly emphasizing the passage of the one time derided culturists from theoretic into actual warfare!"[13] It seems that warfare might indeed have contributed to a wider acceptance of these new directions in art and of what Paul Virilio, following Guillaume Apollinaire, has called an "aesthetic of disappearance."[14] However, despite the parallel that can be drawn between the aesthetics and methods involved in both cubism and camouflage, they had varying aims. While the cubist painters strove to offer new perspectives and readings of their objects, the camoufleurs attempted to shield them from view entirely.[15]

Warfare not only provided modernist patterns to be perceived from the water and land as in New York Harbor and thereby instigate what Oskar Schlemmer in World War II would call "the cult of the surface."[16] While the camoufleurs were struggling to use cubist methods and techniques to break up forms and make the navy ships merge with sea and sky, and artillery and guns with varying landscapes, their colleagues in the air were being trained to differentiate between landscape patterns coded fittingly as "cubist country" and "futurist country." As the art historian John Welchman has observed, these terms used in a 1918 photo atlas prepared by the Royal Air Force to describe "irregularly shaped and dispersed . . . unbounded fields" in the first case, and irregular "abstract-seeming, . . . field patches broken up by occasional roads" in the second, clearly associated the "aerial photograph . . . with . . . Modernism."[17] In the same sense, the English composer and musicologist Norman Demuth compared "the crossing and re-crossing of paths" appearing in aerial photographs with "a spidery drawing by Paul Klee," and claimed that "incidentally, a certain 'Composition' by Fernand Leger is an excellent reproduction of a mid-European ground plan!"[18] While Edward Steichen declared that only his knowledge of the impressionists and cubists enabled him to carry out his aerial reconnaissance mission, Ernest Hemingway in turn claimed to begin "to understand cubist painting" after his first flight in 1922.[19]

In addition to the techniques and aesthetics of abstract art, camoufleurs were also drawn to science. The use of camouflage and mimicry by animals, as illustrated in the 1909 book *Concealing Coloration in the Animal Kingdom*, by the American painter Abbott H. Thayer, had significant impact on the early development of camouflage patterns and schemes.[20] As a painter and naturalist, Thayer himself had been lobbying for the camouflage of American ships since the Spanish-American War in 1898. Principles that belonged to the camoufleur's "ABC," like countershading, color harmony, mimicry, disruptive design, and changes of color to match changing surroundings, could be gleaned from nature directly. The camoufleur was described in a 1917 *New York Times* article as the "military nature faker,"[21] and in 1920 the artist Solomon J. Solomon observed that "a knowledge of nature as pictured from an unaccustomed aspect is the first essential [for camouflage]."[22] It was only a short step for U.S. cavalry officers to suggest in the interwar years that these principles should be used for the camouflage of moving animal targets as well: They proposed that light-colored horses—a security threat since time immemorial—should be dyed "against low-flying aviation attacks."[23]

Research into camouflage lost intensity in all countries after World War I. However, valuable lessons had been learned, and publications like Solomon J. Solomon's 1920 *Strategic Camouflage* attested to the continued interest and apprehension at least of certain individuals. The interwar years enabled professionals from other fields to attend to the research into the scientific fundamentals of camouflage. The idea that camouflage was not only an art, but that it could be greatly enhanced through scientific progress gained momentum. In his 1922 book *Visual Illusions: Their Causes, Characteristics and Applications,* the American scientist Matthew Luckiesh called camouflage "an art based upon sound scientific principles." On the basis of experience during World War I, Luckiesh dedicated one chapter to camouflage. His interest in the fields of infrared and ultraviolet energy led him to draw attention to the fact that chlorophyll and green pigments show different reactions to certain bands of light, an observation that would lead to the development and use of infrared film in reconnaissance photography during World War II. For Luckiesh, the problem of the artist as camoufleur therefore was that "an artist who views color subjectively and is rarely familiar with the spectral basis may match a green leaf perfectly with a mixture of pigments. A photographic plate, a visual filter, or a spectroscope will reveal a difference which the unaided eye does not."[24] The widely perceived consequence therefore was that artists also had to be trained in the science and technology that was aimed at revealing camouflage.

Not the physical properties of visual phenomena but the psychology of their perception was another research area that both informed and was influenced by camouflage. In the 1920s, the gestalt psychologists Max Wertheimer, Wolfgang Köhler, and Rudolf Arnheim discussed what induces us to perceive forms and shapes and how we perceive the relationship between figure and ground. Basing part of his study on Edgar Rubin's "Visuelle wahrgenommene Figuren" (Visually perceived figures; 1921), Köhler, like Luckiesh before him, used the line drawings of the Müller-Lyer illusion, which would later also appear in various World War II publications on camouflage. Köhler, like Luckiesh, also referred directly to camouflage in his work. According to Köhler, intentional camouflage could "disorder" the objects around us that are "very stable wholes . . . we regularly see . . . with their definite forms." Because physical objects were habitually perceived as visual units, "camouflage is a difficult art," Köhler asserted.[25] Camouflage was a figure-ground problem for both its creator and its detector. The confusion of what was ground and what was figure was both an aim of camouflage and one of its dangers. Only from above, in aerial photographs, could the gestalt of the landscape, its plan and pattern, be identified as real or its double, providing that the photo interpreters were adequately trained. Since camouflage makes use of unit-forming factors, various camouflage publications used line drawings, diagrams, and figure-grounds that were similar to the ones used by Wertheimer and Rubin in the early 1910s and 1920s to explain the principles of closure, proximity, and similarity as well as the figure-ground relationship. In this way, the texts on camouflage sought to familiarize readers with the psychology of the visual perception of patterns.[26] Camoufleurs needed to be trained in recognizing what attracted attention and how attention could be diverted.

In Britain, during the so-called Phoney War in the months between September 1939 and May 1940, the zoologist John Graham Kerr and his student Hugh Cott argued that the principles of nature were not being sufficiently observed in camouflage. In a competitive spirit, they suggested that more scientists and engineers than artists should be employed in this area of warfare.[27] A 1940 editorial in the scientific journal *Nature* summed up the problems that resulted from the authorities' neglect of scientific insight into principles such as countershading.[28] In the United States in 1942, Homer Saint-Gaudens, on leave from his faculty position at the Carnegie Institute to serve his country again during World War II, finally noted a turn toward the scientific in camouflage efforts. He observed that the art of camouflage "has been pretty well explored. Now most camouflage activity is turning scientific, for it concerns itself more and more with an elaboration of camouflage technique which requires scientific training."[29] "Starting as an art," Ernest E. Walker summarized, "camouflage planning is today turning scientific for it is concerned more and more with an elaboration of technique which requires scientific training and broad scale planning."[30] Robert P. Breckenridge, a major in the Corps of Engineers, the unit responsible for the preparation of training instructions in camouflage, omitted "art" from the title of his lauded 1942 book entirely and described camouflage as "the new science of protective concealment," provoking General U. S. Grant to disagree with this classification in the book's foreword.[31]

By the outbreak of World War II, most camouflage officers agreed that camouflage required scientific knowledge and artistic, or design, training. Although artists still played a prominent role in the camouflage units of World War II—with Edward Seago and Julian Trevelyan in Britain, Ellsworth Kelly and László Moholy-Nagy in the United States,[32] and Oskar Schlemmer in Germany—men and women from related disciplines became increasingly involved. In Britain, these included the magician Jasper Maskelyne, the film producer Peter Proud, and the theater set designer Oliver Messel. In the United States, the theater set and fashion designers Jo Mielziner, Harper Goff, and Bill Blass, and animation artists and draftsmen from the World Disney Studio and Warner Bros. signed up for camouflage work. Architects like Hugh Casson in Britain and John C. Phillips Jr. in the United States; landscape architects like the Americans Norman Newton, Armistead Fitzhugh, Perry H. Wheeler, and George L. Nason, and the Germans Ernst Hagemann, Hermann Mattern, and Heinrich Wiepking-Jürgensmann; and horticulturists like Leslie J. Watson in Britain also played an important role in their nation's camouflage efforts. The need for both artistic and scientific sensibilities was summarized in 1942 by the American landscape architect Ralph Rodney Root, who noted that "the manipulation of color and form with thorough understanding of their photographic values as seen through the modern camera . . . is a new art and a new science which the modern camoufleur must master."[33]

Despite the questionable and politically motivated classification of camouflage, by the beginning of World War II theoretical discussions about the nature of camouflage gave way to more practical concerns. Due to advanced technology and the development of aviation in the interwar years, aerial attacks and reconnaissance posed a significantly greater threat in World War II. With Germany's first blitzkrieg on Poland, the war-faring countries became aware that this war would likely be decided in the air. Both the use of camouflage to prevent the detection of targets from the air, and aerial reconnaissance that uncovered camouflage became central strategies of warfare.

Camouflage as Regional Planning

Throughout history, warfare has directly and indirectly involved entire territories and geographical regions due to the expanse of the area subject to battles, the movement of troops, and their supply lines. From the time of the American Civil War and the Franco-Prussian War, balloons elevated the viewpoint of wartime reconnaissance missions from hills, mountains, and towers up into the air, thereby broadening the perspective and overview of the theater of war. The Prussian general Carl von Clausewitz defined the theater of war in his early-nineteenth-century philosophical treatise *On War* as "a portion of the space over which war prevails as has its boundaries protected, and thus possesses a kind of independence." The theater of war was defined spatially by "fortresses, or important natural obstacles presented by the country, or even in its being separated by a considerable distance from the rest of the space embraced in the operations."[34] Clausewitz contended that actions in the theater of war could be largely independent of actions occurring outside of it, and he understood the theater of war to be self-contained, enclosed, and as "a small whole complete in itself." In contrast, by the time of World War I and World War II, the use of airplanes as weapons and for reconnaissance missions meant that much larger areas and entire regions became subject to warfare. In the second half of the nineteenth century, the definition of the theater of war had already expanded to encompass "the area or territory in any part of which the hostile forces can come into collision."[35] The theater of war was by this time commonly differentiated into theaters of operation, each subject to the movements of an individual army. Because of the use of airplanes in World War I and World War II, camouflage measures had to take into account the environment surrounding the immediate areas of operation, if not the entire theater of war, and they had to be devised against aerial detection. As the architect André Smith, a first lieutenant in the Engineering Corps of the U.S. Army, pointed out in 1917: "It is the aeroplane that has given to modern warfare a new weapon of defense and protection—camouflage. . . . It is the garment of invisibility that is capable of not only protecting the individual soldier and the furniture of war, but of screening the movements of an entire army."[36]

Among the measures undertaken during World War I to conceal landscapes and deceive the enemy were road shields consisting of camouflage netting stretched between wooden posts alongside and above roads that could hide troop movement from observation on the ground and in the sky. As shown by the British artist Solomon J. Solomon shortly after World War I, the Germans had hidden entire camps by erecting structures on top that simulated harmless rural villages complete with cottages, barns, fields, fruit orchards, and kitchen gardens. To spy on enemy activity, artificial trees that could "house" a soldier for a night and a day were erected in no-man's land, and dummy haystacks disguised gun positions and sharpshooters from both ground and aerial views.[37]

Progress in aviation and aerial photography meant that by World War II concealment from the aerial view not only had to become even more "sophisticated" but that it also had to be practiced on much larger scales than ever before. As the American architecture professor Richard Belcher pointed out in 1942, precautionary camouflage took "the form of regional planning."[38] For camouflage to be successful, more than individual targets needed to be disguised. The airplane had not only introduced a new perspective from which the enemy could be observed and attacked, but it had also changed the dimensions of time and space. It took only minutes to fly over large stretches of land. Therefore, if enemy bombers were to be disorientated and deceived, entire regions had to be studied. The objective was to induce the enemy bombers to lose as many bombs as possible on open fields, where they neither threatened lives nor important production and communication facilities like ammunition factories and railroads. In addition to "horizontal camouflage" (the concealment of structures and soldiers from the view on the ground), "vertical camouflage," or the concealment of military encampments, gun positions, and trenches from the aerial view, became increasingly important. The visibility of structures and buildings on the ground could be prevented through a variety of measures that included their site selection and unobtrusive integration into the respective environment; the preservation of plant materials; new tree and shrub planting; the choice of form, color, and texture; and the use of artificial camouflage like netting, smoke, and decoys. Like theatrical performance spaces, by World War II the spaces of the theater of war required elaborate scenographic treatment that was similarly focused on performance in time and space. However, in addition to the horizontal view, this scenography also had to cater to the vertical view. The reconnaissance pilots, photographers, and bombers acted as both performers and witnesses. Through the development of an elaborate scenography, the areas subject to military conflict were turned into landscapes of war. The diverse means of camouflage had become important and integral parts of tactical and strategic military planning.

Given the expanse of areas that required camouflage schemes as a result of the air war, aerial photography and the production of photo mosaics were necessary for both devising and detecting camouflage. However, seeing the land as a two-dimensional pattern from the air turned out to be insufficient for devising adequate camouflage schemes. By World War II, it had become clear that any land camouflage scheme had to be three-dimensional; painted light and shadow rarely provided adequate concealment. As the architecture professor Konrad Wittmann remarked: "Every observation of nature reveals a composition of light, self-shadow, and cast shadow. An artificial reproduction of nature must compose similar elements—parts which catch light and others which absorb shadow."[39] The American artist Harper Goff pointed out that the "camoufleur . . . should observe from the air the organic structure in the earth which weaves itself like a tapestry across the map."[40]

Since the expense involved sometimes prevented camoufleurs from observing the sites to be camouflaged from the air, three-dimensional contour models were also used, which, in combination with aerial photographs, provided a valuable tool in the research and development of camouflage schemes.[41] Models helped to simulate the view from low-flying planes, as was done at the Scottish Command Camouflage School in Edinburgh by bicycling around the model.[42] At Fort Belvoir in Virginia outside Washington, D.C., models were viewed through a so-called haze box that simulated the aerial vision in cloudy and overcast weather conditions (fig. 52). This prac-

FIG. 52. Viewing a camouflage model through a haze box, which simulated the aerial vision in cloudy and overcast weather conditions. (Robert P. Breckenridge, *Modern Camouflage: The New Science of Protective Concealment* [New York and Toronto: Farrar and Rinehart, 1942], 226)

tice highlighted the atmospheric qualities of the aerial view that could lead to blurry vision, thereby counteracting the aerial view's celebrated precision and factual accuracy.

Models turned out to be an invaluable visual aid because they were three-dimensional, could easily be studied under diverse lighting conditions and from different angles and directions, and could be adapted to various uses by emphasizing or excluding specific terrain features. As a design method and representational technique, models particularly facilitated the flexible shifting between scales, bringing the aerial view into the designers' studio. While they were constructed to facilitate imagining the aerial view, they were also built with the help of aerial photographs. Thus, after the three-dimensional landscape had been flattened into a two-dimensional aerial photograph, the latter was turned again into a three-dimensional landscape, even if it was its artificial miniature.

In many cases, after their contours had been modeled out of hardboard on the basis of maps, aerial photographs that had been scaled to the size of a particular model were dampened and then applied to and stretched across the model. These so-called "photo-skinned" models were painted in transparent colors so that the photographed surface texture of the terrain would remain visible. Vertical structures like miniature buildings, hedges, trees, and fences were added. In addition to the "photographic skin" process used by the British, the United States developed the so-called photo surface model process that was also based upon aerial photographs or photo mosaics. In contrast, the German air force developed a process that used photographs of constructed relief models to overprint contour maps and thereby produced a shaded relief map that simulated aerial photographs of the terrain.

Special units of the British and U.S. Armed Forces consisting of sculptors, architects, set designers, and artists among other professionals also built three-dimensional terrain models to plan military operations and train bomber pilots. Aircrews prepared by studying models and their photographs to memorize their flight path and bombing targets. Large-scale models used in the preparation of air raids often included details such as the façade structure of prominent buildings to facilitate their recognition during bombing raids. Once built, terrain models were photographed under diverse light conditions including the light anticipated for the time of the military operation. Both the models themselves—built with the help of aerial photographs and in some cases "photo-skinned"—as well as vertical and oblique overhead photographs of them were used to brief aircrews. The combined use of aerial photography and terrain models improved the effectiveness of both air-raid protection and air strikes.[43]

Camouflage as Urban Design

Urban areas were the most vulnerable locations with regard to the potential loss of civilian life. If camoufleurs were to save lives and protect important infrastructure, they needed to make cities invisible. Since complete concealment was impossible, however, camoufleurs turned to the production of new urban scenographies aimed at disorientating bomber pilots. In addition, the realization after World War I that the next war would likely be fought as much in the air as on the ground had induced military personnel, architects, and urban planners in a variety of countries to develop urban designs that were less vulnerable to aerial attack. Design professionals cited decreased aerial vulnerability as a factor in their efforts to legitimize both modernist housing schemes and decentralization.

URBAN SCENOGRAPHY

As a result of air-raid protection measures, parts of the urban environment were altered, creating a scenography for both the vertical view of reconnaissance pilots and bombers, and the horizontal view of the citizens on the ground. Perhaps the most spectacular urban camouflage scheme in World War II, and the example described and most often referred to in Allied publications due to its extension and the prominence of the landmark, was the Alster Basin (Binnenalster) project in Hamburg. The Binnenalster signified the "heart" of the city. Much of Hamburg's public social life revolved along its constructed shoreline, the Jungfernstieg with the Alster Pavilion, Hamburg's most well-known café, located on the southern edge of the Binnenalster. The city officials in charge of air-raid protection were well aware that the form of the Binnenalster and its reflecting surface would facilitate orientation in night raids. It was obvious that due to its proximity to the central rail station—one of the likely targets of the raids—recognition of the Binnenalster would easily guide bombers to their targets. At the end of 1940, a first attempt to disguise the Binnenalster was made when a "forest" of Christmas trees was erected on its frozen surface.[44] A more elaborate scheme followed in the spring of 1941. Its intention was to turn the Binnenalster into urban fabric, and create roads that ran across the roofs of the central station and the Dammtor railway station. The railway tracks and the roofs of the stations were painted and covered with painted boards to resemble roads, running across a hill with grass, bushes, and trees. To improve the effect of a continuous urban pattern on the site of the central station, its 300-foot- (91.44-meter-) wide south window was covered and painted to represent a row of houses.[45] The Binnenalster, measuring almost 2,200 square feet (250,000 square meters) was also covered with boards and camouflage netting to resemble urban fabric, following a design by the Hamburg graphic artist Erwin Staub. Hundreds of poles were driven into the basin to sustain the new wooden surface. The basin was covered up to Lombards Bridge, which was made "to appear like a pseudo-Jungfernstieg, even to the extent of a wooden replica of the Alster-Pavillon" (fig. 53 and fig. 54). By building a decoy Lombards Bridge in the Aussenalster, the Binnenalster was seemingly "moved" north 600 yards. The aim was to throw "all bombing calculations . . . off 1,500 feet to the north."[46] Although the Alster project was probably effective in protecting some targets, it was discovered by the RAF early on in its construction, which lasted from January until April 1941. As amusing as this discovery might have seemed to British reconnaissance officers, this "latest trick to which the Nazis [had] resorted" was also regarded with amusement by some Hamburg citizens. One citizen who fled to the United States after the May 1941 raids reported that the small decoy wooden houses and trees that were "planted" on the wooden planks covering the Binnenalster induced "natives to call it 'the negro village,'" using the then-common but discriminatory term for an African village.[47] The amusement caused by Hamburg's altered urban landscape did not last long. The July 28, 1943, bombing raids on the city, Operation Gomorrah, destroyed the inner-city camouflage structures. As Hamburg's police president, Hans Kehrl, remarked in a secret report, the heavy bombing attacks taught a

FIG. 53. (*Top*) World War II: Germany, 1941. A replica of the Lombardsbrücke (Lombards Bridge) and camouflage on the frozen Aussenalster in Hamburg, Germany, designed to disguise the actual bridge from air attacks. Fir trees, branches, and dummy trees were used, and a dummy Lombards Bridge built out of wooden planks. (Photograph by H. Schmidt-Luchs. Ullstein Bild / The Granger Collection, New York)

FIG. 54. (*Bottom*) Decoy urban fabric on the Binnenalster. (Courtesy of Denkmalschutzamt Hamburg / Bildarchiv, Willi Beutler)

lesson about the importance of noninflammable camouflage material. During the raids, "the wood and straw matting used on the inner Alster . . . caught fire . . . so that literally the whole inner Alster was burning and lit up the heart of the city." The police president drew a vivid picture of the violence and terror caused by the raids, drawing comparisons with the Chicago and San Francisco fires, which Hamburg's firestorm "exceeded in effect and extent." His self-serving report described the disaster as a catastrophe resulting from the "murderous lust of a sadistic enemy" that turned the city into "hell"—a hell that it was impossible to escape, no matter how well equipped and prepared the official agencies and citizens were.[48]

FLIGHTS OF IMAGINATION

FIG. 55. Rudolf Stein-
häuser, camouflage
of Charlottenburger
Chaussee, July 1941.
(Courtesy of Landes-
archiv Berlin)

While similar projects were carried out in other German cities like Hannover, where the Maschsee was covered, and Stuttgart, where the central
station was camouflaged, Hamburg's Alster project was one of the most extensive inner-city schemes. Camouflage projects as labor-intensive as this one
were possible only in Germany, where the Nazi officials used forced labor.

In Berlin, where bombing raids began in 1940, the 1.9 miles (3 kilometers) of Charlottenburger Chaussee running through the Tiergarten and
leading into the governmental district in the city center—the east–west
axis in Albert Speer's plan for Germania—was covered with wire-netting
and green cloth. Small artificial spruces were also fastened to the netting to
make it blend into the vegetative pattern of Tiergarten (fig. 55 and fig. 56).
While Charlottenburger Chaussee was rendered "invisible," British intelligence reported that straight, wide aisles imitating the thoroughfare were

FIG. 56. Underneath the camouflage netting of Charlottenburger Chaussee, 1942. (Courtesy of Landesarchiv Berlin)

cut into a forest (possibly the Grunewald) on the city's periphery. The Nazis hoped to deceive British night bombers and lead them to drop their bombs on nonexistent targets.[49] The Allied Forces' strategic bombing targets in Berlin included the television station and fairgrounds in Charlottenburg and the Grunewald Railway Center and Westkreuz, a major interchange point of the S-Bahn network in Wilmersdorf.[50] Aware of the vulnerability of these targets, the German military developed a camouflage scheme aimed at disorientating enemy pilots. A dummy road was laid out across the roofs of the television station and of two large exhibition buildings (fig. 57). The scheme was extended into the adjacent neighborhoods and also affected nearby Park Lietzensee, designed around a central lake in 1919–20 by Erwin Barth, Berlin's director of gardens and parks.

In 1942, camouflage work was under way in the park. The lake was covered with planks and camouflage netting (fig. 58 and fig. 59). A dummy road was laid out crossing the park, including the lakeside walk. The camouflage measures and particularly the dummy road that interrupted the lakeside walk caused citizens to complain about the loss of beauty and the restricted access caused by obstacles like the dummy road. A different type of access restriction—the closing of the park before official blackout time—disgruntled citizens living in the neighborhood and caused complaints

again in 1943, after Berlin had fallen victim to repeated area bombings.[51] The citizens' reactions exemplify the importance attributed to urban public parks during wartime. Park access was considered to have become even more important for recreational purposes since the beginning of the war because many people were unable to travel and take vacations. As soon as area bombings had begun in Berlin, concerned citizens realized that green open areas were in many cases the only resort in emergency situations when bombings caused extensive fires, the melting of asphalt on roads, and air pollution from phosphor. One citizen, recounting an incident intended to convince the authorities to open Park Lietzensee day and night, told of a family in Wuppertal that only managed to prevent eye injuries from exposure to phosphor by lying down on parkland and pressing their faces into the grass for two hours. After more bombing raids in 1943, the citizens' request was finally heard by the authorities, who decided to open all Berlin urban parks night and day due to the increased threat of air raids.[52] Although the camouflage scheme that centered on the fairgrounds and Westkreuz certainly had some effect, it could not prevent bombs from falling on the fairgrounds. Parts of the television station and of the two large exhibition buildings that had been camouflaged with the help of a dummy road running over their roofs were damaged in the raids of 1943 and 1944.[53]

FIG. 57. View from television tower onto camouflaged exhibition buildings of convention center, 1941. (Courtesy of Landesarchiv Berlin)

FIG. 58. (*Above*) Camouflage work in Park Lietzensee, ca. 1940. (Courtesy of Landesarchiv Berlin)

FIG. 59. (*Right*) Rudolf Steinhäuser, camouflage work in Park Lietzensee, June 21, 1941. (Courtesy of Landesarchiv Berlin)

Many aerial bombing attacks were flown at nighttime. The easiest way to make cities invisible therefore was to initiate blackouts. As David Nye has observed, blackouts erased the electrified urban landscape that by the end of World War II had come to be seen as an "emblem of peace" and a "natural state, in contrast to the abnormality of war."[54] In cities under threat from aerial attack, civilians were forced to adhere to a detailed schedule of blackout times that ruled people's lives and to a certain extent determined the rhythm of life in the cities. Cities became ghostly during blackout, when streetlights were turned off and light on sidewalks, streets, and plazas was further diminished by special light-shielding devices installed on traffic lights. Other parts of the urban landscape that needed to be seen even during blackout like curbs, street obstacles, and directional signs were marked by phosphorescent and fluorescent paints and materials or by deep-red lighting. Red and low-intensity white light had proven to provide the best service on the ground while being the least visible from the air.[55]

As in the European theater, the "No. 1 weapon of U.S. civilians in their passive defense against hostile bombers [was] blackout."[56] After the first blackout tests were undertaken in the United States in 1938, they were carried out with greater frequency beginning in 1941, after the attack at Pearl Harbor made bombing seem a realistic possibility. One of the first blackout tests during the war on the East Coast was carried out in Newark. Journalists observing the event from an airplane above the city described it as "great blobs of ink" falling onto and expanding across the city, turning it into a "huge velvety black patch surrounded by the lights of dozens of surrounding municipalities."[57] After a first partial blackout test on December 30, 1941,[58] the U.S. capital finally initiated a comprehensive blackout on April 14, 1942. There, Creville Rickard, who had been a camouflage officer of the Fortieth Engineers during World War I, observed the city's blackout from an airplane. Smitten by Washington's "handsome pattern . . . produced by the chains of lights that marked her circles, her diagonal streets and framed the Lincoln Memorial Area, the Mall, the Capitol, and other landmarks, none of which were of themselves visible," he reported that the blackout signal—causing only few lights to remain—turned the city's neighborhoods into rural communities.[59]

The patterns that city lights formed also led to the idea that light patterns could deliberately be planned and altered so as to change the apparent direction of highways and streets from the air and disorientate approaching bombers.[60] With the help of lights, the Germans were reported to have simulated a number of decoy cities, including a second Cologne, carefully located on a bend of a river similar to the curve of the Rhine at Cologne.[61] In Britain, so-called Starfish sites—fires that were employed to simulate flares dropped by the German pathfinders, thus attracting their bombing load, were erected near cities like Bristol, Sheffield, Birmingham, and Derby.[62] The significance of the night aerial view and the nighttime landscape in warfare even caused neutral Switzerland to order countrywide blackouts. This contested and questionable decision was made after Swiss air neutrality had been breached and the lights of the country's cities, roads, and villages had been used by the RAF for their orientation during bombing attacks on northern Italy.[63]

Since World War I, military officials and architects had been aware of the relationship between building and population density, and the vulnerability of a city, region, or even nation to aerial attack. In the 1930s and increasingly in the early 1940s, when the effects of aerial bombing had been experienced, architects of different countries and convictions predicted that the impact of air-raid protection on urban planning would be comparable to the effect that warfare had had on urban planning during the Middle Ages.[64] Due to the relatively high "aerial vulnerability"—as German officials described the degree of threat posed by air raids to a particular village, city, or region—of any urban area, urban planners in the late 1930s began to discuss the possibilities of dispersing and decentralizing human settlement for the sake of aerial protection. In fact, the early-twentieth-century urban paradigm of airy, sunlit residential neighborhoods with ample greenery that was based on nineteenth-century public health concerns coincided with concerns about air-raid protection. In addition, as the Pratt Institute professor Konrad Wittmann observed, urban planners' long-standing interest in decentralization "for the sake of safety, health, and beauty" received "unexpected support from air-protection design."[65]

Most famously perhaps, Le Corbusier noticed and pointed out this convergence of ideas in his 1933 *La ville radieuse*, in which he referenced some of the latest military concerns about air-raid protection methods and schemes in France and Germany.[66] According to him, the Radiant City, with its 164-feet-tall (50 meters) slab buildings on pilotis placed in ample open parkland, was not only healthier than the dense and dark medieval Parisian inner-city neighborhoods, but it was the only city that could also survive aerial bombardment intact. In the same vein, in 1942, José Luis Sert determined that the least vulnerable residential neighborhoods would be the districts that consisted of "high buildings separated by large spaces." His Corbusian scenario included air-raid protection shelters that were directly accessible from the high-rise buildings by short and in part subterranean routes. While Sert cautioned that city plans should not be developed on the basis of air-raid protection strategies alone, he predicted that they would ultimately transform urban patterns.[67]

The concern about air-raid protection was used to legitimate different urban paradigms. In contrast to the high-rise cities promoted by Le Corbusier and Sert, German architects and planners favored dispersed, low-density plans. In Germany, the experiences of World War I and the air war of World War II inspired various university theses on air-raid protection and city planning. In 1933, Kurt Berg concluded his master's thesis, "Luftschutz im Städtebau der Neuzeit" (Air-raid protection in town planning of the modern era), with the recommendation that all city planning and construction in Germany be based on the aerial view. Berg proclaimed that camouflage had to be integrated into city planning.[68] The relationship between city planning and "aerial vulnerability" was also discussed some years later during the war by Rudolf Hammerling in his doctoral dissertation titled "Luftschutz und Städtebau" (Air-raid protection and city planning) submitted to the Technical University of Breslau in 1941. In addition to the principles of functional separation, dispersion of residential neighborhoods and traffic, and camouflage of military facilities and industry, Hammerling discussed the protective value of diverse ideal city planning concepts such as the concentric, the star-shaped, the linear, and the satellite city. As the most protective settlement pattern, however, Hammerling promoted the "city landscape" (*Stadtlandschaft*), a term and paradigm first coined and developed in the 1920s by German geographers, most notably Max Eckert and Siegfried Passarge, before German city planners began using it in the late 1920s and early 1930s. The "city landscape" was to consist of a decentralized and spread-out urban fabric that was adapted to the topography and whose various parts, divided by greenways, accommodated different urban functions. This concept was later further elaborated, providing the basis for the 1940s Nazi plans to reorganize big cities into many so-called settlement cells. Each cell would contain about eight thousand inhabitants and would be just large enough to be organized around party headquarters, Hitler Youth facilities, a community center, and parade grounds, and small enough not to attract enemy bombers.[69]

Berg's and Hammerling's works reveal more than the importance attributed to air-raid protection by architecture schools and by professionals dealing with the built environment in the late 1930s and early 1940s.[70] As much as these projects reflected the immediate effects of the first bombing raids on German cities, they were also based on the longtime fear of Germany being the European nation most vulnerable to aerial attacks. Ever since the Versailles Treaty had prohibited the creation of a German air force, Germany had invested much thought into other means of air-raid protection. Besides the German Red Cross and a couple of other aid organizations, in the 1920s a number of private associations like the Deutscher Luftschutz e.V. (1927) had begun to explore construction and planning measures for air-raid protection. Once the Nazis came to power, air-raid protection became a central element in the German state's organization of self-defense and preparation for war. Air-raid protection strategies and measures therefore received increased attention after 1933, and instructions regarding the dispersion and decentralization of housing and new settlements already existed years before Germany declared war on Poland.

It was determined that settlements could be best protected from aerial attacks if they blended into the surrounding landscape. The "natural camouflage" offered by woods, trees, and shrubs should be exploited. New settlements should not go beyond a certain size, and if they did, wide roads and greenbelts needed to separate individual residential areas to prevent fires from spreading easily. Vulnerable land uses such as industrial plants and hospitals were to be located outside of the cities and surrounded by green areas and parks. These principles were also valid for all rural settlements that were planned for the annexed eastern territories: instead of dense villages formed around a center, open, dispersed settlements were to be built. Many of these strategies coincided with the principles that were generally acknowledged at the time to create healthy, livable cities. While greenbelts could provide camouflage, fire breaks, air reservoirs in the case of gas bomb attacks, and the necessary space for the erection of anti-air-raid guns, they were also valuable park spaces that brought fresh air and recreational opportunities into the cities in peacetime. Ponds and small water features provided not only aesthetic delight and cooler areas in hot summers, but they could also function as water reservoirs for extinguishing fires after aerial attacks. Small public urban parks, gardens, and allotment gardens were considered precious assets of a hygienic city in peacetime and areas for the construction of air-raid protection trenches during wartime. The decentralization and the dispersal of buildings and settlements corresponded to the ideas of many groups like Kampfbund Deutscher Architekten und Ingenieure that were guided by strong anti-urban sentiment. The Nazis used this sentiment for their own purposes and proclaimed the traditional small rural town as their ideal. In 1933, Kurt Berg had identified the garden city as a model for the "air-protected city" (luftsichere Stadt). When the master plans were drawn up for the redesign of the German cities that Hitler had declared were the representational centers of the new Germany—Berlin, Hamburg, Munich—they included extensive air-protection measures. Much attention was directed toward what was called "constructive air-raid protection" (baulicher Luftschutz), a term that implied the provision of existing spaces like basements and cellars, and the building of different types of bunkers and flak towers. In cities like Hamburg and Berlin, vacant lots were used to build bunkers. To keep the citizens' spirits high and calm them down on the one hand, and to camouflage the buildings on the other, various means were used to integrate the buildings into the existing urban fabric. The architects used building heights and volumes, and façade structures and materials that blended with the surroundings. Vernacular architecture and medieval military architecture provided the models. While architects orientated themselves toward vernacular building styles to create harmonious ensembles in keeping with the teachings of Camillo Sitte, bunkers modeled on medieval fortifications were thought to make them and their protective function easily recognizable for the citizens. As a directive by Hamburg's architect in charge of the city's redesign demanded, air-raid shelters were to close gaps between buildings and blend into the surrounding architecture, thereby contributing to the image of a regular, even street alignment and urban fabric.[71]

While air-raid shelters were actively used as urban design elements that complemented existing buildings, the necessity for open space was likewise recognized. When Albert Speer began to develop plans for Hitler's Germania in 1937, he also initiated the drawing up of an open space plan for Berlin. Speer was aware that his design, which was intended to turn Berlin into the world capital for 10 million inhabitants by 1950, would be incomplete without the provision of open space in the form of squares, plazas, and large people's parks for recreation and air-raid protection. He envisioned Tempelhof airfield transformed into a large pleasure garden modeled on Copenhagen's Tivoli, and the extensive Grunewald becoming a new people's park, a kind of Bois de Boulogne with trails, restaurants, and a number of recreational facilities including sports grounds.[72] The city was to be structured by green radial wedges that would not only provide such recreational opportunities but also the grounds necessary for aerial protection. Early on in the development of the open space plan, the air force was asked to comment and pass on their requirements for the provision of air-raid protection measures. It became clear that public parks would need to be distributed in a way that catered not only to all citizens' recreational needs but also to the effective positioning of anti-air-raid lights and guns. Furthermore, it was determined that Berlin's ring roads would be needed for barrage balloons and that public parks could act as valuable firebreaks in the case of aerial attack with fire bombs. Based on the principles of modern city planning and air-raid protection, all redesigns for residential neighborhoods avoided high multistory buildings, the closed block structure, and enclosed front gardens. Instead, streets, sidewalks, and adjacent front gardens were to be turned into one green, park-like environment.[73]

In the United States in 1943, the American Office of Civilian Defense (OCD) envisioned how much better London would have fared in the 1941 bombing raids if the capital had consisted of thirty separate small cities, offering Norman Bel Geddes's Futurama at the 1939 World's Fair in New York City as an example of such dispersion. Bel Geddes presented the public with an aerial vision of The World of Tomorrow that featured as one of its most important pieces an extensive highway system designed to boost General Motors' car sales.[74] The highway system enabled dispersed settlement patterns, and the Futurama displayed numerous scattered small towns, also well-suited for air-raid protection (despite the building height, which the OCD still considered too high). In the United States, therefore, commercial interests and regionalist ideologies coincided with the federal mandates for air-raid protection. The OCD noted that the ideal town would "be generally informal in layout . . . ; and it should contain considerable foliage, for from the oblique angle of bombing approach, trees hide from view much of the wall surfaces of buildings and the widths of streets. . . . Streets, like highways, should be double-laned, with planting strips between, and would be better curved than straight. Walls and roofs should be of low visibility materials, colors, and textures. . . . Figuratively man's earth has been shrinking, and the more we achieve decentralization, the more widely will the enemy have to spread his bombs in his attempts to destroy, or to disrupt, the nerve centers of our great land."[75]

Only a few years after World War II, with the beginning of the Cold War, the fear of atomic warfare led to the revival of discussions regarding the necessity of decentralized city building. In the United States, the atomic threat from above led many city planners to embrace and further develop ideas of settlement dispersal, using aerial photography as a planning device.[76] "Defensive dispersal" provided an additional justification for comprehensive dispersal plans that many planners had already promoted before World War II. Models discussed among city planners and atomic scientists ranged from "cluster cities" and satellite towns to "rod" and "doughnut" cities and were in many cases based upon Howard's garden city concept and Frank Lloyd Wright's Broadacre City. In 1948, Tracy B. Augur, a member of the Regional Planning Association of America (RPAA), which had been founded in 1923 with the intention of promoting decentralization and regional planning as a means to reconnect humankind with nature, was among the city planners who played a central role in shaping federal policies with regard to "defensive dispersal," which ultimately facilitated suburbanization. Atomic threat provided a welcome justification of RPAA's goals, and Augur promoted his idea of the "cluster form city," made up of twenty settlement units that each measured just over three square miles and were distributed over an area of 886 square miles.[77] Not only would this reduce vulnerability to aerial attack, but everyone would live within a mile of the open country. Thus, as conceptualized by Augur, urban settlement was not only dispersed across the landscape, but the landscape was brought into the urban settlements. In addition, Augur considered his city model a defensive measure against "internal enemies" and "internal disorder and unrest," which many at the time feared would be caused by the racial minorities in the urban centers and by communist infiltration.[78] In addition to cluster and satellite cities that in many ways corresponded to the "city landscape" already promoted by German planners during World War II, other already existing visionary and utopian ideas proved useful as models for the defensible city. Similar to the Spanish urban planner Arturo Soria y Mata's nineteenth-century concept of the Linear City, the Rod City proposed in 1949 by the atomic scientist Ralph

Lapp consisted of a 50-mile-long, 1-mile-wide linear urban agglomeration, whereas his Donut City was a city whose core had been replaced by a park or an airport. While American planners did not pursue Lapp's ideas, in the German cities of Berlin and Hamburg, in which the centers had largely been destroyed by Allied bombing raids, the architects and planners in charge of reconstruction briefly entertained similar ideas.[79]

Not parks but greenbelts were the characteristic open space elements in a plan that the mathematician Norbert Wiener developed in 1950 with his two colleagues, the political scientist Karl W. Deutsch and the historian of science Giorgio de Santillana at MIT. Published only in an article in the popular magazine *Life*, their plan was based on the concept of the "city as a net of communications" and was primarily concerned with protection against a breakdown of the flow of information and traffic. Therefore, besides greenbelts, which would act as fire breaks and land for tent cities, eight-lane expressways and six-track rail beds surrounded the city at a distance sufficient to save them from the devastating effects of an atomic blast. Hospitals, warehouses, truck depots, shopping centers, fuel storage facilities, and emergency power stations would be located along the expressways ten miles from the edge of the built-up area. Drawing upon analogies with the human circulatory system, Wiener and his collaborators argued that a resilient and uncongested transportation network was the most important element in creating a defensible city.[80]

Combining both new communication systems and population dispersal, the ideas put forward by the planners Donald and Astrid Monson in 1950 and 1951 were more realistic than Wiener's "Civilian Defense Plan." However, like many comprehensive planning schemes developed at the time, the Monsons' ideas disregarded the social implications and neglected the social and cultural values of urban core areas. Sharing Augur's belief in satellite cities, they proposed a five-point dispersal program that included directing new war industries to small centers, constructing express highways through existing cities, and reducing the population density in the city centers through control of all rebuilding. Although many planners had realized by the early 1950s that all settlement plans would be more or less futile in the event of an H-bomb explosion that would be even more powerful than explosions of atomic bombs, these ideas found their realization in President Truman's Industrial Dispersal Policy at the beginning of the 1950s, the 1954 Housing Act, the 1956 Interstate Highway Act, and in policies based upon the 1949 federal Urban Renewal legislation.[81]

The ideas discussed in the United States also reached receptive ears abroad. In Italy, where the futurist air painters had envisioned and captured on canvas the kinetic experience of flight above cities and where Mussolini's interest and practical experience in aviation had led to an aerial cult in the

1920s, the urban planner Domenico Andriello published his thoughts on the "reciprocal relationships between airplane and city" in a thin 1947 volume entitled *Aerourbanistica,* a term he used to describe the part of urbanism that studied the transformation of human settlements resulting from the military and civilian use of aviation. Andriello anticipated that aviation, with its influence on the relationship between time and space, would determine the building and structure of cities, no matter whether the future decades would come to be described as the air age because of aviation's peacetime functions or as the atomic age because of its role in war. Andriello considered the most convincing principles of a military "aerourbanistica" for the protection against nuclear attack to be a loose urban fabric, the creation of housing and other facilities underground, the siting of new cities near mountains and hills, and the planning of "regional cities." Mountainous terrain and coastal cliffs could offer natural grottos for the creation of underground shelters. In the case of the development of new urban centers, therefore, the geology and soil quality of their location was to be taken into account.[82]

While Italian planners were looking toward the United States for new city models, the United States finally began implementing its interstate-highway program, which was bolstered by the 1956 Interstate Highway Act and supported by the American Road Builders Association, the auto, trucking, oil, tire, asphalt, cement, steel, lumber and construction industries, and their unions. In Germany in the meantime, city planners continued to develop urban plans based upon the paradigms that had been developed during the 1930s and 1940s. Besides Göderitz, Rainer and Hoffmann's oft-quoted plans for the "structured and decentralized city" (*gegliederte und aufgelockerte Stadt*) and Hans Bernhard Reichow's "organic" city plans, in the 1950s the industrialist Heinrich Dräger propagated the concept of the *Schnellbahnstadt* (fast-track rail city). In this concept, satellite cities were supposed to be constructed 9.3 to 18.6 miles (15 to 30 kilometers) from a *Schnellbahnstadt,* a central city to which they were connected by a fast railroad. Similar to Howard's diagrammatic concept of the garden city, an ample greenbelt was to be located between the central city and the satellite cities. A radial light-rail system fed by atomic energy would connect the satellite cities with the central city, eventually eliminating much of the private automobile traffic.[83]

While parks, greenbelts, and tree-lined streets were considered fundamental components in all new anti-air-raid settlement plans that were drawn up during and after World War II, efforts outside cities had to be undertaken to camouflage the facilities that had already been decentralized or intentionally located outside of the populated areas. Industrial areas and airfields faced a particular threat during World War II, and landscape architecture offered a particularly suitable means to help render them invisible, or at least inconspicuous.

Camouflage as Landscape Architecture

Before aerial attacks were flown against civilians and area bombing was carried out as a last resort to demoralize the enemy's entire population in urban areas, strategic bombing was used to destroy the enemy's production plants and military bases, which were often located outside of the cities and in rural areas. Factories, power plants, and airfields in particular needed to be protected against aerial attack. The Germans had realized even before the war that the bird's-eye view had to be considered in the siting and concealment of their industrial plants. Beginning in 1934, they undertook extensive programs to green factories and blend them into the surrounding countryside.[84] The 1938 guidelines for air-raid protection regarding town planning included the planting of trees near industrial plants so that the trees would disrupt shadows. As soon as the war began, England and the United States raced to catch up. By World War II, landscape architecture in particular appeared closely related to camouflage work due to its planning and design of landscapes of different scale and type, its preoccupation with masking what was considered "unseemly," its work with plants, and its foundation in both art and science. Like their colleagues in other design disciplines, many landscape architects eagerly sought to serve as camouflage officers in the military. Not only could their training benefit them in camouflage work, but this occupation was likely to help them avoid duty on the front lines. Design professionals too old for active duty were eager to offer their services to the military as a result of the scarce employment opportunities during wartime and a patriotic desire to serve on the home front.

LANDSCAPES OF WAR

Besides the camouflage and photo intelligence research units that were set up by the respective militaries, educational institutions joined the task force and developed research programs and courses in camouflage. Concentrating on industrial camouflage in the United States, the Pratt Institute in Brooklyn initiated research into this area in 1940 by setting up a laboratory under the guidance of the architect Konrad Wittmann, who collaborated with the engineer William McGuiness and the "theater man" William Goodridge.[85] As Wittmann poignantly observed, "until now, we designed a factory with ground-plan and elevation, but it is no longer unimportant how it looks from the sky."[86] He published the research results in 1942 as *The Industrial Camouflage Manual*, intended for distribution throughout the United States.[87] The manual advised that industry should be housed in inconspicuous, low, flat-roofed, and widely dispersed buildings. This not only made it easier to blend the buildings into the landscape pattern, but in the event of exploding bombs, it allowed their air pressure to escape more easily than in confined spaces surrounded by tall buildings. Industrial plants were no longer to be seen as contrasting with nature, or even as "a design of dreary industrialization hostile to nature."[88] Instead, factory buildings were to become "part of the landscape"[89] by situating them along the contour lines, preferably with the widest façade oriented east–west to reduce shadows, and by choosing façade patterns, colors, and textures that easily merged with the surrounding landscape. Their siting in woods or on the edge of woodland was considered particularly suitable because of the trees' absorption of shadows. Roads leading to the factory buildings should follow the contours and only be one-way to make them as inconspicuous as possible. Parking areas also needed to be dispersed and protected from view by irregularly spaced groups of trees. Artificial and live tree and shrub plantings surrounding the buildings were proposed to distort the form and shadow of the buildings. Building forms could also be distorted and shadows prevented in the first place by covering the roofs with camouflage nets that expanded to the ground at an angle at the side of the buildings and whose texture resembled that of the surrounding land. While a fitting texture could be achieved with rubbish, excelsior, wood shavings, dry shrubs, hardy bushes, pine branches, and Spanish moss—which could actually be grown on netting—(the common heather, *calluna vulgaris,* was used in Europe), it was found that roofs could also be planted with live grass and shrubs. Finally, it was discovered that the grading of the terrain at an angle of 10 degrees could also eliminate shadows.[90]

When large areas needed to be concealed with camouflage nets, it was advised that a decoy landscape be constructed on top.[91] A British series of drawings illustrated the procedure for camouflaging an entire supply camp (fig. 60). The camp was covered with a net-and-plank construction that provided the "ground" for an entire ensemble consisting of a dummy cottage, barn, kitchen garden, orchard, and dummy hedges delineating fake fields. Two of the most impressive schemes of this type in the United States were carried out on the West Coast in the spring of 1942, in anticipation of Japanese air attacks. Both the Lockheed and the Douglas aircraft factories in Burbank and Santa Monica were assumed to be likely Japanese bombing targets. In the months between April and September 1942, painters, set designers, illustrators, and other staff from the Hollywood studios disguised the aircraft production plants as suburban neighborhoods (fig. 61). In addition, a decoy replica of the Douglas plant was constructed in open fields near the actual factory.[92]

Besides industrial areas, airfields belonged to the more extensive grounds that needed to be concealed at least well enough to confuse bomber pilots, if not deceive them entirely. Airfields posed a double challenge to the camoufleur: while they were to be rendered invisible to the enemy, they needed

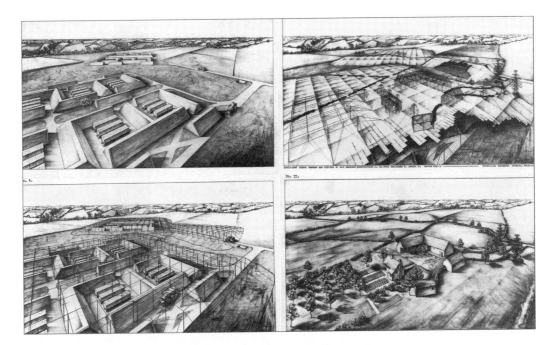

FIG. 60. (*Top*) Suggested camouflage for a supply camp. (Major J. Gray, 83/38/1, Department of Documents at the Imperial War Museum)

FIG. 61. (*Bottom*) The Lockheed aircraft factory in Burbank, California, camouflaged to resemble a suburban neighborhood. (National Air and Space Museum [NASM 9A08799], Smithsonian Institution) to be recognizable to the pilots of one's own nation. When the American CBS correspondent William Shirer was flown into Ghent in a German Army Transport Plane in August 1940, he noted that the camouflage almost prevented the pilot from finding his landing field: "From the air . . . it looked just like any other place in the landscape, with paths cutting across it irregularly as though it were farm land." Once on the ground, Shirer could observe the "mats plastered with grass" that hid the planes. Other aircraft were hidden underneath the trees in the woods, near small clearings that had been cut to make these hiding places accessible. Between Calais and Boulogne, Shirer observed that the Germans were using wheat fields as temporary airfields with "the shocks of wheat . . . left in the field, with only narrow lanes left free across the field for the planes to take off from and land on." In Germany itself, most airfields were established on farmland and on sites with favorable soil types and drainage conditions for turf fields, thus eliminating the need to construct highly visible concrete runways and facilitating camouflage.[93]

Concealing concrete runways and blending existing airfields into the landscape proved to be a greater challenge, requiring a number of strategies that involved the invention of several artificial surface coatings and the coloring and chemical treatment of vegetation. Mobile hedges were used in Britain to blend airfields into adjacent field patterns. These hedges on wheels, consisting of dry brush and branches, were positioned on the runways to complement the surrounding field pattern and could be temporarily removed whenever a plane needed to land or take off. Merrill E. De Longe reported that Germany had perfected the creation of mobile landscapes on and near its airfields, "using all types of buildings and even movable boxed trees." According to his reports, the Germans had "even gone so far as to have smoke coming out of the chimneys of these make-believe houses, which are lined up along runways, with trees growing in front of them, much as they would appear in a typical town." All structures were mounted on slides or rollers so that they could be pulled off the runways when planes needed to land or take off. In many cases, decoy airfields were constructed three to five miles from the actual airfield. To appear as realistic as possible, not only their size, orientation, and the nearby landmarks had to resemble those of the original, but the dummy fields also had to be subject to an easily detectable camouflage scheme. While the first national competition in airport design in the United States in 1929 produced plans and designs with elaborate Beaux-Arts ground patterns and highly visible concrete runways, little more than a decade later De Longe criticized these "monument[s] to the engineering and architectural genius of our nation": airfields needed to be as inconspicuous as possible.[94]

As soon as the attacks on Pearl Harbor on December 7, 1941, had made the United States aware of its own vulnerability, camouflage in this country entered a more productive phase. The War Department issued a directive "to comply with the dispersion, concealment, and camouflage of all camps and stations under construction or to be constructed." In the United States, this included ground stations within 200 miles of the Atlantic and Pacific coasts, and air stations within 350 miles of the Atlantic or Pacific Oceans, and within 300 miles of the Gulf of Mexico. From 1940 onward, the Corps of Engineers had been pressing for the camouflage of airfields in critical coastal areas on the east and west coasts. Due to the events of war, by the end of 1942 the first twenty airfields located within 300 miles of the U.S. coastlines had finally been camouflaged.[95]

Bradley Field near Windsor Locks (today Bradley International Airport) was one of the first existing airfields to be camouflaged in the United States. The 1,600-acre field had been acquired by the State of Connecticut as an airport in 1940 and was leased to the U.S. government for army use shortly thereafter. In 1941, plans were drawn up to render Bradley Field "invisible" to the aerial view (fig. 62). As with all such schemes, Bradley Field's camouflage was based on the idea of blending the airfield into the surrounding countryside. The airfield was located in a rural area characterized by a closely knit field pattern and orchards. To simulate the land-use pattern with its orchards and plowed and strip-planted fields, different hardy grasses and other crops were planted adjacent to the runways. The effect of orchards on fields was achieved by outlining the approximately 25-foot perimeters of the tree crowns on the ground with lime. The circular areas representing the tree crowns were treated with a grass-killing solution consisting of sodium chlorate and water. The fake horizontal tree crowns were then covered with brush piles that were burned, with the fire being extinguished as soon as the brush was charred. Smaller brush piles were placed south of the fake tree crowns and spray-painted green. The grass was kept short, and the brush piles were spray-painted at regular intervals until midsummer, after which the paint was allowed to fade until the winter months, thus mimicking the seasonal changes of the vegetation. While the same general technique was employed for simulating hedgerows, the field pattern was continued across the runways by applying asphalt with wood chips, slag, or high-pressure steam cinders and aggregate to their surface. Plowed fields and strip-planted fields required additional treatment with brush that was first laid out in strips two feet wide and two feet apart and then charred so that the strips were stained black. The strips between the brush that aligned with the charred strips on adjacent simulated field areas were spray-painted with a black bituminous emulsion. Existing farm buildings in the area were converted into the necessary facilities for the station, and additional buildings were dispersed.[96]

Living Camouflage

Although the camouflage measures described above involved chemicals and more inanimate than living materials, some military officials quickly realized the benefits of using natural and living materials in their camouflage schemes. That nature had always been the "master camoufleur" had been remarked by the American artist Eric Sloane in 1942, who also noted: "Nature if given half the chance, will make our job an easier one."[97] In World War II, "cooperating with nature" was considered one of the fundamentals of camouflage. As one *New York Times* journalist put it: "In the year 1941 camouflage, whether industrial or strictly military, goes with marked singleness of purpose 'back to nature.' . . . Broadly phrased it may be said that the camoufleur paints a picture. . . . [I]t is a matter of covering areas that are often enormous. It is three-dimensional."[98]

Landscape architects in particular were very familiar with animate and inanimate materials used to imitate landscape features, mask objects, or blend them into their respective environments. These activities had a long history, and the similarities between camouflage and landscape architecture did not go unnoticed. In a 1943 article in *Landscape Architecture,* the American landscape architect Armistead Fitzhugh analyzed the similarities and differences between landscape architecture and camouflage. Working for the Camouflage Section of the Engineer Board in the development of camouflage design for airports, industrial units, and barracks and preparing plant lists for camouflage schemes along seacoasts, Fitzhugh was well versed in the subject matter. "Camouflage, like the practice of landscape architecture," he argued, "deals in large measure with the creation of environment and the organization of land-space." "Both jobs," he observed, "require a balanced artistic and scientific approach,"[99] and he drew attention to the fact that camouflage adapted "the basic principles of landscape architecture."[100] Looking into the future, he speculated that "camouflage . . . may have direct effect on man's style of architecture and may cause certain modifications in the use and organization of land." Observing the policy of decentralization, he assumed that "land-use or land-space planning may come into its own [as a] . . . positive action."[101] Thus, it was only logical for him to argue that landscape architects had much to contribute to camouflage. According to Fitzhugh, they could approach problems in an inclusive and comprehensive way and "visualiz[e] in terms of space and space relationships between the accents, such as dark spaces between accents of light."[102] They also had the practical experience needed for the proper selection and use of camouflage materials. In fact, Fitzhugh noted, "preliminary training for techniques for military site selection, camouflage discipline, and the use of camouflage materials is developed incidentally in professional practice of landscape architecture."[103]

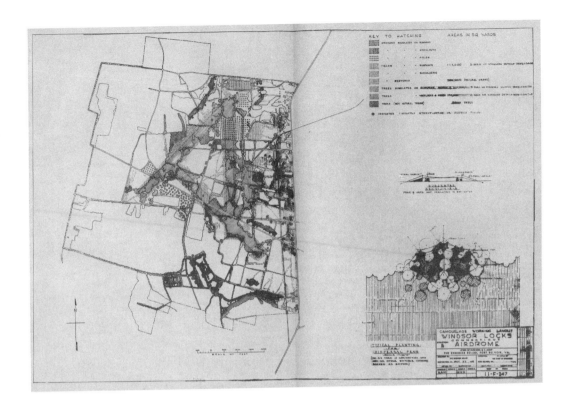

The British architect and camouflage officer Hugh Casson humorously observed the similarities between design principles of the English landscape garden and camouflage, suggesting the latter could remind the landscape gardener "of Price, and Sir William Temple's 'Sharawaggi.'"[104] Imitation, illusion, and deception, methods used in eighteenth-century picturesque garden landscapes promoted by Uvedale Price and William Temple in Britain, figured prominently in twentieth-century camouflage work. While the ideology underlying eighteenth-century picturesque landscape gardens was different from that generating twentieth-century camouflage schemes, the aesthetic intent was the same. Artificial landscapes were to look as natural as possible. In their imitation of nature, including human settlements, they were to deceive the viewer. It is therefore no wonder that Robert P. Breckenridge's thumbnail illustration of a suggested camouflage planting scheme (fig. 63) resembled an image provided by John Claudius Loudon in the early nineteenth century to illustrate the picturesque way of planting trees (fig. 64). Nor is it surprising that toward the end of the war, German intelligence used paint and netting to "improve" the ruined and abandoned appearance of bombed factories that were continuing production under blasted roofs. Like the fake ruins in some late-eighteenth- and early-nineteenth-century landscape gardens that surprised garden visitors by providing com-

FIG. 62. Camouflage plan for Bradley Field, Connecticut, 1941. The three landing strips are barely visible. (Folder 5, box 1, Edward M. Farmer Papers, Hoover Institution Archives, Stanford University)

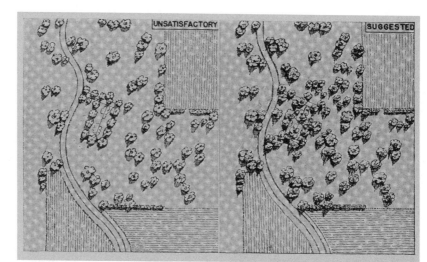

FIG. 63.
(*Top*) Camouflage instruction. The camouflage planting on the right was considered more effective. The irregular groups of trees mask the rectangular building near the left edge of the illustration. (Robert P. Breckenridge, *Modern Camouflage: The New Science of Protective Concealment* [New York and Toronto: Farrar and Rinehart, 1942], 108)

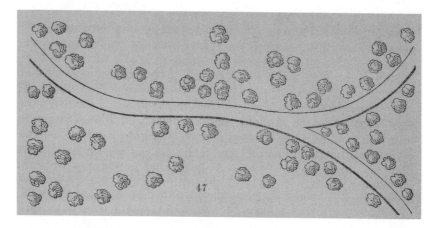

FIG. 64.
(*Middle and bottom*) John Claudius Loudon. Sketches illustrating the "gardenesque [*top*] and picturesque [*bottom*] way of planting trees". (John Claudius Loudon, *The Suburban Gardener and Villa Companion* [London, 1838], 165)

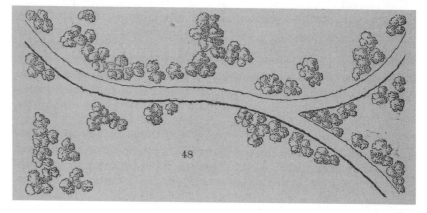

fortable furnished rooms behind their façades, the German factories camouflaged as ruins were meant to deceive.

By the end of the eighteenth century, it had become a generally accepted notion that landscape gardening belonged to the arts. It was considered an art to turn a piece of land into a landscape garden that imitated nature. This artful imitation of nature, like the artful imitation of objects in a still-life painting, could provide pleasure. In his 1757 *Philosophical Enquiry into the Origin of Our Ideas of the Sublime and Beautiful*, Edmund Burke described imitation as "the second passion belonging to society."[105] He stated that "no work of art can be great, but as it deceives; to be otherwise is the prerogative of nature only. A good eye will fix the medium betwixt an excessive length, or height, (for the same objection lies against both), and a short or broken quantity."[106] Thus, according to Burke, deception lay at the heart of all art; and perhaps more implicitly than in any other, deception was a means used in the art of landscape gardening. Burke contended that for an artwork to produce a pleasurable effect it needed to offer the viewer opportunities to complement the picture—the "gestalt," in the words of the later gestalt psychologists—with his own imagination. Burke was already expressing the basics of an idea that the gestalt psychologists Max Wertheimer, Wolfgang Köhler, Kurt Koffka, and later Rudolf Arnheim would describe as the process of "unit forming" and "visual thinking" more than 150 years later and that was considered central to camouflage.

Burke's observation was further elaborated by his contemporary Thomas Whately. Writing on gardening, Whately argued that in the creation of artificial ruins, lakes, and rivers, an "overanxious solicitude to disguise the fallacy is often the means of exposing it; too many points of likeness sometimes hurt the deception; they seem studied and forced; and the affectation of resemblance destroys the supposition of a reality. . . . When imitative characters in gardening are egregiously defective in any material circumstance, the truth of the others exposes and aggravates the failure."[107] Whately's observation reverberated in one of the central principles of camouflage, as described in a publication issued by the U.S. Office of Civilian Defense: "Plants wrongly used, in a camouflage installation, may be as dangerous a tell-tale as any misuse of paint."[108] After all, camouflage did not necessarily aim at objects not being seen but at making them seem ordinary and "natural."

Considering the affinity between landscape gardening and camouflage, it is not surprising that by the beginning of World War II, army officials had begun to realize the benefit of employing landscape architects as camoufleurs. Landscape architects themselves realized the opportunities their training provided them with in regard to the war effort and air-raid protection measures. In an increasingly tight economy, many landscape architects began to offer their services to the military. In Germany, they began to work for Nazi programs like "Schönheit der Arbeit" and "Kraft durch Freude," initiatives that, besides lifting public morale and spirits, were intended to "camouflage" camouflage measures.[109] In 1936, Christian Urhammer argued in the German journal *Gartenkunst* for "a new type of landscape designer" with a sense for aesthetics as well as for the practicalities of air-raid protection.[110] The establishment of luscious gardens and parks surrounding industrial buildings, and the Reichsbahn's efforts to promote the planting of trees and gardens along its railway embankments were indeed more than the mere physical manifestations of Nazi social politics and political ideology — attempts to steadfastly root Germans in their homeland and reconnect them to nature. As the caption of a photograph showing trees along a railway embankment that illustrated a 1935 article on landscape gardening for the German Reichsbahn made clear: "This stock of oak trees is not only pretty but also serves to camouflage the tracks against air raids."[111] Landscape architects like Hermann Mattern were commissioned with landscape designs for factories as part of the nationwide program "Schönheit der Arbeit" for the beautification and improvement of workplaces and environments.[112] While intended to provide landscape architects and contractors with work and factory workers with healthy, uplifting break spaces that instilled in them a feeling for the nature of their homeland, the greening of industry had an equally, if not more important, side effect: air-raid protection.[113] Using vacant urban lots in camouflage and air-raid protection schemes and turning them into "green arbors" also provided ample ground for the employment of landscape architects, according to Alexander Löftken, a senior official in the Air Ministry.[114] Some collaborators of the German landscape architect Alwin Seifert were commissioned with camouflaging the Westwall, a line of bunkers and tank traps built as protection against French invasion after 1938.[115]

The Nazi follower Heinrich Friedrich Wiepking-Jürgensmann explained in his *Landschaftsfibel* how victorious warfare was directly dependent on the existence of ample forests, hedgerows, and tree rows. Treeless open stretches of land like the Magdeburger Börde were not easily defensible against aerial attacks. In a series of sketches, he illustrated how rows of hedges and trees as well as trenches along roads could not only benefit the economy by providing beneficial microclimates for crops and protective shields against inclement weather for villages, but could at the same time form obstacles for tanks and protection against ground and aerial observation. Wiepking-Jürgensmann's ideal scenario was a "defensive planting" consisting of dense, thick forest swaths that encompassed a main road and two minor roadways that ran loosely along either side of the main road layout. He argued that defensive measures against the enemy were congruent with measures to protect the land against damage caused by wind, water, and sun. He claimed that "the more we build a landscape against the enemy, the more we protect it from weather damage! True to nature and defensive are one and the same!" Wiepking-Jürgensmann used the Finnish people to illustrate the intrinsic relationship between a victorious people and its habitat, which in the case of Finland consisted of—as he put it—"unmanageable, hard to penetrate, thick and cohesive woods." He believed that landscape had to be planned and designed according to military requirements as much as it had to respond to economic and aesthetic considerations.[116]

Wiepking-Jürgensmann's ideas were used by several landscape architects working for the Nazi civil and military engineering group Organisation Todt, who were particularly involved in projects that built upon their knowledge of bioengineering—the use of natural materials for soil reinforcement and stabilization. As a brochure published by Organisation Todt in 1944 testified, bioengineering was considered a technological means of warfare: besides being used for keeping supply roads open during snowstorms, for military surveying, and for the design of "defensive landscapes" (*Wehrlandschaften*), it could be used in camouflage against ground and aerial threat. The brochure pointed out how live plants that had traditionally been used for earth stabilization in road building and hydraulic engineering could also play a role in the construction and treatment of military emplacements and strongholds. "Living camouflage" (*lebendige Tarnung*), as the concealment with live plant materials was called, required not only knowledge of the techniques of deception and optical illusion and of the function of the buildings to be camouflaged, but also thorough knowledge of the soil and of the ecological conditions of a given area. The brochure's author, Alfred Becker, was therefore inclined to speak of camouflage planting as "landscape art." Knowledge in phytosociology was considered of the highest importance for camouflage and for military action in and the conquest of enemy territory.[117]

The foundations of the German reconnaissance and camouflage missions were largely based on developments in geography and specifically landscape ecology, which had used aerial photography for the purpose of surface-pattern recognition as soon as it had become more readily available in the 1920s. The geographer Carl Troll, who coined the term "landscape ecology" in 1938, was eager to secure a leading position for his field among the sciences considered relevant for warfare. In 1939, he had already pointed toward the annexed eastern territories as an ideal testing ground for the application of his aerial photo research, but to no avail.[118] The German Air Ministry only became interested in it in the 1940s, after a special research task force of the German Army High Command (Forschungsstaffel z.b.V. [zur besonderen Verwendung] des OKW) had been formed under the direction of the zoologist, pilot, and lieutenant Otto Schulz-Kampfhenkel. Due to their knowledge of phytosociology and ecology, some German landscape architects like Hermann Göritz were employed in this research task force along with plant ecologists, soil scientists, geologists, biologists, cartographers, photogrammetrists, and geographers, some of whom were Troll's students, collaborators, and colleagues. The men were charged with field reconnaissance missions and using aerial photographs for the terrain evaluation and mapping of little-known and inaccessible terrain for military use and with the development of camouflage instruction between 1943 and the end of the war.[119] They were tasked with aerial and ground surveying of enemy territories, and their methods were not dissimilar to those used in landscape ecological research. As in the nascent field of landscape ecology, aerial photographs were used to identify plant societies, from which information on soil conditions could be inferred. The maps produced by the special research unit on the basis of an analysis of the terrain's natural cover, soil profiles, and water conditions were to illustrate its trafficability, its camouflage possibilities, and its suitability for building hideouts and emplacements.

Landscape architects were also employed in Italy, where German air-protection measures were eagerly observed by the military and landscape architects alike. In 1937, Maria Teresa Parpagliolo reported on the green open spaces in German cities. She pointed out that besides reeducating the population about a healthy active life and reinstilling in the citizens a love and respect of their own country, vegetation had a new task: that of the defense of the citizens against aerial and gas attacks in the case of war. She indicated that this was why tree plantings surrounded industry and military constructions of any kind. This functional motivation together with aesthetic intentions, she concluded, made nature the true and most effective friend of all humans. Parpagliolo's colleague Pietro Porcinai offered his services to the Italian minister of war in 1942 and developed a patent of living camouflage (*brevetto di elementi mimetici per mascheramento con vegetazione naturale*). In France in 1940, Le Corbusier was commissioned by the Ministry of Defense to design an industrial complex for war production that was intended to reform industrial building. Called the "Green Factory" (L'Usine Verte) because its siting took into account the terrain features, natural light, and landscape scenery, the plant design was intended to promote the workers' physical and spiritual well-being. Like industrial building in Germany at the time, however, its implicit objective very likely was air-raid protection.[120]

In Britain, military officers who were inspired by intelligence reports on German treatment of industrial plants also reached out to landscape architects and horticulturists for their expertise in "living camouflage." The biggest advantages of live plant material were considered to be its "more convincing" nature, its permanency, its improvement and development from camouflage to concealment over time, and its seasonal change, "ren-

FIG. 65. Experimenting with "Watson's Pots,"
the method of disguising concrete runway
with grass-filled holes, 1942. (HO217/7, The
National Archives, Kew, UK)

dering the ground patterning entirely in harmony with the surrounding
country."[121]

In 1939, the English garden architect James Lever, from Angmering Green
in Sussex, and O. C. A. Slocock, the president of the Horticultural Trades
Association, advised Major D. A. J. Pavitt on plant lists and designs for living
camouflage. As numerous camouflage manuals at the time advised, plant
materials were used to screen objects from observation, to break up and
distort shadows, and to provide easily maintained, colored texture. Lever
established lists of trees and shrubs that distinguished between leaf colors
and deciduous and evergreen species. Inspired by German examples, Pavitt
and Lever aimed at enclosing industrial grounds with forested areas—living
camouflage belts—that could provide the nursery stock for future camouflage measures in other locations. Lever based his planting design on the aerial view of "a typical English wood of long standing [that] shows up from the
air as a blackish brown mass, due to the great density of—to coin a word—
twigage [sic]." He recommended the use of native plants because they had
smaller leaves and provided "that dense mass of black brown twiggage [sic]"
that provided better concealment throughout the entire year.[122] The British
horticulturist Leslie J. Watson was employed to research suitable plant materials and their reaction to diverse chemicals under various conditions. One
of the inventions with which he is credited, however, also involves concrete.
Watson suggested boring holes into concrete runways and filling them with
soil and tufts of grass (fig. 65). This type of runway had the advantage of

appearing similar to grassland from low angles of vision while providing a hard landing and takeoff surface that drained easily and did not dust.[123] "Watson's Pots," as the concrete-grass surface was called after its inventor, seem likely to have been a precedent for the permeable pavers often used for today's parking lots.

Although landscape architects and horticulturists played important roles in all war-faring countries, the U.S. military found these professionals and the method with which they were associated—living camouflage, or camouflage with planting, as it was called in the United States—of special importance. The United States lagged behind the other Allied nations in preparing for the war, and camouflage only became of wider concern after the December 1941 bombing at Pearl Harbor, when aerial attacks first began to be perceived as a serious threat. On the North American continent, however, aerial bombings never posed as acute a threat as in the European theater of war. The U.S. military may have been aware, therefore, that it could and should also work with long-term camouflage measures like plantings. Plant materials were also more suitable for camouflaging extensive military and industrial areas, common in the United States, where land was abundant. Numerous articles in specialist journals and publications like Robert P. Breckenridge's *Modern Camouflage* therefore either specifically pointed toward the landscape architect as the expert camoufleur, or extensively treated the subject of camouflage with planting. "The knowledge of the basic fundamentals of landscape architecture and its habitual use of site planning technique is very helpful to the camoufleur," one lecturer pointed out, and another observed that the landscape architect was in the advantageous position "to play a double role, on the one hand contributing to the cause of obscuration, and on the other, bringing to many a bleak spot a measure of aesthetic improvement." In 1943, the Office of Civilian Defense acknowledged that the modern landscape architect's "training is excellent preparation for the understanding of camouflage in terms of handling terrain" and that "a qualified landscape architect should have charge of the designing of planting."[124]

Entering the military ranks as a camouflage officer, however, proved to be complicated, and it took a fair amount of lobbying by American landscape architects to evoke statements like the ones quoted above. In 1940, the American Society of Landscape Architects (ASLA) not only signed a memorandum that clearly differentiated between the work to be conducted by landscape architects on the one hand and city planners on the other with regard to defense projects, but it also issued a pamphlet that enumerated the qualifications of landscape architects in national defense, including their employment in camouflage. In March 1941, ASLA predicted that camouflage would become a growing occupation for landscape architects "if conditions become more serious."[125] Armistead Fitzhugh was still encouraging his colleagues by

noting the military's big demand for "education in . . . site planning and the full meaning of adaptability to [the] environment." "Being well grounded in land planning already, the ASLA," he advised, "might do well to become air-minded and visualize the landscape from the bomber's point of view."[126]

But by this time, landscape architects had already become involved in protective concealment in a variety of ways. In 1940, the landscape architect Chester W. Nichols lectured on the "art of camouflage" and the necessity of decentralizing buildings at Harvard University. His colleague Edward L. Packard reported on the construction of Westover Airport at Chicopee Falls, Massachusetts, where buildings were staggered to reduce the possibility of them being hit by a string of bombs, and where the entire airfield and base were designed to merge with surrounding landscape features. Selected faculty and staff at Harvard University and the Massachusetts Institute of Technology, including the Fogg Art Museum director Edward W. Forbes, were "anxious to make, if possible, some contribution to the study of problems of camouflage."[127]

These first stirrings finally led to the establishment of one of the first two camouflage courses in the country in 1941. Geared primarily toward students and professionals of the design, architecture, and engineering professions, the courses were held in the Harvard Department of Fine Arts and taught by the drawing and design instructor Winthrop O. Judkins (fig. 66).[128] But although landscape architects like the Harvard graduate Vincent N.

Merrill posited that "the landscape designer is the artist whose training and experience provide the best all-round background for camouflage," Merrill and many of his colleagues could not as easily accept that their artistic and scientific skills should be used in warfare. After all, Merrill asked, wasn't it the landscape architects' goal to design gardens and landscapes that attracted rather than diverted attention? As one of the few public commentators on camouflage who addressed the "dark" side of military action, including camouflage, Merrill pointed out the difference between wartime camouflage and peacetime landscape design. Whereas activities like masking were honest, playful, and geared toward aesthetic goals in peacetime, in wartime they were carried out with seriousness and deceit.[129]

In contrast, Merrill's colleague Ralph Rodney Root did not consider this issue an ethical dilemma. He argued for large-scale projects that provided protection in war and "decorative landscape treatment during peace times."[130] *Camouflage with Planting* was the title of his 1942 book on the use of plant materials in camouflage, or protective concealment, as it was officially called. Trained at Cornell and Harvard, Root had founded the University of Illinois's landscape architecture program in Urbana in 1912. He served as head of the program until 1918, when he went back into private practice. His book on camouflage followed a number of publications in which he dealt with country estates, garden history, and landscape gardening. The aerial view and camouflage had already played a role in Root's 1941 book *Contourscaping*. To distance landscape architecture from ornamental "landscaping," secure its standing among the learned professions, and modernize it, Root coined the term "contourscaping," which he defined as a fine art that worked with "color form plant material [sic] and light."[131] In rather contorted language with a clearly modernist bent, Root showed that all outdoor designs could be thought of as abstract compositions of volumes, outlined by the contours of spaces and objects. He argued that aerial photographs could facilitate the recognition of the contours of different vegetation and land-use patterns. It was in this connection that he pointed out that "successful camouflage work uses the same [work] methods . . . as contourscaping,"[132] meaning simply that landscape architecture employed many of the same techniques used in land camouflage. Root's preoccupation with figures and their contours, and with the ground plane faintly recalled the visual theories of the gestalt psychologists.

With his subsequent booklet *Camouflage with Planting*, Root provided a how-to manual. He argued that all vulnerable structures had to be concealed by blending them into the existing landscape pattern as seen from the air. Thus, all planned structures had to be sited along the contour lines, and "landscape planting should be used to break up shadow patterns and secure an unobtrusive monotony in the airman's view of the project."[133]

To facilitate the work of the camoufleur, oblique and perpendicular aerial photographs, including infrared photographs, would be needed. The latter were necessary to determine the types of plants to be used in camouflage plantings since it had been found that the infrared reflective properties of foliage differed depending on the plant species. No longer was aerial reconnaissance confined to panchromatic images only. Although aerial infrared photographs had already been used during World War I, advanced technology made infrared photography more affordable and more easily available during World War II. The different ways of seeing therefore had to be anticipated in the choice of plants for camouflage schemes, and they led to the development of paint that reflected infrared light the way that vegetation does. This green camouflage paint that contained chromium oxide photographed on infrared film with the same color tone as adjacent vegetation.[134] Authors like Root, however, argued that despite the constrictions imposed by the principles of functional camouflage design, landscapes could be both useful and beautiful: after all, Root remarked, camouflage with planting produced a landscape "appropriate to its locality and adapted to the life of the people who use it."[135]

In the July 1942 issue of *Landscape Architecture,* seventy-seven "recent references on camouflage" were listed to keep professionals up-to-date with camouflage developments.[136] If they were not directly employed by the War Department in the Camouflage Section of the Engineer Board like George L. Nason, Armistead Fitzhugh, Harold W. Graham, and Perry Wheeler, landscape architects participated in industrial camouflage courses, like Marjorie Sewell Cautley, and in the civilian camouflage courses held at the Engineer School at Fort Belvoir under the auspices of the Office of Civilian Defense (OCD), like Henry L. Hornbeck, Lawrence G. Linnard, Sidney N. Shurcliff, A. F. Brinckerhoff, and Leland Vaughan.[137] In 1942, a consortium of universities gained permission from the OCD to offer camouflage courses for professional candidates including landscape architects, engineers, architects, industrial designers, and other professionally qualified candidates if at least one university staff had been trained in the OCD's industrial camouflage course at Fort Belvoir. Numerous landscape architecture faculty took advantage of this opportunity.[138]

The heightened interest in camouflage planting by engineers, architects, and landscape architects went hand in hand with an increasing awareness of the nursery industry. As in Britain, where camouflage belts were to be established that at the same time functioned as nurseries, the U.S. military realized that appropriate plant stock needed to be cultivated. In 1940, it was already assumed that tree nurseries would play an important role in warfare, leading the State Institute of Agriculture, in Farmingdale, New York, to offer a weekly lecture course of about four month's duration on camouflage techniques.[139] Plants were considered superior to artificial materials because they changed with the seasons and because of their masking ability with age. The plants used in camouflage needed to have the same appearance from the air as the plants growing in the surrounding area. To facilitate protective concealment, the Camouflage Section of the Engineer Board at Fort Belvoir developed an annual manual in collaboration with the American Association of Nurserymen that listed available plant materials for camouflage according to their type, size, type of foliage, growth habit, and availability in different areas of the United States. Botanists and foresters at Harvard University's Arnold Arboretum and the Harvard Forest at Petersham conducted research into plant materials for camouflage. For the disguise of harbors and large water surfaces, experiments with surface-covering water plants were undertaken. In 1943, an unofficial newsletter produced by the graduates of Fort Belvoir announced that the breeding of plants like water hyacinths and "duck weed" for salt water was being considered. The reported plan was to use these plants to disguise entire harbors, wide rivers, and shorelines as solid land.[140]

Live plants could not be used for camouflage purposes in all cases. All war-faring countries therefore produced a variety of dummy trees and shrubs especially for the use in the field. The Camouflage Board at Fort Belvoir developed tree varieties out of empty ration tins, steel wool, pipe and wood frames, chicken wire, and cloth strips. Along the front lines, cut branches and foliage were often used to garnish camouflage nets, vehicles, and gun positions. Wilting and loss of color were the result and the challenge that camoufleurs had to confront on a regular basis. Harvard botanists and foresters therefore also began to tackle this problem, drawing up tables on the "lasting period of cut foliage" of different species.[141] Supported by the Maria Moors Cabot Foundation for Botanical Research, the Harvard Camouflage Committee, chaired by the director of the Arnold Arboretum Elmer D. Merrill, summed up its research in two manuals that were sent to Fort Belvoir in 1943. Of course, it was not surprising that the committee suggested the use of uncut vegetation as the best camouflage measure. However, if the use of existing vegetation without cutting was not possible, it found that, in Europe and northeastern America, softwoods like pine, juniper, and cypress could be used for long-lasting camouflage effects as long as they blended into the surrounding vegetation. Hardwood foliage wilted faster than that of softwoods, and due to their especially fast wilting process, it was determined that willow, aspen, butternut, walnut, and American ash were completely useless for camouflage projects. Other hardwood species, it was pointed out, needed fresh, clean water to sustain them for longer periods. The manuals also drew attention to the fact that cut branches needed to be positioned according to their natural growth and orientation so as to prevent the tender undersides of leaves from browning in direct sunlight. Finally, the manuals advised that plants should be cut at night, early in the morning, or during a rainstorm, and that stems should be recut under water to slow down the wilting process. The first manual was supplemented by a publication with advice regarding the vegetation on the tropical Pacific islands. Based on experiments at the USDA Plant Introduction Garden in Coconut Grove, Florida, the Camouflage Committee determined that the coconut palm, banana, screw pine, and Australian pine, among other species, provided the most valuable and resistant camouflage material in the tropical and subtropical theaters of war.[142] Although the initial objective of the handful of faculty and researchers who voluntarily formed the Camouflage Committee in 1942 was to carry out a broad but integrated research program in cooperation with army authorities, Merrill and his colleagues soon realized that the military was much harder to approach and impress than they had initially imagined. The project itself withered by the end of 1943 and was subsequently dissolved.

Although sprays that prevented wilting for some hours or days, depending on the plant species, were already available in the first war years, they only deferred the problem for a short while. It was not until 1969 that the *New York Times* reported that a preservative had been newly created to "prolong the life of various kinds of foliage used to camouflage military installations." Consisting of a mixture of organic chemicals and metallic salts dissolved in alcohols, it prevented foliage of hemlock, birch, oak, maple, holly, and beech trees from wilting and losing color for up to six weeks.[143]

Insect pests posed another challenge to living camouflage materials. Like the trees along German railways, the shade trees along U.S. roads were frequently identified as cheap and attractive air-raid protection. Trees were to be preserved along the new defense highways and their roadsides to be planted with additional grasses, legumes, and vines to render them less conspicuous.[144] While trees could provide protection, they were themselves often threatened by insect pests. Various authors therefore argued that the limited insecticides available should not be allocated entirely to the protection of food crops. After all, noted Cynthia Westcott, healthy "shade trees may save more lives than wormless apples."[145] The immediate concern with survival was very strong, and questions about the larger environmental effects that could result from the extensive chemical treatment of plants and wide stretches of land did not surface until the postwar years. Thus, different types of fertilizers were indiscriminately used on extensive areas to simulate different field patterns and shadows: sodium arsenate, which killed grass tops; ammonium thyocyanate, which turned grass brown and then white; and iron sulphate and tannic acid solutions, which turned ground cover black. In addition to these chemical ground and surface treatments, different mechanical methods were developed that would provide a variety of textured patterns when seen from the air. Among these were "scarification," a breaking up of the surface of the ground and "rooting," "which produced a rough, coarse texture without geometrical pattern."[146]

Camouflage for Peacetime

Not only was camouflage considered a vital wartime necessity, but it was also seen by some as a means to advance art and culture. While art was recognized as informing camouflage work, the latter could also inform art. Milton S. Fox believed that the study of camouflage would emphasize the importance of interdisciplinary work and would give new importance to occupations and fields as diverse as chemistry, mechanical engineering, architecture, mathematics, woodworking, modeling, casting, photography, surveying, landscaping, and gardening.[147] A motivation for camouflage research and civil and military camouflage discipline during the war years was provided by the assumption held by many professionals that camouflage would prove useful in peacetime projects as well. In 1942, Robert P. Breckenridge was already asking, "What of camouflage *after* the war?,"[148] only to argue that the decentralization of settlements, the dispersion and irregular siting of buildings, their blending into the landscape, and the preservation and use of plant materials were objectives of both camouflage and city planning. Thus, Breckenridge noted, "the camouflage planner is contributing not only to the safety and protection of our people today, but also better living and working conditions tomorrow."[149] The argument that camouflage measures would also be beneficial in peacetime was used to entice industry to participate in wartime camouflage measures. Camouflage, it was said, was not only a protective but also an aesthetic and sanitary measure. The American artist Eric Sloane warned that as the result of increasing air travel, "the factory of the future will be seen from the air as much as from the ground," and what factory owner did not want his plant to be "presentable to passenger air traffic"? Sloane pointed out that to secure landscape amenities, the job of the camoufleur in peacetime would also include the concealment of the "maze of gas tanks, power plants, garbage dumps and industrial disposal areas" that were building up around "such national landmarks as Niagara Falls, New York Harbor and the Mississippi River."[150]

The same Francis Keally who in the 1920s had produced visionary airport designs (see chapter 1) and in the 1940s had assumed the chairmanship of the New York Civilian Camouflage Council believed that the wartime camouflage experience would lead to "more consideration . . . given to beautiful landscaping" in peacetime and that "not only the towns but the spaces between the towns w[ould] be made more beautiful and attractive." In Britain in 1944, Hugh Casson also looked ahead. How would the lessons learned from camouflage contribute to the design of postwar landscapes? Camouflage, he argued, could "help—not in its narrow war-idiom—but in the broadest sense, as the scientific use of texture, tone, and colour, to complement instead of to disguise form." Casson pointed out its potentials for architecture, urban design ("street picture making"), and industrial landscapes. Camouflage could now help to site factories in a way that would make them inconspicuous. "If they are also simply designed, well built of sound materials and not too untidy in their habits," he argued, "they should be no intrusion upon the country scene."[151] When the landscapes of war were turned into what Sylvia Crowe in Britain called a "landscape of power"—characterized by power stations, power lines, transformers, telegraph poles and wires, radio masts, and airfields—principles were used that had been employed in camouflage.

LANDSCAPES OF POWER

In the United States, Breckenridge had noted that one of the greatest challenges would be posed by the increasing number of airfields and highways, transportation structures that were extremely conspicuous from the air. In Britain, not new airports, but the numerous existing military airfields posed a significant albeit different question shortly after the war. What to do with the many airfields that had become obsolete preoccupied the British Parliament in 1945. The landscape architect Brian Hackett deplored the damage that had been done to the landscape through the building of airfields that involved "the removal of hedges and banks, the piping and filling in of ditches, filling in of ponds, cutting down [of] trees."[152] He argued that the airfields should be retained or returned to agricultural use, or that they should be converted to sites for housing or a recreational center. In accordance with the wartime camouflage principles, retained airfields and airfields turned into villages would have to be "marr[ied] with the existing landscape as far as possible,"[153] using shrubs and tree clumps, and painting the buildings with colors that easily blended into the landscape. New buildings should be adapted to the local landscape character and color. The conversion of airfields into recreational centers with boating lakes, playing fields, and parade streets and auto- or bike-racing tracks on the former perimeter tracks and runways called for a comprehensive design that merged the center with the surrounding countryside. Hackett therefore argued for the employment of landscape architects as regional landscape advisers to support the regional officers of the Ministry of Town and Country planning, and as land utilization officers to assist in rehabilitating Britain's military airfields.[154]

Hackett's British colleague Sylvia Crowe also considered military airfields to be "littering" the British landscape. Crowe proposed that airfield buildings should be sited "against the background of trees, or within their shelter," and that surrounding fences should run along or within the edge of the planting. As in wartime, the airfield buildings were to be made as unobtrusive for onlookers as possible. Another way to achieve this objective was to work with earthworks, plantings, and existing landforms. Crowe was unrelenting when it came to military airfields: They "should . . . disappear into the landscape."[155] Although she embraced many of the "new shapes" evolving out of transportation and industry and argued for aircraft hangars in "a shape expressive of a machine rising from the ground, or alighting from the sky,"[156] Crowe approached many of her postwar commissions for the British Forestry Commission and the nationalized Central Electricity Generating Board (CEGB) founded in 1948 like a camouflage officer. This might not surprise since she probably had occasion to witness land camouflage during World War II, when she served as an ambulance driver in France and in the Auxiliary Territorial Service on the English South Coast and later in Gravesend.

Crowe's postwar agenda was determined by the idea that the buildings and structures of new industries like nuclear power, communication, and transportation needed to be assimilated into the landscape by preserving and redesigning, where necessary, "the entire surface-cover of the land into one flowing comprehensive pattern."[157] Like the work of some of her colleagues such as Geoffrey Jellicoe, Crowe's projects for the CEGB were guided by the Generating Board's acknowledgment of the "conflicting demands of industry and amenity" and by the consequent task to harmonize "modern power with ancient beauty," as expressed by the conservative Minister without Portfolio William Deedes at the opening of the 1963 RIBA exhibition entitled *The Architecture of Power.*[158] Providing a coordinated and economical power supply while at the same time conserving landscape amenities and the environment was considered a challenge that had led to the CEGB's employment of landscape architects in the first place. Wartime reports on the state of the land and country like the 1937 Barlow Report and the 1942 Uthwatt and Scott Reports as well as planning initiatives for reconstruction in the postwar years motivated by the 1947 Town and Country Planning Act had set the stage for the CEGB's greater concern for the public interest and the environment. It had become clear that the generation, transmission, and distribution of energy required national and regional planning. Landscape architects, like architects, understood the challenge to "marry" industry and landscape as an opportunity to explore new professional possibilities.[159] Sylvia Crowe appreciated these opportunities for creative design, and anticipated that the "18th-century landscape tradition" could be resumed on a new scale by dealing with industrial landscapes using heavy machinery for the sculptural treatment of the ground.[160]

Like camoufleurs during the war, Crowe considered the landscape a pattern "always open to the sky, . . . a free, flowing rhythm, based on organic nature."[161] The power and transformer stations she was working on in her commissions were to be absorbed into this landscape. In this way, the landscape, which according to Crowe, had "lost its continuous web of pattern" and had "disintegrated like an exploding atom," needed to be woven together again, "sometimes into a variation of the old pattern, sometimes into a completely new one."[162] To achieve this, the form of power and transformer stations, for example, had to suggest "an extension of organic nature, rather than the imprint of human proportions."[163] Crowe maintained that "the surroundings can then be modelled to link nature and construction together into the rhythmic flow of a true landscape."[164] Like the early camoufleurs and their observers during World War I and World War II who had noted parallels between camouflage work, landscape patterns, and modern abstract art, Crowe compared the patterns of the "landscape of power" with Paul Klee's composition of arrows and interpenetrating lines. The interlocking shapes and lines of abstract art had so far only been translated into garden designs, for example, by Roberto Burle Marx in Brazil and by Thomas Church in California. Crowe aimed at using "patterns of interlocking shape" to transform entire landscapes.[165] Following the principles of industrial camouflage during World War II, several of her drawings illustrate how power and transformer stations can be unobtrusively integrated into the existing landscape pattern (fig. 67). Crowe found confirmation for her preoccupation with landscape pattern and the humanistic domestication of the landscape of power in Gyorgy Kepes's publication *The New Landscape in Art and Science* (1956). Based on an exhibition at the Massachusetts Institute of Technology, the book illustrated patterns on a variety of scales seen through microscopes and telescopes.[166] The work was favorably received in landscape architecture circles not only because of its presentation of natural phenomena as abstract patterns and ordered structures, but because of its programmatic intent to facilitate bridging the spheres of science, technology, and art.[167] Kepes also argued that "the new landscape," that is, the technological landscape, had to "be brought into harmony with the rhythm of the seasons, with the openness of the sky and with the opportunities of the land." He maintained that art could produce a balanced "human-made environment" with "a new texture that buil[t] upon the scientific knowledge of our needs" and in which human scale was applied to the material world.[168] Crowe sought to achieve this same goal in her treatment of the new industrial landscapes in Britain.

Along with their integration into a pattern seen from the air, building masses and forms also had to blend into the landscape from the ground view. Again, the design principles suggested resembled those of military camouflage. Planting, siting, excavating, and "sinking" could, for example, be used

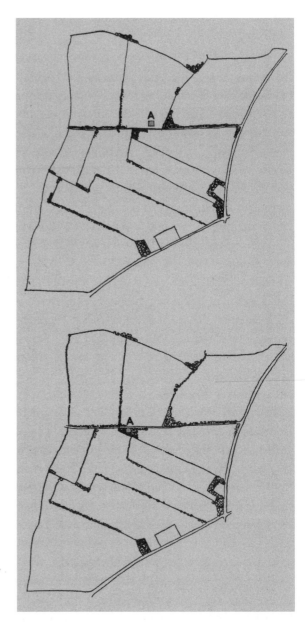

FIG. 67. Example of the unobtrusive integration of a transformer station (*A*) into the landscape pattern. Drawing by Michael Laurie. (Reprinted Sylvia Crowe, *The Landscape of Power* [London: Architectural Press, © 1958], 93)

to "camouflage" and screen transformer stations. The landscape should not be leveled, and the stations could be partly screened to make them merge with the surrounding landscape more easily and give them the appearance of having "sprung from the earth."[169] Trees surrounding industrial buildings and power stations could provide a "unifying background to the tiresome poles and wires" and could form a "counterpoise to the great height" of vertical buildings like cooling towers. According to Crowe, tree masses in this context could also fulfill "the rôle of a recumbent unifying element." Crowe advised how plantings of vegetation that corresponded to the types already growing in a given area could be used to tie industrial buildings into their surroundings. It was important that the plantings not follow the line of the object to be screened, but rather related to the surrounding landscape.[170] In keeping with traditional British landscape, Crowe also promoted the adoption of the eighteenth-century ha-ha to blend buildings with the landscape contours, a practice also included by the CEGB in one of their design memoranda. "This is," she argued, "a useful device when the building requires the appearance of rising cleanly from the open ground, with the landscape sweeping up to it, without planting or walls."[171] Among the camouflage principles Crowe embraced in her postwar work were the disruption and breaking up of clear edges, forms, and silhouettes of large buildings through plantings and landforms; the use of colors that matched buildings to their surroundings; and roads and fences running parallel to contour lines. In camouflage advice similar to that given in World War II, Crowe also maintained that concealment was not in all cases the best solution. Some buildings needed to be made "less disruptive by making them appear as a part of the landscape composition." Furthermore, in accordance with World War II industrial camouflage principles, Crowe suggested surrounding industrial buildings with more intricately formed human-scale landscapes that not only accommodated car parks and gardens for the workers, but that integrated the buildings into the larger landscape pattern. Despite the more intricate landscape design surrounding the industrial building, it was the "organic pattern" of the rural surroundings that should impose itself on the industrial plant.[172]

One of the sites where Crowe strove to achieve "a direct union between the main buildings and the surrounding Welsh mountain landscape" by carrying the "wild landscape . . . right up to the structures" was Trawsfynydd in Merionethshire in Welsh Snowdonia, the fourth nuclear power station of Britain's 1955 nuclear power program, devised to respond to the increased demand for electricity in the postwar years (fig. 68 and fig. 69). Construction began in 1959 on the shore of Trawsfynydd Lake, a large reservoir that had been built three decades before for the Maentwrog Hydroelectric Power Station and that would provide the nuclear power station with the necessary cooling water. The pump house was sunk below ground level; the approach road was unlit, uncurbed, and laid out along the contours; and the substation was sited on low ground with its surface partly sown with dwarf clover "to break up the great expanse of hard surface as seen from higher viewpoints." Ground modeling, using the soil and peat that was removed for the excavation for foundations, was employed to merge the buildings with the surrounding landforms. The ground between the turbine house and the substation, for example, was modeled so as to appear as a spur of

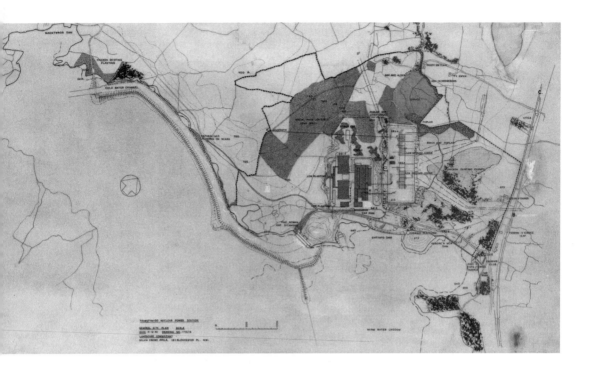

FIG. 68.
Sylvia Crowe, land-
scape plan for Traws-
fynydd nuclear
power station, Wales.
(Sylvia Crowe Collec-
tion; Reproduced
with permission
of the Landscape
Institute)

the surrounding hills. At the northeast corner of the substation, tree-planted mounds were built to conceal parts of the power station from the road. Furthermore, the reactor buildings were designed so that they would not tower above the outline of Craig Gyfyns, and the concrete building façades were colored gray to match the rock in the immediate environment.[173]

Another example of the principles put forward by Crowe and some of her landscape architecture colleagues was Geoffrey Jellicoe's design for the landscape treatment surrounding a nuclear power station at Oldbury, located on the River Severn between Gloucester and Bristol, that opened in 1967 (fig. 70). The nuclear power station was positioned on a platform made from dredged soil. In 1945 Jellicoe had already expressed his conceptual ideas regarding the landscape treatment of power stations in an article published in the *Architectural Review*. He considered the "wildest" landscape and sites located farthest from human habitation as the most ideal locations. In his conceptualization, powerful energy found a metaphorical equivalent in powerful nature. The power station and its environment were to be conceived as one landscape design. The flat, open Oldbury site fit his ideas well, since he had also posited that "the ideal location for industrial buildings beyond human scale is an open landscape." Keeping in mind the aerial perspective, Jellicoe designed an abstract field pattern for the terraces surrounding the station's platform. This field pattern, structured by hedges and cultivated with different crops and orchards, was connected to the historically grown,

FIG. 69.
Sylvia Crowe, sketches illustrating views from roads approaching and passing Trawsfynydd nuclear power station, Wales. (Sylvia Crowe Collection; Reproduced with permission of the Landscape Institute)

more intricate and irregular field pattern of the surrounding countryside by a ring of pastureland. Jellicoe wanted his rectangular field terraces to mediate between the small-scale irregular field pattern of the environs and the monumental clear shapes and forms of the power station. While it was hardly possible to conceal a nuclear power station from the horizontal view in the flat landscape of a river estuary, the field pattern and associated colors Jellicoe used for his design aimed at blending the station's structures into the existing landscape pattern, both visually and on an emotional level. As he had remarked in 1945, a functional "tree plan" designed for wind shelter and shade, "dust filtration and . . . camouflage of inevitably dirty corners" would with its natural development over time create an "emotional bridge between the turbines and the cows."[174]

Industrial landscapes and their camouflage continued to preoccupy land-scape architects throughout the 1960s and 1970s. The concern that guided Sylvia Crowe and many of her colleagues at the time was the "breach be-tween the artist and the scientist."[175] As a new group of experts who had attained public recognition, particularly following the 1951 Festival of Brit-ain, where they had been responsible for much of the open space design, landscape architects joined a discussion that was dominating much of intel-lectual culture and the media. In 1946, the BBC had "called the division be-tween scientific and humanistic thought 'the challenge of our time.'"[176] The

FLIGHTS OF IMAGINATION

British physicist and novelist Charles Percy Snow had begun to elaborate on the "two cultures" in the *New Statesman* in 1956 and more famously in his subsequent 1959 Rede Lecture at Cambridge University, thereby leading an old discussion about the relationship between the arts and the sciences to a new high point and sparking what has become known as the "two cultures" controversy. Criticizing the intolerance and the chronic—and in part— wanton misunderstandings between scientists and artists, Snow insisted that communication and interaction between the two groups was vital, not least for tackling and overcoming world problems like the "H-bomb war, over-population, the gap between the rich and the poor."[177]

Even if they were concerned more with local, regional, and national issues, some landscape architects at the time realized that they could contribute to reestablishing the lost connections between art, science, and technology, and attempt to reconcile scientific and artistic endeavors. In *The Landscape of Power,* Crowe mused that "it may be that it is the role of landscape design to bridge this gap, for landscape architecture is rooted equally in art and science, and has as its aim the reconciliation of artifice to nature, and of art to science."[178] This had also been landscape architecture's call in camouflage work. Landscapes of war and power offered a chance for landscape architects in all countries to assume new perspectives and to further emancipate themselves and promote their young profession, which had only been institutionalized in Britain in 1929. As much as the aerial view was a tool in camouflage work that can be seen as a form of landscape architecture, it also led to the development of camouflage in the first place. After World War II, aerial views were also used for more peaceful endeavors that involved protecting and conserving the land. However, aerial photography continued to be employed to support militaristic rhetoric when it came to redesigning cities, and it continued to be used to facilitate regional landscape planning.

Five | Conserving the Land

THE AERIAL VIEW AND ENVIRONMENTAL
PLANNING AND DESIGN

In 1955, the German-born architect-turned-writer Erwin Gutkind gave the introductory lecture at the international conference "Man's Role in Changing the Face of the Earth" held at Princeton University. Sponsored by the Wenner-Gren Foundation for Anthropological Research in New Jersey to initiate a discussion on the wise and sustained use of the landscape, the conference was organized by a small group of researchers from the sciences and humanities: the geographer Carl O. Sauer, the zoologist Marston Bates, and the historian Lewis Mumford. Gutkind's lecture was entitled "Our World from the Air: Conflict and Adaptation."

That the Princeton conference was introduced with a lecture on the visual appearance of the planet from the air reveals the epistemological and methodological importance attributed at the time to the aerial imagination and representation for understanding, mitigating, directing, and shaping humankind's impact on the earth. Gutkind was writing after the aerial reconnaissance and bombardment of World War II had caused unprecedented harm to people, their homes, and the environment in Europe and Asia. He was also writing in light of the unprecedented technological development and population growth of the postwar years, which had led to heightened awareness of the quality of the human living environment and of the inherent worth and value of nonhuman nature. Although aerial photography had been used as early as the 1920s to detect what were considered to be the detrimental effects of human settlement on the earth, in the postwar years its use in the identification of illegal and deteriorating buildings, air and water pollution, and diseased vegetation significantly increased. The aerial view captured in photographs also became a visual rhetoric used to draw attention to technological progress and the inherent value of the earth on the one hand, and to alert the public to the environmental destruction caused by humankind on the other. On a larger scale than ever before, aerial and satellite photographs became a technological tool for analyzing, planning, and designing our living environment, in many cases with the intent to protect and conserve the land. It literally and figuratively reached new heights when the Soviet Union launched *Sputnik* in October 1957, initiating the space race and leading the United States to develop their LANDSAT program, launched in 1972.

Gutkind's lecture was an elaboration on the introductory chapter of his picture book published three years before and entitled *Our World from the Air: An International Survey of Man and His Environment*. Believing in the social agency of architecture, he had designed and built numerous modernist buildings and entire residential neighborhoods in Berlin before emigrating to England, and had already begun work on the book before World War II. In his effort to describe humankind's attitude toward its environment through aerial surveying, Gutkind had collected vertical and oblique aerial photographs illustrating settlement forms and landscapes from around the world. His study was supported by the British Institute of Sociology, an institution closely affiliated with Geddes's work.[1] Although Gutkind, like his contemporaries Brunner and Ewald in the late 1920s, used aerial photography to reveal urban form and the human adaptation and cultivation of the land, his intention was not to foster particular national or regional identities. In contrast, using selected photographs that spanned the entire globe, he argued for a world citizenship that cared for its living environment through rational comprehensive regional planning. He considered the synoptic aerial view of extensive areas an aid in grasping past mistakes and an inspiration for future human activity that needed to be based on "foresight and co-ordination." Aerial photographs allowed Gutkind to produce an illustrated survey that considered both the destructive and constructive aspects of humankind's past, present and potential future relationship with its environment.

The Princeton conference gave Gutkind the chance to further elaborate on his ideas and insights about the conquest of the air and the aerial view. He pointed out that the aerial view provided global awareness and showed that "the whole world is our unit of thinking and acting." He observed that "nothing can develop in isolation, and the transformation in one country produces direct reactions on the physical and social structure of all the others." In a Geddesian spirit, he stressed that aerial vision provided an overview of nature's "environmental patterns" and "dynamic relationships" on earth. Since humankind was a part of nature, Gutkind argued for a new discipline—"social ecology"—that included "those branches of the social and natural sciences which have a more or less direct bearing upon the role of man in re-forming his habitat."[2] Gutkind also held that the elevated synoptic view was a tool for both analysis and synthesis. To his mind, it provided rational knowledge and creative potential. Furthermore, the aerial view offered insights into a new understanding of space and scale. It could "reconcile . . . the infinitely large and the infinitely small," and it could bridge "the gap between the smallest social unit, the individual human being, and the largest unit, the universe—between, as it were, the social microscope and the social telescope." Finally, Gutkind believed that the aerial view and the new space-time relationship created by the airplane would enable and strengthen regional unity and a balanced decentralized structure of settlement.[3] Predicated on holistic thinking, his work built upon ideas that had been developed in the early twentieth century and that shaped many of the events in its second half.

Aerial Photographs as X–Rays of the Urban Condition

In his lecture, Gutkind argued for a balanced decentralized structure of settlement, an idea that he shared with many landscape architects, architects, and urban planners who were, among other things, concerned about protecting their countries against aerial attack. However, in the postwar years it also became clear to urban professionals in Europe and in the United States that urban centers needed improvement and renewal as well as dispersal. The aerial view played an important role in this work. In fact, the view from above captured in aerial photographs was the primary perspective assumed in planning after the war. The beginnings of this use go back to the 1920s, but after World War II, aerial photography began to be used on a much larger scale. As in the 1920s, it also supported the philosophical holism and organicism that in the second half of the twentieth century still underlay the conception of the city. Many scholars and professionals who dealt with the study, planning, and design of cities in the postwar years entertained the idea that the whole was greater than the sum of its parts. They built upon the theories and concepts that had been developed by sociologists and geographers at the University of Chicago who had been searching since the 1920s for models to analyze and describe life in cities. These sociologists and geographers used ecological terms and drew analogies with organisms of the natural world, building upon similar comparisons that had been made since classical times and especially in nineteenth-century literature. As noted in chapter 2, urban professionals soon realized that these verbal analogies and metaphors could be readily supported visually by the aerial view.

While the Chicago sociologists Robert Park and Ernest Burgess had used planners' maps for their work and had illustrated their ideas in concept diagrams that showed the entire city,[4] in France after World War II, the sociologist Paul Henry Chombart de Lauwe promoted the use of aerial photography as a method in sociology, human geography, and ecology. In contrast to plans, which he considered insufficient to reveal "the details of life of the housing blocks and labyrinthine streets,"[5] aerial photographs were "more complete and lively" documents.[6] In turn, the planners and officials who began to build upon human ecology in subsequent decades not only developed diagrams reminiscent of those of their scientist colleagues,[7] but they also made additional use of aerial photographs. For them there was no better means to show a city as a whole and to illustrate the "organic re-lationship"[8] of individual planning areas to the city in its entirety. In 1971, the American city planner Melville C. Branch therefore remarked that "an aerial photographic view of the city as a whole is essential for comprehensive study and understanding of the urban organism and the formulation of realistic programs for directing its growth and development."[9] Aerial views, Branch argued, showed the "most essential physical-spatial characteristics and form" of cities, revealing their socioeconomic-political realities. In his and his colleagues' eyes, aerial views were "constant reminders of the necessity to consider the total anatomy of the urban organism if citywide planning is to be more than a delusion or ineffective patchwork."[10]

The organicist and biologistic analogies have come to the fore especially on occasions when cities and urban life have been considered to be in crisis and methods were sought to describe the processes that led to these situations. Planners and officials responsible often used organicist metaphors when they wanted to relinquish all responsibilities for certain developments. As an organism, they argued, the city was self-organizing and had a life of its own, and the best they could do was to control or direct its development. Given the nature of these analogies, it appears only logical that medical terminology would be used to describe what were perceived to be urban problems and to suggest how they could be alleviated. In the postwar United States, as in Europe, cities were considered to be sick and diseased organisms that required treatment. Aerial photography, therefore, was imagined as X-rays or a giant microscope "looking *down-and-in*"[11] to discover a city's syndromes and symptoms. Aerial urban photography thereby displayed its ambiguous nature, on the one hand providing an instrument to observe, "dissect," and analyze the urban environment, and on the other hand rendering everything on an equal scale. Within the framework of what in the United States was called "urban renewal"—a term coined in 1953 by the housing economist Miles Colean and first officially used in the 1954 Housing Act to describe the rehabilitation and conservation of deteriorating areas and the clearance and redevelopment of run-down areas[12]—"surgery" and "face lifting programs" were "prescribed" and "city clinics" were established. The contagion was termed "blight." To fend off blight while working within the parameters of federally funded renewal programs that required citizen participation, many cities established "city," "housing," and "urban renewal clinics" to educate citizens on how to abide by housing codes and improve their neighborhoods. The Chicago Land Clearance Commission, an independent municipal corporation charged with the acquisition and clearance of deteriorated areas and their resale to private and public developers, identified blight as "a municipal cancer . . . [and] disease [that] spreads from block to block, leaving decrepit and dangerous buildings, unhappiness and torn lives in its wake."[13] The non-profit American Council to Improve Our Neighborhoods (ACTION) that was founded in 1954 to help conserve and rehabilitate existing houses and neighborhoods and to remove "slum conditions" considered blight to be "the insidious decay which can attack anyone's home or community—even the finest." According to ACTION, blight "sets in wherever people neglect their homes or allow their neighborhoods to decline."[14] Implied in these definitions was the idea that a deteriorating area, if not properly treated, could negatively affect an entire city—the "organism." Consequently, planners like Tracy Augur demanded that decline and neglect be "dealt with on the scale of the whole city or the whole metropolitan area or urban region."[15]

Many city and government officials believed that blight as a phenomenon of the natural life cycle of cities could be reversed, slowed, halted, and defeated by diverse means, including "surgical" measures.[16] Thus, the Chicago Land Clearance Commission "prescribed surgery" for the city, and a 1954 article describing its activity was illustrated on the first page with an aerial view of Chicago's urban core, two pairs of surgeon's scissors, and a scalpel that had cut out part of the aerial photograph (fig. 71). The photograph's caption read: "From the lake, Chicago's skyline is a magical thing. Behind the façade, blighted areas crowd the loop."[17] The illustration's message was clear: the blighted areas had to be cut out; they had to be cleared and redeveloped. As noted in chapter 2, aerial views captured in photographs had been used in the late 1920s to "indict" the city and to identify its problems with regard to urban form, congestion, and bad construction. At that time they also became a favorite means to illustrate both run-down and projected areas of cities. In his eighth French edition of *Urbanisme* in the 1920s, Le Corbusier had used organicist rhetoric in suggesting "surgery" for the "sick" city of Paris.[18] By the postwar years, when aerial photographs had become more readily available, they became a common tool for the planner—the surgeon—to identify problems and treat the city, his patient. As the illustration on the first page of the 1954 article showed, the city was not only seen as an organism with a life cycle that consequently attracted organicist and biologistic analogies,[19] but it was also perceived as a collage of patterns.

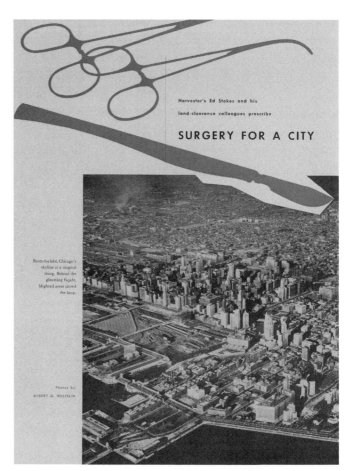

Harvester's Ed Stokes and his land-clearance colleagues prescribe

SURGERY FOR A CITY

From the lake, Chicago's skyline is a magical thing. Behind the gleaming façade, blighted areas crowd the loop.

Photos by
ALBERT G. WESTLIN

FIG. 71. "Surgery for a City," illustrating urban renewal initiatives in Chicago, 1954. ("Harvester's Ed Stokes and His Land-Clearance Colleagues Prescribe Surgery for a City," *Harvester World* [October 1954]: 12–17; Used by permission of CNH America LLC)

The surgeon's scissors could cut out pieces of the city's tissue that were to be replaced by new tissue, or patterns, perceived as the figure grounds of new developments. Little attention was paid to the fact that the excision of two-dimensional patterns representing urban space involved the displacement of the citizens who lived there.

In city planning, the aerial view therefore continued to be both a means of seeing and knowing, and a means of envisioning. In urban redevelopment and renewal, aerial photographs turned out to be especially valuable because most projects for land clearance and redevelopment covered large areas. For this reason and because of aerial photography's efficient provision of information on land characteristics like surface utilities, structural conditions, unknown or legal land uses, fire hazards, and drainage courses, Joseph T. Bill, the executive director of the Sacramento Redevelopment Agency, promoted the use of aerial photography in urban redevelopment in 1951.[20] In the subsequent redevelopment and renewal practice, aerial photographs were also used to visualize urban change. Oblique and vertical aerial

FIG. 72.
Vertical aerial photograph overlaid with new buildings proposed in the urban renewal scheme for Southwest Washington, D.C., 1950s. (Webb & Knapp, Inc., *A Redevelopment Plan for Southwest Washington, D.C.*)

views of parts of cities were often overlaid with lines and colored patches to mark the areas needing treatment (fig. 72). This analysis was followed by renderings inserted into oblique and vertical aerial photographs that showed the envisioned new areas for the city. Aerial views not only provided orientation and regional context, they also offered views into the future.

In the United States, the urban renewal programs made ample use of aerial photography. The identification of declining neighborhoods and substandard housing, one of the first steps in the process, was facilitated by the aerial view. Aerial photography, which had become an indispensable means of warfare during World War II, was now used to "attack" the "ills" of the city, as some urban professionals said at the time.[21] Thus, aerial photography lay at the basis of many of the activities promoted by both military officials and urban professionals for use in peacetime and future warfare. In cities, the disembodied, detached aerial view that supported the holistic and organicist understanding of the city became a tool that readily facilitated and fostered authoritarian planning. As had been discovered in the 1930s (see chapter 2), aerial views also facilitated the identification of illegal behavior.

As an instrument of power, they could be used just as easily for planning and surveillance purposes in the domestic sphere in peacetime as abroad during wartime. Aerial photographs were used to detect building-code and tax violations, fire hazards, trash and water pollution, as well as urban disaster damage resulting from fires, earthquakes, and cyclones, among other things. They were also used to prepare planning measures without letting landowners know; thus the aerial view as a means of authoritarian planning could both veil and unveil the planning process itself and its objects.[22]

As Jennifer Light has shown, in the postwar years officials in the military and urban planning fields collaborated and influenced each other's work. As members of the military-industrial-academic complex, they engaged in the transfer of technology between the fields.[23] The aerial imagination and the view from above as first captured in the aerial photographs of World War I, by reconnaissance and LANDSAT satellites after World War II, and as provided and distributed by computer programs like Google Earth™ since 2005 have played an important role in connecting the military and civilian planning fields throughout the twentieth and twenty-first centuries.

Many of the proponents of the use of aerial photography in planning had a personal background as officers and photo interpreters during the war. One of the first book-length investigations into the use of aerial photography for city planning in the United States in the postwar years was undertaken by the city planner Melville C. Branch, who had trained in the U.S. Navy Air Combat Intelligence School on Rhode Island from 1943 to 1945. Published as a volume in the Harvard City Planning Studies series, Branch's 1948 *Aerial Photography in Urban Planning and Research* promoted the use of aerial photographs by "planning agencies and research organizations engaged in various phases of urban study."[24] Branch pointed out the advantages of aerial photography in providing comprehensive, contextual, and composite views of entire urban regions; in providing ostensive illustrations that could convey an "impression of actuality" for use in professional and public meetings and as a basis for the construction of study models; and in providing demographic and socioeconomic information. He argued, for example, that aerial photographs were the best available means to identify the pattern, function, and interrelationships of open space throughout a city. Aerial photographs in general offered a "view of the urban region as a whole," which he considered "essential for the comprehensive study of the community and the development of a basic program of gradual reorganization."[25] Because of their photographic realism, aerial photographs were more easily understandable for the citizens and could consequently play a significant role in establishing ties with the public and keeping it informed about planning decisions.[26] Although this use made aerial photography appear as a harbinger of community involvement and participation, at the same time Branch promoted it as a convenient, implicitly covert, authoritarian means of insight into the socioeconomic structure of neighborhoods. He drew attention to the fact that "although photographic representation is of the physical corpus and does not reveal economic, sociological, or governmental material directly, a surprising amount of indirect information pertaining to these fields is reflected in the three-dimensional characteristics of the community."[27] Thus, social structure and land values could be deduced from the location, topography, and the building patterns and coverage of parcels. Furthermore, behavioral structures and attitudes could be inferred from aerial photographs that revealed "informal walkways established as shortcuts or as preferable routes" and worn "grass areas used for group games."[28] While these observations could lead to a variety of conclusions, some designers simply suggested that the spontaneous movement patterns and desire lines, or trails, visible in aerial photographs should be used as the basis for path designs.[29]

AERIAL SLUM-SPOTTING

Branch anticipated that socioeconomic data relevant to the urban planning process, including what would a few years later be called urban renewal, could be derived from aerial photo interpretation. He was, in fact, voicing an assumption that attracted sociological research at the time. In France, shortly after World War II, the sociologist Chombart de Lauwe praised aerial photographs as one of the best means to document social processes and social space.[30] In the United States, the air force initiated research into the use of aerial photography for the identification of urban demographics on enemy terrain. Knowledge gained about the urban populations in adversary countries was believed to be helpful for long-range intelligence planning as well as for target selection and analysis in strategic bombing and psychological warfare. For urban sociologists and geographers, aerial photography promised a relatively cheap, easy, and fast means to collect relevant data that could ultimately also be used by urban professionals concerned with the future improvement and design of the urban environment. Like their colleagues in the natural sciences, social scientists appreciated that aerial photography could reveal "the urban area as a total configuration in all its complexity" and that it enabled seeing the "spatial units of the city . . . in their true relationships to each other and to the natural environment."[31] The aerial photographic view of a city, it was pointed out, provided "a 'gestalt' view of urban neighborhoods and their surrounding interrelated areas."[32] Like urban planners and designers, social scientists valued aerial photography because of its flexibility of scales. It could, on the one hand, enable "micro-ecological,"[33] or "microscopic studies of individual blocks within a larger area of transition."[34] On the other hand, aerial photographs also facilitated a more "generalized appraisal[s] of ecological patterning,"[35] such as "the ecological location of a prominent community sub-center, in relation to the total urban configuration."[36]

Having used aerial photographic interpretation for the selection of targets and the appraisal of damage during World War II, the U.S. Department of Defense promoted research into the use of "aerial photography as a means of providing social-psychological, economic, and demographic intelligence" beginning in 1950.[37] Major Norman E. Green, who had served in photographic reconnaissance aviation and interpretation during World War II and later elaborated on this research in his 1955 Ph.D. dissertation at the University of North Carolina, and Lieutenant Robert B. Monier began to research photo interpretation methods for the collection of demographic and sociological information in the early 1950s.[38] Conducted from the Air Force and Training Research Center at the Maxwell Air Force Base in Alabama, and named POP KEY (short for aerial photographic population keys to urban areas), their project tested the reliability of aerial photography as a source of information on housing and population numbers, and density and distribution patterns.[39] The pilot study test site was Birmingham, Alabama. The central question underlying Green and Monier's study and all studies that followed was to what degree physical urban structure that was identifiable by skilled aerial photographic interpretation could lead to reliable demographic and social information. In other words, could the identification of urban physical-spatial features lead to an understanding of the social structure of a city, and would aerial photography as a research method affirm Robert E. Park's 1926 thesis that the "physical" and "social systems" of a city were interrelated? While the sociological literature at the time suggested just that,[40] aerial photography was considered a new method of data collection to substantiate this hypothesis. As in many cases with regard to the urban environment, the aerial view was used to legitimize and confirm accepted notions and opinions rather than to criticize them. The study of aerial photographs of Birmingham correlated with census data, and data collected by ground observation revealed that the population density could indeed be derived from the identification of built structure and that in this southern American city, "'high' and 'low' dwelling-unit density essentially defined the 'ecological' pattern of racial segregation."[41] Further studies that involved a variety of urban centers in the United States led Green to conclude that the physical and social structures of a city were related and that "the aerial photographic method may be adapted as a useful research tool in urban sociology."[42] Although Green and many other social scientists admitted that the unique characteristics of each city challenged the establishment of a universal interpretative key, they argued that photo interpretation was nevertheless a valuable tool to describe urban morphology, test theories of urban growth and structure, measure traffic as a function of land use, plan for civil defense, appraise the risk of home mortgages, locate stores and industrial plants, estimate the public utilities requirements, and analyze fire susceptibility.[43]

One of the consequences of studies like Green and Monier's was that aerial photography came to be considered a scientifically sound tool in identifying derelict residential areas, or, as one author bluntly put it, a tool for "aerial slum-spotting."[44] An urban poverty study published in 1967 by L. Mumbower and J. Donoghue found that poverty indicators identifiable in aerial photography included "structural deterioration, debris, clutter, and sometimes the lack of vegetation . . . , walks, curves, and paved streets." Furthermore, they found that "junk yards, warehouses, and small businesses" were often interspersed in poor neighborhoods and that the lack of parking spaces at apartments was an indicator of public housing projects.[45] Mumbower and Donoghue's study also found that aerial photography confirmed the correlation between urban poverty and residential areas in proximity to central business districts, industry, and major transportation arteries, an observation that attested to their belief in aerial photography as a "unique source of . . . data" that could "facilitate the analysis of a variety of socioeconomic aspects of the city."[46] The researchers touted aerial photography as "unbiased recording of information" that facilitated "the continuing examination of changes in our urban environment."[47] Similarly, the geographer Duane Marble, working at Northwestern University under a NASA grant to explore the potentials of reconnaissance satellites for urban planning, came to the conclusion that aerial photographic interpretation was more accurate in its identification of substandard housing conditions than surveys and observation on the ground.[48] Paradoxically, despite the attention paid by sociologists, geographers, and planners to the substandard living conditions in many cities, in the postwar years the use of the aerial view by planners and researchers on occasion led to their increasing detachment from life and the actual conditions on the ground, both literally and figuratively.

CRITIQUE OF "PLANNING FROM THE AIR"

During the period of urban redevelopment and renewal in the United States, the aerial view became an instrument of authoritarian and capitalist planning, a political potential noticed as early as the 1930s. Already then, aerial photographs were used to select the property that needed to be condemned for the construction of the Triborough Bridge in New York City, and near Manchester, United Kingdom, a housing development was planned and revised from the air.[49] Planning from the air became a common procedure in the United States and in other countries during the postwar years,[50] so much so, in fact, that planners and architects themselves voiced concern and began critical discussions about the new opportunities offered by aerial views. At a 1946 meeting of the Royal Institute of British Architects, the town planner Max Lock contemplated the "danger of going up and taking photographs, and planning schemes from the air for clients who will only be able to appreciate them from the street."[51] In contrast, the architect Rolf Hellberg believed that no architects in their right mind would exclusively plan for the aerial view and that aerial surveys were "only an ancillary to ground survey."[52] In the United States, Melville C. Branch warned that using false-color infrared film to identify low-income, socially depressed areas was justified only as a research effort, and that data collected from aerial photographs needed to be cross-checked by ground survey.[53] More generally, he cautioned that photo interpretation was more difficult without ground observation and knowledge of the local conditions and culture.[54]

Despite these warnings and although many urban renewal planning studies and reports also included individual photographs showing extant conditions on the ground, these, like the aerial photographs used, tended to be of an investigative reporting nature and focused on the urban fabric and form rather than on the livelihoods of the people who lived, or had previously lived, in these areas. Thus, the photographs used for urban renewal projects were often used outside of the context of "social experience,"[55] and they were mostly used in what John Berger has called a "unilinear way," that is, to marshal support for an argument.[56] In the same vein, the social scientists Timothy Ingold and John Urry have more recently pointed out that while it is becoming easier to visit, appreciate, and compare places, even from above, they are "not really known from within."[57]

In contrast to these criticisms, the aerial view captured in aerial photographs was also held up as a tool that promoted flexibility in planning, in both scale and time. Aerial photographs could be enlarged and scaled down, and they could provide both detailed and broad views. Taken at intervals over many years, they offered a historical record of changes in land use, development patterns, and vegetation growth, a capability already pointed out in this context as early as 1909.[58] In this way, they recorded processes in time and space, and they provided a continuity of time and space. The availability of regularly updated photographs could therefore support "continuous master planning," an idea that Branch advanced beginning in the 1950s and elaborated on in the 1970s. Branch promoted planning as a continuous process rather than as a practice that prepared plans for finite developments. He foresaw that the future planning process would depend upon simulations "handled . . . on output-display devices connected with electronic computers and videotape storage"[59] that continuously needed updated information. Branch, who had attempted in 1957 to draw connections between planning and operations research, saw cities as complex systems whose development was open-ended and therefore needed flexible management. Underlying this idea was a holistic and dynamic notion of the city that required comprehensive planning of a physical environment in time: according to Branch, city plans had to "incorporate information and projections for each principal urban element separately, and portray their synthesis into a combined pattern of actions and objectives over time for the best benefit of the city as a whole."[60] Aerial photography was a means to this end because it could be used to update information of vast areas in a short time.

Given the overlap of military and space research with urban planning interests in particular during the years of the Cold War and given Melville Branch's own biography, it becomes understandable that in a new 1971 edition of his book he suggested that city planning offices should be organized and set up like the NASA spaceflight center.[61] Branch had suggested in 1957 that both "planning rooms or military control centers [were] . . . special forms of analogic representation."[62] He had compared systems analysis with the principal mechanisms of operations research, arguing that the studies of the operation of a system used by the military during World War II could also be applied in planning.

Aerial Photography, the Environmental Movement, and Landscape Planning

Landscape planning, also described as environmental, ecological, or natural resources planning, which proliferated in the 1960s as a result of the maturing environmental movement, also relied heavily on the methods and tools developed by the military during the Cold War, in particular on aerial and satellite photography.[63] Peder Anker has compared landscape planners like Ian McHarg to "cabin ecological engineer[s] who managed and surveyed the environment in the same way that NASA's ground controllers in Houston kept a close eye on the cabin ecological circulation of energy and materials within a spaceship."[64] The perspective assumed by the landscape planners who surveyed, analyzed, and drew up plans for entire regions was aerial. As for their urban counterparts, aerial photography turned out to be an indispensable tool for landscape planners, who also relied on philosophical holism to explain their practice.[65] On both sides of the Atlantic beginning in the 1960s, landscape planning was largely based on landscape ecology, which had likewise always used aerial photography and fostered holistic beliefs (see chapter 2).[66] Landscape planners shared landscape ecologists' holistic "approach, . . . attitude [and] . . . state of mind."[67] After all, the latter considered their field not only as a "formal bio-, geo-, and human science"[68] but also as an approach to understanding the environment as "a kind of whole that cannot be really understood from its separate components."[69] Landscape planners were also influenced by the systems theory and cybernetics being used at the time by engineers and computer scientists.[70] Coined and elaborated on first by Norbert Wiener at MIT, cybernetics was understood as an epistemology that sought to explain both machines and human life in terms of abstract communication, control, and feedback systems. While cybernetics and systems theory, as developed beginning in the 1930s by Karl Ludwig von Bertalanffi, implied a holistic, interdisciplinary point of view that sought to construe the general principles of different kinds of systems, they also provided a legitimization for understanding landscape planning as a data-based science. Furthermore, systems theory and cybernetics led landscape planners to experiment with the use of computers for the analysis of geographical data. Aerial photographs played an important role in this, giving insight into the hydrological, geological, infrastructural, and social systems of particular regions. As shown by a 1969 comparative study of sixteen resource analysis methods that was conducted at Harvard University's Graduate School of Design for the Department of the Army New England Division in connection with research into computer application, aerial photo interpretation could provide much of the data needed.[71] Planners like Carl Steinitz at Harvard University showed that data from aerial photographs fed into the computer could help generate visions of future regional landscapes. At the same time, aerial photographs issued by NASA provided a visual rhetoric that testified to the necessity of environmental and natural resources planning in the first place.

Denis Cosgrove has shown how the first photographs of the earth taken by humans on NASA's Apollo missions illustrate the "contested global visions" of the late 1960s that were based on environmentalism on the one hand, and technological progress on the other. The world-famous photographs number AS8–14–2383—entitled "Earthrise"—and number AS17–148–22727 were taken on Apollo missions 8 in 1968 and 17 in 1972. Their viewpoints from lunar orbit made the earth appear both sublime and vulnerable, a perception furthered by some of the astronauts' comments: William Anders referred to the earth seen from space as a "fragile Christmas-tree ball which we should handle with considerable care."[72] As Cosgrove and other authors have therefore argued, these images as well as aerial photographs in general helped the environmental movement to make its case.[73] Photograph number 22727, which shows the illuminated sphere of the entire earth floating in dark space, has been widely reproduced on postcards, calendars, political manifestos, and commercial advertisements ever since it was taken.[74] It was reproduced on the Earth Flag created for the first Earth Day held on April 22, 1970. In contrast to "Earthrise," which was seen in 1968 as figuratively illustrating "dawn"[75]—a new horizon of human technological progress—photo 22727 became an icon and a symbol of the environmental movement that set out to rescue a "doomed" earth.[76]

If these photographs from outer space encouraged a detached, disengaged global consciousness at the expense of actual local engagement and awareness, as various authors have argued,[77] aerial photographs taken from lesser heights could translate this consciousness to the regional and local levels by directly pinpointing what environmentalists and environmental organizations considered "environmental sin." For example, in 1960 the Sierra Club used William Garnett's aerial photographs of the monotonous suburban pattern of the Los Angeles suburb Lakeside to illustrate the "hell we are building here on earth."[78] These aerial photographs, which had originally been taken in 1950 to illustrate the progress of industrialized housing, showed the track patterns of bulldozers, the houses in an unfinished state of assembly, and, finally, the earth covered with seemingly never-ending rows of recently constructed tract houses. The photographs were reproduced in a number of books in the 1960s that criticized the depletion and destruction of the land and soon became iconic.[79] With the aerial view in mind, the Danish landscape architect C. Th. Sørensen criticized a similar phenomenon in Europe, commenting in 1966 on the monotonous impression that a district of single-family homes produced no matter whether one walked through or flew over it. The Scottish-born landscape architect and city planner Ian McHarg used aerial photographs in particular to illustrate "the plight" of cities and land use in his 1969 book *Design with Nature*.[80] He insisted that only the view from an airplane could properly reveal the human land-use pattern and humankind's impact on the earth. For McHarg, aerial photography rather than maps offered the true face of the land, an observation that may also have been grounded in his experience as a parachutist for the British army during World War II.

In his book, which quickly became a best seller and has since its publication strongly influenced the planning and design fields, McHarg also used several NASA photographs that showed the earth from outer space, including photo 22727. On the back of the dust jacket, it illustrated the book's and its author's environmentalist bent. The book's intent was to make the planning professions more aware of the environment and to give examples of how planning could be linked to the ecology of the land. McHarg bemoaned the absence of natural scientists in planning and saw in their inclusion an opportunity to improve both human and planetary health. After all, McHarg argued, while the astronaut depended on the space capsule for his survival, humankind's primary capsule was the earth, which therefore deserved special attention. Ecological planning of the land on earth seemed to McHarg a more worthy objective than the conquest of space. However, as McHarg himself noted, the research conducted into space ecology at the time influenced his ideas. Like the space cabins and colonies that were designed and envisioned in the 1960s as artificial closed ecosystems, McHarg and his collaborators based their projects on the understanding of the earth as a similarly manageable ecosystem.[81]

McHarg wanted to sustain "nature as a source of life, whole milieu, teacher, sanctum, and challenge."[82] In a quasi-religious tone, he criticized humankind—"man"—for its insensitive and wasteful treatment of the earth and its resources. To counter this development, McHarg argued, humankind had to both "become the steward of the biosphere" and "design with nature."[83] Designing with nature meant creatively "fitting" together land uses with their proper locations in such a way that the human impact on the earth would be minimized while human desires and needs were satisfied. Thus, landscape architects designing with nature had to be "conservationists by instinct, . . . who care not only to preserve but to create and manage."[84]

In *Design with Nature* and numerous publications preceding and succeeding the book, McHarg explained and illustrated how he thought this could be achieved. The "ecological method" was his solution to the problems that humankind was facing on earth, including the increase of population with its consequences of urban and suburban growth, pollution, and the accommodation of new technologies like atomic energy. McHarg believed that ecology provided the "single indispensible basis for landscape architecture and regional planning."[85] This authoritarian, dogmatic, and exclusionary view led McHarg to value only nature and natural processes as "formgivers" in landscape architecture, and to condemn many of the masterworks of Western landscape architectural history. His ideology therefore not only reinforced but also reestablished the role the natural sciences played in landscape architecture and planning.[86] Although McHarg, who had been taught at Harvard University under Walter Gropius, claimed that the use of ecology would integrate the sciences, humanities, and the arts, his work ultimately "contributed to a culture of scientific technocracy among environmentalists . . . at the expense of humanism."[87] His message to focus projects on ecology in many cases led to the neglect of cultural, aesthetic, and social issues.[88] In McHarg's work, ecosystems became a conceptual and managerial tool.[89]

Central to his "ecological method" was the inventory and analysis of biotic and abiotic systems that was carried out with the help of satellite and aerial photography in combination with field research on the ground. The aerial perspective, including the high-altitude view of the astronaut floating in outer space, not only revealed how polluted and exploited the earth was, but it played an important role in understanding the ecology of entire regions. Offering a holistic view, it both illustrated the decay and alarming state of the earth and provided an agent for improving upon this situation. By drawing attention and awareness to the larger context of and the relationship between ecosystems, the aerial view was thought to play an active role in remediating the negative consequences of human behavior. The importance attributed at the time to the aerial view in general, and to remote sensing in particular, was also revealed in McHarg's attempt in 1966 to hire a specialist in computation and remotely sensed imagery at the University of Pennsylvania, as well as a biometeorologist, a geologist, a hydrologist, a soils scientist, and plant and animal ecologists. McHarg, who had built the Department of Landscape Architecture at the University of Pennsylvania beginning in 1954, anticipated that these expert faculty from the natural sciences would become the core of a new Department of Regional Landscape Planning. This department was in turn to form a bridge between the natural scientists and the social scientists in the existing Departments of Regional Science and City Planning, which were mainly focused on economic aspects of urban and regional development.[90]

Although only part of the project could be realized due to lack of funding, during the 1960s in the United States, air photo interpretation became standard in every regional planning project. McHarg used aerial photos as aids for his "ecological inventories" and the description of "natural processes" that formed the basis for his regional landscape plans.

His idea for ecological inventories was based on research that had been conducted by his colleague Philip H. Lewis at the Universities of Illinois and Wisconsin.[91] Lewis used aerial photography to identify "natural and cultural [resource] patterns"[92] of a particular region, in particular its unique scenic, geological, ecological, and historical landscape features.[93] Beginning in the 1950s and throughout his career, Lewis developed the "regional design process," describing it as "total environmental design"[94] and "a holistic approach to design and planning for sustainable land use."[95] He and his followers considered aerial photography "one of the best hopes for efficient data collection."[96] In the 1960s, he also hoped for what today has become a reality in the form of Geographical Information Systems (GIS), "a sensor system placed in a stationary satellite [that provides] not only current data but, linked to a regional computer graphic system, offer[s] new and changing patterns as they evolve."[97]

The aerial view supported McHarg's and Lewis's holistic worldview, and aerial photographs provided the tools for their scientific analysis. Like many other landscape planners at the time, McHarg and Lewis believed that landscape was "a pattern of ecosystems which are investigated at those levels of differentiation which facilitate an understanding of the processes and products of ecosystem behavior as a 'whole' within a hierarchical series of wholes."[98] Believing in creative evolution, a holistic theory developed by biologists and philosophers at the turn of the century as a reaction against mechanistic analysis, McHarg saw the world as a "single super-organism" and as "the sum of the yearnings of all life in all time."[99] Like many landscape ecologists, landscape planners considered ecosystems "a geographic totality"[100] and "a whole which is greater than the sum of its parts."[101] They considered "landscape as a holistic entity, made up of different elements all influencing each other."[102] The aerial view was an excellent means to investigate this "landscape totality"[103] and distinguish and identify the landscape ecological patterns and mosaics.

McHarg and Lewis combined the holistic view of landscape with a modern positivist assumption that science would provide answers and solutions to world problems. Their colleague Garrett Eckbo described landscape planners' environmental design concepts as "based upon comprehensive ecological and behavioral analysis" and coming "equally from reason and intuition, analysis and inspiration, intellect and imagination."[104] McHarg's and Lewis's plans were, however, heavily based upon ecosystem analysis. They used what they considered an analytical approach based on science, and believed that ecology and "natural patterns," as discovered in aerial photography, should be the "form determinants" of development in rural and urban areas.[105] Their ecological approach was akin to the regionalist planning tradition in the early twentieth century promoted by Benton MacKaye, Clarence Stein, and Lewis Mumford. In contrast to the "metropolitanist" approach to regional planning, the regionalists supported planned dispersed settlements in an open and green environment that were connected by regional transportation and utilities networks.[106] At the same time, however, McHarg's and Lewis's planning approaches sought to accommodate both urbanists and environmentalists by strengthening regional centers and limiting growth at the edge. Lewis proposed that ecological inventories be produced for 45-mile belts around each metropolitan region. He argued that the landscape patterns could serve as urban form determinants and proposed that "environmental corridors" could be left in a natural state and that natural drainage systems be protected rather than replaced with concrete systems.[107] On the scale of entire states, Lewis proposed the determination of what he called "environmental corridors," land reserved for recreational open space and environmental planning.[108]

McHarg and Lewis both worked with the overlay method, also called "layer-cake representation" by McHarg, which produced composite maps. Each inventoried factor like topography, hydrology, plant associations, and historic sites was rated using a range of values that were represented in different tones of one color on a transparent film that could be placed over a base map. The darker the tone used in the factor's representation, the higher its value. In the composite map, areas suitable to development would appear as lighter tones. The areas least suitable to development would appear as the darkest tones on the map. As their colleague Angus Hills observed, after having acted as an "'evaluator' of normative values of various kinds: social, economic, aesthetic, juridical, etc.," the landscape planner "creatively incorporate[d] these values into the landscape plan."[109]

The analytical overlay method based on both empirical data sets for landscape evaluation and on a holistic worldview was neither new nor unproblematic. Cultural issues in particular were often too complex for adequate mapping. Furthermore, although the method was hailed as an objective procedure, it is, of course, well known that any kind of map is an interpretation and a subjective compilation and representation of information. Rather than providing a suitable means to present what the authors considered dynamic natural processes, maps were also a static medium that "froze" conditions in time. In landscape architecture, a resource pattern analysis and subsequent environmental system overlay had already been practiced in early landscape and regional plans, for example, by the landscape architects Charles Eliot and Warren Manning, and by the committee for *The Regional Plan of New York and Its Environs*.[110]

However, the breadth and combination of issues that the overlay method addressed was unprecedented. Like aerial photographs that lay at the base and heart of the overlay method, the maps it produced made patterns and relationships among them visible.[111] As Lewis showed in an early 1961 study of Illinois, the method could also be used for historical land-use and ecological analyses. The study showed the impact that the establishment of two thousand sawmills had had on vegetation patterns between 1812 and 1960. Lewis revealed that the "timber pattern had been reduced to a linear system, following most of the flood plains where the ground is too wet to get it to cut, or, situated in larger areas in the national forests."[112] In response to the observation that most historical and archaeological sites as well as most state parks were located within these linear corridors, Lewis proposed that the corridors be protected and reserved for recreational purposes. The different resource patterns that Lewis identified in his work also included cultural factors connected to different ethnicities—their foods, dress, handicrafts, festivals, and architecture—and what he called "visual landscape personalities," areas characterized by specific landscape features.[113]

The identification of landscape patterns and their use in land-use development was the specialty of Douglas Way at Harvard University's Landscape Architecture Department in the late 1960s and early 1970s. Aerial photographs and remote sensing lay at the basis of his work. Way led the way at a time when it was still difficult to find the appropriate sources for aerial photography. In 1968, he produced a manual for the identification of specific landforms in aerial photographs. He considered the different visual qualities of vegetation and land use, topography, erosion gullies, and drainage patterns to be signifiers for different landform types. To facilitate air photo interpretation, Way used line drawings that showed in abstraction the drainage patterns seen on air photographs. The abstracted line drawings described and represented in image the drainage patterns defined by terms like "deranged," "annular," "barbed," and "pinnate." Way's "terrain analysis" with the help of stereoscopic aerial photographs could not only provide an economic means for land planning by saving time, but it could also easily record "ecologically related landscape elements."[114] For Way, landforms therefore were "terrain features formed by natural processes" that could be defined and recognized on the basis of their physical and visual characteristics seen from the air. Environmentally sensitive and conscious site development was considered to be possible and effective only with the help of aerial photographic interpretation of land patterns and additional field surveys. When satellite imagery became more readily available after the launching of the first LANDSAT satellite by the United States in 1972, Way also began to employ remote sensing to facilitate the identification of geological and geomorphological patterns on larger scales. LANDSAT was able to provide almost instantaneous images of areas measuring 115 square miles and therefore provided a quicker, cheaper, and more effective substitute for photo mosaics.[115]

The use that McHarg, Lewis, Way, and other landscape planners made of aerial photography in their work built upon the way it had first been used in geography, forestry, and (landscape) ecology. It supported a holistic approach to landscape planning and contributed to strengthening the region as a basic planning unit. The region had already played an important role as a spatial-temporal unit in early ecology in general and in landscape ecology in particular.[116] As in landscape planning, the region has remained the preferred study unit in landscape ecology. After Troll argued that aerial photography had led to the "natural regionalisation of the earth,"[117] his Dutch colleague I. S. Zonneveld pointed out in 1972 that landscape ecologists studied land as "a holistic entity" and as "the total character of a region."[118] More recently, Richard Forman has suggested that "landscape ecology focuses on analyzing and understanding land mosaics, large heterogeneous areas with important natural systems viewed at the human scale, such as landscapes, regions, or the area seen from an airplane window or in an aerial photograph."[119] Similarly landscape planners, following Patrick Geddes, understood a region to be a natural drainage basin or a continuously urbanized (metropolitan) area.[120] Thus, landscape was seen as a "regional matter,"[121] as the whole of a land surface formed by "natural forces and human activities,"[122] including farming and settlement patterns. Landscape planning, it was believed, could "establish reciprocal harmonious relations between the conservation of the good things which exist and the designed development of good things we never knew we could have."[123] The landscape planning promoted by McHarg, Lewis, and Way in the twentieth century had been pioneered in the late nineteenth century by the landscape architects Frederick Law Olmsted, Calvert Vaux, and Charles Eliot when they lobbied for and finally carried out the municipal and metropolitan park system plans for Boston. These plans set the stage for others to follow. In 1901, the eminent *McMillan Plan* for Washington and in 1909 the *Plan of Chicago* also included metropolitan park system plans. Although these plans show that initiatives for regional planning predate powered flight, aerial views and the aerial imagination were already important prerequisites, as described in chapter 2. Aerial photographs further facilitated the identification of landscape patterns and the development of landscape planning based on a regional scientific analysis.

The Aerial View as Magnifying Lens

While the aerial view supported a new spatial imagination based on the unit of the region, it also enabled—and in certain situations even required—switching flexibly between scales. This had already become apparent at one of the first public exhibitions of a large photo mosaic map in the United States in 1935. The map, which had been recommended by the Connecticut governor Wilbur L. Cross as a planning tool a couple of years earlier, illustrated the state of Connecticut and was described in a press release by the Fairchild Aviation Corporation as the "world's largest photographic wall map." It measured 18 by 13 feet (approx. 5.5 by 4 meters), covering 234 square feet (21.7 square meters) on a wall of the Hartford Armory, the venue of the State of Connecticut Tercentenary Industrial Exhibition. Showing minute details of the 5,004 miles of state territory, the map was so large—or, one could say, the extensive area of the entire state was depicted so small—that it could be viewed "most effectively only through field glasses" (fig. 73). Spectators were advised to study the mosaic "by means of field glasses, which will slightly magnify the detail,"[124] an activity that incidentally simulated the experience of early-twentieth-century surveyors. Large-scale aerial mosaic maps both made extensive stretches of terrain appear as abstract patterns, or ornamental "mosaics," and provided sufficient detail for onlookers to identify particular landscape elements. The detail and high resolution typically offered by aerial mosaic maps would have aroused the curiosity of the spectators and drawn their gaze into the fictitious depth of the image. The advice to use field glasses to zoom in on details of the Connecticut map likely further amplified the natural movement of the exhibition visitors, who, viewing the map by moving toward and away from it, would have zoomed in and out to grasp details and put them into context.

Aerial photographs could be used as a magnifying lens in a double sense. On the one hand, they magnified and enlarged the field of vision, thus offering a broader outlook onto the land of an entire region. On the other hand,

FIG. 73. Looking at the aerial mosaic of the state of Connecticut through binoculars, 1935. (Box 3, record group 56, Connecticut Tercentenary Commission, State Archives, Connecticut State Library)

they also offered such a precise and detailed representation of the earth's surface that new knowledge concerning individual landscape features could be gleaned from them. In 1948, the French sociologist Paul Henry Chombart de Lauwe pointed out how, among scientific discoveries, aerial observation was situated in direct contrast to the microscopic view. Humankind at the time seemed to be "attracted to the atom and the galaxy, towards the infinitely small and the infinitely big," he posited.[125] But the aerial view and the shifting between scales not only benefited the natural and social sciences; it also inspired designers and artists. In fact, Gutkind's belief that the aerial view could provide both rational knowledge and creative potential, that it could "reconcile" art and science as well as the different scales with which humankind was confronted in the modern world, led to a number of responses from artists and designers involved in shaping the environment. Switching flexibly between scales was, of course, fundamental in design practice so that the appeal of aerial photography to designers and the professional opportunities it created for them were only logical. However, the perception of the aerial view as a magnifying lens was equally important because of its philosophical implications. The aerial view could place humankind into perspective, and it could mediate between the two spheres that are so important to human life and culture: art and science. The use of aerial photography and the view from above in both art and science appealed to design practitioners, who themselves sought to straddle these different and seemingly opposing spheres.

In 1951, the Hungarian-born painter and designer Gyorgy Kepes curated an exhibition at MIT entitled *The New Landscape*. Kepes's "new landscape" was in part what Sylvia Crowe a few years later began to call "the landscape of power": the industrial and technical landscape characterized by power pylons, telegraph poles, factory chimneys, and television antennas (see chapter 4).[126] Kepes wanted his audience to better understand the visible forms of new technology and of new scientific accomplishments, so that they might inspire new artistic expression. He argued for the reconciliation of the arts and sciences. After all, he pointed out, "history" had shown "that these two creative human activities are interdependent."[127] The new landscape was a balanced landscape that included technology.[128] To develop a figurative and literal new landscape, artists, architects, and designers needed a "new vision" that Kepes saw realized through the optical techniques offered by the telescope and the microscope and by the new perspectives provided by airplanes and rockets. By reducing distance and increasing size, these instruments and vehicles offered vertical views in "new orders of magnitudes."[129]

Like the exhibition, Kepes's homonymous book, begun in 1947, completed five years later, and finally published in 1956, mainly consisted of pictures that showed aerial, telescopic, and microscopic views that were taken by artists and by scientists for scientific research purposes. Among the exhibition's photographs were aerial and telescopic photos showing driving patterns in a ploughed field, strip cropping and contour cultivation, a nebula, the moon, the Alaskan coastline, and the ocean. The photomicrographs on show included depictions of part of a deer tongue, stamina hairs of plants, slime mold, blood vessels, and the dendritic structure of white cast iron. Kepes had inherited his interest in and infatuation with the patterns and forms of both the natural and the technical world from his mentor, László Moholy-Nagy, who had published *Von Material zu Architektur* in 1929, translated into English as *The New Vision* in 1938. In fact, as the English titles suggest, Kepes's book *The New Landscape* can be read as a sequel to Moholy-Nagy's *The New Vision* and his subsequent 1947 book *Vision in Motion*. It also recalls an attempt ten years earlier by the nationalist German author Hans Ludwig Oeser to use microscopic and telescopic photographs to "grasp a little more of the layout and structure of this world."[130] Oeser, who also produced photo books that served Nazi ideology, was inspired by the new opportunities offered by photography and its application in scientific research. He argued that each photograph and its relationship to other photographs was a piece in the puzzle of the world. Photography could render the small big, and the big small.[131] He posited that the visually perceptible world together with the part of the world that was imperceptible to humankind formed a whole. Humankind was positioned in between the big and the small, and Oeser laid out his teleological belief by arguing that while humankind was using and attempting to dominate nature, nature was probably using humankind.

While Oeser had described aerial, telescopic, and microscopic photographs as beautiful on account of their depiction of nature,[132] Moholy-Nagy's and Kepes's work elevated scientific microscopic and aerial photographs to art by revealing their abstract qualities and patterns and by presenting them as a disembodied and detached "new vision." Whereas throughout the second half of the nineteenth century photographs for scientific purposes, so-called "mechanical photography," had still been considered as standing in contrast to "aesthetic photography" and artistic production as a whole,[133] Moholy-Nagy's and Kepes's presentations had finally rendered them into artworks.

The ability to zoom in and out, to visualize details in microscopic views, as well as to show these details in their context fascinated artists, scientists, and design professionals alike. In 1968, the year before the astronauts Neil Armstrong and Edwin Aldrin planted the American flag on the moon, the audience of a short film by Charles and Ray Eames was taken on virtual rides into space and into the human body. Inspired by the Dutch author Kees Boeke's 1957 book *Cosmic View: The Universe in 40 Jumps*, the American designers produced *A Rough Sketch for a Proposed Film Dealing with the Powers of Ten and the Relative Size of Things in the Universe*. This first version of what would ultimately become their film *Powers of Ten* lasted eight minutes and was made for the Commission on College Physics with the goal of appealing to both a ten-year-old and a physicist. Building upon microscopic and telescopic images produced by scientific research, like Moholy-Nagy's and Kepes's work, Eames's film bridged art and science. Camera zooms take the viewer on a journey along a straight vertical line from a man sleeping on a golf course in Miami into space beyond the Milky Way, and back again into the man's body, into his cells, and into the carbon atom of his DNA. Zooming out, every ten film seconds the viewpoint onto the sleeping man becomes ten times farther distant. Moving inward into the hand of the sleeping man, every ten seconds the images show a magnification of ten. This information in addition to the total distance traveled, the traveler's time, the earth time, and the percentage of the speed of light is given by numbers that appear on a dashboard on the screen and by the monotone female voice of the narrator. As one of the contemporary critics of the film commented, the information provided could not be grasped in one viewing alone, and the fantastical "inter-stellar roller-coaster ride of Powers of Ten" overwhelmed the viewers' mental and emotional capabilities.[134]

The film and a second version that came out in 1977 were well received and were used by professors from a variety of fields, including psychology, medicine, and astronomy, in their classes. In addition to the imagery itself, which included new maps of galactic clusters and the Milky Way—the products of large-format aerial and satellite photography and of optical electron scanning and transmission microscopy—these specialists appreciated the film's placement of humanity within the universe. Although the entire film conveyed an anthropocentric and geocentric view in that it was centered on a man lying in the grass and consisted of zooming out from and back into this human subject, at the same time the aerial and microscopic views also distanced the viewer from it and placed humanity into a cosmic order. The film was a disembodied view of and finally also into the human body. It showed what the progress of modern science had demonstrated by that time: to use Hannah Arendt's words, it showed "to what an extent this . . . universe, the infinitely small no less than the infinitely large, escapes not only the coarseness of human sense perception but even the enormously ingenious instruments that have been built for its refinement."[135] As the MIT psychology professor Stephan L. Chorover noted in response to the 1977 version of *The Powers of Ten*, paraphrasing the lyrics of the Beatles' song "Within You Without You" from the band's 1967 album *Sgt. Pepper*, the film reminded one that "the universe goes on within you and without you."[136]

As much as *The Powers of Ten* encouraged humility and the environmentalist spirit, it was also a product of the progressive spirit of its time, using the latest telescopic and microscopic photography available. It therefore merged what Denis Cosgrove has called the "contested global visions" of the late 1960s that were based on environmentalism on the one hand, and technological progress on the other. In two different ways, therefore, "the downview" expanded "head-on evidence," as Arthur Drexler, the Museum of Modern Art's director of architecture and design, put it in 1964.[137]

The Landscapes of "Aerial Art"

In 1966, Robert Smithson developed what would become a key project in the nascent earth art movement.[138] His artwork not only counted on aerial vision but was also created for an airport site.[139] Smithson described it as "aerial art," "a total engagement with the building process from the ground up and from the sky down."[140] The project grew out of Smithson's consultation on the preliminary studies and concept plans for Dallas–Fort Worth Airport undertaken by the Manhattan-based architectural and engineering firm Tippetts-Abbett-McCarthy-Stratton. The airport project provided Smithson with a new scale and a new perspective and led him to what he in 1969 called the "earth project situation."[141] It also confronted him with the airport as "created world . . . without tradition" and an "artificial landscape without cultural precedent,"[142] a situation that had already been observed by landscape architects in the early twentieth century and again in the postwar years when the use of many abandoned military airfields had to be determined (see chapter 4). The Dallas–Fort Worth Airport not only inspired Smithson to experiment with large sites, physical (earth) masses, and the aerial perspective, but he also involved his artist colleagues Carl Andre, Sol LeWitt, and Robert Morris, providing them literally with a first experimentation ground for works made directly on and in the earth.[143] In 1969, another colleague, Dennis Oppenheim, posited: "I'm to the point now where I see the earth as sculpture—where flying over the earth is like viewing existing painted areas or pictorial, painterly surfaces."[144]

Smithson's aerial art is important in the context of this book because the earth art movement it inspired has been important for landscape architectural practice ever since.[145] Earthworks and their wide distribution in aerial photographs and film contributed to landscape architects reconnecting aesthetic and ecological concerns in their practice. Engaging with a variety of outdoor sites, many earthworks artists created aesthetically appealing works. While many of these were statements against the traditional workings of the art market and the division between subject and object as well as art object and art connoisseur that still dominated the art world, they were also driven by the artists' concerns about environmental destruction and humankind's relationship with the earth.

Under the influence of the earthworks created by artists in the United States and Europe in the 1960s and 1970s, landscape architects began to explore how human perception and knowledge of actual site conditions and existing ecological processes could inform design. In the 1980s, landscape architects like George Hargreaves, Michael Van Valkenburgh, and Richard Haag no longer concentrated either on visual artistic expression as heralded in the United States by Peter Walker or on ecological issues as promoted by Ian McHarg in his conceptualization of regional landscape planning. Instead they strove to bridge these two design approaches by observing and analyzing the site conditions to create aesthetically interesting designs for places in which people would be both exposed and reconnected to the natural elements, the ecological processes, and other characteristics of the site. The aerial view became instrumental in establishing this new paradigm in landscape architectural practice because it could both promote the artistic approach by exposing intricate ground patterns and sustain ecological thinking by showing environmental context. Although environmental art and landscape architecture developed a strong emphasis on the phenomenological qualities of their works by paying attention to bodily movement through the site on ground level, the aerial view was considered a necessary means of analyzing and knowing the cultural and the natural worlds in the first place.

When Smithson was introduced to the site and plans of Dallas–Fort Worth Regional Airport, he was fascinated with the extent of the new airport's runways, which, as he pointed out, spanned the length of New York City's Central Park. Smithson's ideas for the airport that he developed between 1966 and 1967 revolved around works intended to be viewed from above from landing and departing airplanes. For him, "aerial photography

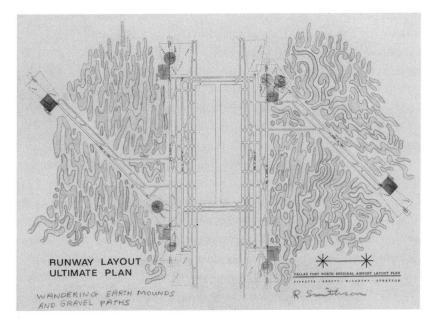

and air transportation [brought] into view the surface features," and "the
world seen from the air [was] abstract and illusive."[146] The new "aerial art"
inspired by the aerial view, the idiosyncratic site conditions, and individual
site perceptions replaced the "naturalism of seventeenth-, eighteenth- and
nineteenth-century art." In "aerial art," Smithson contended, "the landscape
beg[an] to look more like a three dimensional map rather than a rustic garden."[147] While he developed a number of different sculptural interventions
for the areas in between and surrounding the runways, they were all designed for the aerial view, and none required verticality. Through his and
his fellow artists' projects, Smithson strove to "define the limits of the air
terminal site in a new way" and to "set a precedent and create an original
approach to the esthetics of airport landscaping."[148] Among Smithson's own
ideas were large, shallow horizontal glass-covered boxes embedded in the
earth and containing rows of "yellow fog lights," patterns of large square
asphalt pavements and a web of white gravel paths. His last design proposal,
Aerial Map, was for a vast spiral consisting of triangular concrete panels laid
out on the ground so that it could be seen in its entirety only from the air.
While this work can be read as a forerunner of his *Spiral Jetty* in Utah's Great
Salt Lake (1970), more influential for later landscape architectural practice
was his proposal for *Wandering Earth Mounds and Gravel Paths* (1967; fig. 74).
In this design, a pattern of low amoeba-shaped earth mounds covered the
clear-zones and surrounded the runways.[149]

Given the vastness of the airport site and the new medium and perspective with which he was working, Smithson's preoccupation with scale only

appears logical. The potential to see the airport site from the airplane at various heights and the telescoping and contextualizing effect this could have drew his attention to the relativity of human life and its insignificant position in the universe on the one hand and to the actual environmental and ecological conditions of the site on the other. Again the aerial perspective had the effect of broadening the view and providing context while at the same time focusing the view on the object itself. The airport project led Smithson to consider the task at hand in a holistic way and inspired him to explore the relationships between things and between objects and their environment. "This airport is but a dot in the vast infinity of universes," he wrote; "[it is] an imperceptible point in a cosmic immensity, a speck in an impenetrable nowhere," and he pointed out that "aerial art reflect[ed] to a degree this vastness."[150] The aerial perspective was a way for Smithson to explore not only new spatial but also new temporal scales. Similar to the *Powers of Ten,* the film Smithson produced to accompany his 1970 work *Spiral Jetty* placed humankind into a geological time frame and a universal perspective. The last part of the film showed aerial shots from a helicopter circling the spiral, which, after having shown the artwork in its entirety, zoomed onto the spiral path and finally up to the individual salt crystals. When Gyorgy Kepes invited Smithson to contribute to his 1972 book *Arts of the Environment,* Smithson included stills of the film throughout his essay on the *Spiral Jetty.* Like the film, the essay therefore moves from more extensive vertical aerial and horizontal ground shots to microphotographs of salt crystals that form the jetty's material. Aerial, and in the case of the *Spiral Jetty,* microscopic, photographs became an indispensable means of documentation, exposure, and distribution of the earthworks that, like the *Spiral Jetty,* were often located in remote or even inaccessible places and would therefore only rarely be seen directly by visitors.[151]

Kepes, who in 1967 had founded the Center for Advanced Visual Studies at MIT to forge fruitful connections between art and science and to further public environmental awareness and ecological consciousness through art, had become aware of Smithson's work some years before. The artists shared an affinity for abstraction furthered by micro- and telescopic aerial views and to environmental art, but they disagreed on the functions this art should fulfill, giving voice to the varying degrees and shades of environmentalism summed up by Cosgrove as "contested global visions." As an acute observer of the deteriorating environmental conditions, Kepes wanted artists to become environmentalists who would use their skills for such projects as developing publicly accessible water-purification plants that had aesthetic and experiential potential in addition to their obvious functions.[152] Smithson, in contrast, criticized the use of art for the celebration of technology as a "sad parody of NASA." He did not share Kepes's ordered, organic worldview and was more interested in environmental entropy—the popular notion of irreversible disorder, uncertainty, and decay in environmental systems. When Kepes invited Smithson to participate in the group show representing the United States at the 1969 São Paulo Biennial, Smithson was among the artists who pulled out of the show to protest the Vietnam War and the political repression and censorship of the arts in Brazil. However, another reason to recall his participation was Kepes's group effort for the Biennial, which Smithson deprecatingly likened to the "crewcut teamwork" of "NASA's Mission Operations Control Room."[153] Despite his different approach to environmental art, Smithson later argued along Kepes's lines that art could "mediate . . . between the ecologist and the industrialist" by developing projects for the remediation and recycling of polluted water and land.[154] Smithson's projects for the recycling and remediation of mining areas as well as the aesthetics of his and other artists' earthworks have inspired many landscape architects since the 1980s.[155]

Although the aerial view could facilitate physical and mental detachment from life on earth, in the case of many of Smithson's and other environmental artists' works, it attracted attention to life on earth instead. In fact, aerial vision was used by many artists to gain access to the "hidden" qualities of the site. The locations of many earthworks were found and determined from the air.[156] However, while their physical extent was most easily perceived from the air, in many cases, their creation was as much if not more inspired by the immediate physical qualities and phenomenological observations found on the ground. As Robert Irwin explained, most earthworks were "site specific," which means that they were "conceived with the site in mind," or they were "site conditioned/determined" and depended on the qualities of the site.[157] Like Smithson when working on his airport project, many earth artists developed their work "from the ground up and from the sky down." They used form "to focus attention on a place and its particular qualities—its ancient natural histories, its deep time, its recurring natural cycles and processes."[158] Landscape architects in the 1980s were attracted by the interesting and appealing graphical patterns that earthworks provided to the aerial viewer, by the earthworks' environmentalist motivation, their acknowledgment of landscape transformation and change, and their potential to appeal to human affect, empathy, and sensual perception and physical immersion on the ground. Furthermore, the synthetic method of working from the ground up while not losing sight of the site's larger implications provided landscape architects with an alternative to the comprehensive landscape analysis conducted for entire regions that was largely based on map and aerial photographic analysis and interpretation. Inspired by some of the early earthworks, therefore, landscape architects attempted to create places that forged meaningful relationships between people and their natural and cultural environment by incorporating and emphasizing the natural and cultural processes germane to the site.

Although many landscape architects including Laurie Olin, Richard Haag, and Michael Van Valkenburgh were inspired by earth art to merge environmental and aesthetic concerns, Hargreaves Associates' design for Byxbee Park provides one of the more explicit examples of the many direct and indirect connections between both landscape architecture and earthworks, and landscape architecture and the aerial view.[159] Hargreaves Associates, in collaboration with the environmental artists Peter Richards and Michael Oppenheimer, created Byxbee Park in Palo Alto in the 1980s to remediate a former landfill and accommodate the recreational interests of local joggers, walkers, and bird-watchers. The park covers 45 acres (18.2 hectares) of a former landfill and is located adjacent to a tidal creek, a sewage treatment plant, and an active landfill on the South Shore of San Francisco Bay. It is surrounded by remnants of marshland crossed by high-voltage transmission lines and lies underneath the flight path of small planes that land and take off at Palo Alto's municipal airport located northwest of the park. To turn the landfill into publicly accessible parkland, it had to be capped with one foot of impenetrable clay and covered with two feet of earth. To protect the cap and prevent toxic substances from leaching into the bay, the designers had to create a park without trees and artificial irrigation. They adopted a sculptural approach that was generated by the site's environmental conditions including wind, its shallow soil, its land-use history, and by the aerial view. While ground modeling and all sculptural interventions like the 30-foot-high installation *Wind Wave Piece* and the field of regularly spaced wooden telephone poles provide interesting and captivating phenomenological experiences on the ground, some were also designed for the aerial view. Thus, a row of standard precast concrete highway barriers is positioned in such a way on one of the slopes underneath the flight path to Palo Alto Airport to form the aeronautical symbol typically found on the blast pads at the beginning of airport runways (fig. 75). On the ground, the concrete barriers slow down runoff, diminishing the amount of polluted water running into the bay and creating humid micro biotopes. Other processes on the site are made visible by a flame that burns the methane gas produced by the disintegration of the fill underground and by its underlying bed of white gravel. The keyhole shape of the bed of white gravel is only perceptible from the air.[160] Its orientation takes into account the main direction of airplanes coming in to land at the Palo Alto Airport. Although it seems unlikely that pilots unaware of the history of the land they are traversing will easily grasp the subtle visual metaphor suggesting that they are peering through a keyhole into the underground of decomposing trash, the keyhole, like the concrete barriers, provides pilots with a distinct landmark for orientation.[161]

The role of the aerial view in the development and dissemination of earth art and its subsequent use for design inspiration in landscape architecture speaks less to the use of the aerial view as a means of power, dominion, control, and surveillance than to its capacity to evoke awe and humility, and to its use by the environmentally conscious to appeal to human affect and empathy. From the time that aerial photography became more available to architects and landscape architects in the 1930s, it has therefore not only furthered a detached and disembodied view onto the earth, but it has also invited criticism of this same view and has induced a renewed focus on the phenomenological qualities of our immediate living environment as they are perceived through the body on the ground. In the 1960s, Maurice Merleau-Ponty criticized "high-altitude thinking"[162] and "scientific thinking, a thinking which looks on from above" and suggested that it "must return . . . to the site, the soil of the sensible and opened world such as it is in our life and for our body."[163]

At various moments throughout the latter half of the twentieth century in particular, architects' and landscape architects' enthusiasm for the aerial view was followed by their renewed attention to the ground view and the sensory qualities of living through and inhabiting a space on the ground. This became particularly manifest in landscape architects' work in the 1980s that was influenced by the 1960s and 1970s earthworks and phenomenological theories such as Merleau-Ponty's. It is also evident more generally in the recent program developments of Google Maps™ and Google Earth™. In addition to its satellite images and maps that were launched in 2005,

FIG. 75. Byxbee Park, Palo Alto, California. Highway barriers laid out to imitate the chevrons typically painted in yellow on the blast pads of airport runways. The plane is on a landing course for Palo Alto Airport. (Photograph by the author)

since 2007 Google Maps™ and Google Earth™ have been offering Internet users Google Street View™, the possibility to virtually position themselves on a city street and view the streetscape as if they were standing or walking in it. Thus, the recent history of the use of the aerial view as captured in aerial and satellite photography in architecture, landscape architecture, and city planning is repeating with modern technology the centuries-old practice of illustrating projects with a series of plan views—views from above—followed by sections, elevations, and perspectives that show the project from various viewpoints at eye level on the ground. In design representation, therefore, the plan, or aerial view that provides an overview and context, is typically complemented by images that reveal the more immediate bodily experiences in the envisioned and projected spaces and landscapes.

Google Earth™, initially developed by Keyhole Inc. with support from the CIA and called Earth Viewer 3D, has provided Internet users with the ability to virtually travel across the globe, zooming in and out of locations as they please with a "subtle aura of techno-scientific authority."[164] Also, although the structure of the program largely determines its use and privileges those in power, users can subvert this same techno-scientific authority by becoming "embodied interactors"[165] who generate their own content and communicate in the "Google Earth Community," a social online network that has developed as a result of the program's appeal to Internet users worldwide.[166] The "free movement" of Google Earth™ users across the globe has not only led them to create map overlays that would fall under the category of critical geography, for example, by illustrating the growing world population, wealth, and Internet access, and showing their correlations. It has also caused more explicit scandal and public outcry, as, for example, in 2006, when Google Earth™ users began commenting on how much a formation of buildings at Coronado Navy Base in San Diego seen from the air resembled the shape of a swastika (fig. 76). Because the buildings' form had not been noticed by the U.S. Navy until after groundbreaking in 1967 and because it was not visible from the ground, no changes were made at the time. The situation changed forty years later, however, when millions of Internet users had free access to satellite and aerial photographs of the base that revealed the buildings' swastika shape. Now the aerial view did matter, and the protesters did have a point since a variety of projects in 1930s Germany had been based upon the aerial view of the swastika. While a group of private homes in Munich's district of Bogenhausen was intentionally built in the shape of the Nazi symbol in 1934, in 1992 a swastika-shaped patch of larch trees in a pine forest was discovered near the town of Zwernikow in the region of Brandenburg. The trees had probably been planted by the landowner, Hans von Wedels, in 1938 as a sign of his allegiance to the Nazi regime, and they had survived four decades of East German communist

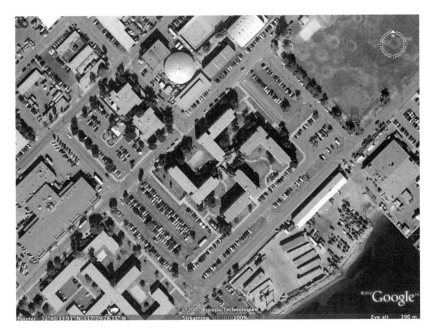

FIG. 76.
Google Earth™
image of the
Coronado Navy
Base in San Diego,
California.

rule. While the trees in Germany were finally felled in 2000, in San Diego the U.S. Navy responded to the public attention generated by Google Earth™ users by making plans to "camouflage" the swastika-shaped building, using landscaping and rooftop photovoltaic cells to prevent offensive and unintended associations.[167]

Although the aerial imagination has effectively existed for thousands of years, a century after the invention of powered flight the aerial view still causes moments of excitement, enthusiasm, and fascination. This can largely be attributed not only to the quest for knowledge, but also to the thrill of what seems an instrument of power, authority, control, surveillance, and voyeurism that has, by the beginning of the twenty-first century, become available to Internet users around the world. The fundamental character traits that attract people to the aerial view and aerial photographs have not changed. Thus, at the beginning of the twenty-first century, Google Earth™ builds upon the technological accomplishments of the twentieth century in a variety of ways. By offering a "Google Sky" function that enables users to "fly" into outer space and visit the moon and mars in addition to navigating the earth, and through the users' ability to zoom in and out, Google Earth™ has added technological prowess, accuracy, ambience, user autonomy, and flexibility to the "inter-stellar roller-coaster ride" of *The Powers of Ten* in the 1970s. As the Eamses' film put humankind into perspective, so Google Earth™ has provided individual environmentalists with a medium and platform to visualize and disseminate the consequences of different types of human impact on the earth, like land-use decisions and climate change.[168] The geographical information system has also taken the compression of time and space that occurred in the first photo mosaics in the 1920s to another level by creating a mosaic that consists of thousands of aerial and satellite photographs taken at different heights and at different times. Not only is the time-space compression present in the virtual movements of the Google Earth™ users themselves, who can fly around the earth in seconds, but it is also pictorially represented in Google Earth's™ mosaic of aerial and satellite images that were taken at different times. The virtual globe presents an extreme case of constructed synchrony and contemporaneity. Overlaps of historic and current imagery that have been created for various locations make explicit use of this patchwork that first developed out of practical necessity.

The firm GeoEye and its not-for-profit foundation, which provide high-resolution satellite imagery for use by defense, intelligence, and mapping agencies; the mining, oil, gas, and forestry industries; architecture, engineering, and construction companies; and in disaster response and environmental assessment, has in the last years provided before-and-after high-resolution aerial imagery of disaster zones, such as the areas in Haiti struck by the January 2010 earthquake and the regions affected by the April 2011 earthquake and tsunami in Japan. GeoEye capitalizes on the aerial representation of landscape change and transformation whether it be extremely immediate, as in these cases, or more gradual, as in the case of climate change. Embedding GeoEye Haiti images into its website in January 2010, the *New York Times* provided Internet users with an interactive feature. Choosing between different landmarks in Port-au-Prince, users could view them in before-and-after satellite images, comparing these by using the cursor to "slide" an aerial image of the scene before the earthquake over the image produced of the same location after the event. While this technology creates and further supports awareness, at the same time it also renders disasters into spectacles that can be viewed safely from thousands of miles away.

Thus, the affective qualities of aerial imagery first pointed out by architects in the 1920s have also reached new levels with programs like Google Earth™. Through its technical beauty and easy operation, Google Earth™ powerfully connects people visually to real places and fosters a close identification with their home and places they have visited.[169] Whereas in the 1920s and 1930s designers developed buildings and landscapes for the aerial view only on rare occasions, due to geographical information systems like Google Earth™ and its followers like Maps-Live, designers today must expect that all their designs will be subject to the aerial gaze.

Some have taken up the challenge, developing projects in both urban and rural environments with Google Earth™ in mind. In the summer of 2010,

the air sightseer above the floodplain of the small municipality of Datteln in the German state of North Rhine–Westphalia was greeted for the first time by the face of a young woman, the ballet dancer Alexandra from Berlin (fig. 77). Alexandra's face in Datteln consists of a vegetation pattern laid out and planted with the help of the Global Positioning System (GPS), created by the U.S. Department of Defense and first declassified for public use in 2000. The face covers an area the size of one of the region's grain fields. It becomes visible when viewed from a certain vantage point from the air and will become apparent to Google Earth™ users worldwide once Google has updated its satellite images of this German region. As part of the initiatives undertaken to mark Essen's selection as a European Cultural Capital 2010, this permanent art project entitled *Lippe+* was intended to attract tourists to boost the local and regional economy. At the same time, however, it had an ecological purpose and a didactic mission. As part of a nature reserve, the groves and riparian forest planted to give contours to Alexandra's face when viewed from the air were part of an environmental compensation measure intended to interest visitors on the ground in their native natural heritage.[170] The landscape architect and the geographer in charge of the project used the newest technology to fuse art and science, culture and nature.

While *Lippe+* attests to the influence of the global economy and the ubiquitous aerial view offered by Google Earth™, it unwittingly links earth artists and initiatives in social and environmental planning and protection to NASA's space exploration of the 1960s. These developments used, benefited from, and in part were even sustained by the aerial view. Furthermore, the

FIG. 77. The face of the ballet dancer Alexandra as a vegetation pattern laid out and planted with the help of the Global Positioning System (GPS) near Datteln, Germany. (© landscape architect Ulli Pinick, HVG Grünflächenmanagement GmbH)

project works on and with different scales. While it appears from the air at a height of up to 2.5 miles (4 kilometers) as a piece of living graphic art, it is also a functioning ecosystem in which the smallest organism depends on a variety of biotic and abiotic factors that make up the regional watershed. What differentiates *Lippe+* from other contemporary art for the aerial view, for example, the New York City artist Molly Dilworth's "art for satellites"—large-scale rooftop paintings for Google Earth™—is that it is a three-dimensional living ecosystem. Furthermore, in contrast to crop art, *Lippe+* is not a temporary installation but a permanent, even if changeable, landscape. Finally, the project contrasts with some of the earlier earth art projects, for example, Smithson's *Wandering Earth Mounds and Gravel Paths* and Stan Herd's portrait of the pioneering aviatrix Amelia Earhart in a field near her birthplace in Atchison, Kansas, in that it is not only intended to "cultivate beautiful air views" but also to restore a riparian ecosystem.

As *Lippe+* attests, throughout the second half of the twentieth century and into the twenty-first, the aerial view has continued to be used to shift perspectives, to zoom in and out, and it has played an important role in attempts to reconcile the arts and sciences on a theoretical level. In more practical terms and as a tool, it has among other things been employed in landscape and environmental conservation as well as in regional, landscape, and urban planning efforts. After World War II, the ability to use aerial photography as a magnifying lens in a double sense—to zoom in onto individual objects and to zoom out to show these objects in broader context—led a number of different agencies concerned with environmental and urban planning to take further advantage of the aerial view for various planning and surveillance purposes during peacetime. While the superpowers were trying to use the scientific and technological knowledge gained during World War II for space flight and research as well as surveillance of the respective enemy during the Cold War, the advantages of aerial photography and remote sensing for seemingly peaceful terrestrial endeavors like urban renewal also gained momentum. Due to the time saved and the comprehensive overview offered by aerial photographs, air photo interpretation was considered indispensable for environmental and urban planning in particular. In 1972, remote sensing provided new tools for these fields. When, in 1930, William Mitchell described the pilot's views of the earth at different heights, he favored the altitude of 20,000 feet (between 4 and 4 miles/4.8 and 6.4 kilometers) for earth observation because "prominent objects such as cities, rivers, lakes and forests are very easily distinguished,"[171] whereas above that height these features seemed to merge into each other. In contrast, from the early 1970s onward, satellite pictures from much greater heights have provided crisp and clear small-scale synoptic views that have enabled the discovery and exploration of geographical features such as fault lines. Satellite imagery from heights of more than 500 miles (800 kilometers) has uncovered physiographic and cultural regional patterns and has consequently been used in regional planning.

As in the first decades of the twentieth century, the aerial view after World War II continued to provide both aesthetic inspiration and a critical-analytical tool. The aerial view has not only offered new perspectives *on* human life and its relationship to nonhuman nature; it has also put humanity *into* perspective. The aerial view has therefore not only been beautiful and presented attractive new patterns; it has also been merciless. Better than any other perspective, it reveals humankind's changes and damages to the earth. As noted in chapter 2, aerial photographs began to be used in the 1920s for such purposes as the detection of water pollution and crop damages by insect pests in agriculture. Paradoxically, by the twenty-first century, the aerial view that witnesses the manifold effects of environmental destruction and pollution has also come to provide a means for the production of aesthetically appealing photographic art that attempts to create environmental awareness as in the case of the contemporary artists Alex McLean, Emmet Gowin, and, more recently, J. Henry Fair and the young German graphic artist Christoph Engel. As detached aerial views, these photographs intend to inspire the viewer to care about the use and shape of the land on the ground and to continue the work in environmental remediation.

Six | *From Airfields to Green Fields*

RECLAIMING AIRPORTS AS LANDSCAPES FOR URBAN ECOLOGY

Throughout their existence, but especially since they came to occupy such a dominant position in our mobile global world as sites for mass travel in the second half of the twentieth century, airports have inspired thought about landscapes and about the creation of new landscapes in fields as diverse as geography, wildlife biology, and art. An increasing awareness of the environmental impacts of aviation facilities and aircraft has encouraged the conceptualization of the airport as landscape, and as a component in the landscape mosaic. Wildlife biologists and ecologists have developed elaborate wildlife management schemes for airports and their surrounding areas.[1] These schemes are the result of the threat that certain wildlife species pose to flight security on the one hand, and of the realization that many airports provide habitats for endangered flora and fauna on the other.

At the beginning of the jet age, Robert Smithson looked at the airport landscape from the detached, critical perspective of the artist and discovered the potential of the airport for his work. His work on the airport project at Dallas–Forth Worth led Smithson to think about landscape in a new way. For him "landscape" now no longer implied "a rustic garden." Instead, it appeared to him "more like a three dimensional map."[2] Smithson broke with the tradition of seventeenth-, eighteenth-, and nineteenth-century landscape art and with the way of seeing that this art implied. As noted in chapter 5, Smithson's "aerial art" favored the vertical view. He developed artworks for the direct view from approaching and departing airplanes and for their view mediated through video in the terminal building. Some decades later, in the 1990s, when the air carrier industry in Europe had been deregulated, observations on airports in general and Heathrow Airport in particular inspired the cultural geographer Denis Cosgrove to explain what by this time had become the extended meanings of "landscape." Studying an airport could "recover landscape as a synthetic idea, a flexible concept,"[3] he posited, that included social, political, and economic worlds. Like Smithson, Cosgrove compared the airport with a rustic garden, in his case with a Georgian landscape garden. Unlike Smithson, however, he described the airport as a landscape by drawing attention to the conceptual *similarities* between airports and landscape gardens. For example, like a Georgian estate in the eighteenth and nineteenth centuries, Heathrow Airport today is a major economic motor of the country. Cosgrove compared the Georgian estate's main house to the airport's terminal building. Similar to the maps and paintings that were part of the interior designs of Georgian country homes and that indicated their power, plans and schedules are displayed in the airport terminal to inform and orientate passengers. Cropped grass surfaces play an important role both in estate and airport design, which also controls sightlines and movement. While meadows and grass lawns were parts of the picturesque and pastoral scenery in landscape gardens, at airports they also fulfill more practical purposes, collecting runoff and dust on the one hand, and, due to their low cover, preventing birds from hiding and nesting, thereby decreasing the risk of bird strike.[4] While Cosgrove's comparison might have seemed far-fetched to many of his readers given the technological environment of today's major airports, the history presented in chapter 1 of this volume shows that airports have always been envisioned as landscapes by some architects, landscape architects, and critics and even went through what Reyner Banham in 1962 called an "almost pastoral phase."[5] In the 1920s and 1930s, when airplanes were still "light and slow-moving on the ground,"[6] a flock of sheep would often be kept to "mow" the grass and compact the soil.

Since the 1990s, flocks of sheep have been returning to some former airfields, and the early proposition expressed in the 1920s *Regional Plan of New York and Its Environs* to convert airports that become outdated and unnecessary into "permanent public open space" has become a reality.[7] Furthermore, the conceptual analogy that critics and airport architects drew implicitly and explicitly between airports and Versailles in the 1920s has again played a role in the more recent context of airport conversion into parks. The landscape architect Eelco Hooftman, principal of the firm Gross.Max., whose design for the decommissioned Tempelhof Airport was commissioned in 2011, has pointed toward this analogy that seems particularly pertinent in the case of Tempelhof.[8] By embracing the open, seemingly level field and providing a threshold between the city and the landing field, Tempelhof's monumental terminal building, designed by Ernst Sagebiel and built beginning in 1936, conceptually resembles the Palace of Versailles, which is similarly located, acting as hinge between the city and extensive gardens.

Due to the expansion of domestic and international air travel furthered by new technologies, global markets, and airline deregulation, many cities have built new international airports farther outside the urban areas and have closed down their former commercial airports. Many military air bases have also been closed as a result of the changing geopolitical power structure and savings measures. Numerous decommissioned commercial and military airports like Chicago's Meigs Field; Stapleton in Denver; Crissy Field in San Francisco; El Toro Air Base in Orange County, California; Downsview in Toronto; Hellenikon International Airport in Athens; Fornebu International Airport in Oslo, Norway; Francisco de Miranda Air Base in Caracas, Venezuela; Mariscal Sucre International Airport in Quito, Ecuador; the Gatow, Tempelhof, and Johannisthal Airports in and near Berlin; and Riem in Munich have been, are being, or are planned to be turned into parks. In many cases, as in the ones in Berlin, Germany, and Orange County, California, further discussed in this chapter, these developments include new neighborhoods and the provision of nature reserves. As this chapter shows, the design opportunities they involve and their central position for urban development make former airports turned into parks ideal subjects for the examination of contemporary approaches in urban park design and of our current relationship with the environment and nonhuman nature.

LIKE MANY EARLY public urban parks and like parks on former industrial sites, decommissioned airports are often located on the periphery of urban areas, or in areas that were once peripheral but during the twentieth century became surrounded by new industrial, commercial, and housing developments. Park designs for a number of former air bases like Gatow near Berlin, the Maurice Rose Army Airfield near Frankfurt, and the former Munich-Riem Airport in Germany intentionally attempt to create links connecting urban and rural areas and have become parts of the cities' metropolitan park systems. Like many former industrial sites, these former airports also have a high percentage of impervious surfaces and contaminated soils resulting from oil, gasoline, and deicing fluids. While the remediation of pollution on former airport sites poses challenges, their vast open space provides the cities with new opportunities. Some of the biggest urban parks that have recently been created or are under construction are located on former airport and airbase sites. Not only their peripheral location and the history of their inception, but particularly their size, openness, and flatness distinguish these sites from many other urban parks. In recent decades, a number of parks have been created on other transportation sites as well, in particular railroad sites. In contrast to parks on former airport sites, however, parks on railroad sites tend to be linear, following the tracks, as in the case of the Promenade Plantée in Paris (construction 1989–94), the Natur-

Park Südgelände on a former switchyard in Berlin (construction 2000), and the Highline in New York (construction begun 2006), and they are often also more centrally located, as in the case of the Railyard Park near the center of Santa Fe, New Mexico (construction 2006–8), the Railroad Park in downtown Birmingham, Alabama (construction 2008–10), and the Park am Gleisdreieck in Berlin (construction 2009–13).

The openness and relative flatness of abandoned airport sites in many ways provide designers with a blank slate. Whereas the sites for the first urban parks were often selected on the basis of their unsuitability as building sites as a result of their topography (Central Park) or for their attractive topographical features (Englischer Garten, Prospect Park), former airport sites lack notable topography and have been cleared of shrubs and trees. They are characterized by a lack of vertical features, and their buildings are limited to the edges of the open field. They provide twenty-first-century planners with the vast openness that avant-garde architects and urban planners like Le Corbusier sought for their work at the beginning of the twentieth century. Decommissioned airports have offered cities new opportunities for growth and development, and they have led to projects like Hellenikon Metropolitan Park at Athens's former international airport south of the city center and Orange County Great Park on California's El Toro Air Base outside Los Angeles being advertised respectively as the biggest metropolitan park project in Europe and the "first metropolitan park of the 21st century." With 1,325 and 1,347 acres respectively (536 and 545 hectares), these sites are indeed bigger than some of the largest eighteenth- and nineteenth-century urban parks, for example, Central Park (843 acres, 341 hectares), Munich's Englischer Garten (900 acres, 364 hectares), and Golden Gate Park (1,000 acres, 405 hectares). And while it varies how far outside the central district they are located, parks on former airports do in many cases cater to an entire metropolitan area rather than to only the central city. Similar to the nineteenth- and early-twentieth-century park projects, however, they are instruments of urban boosterism, or place-marketing. Parks on former airport sites are part and parcel of the increasing commodification of urban life, and they are frequently connected to urban housing development by private investors whose taxes are intended to finance the public park development.

City and federal governments and agencies, and development corporations are promoting these new parks as sustainable, future-oriented projects. It is true that the parks provide many citizens with access to new large public open space for recreational pursuits, reduce the urban heat island effect, and provide fresh air and many plant and animal species with areas for retreat. Due to their particular site conditions on higher and relatively flat ground without shrub or tree cover, former airports often also present a rare habitat for endangered species. At the same time, however, these park projects become catalysts and platforms for capitalist urban development (as in earlier times) and for neoliberal politics.

Most parks on former air bases and airports fall into what the environmental sociologist Galen Cranz and Michael Boland defined in 2004 as the "sustainable urban park" and what a 2007 volume on new park landscapes simply called "large parks," parks of 500 acres (202 hectares) or larger.[9] Like the ideal type of "sustainable urban park" that Cranz and Boland described, many parks on former airport sites use site-specific plant materials, sustainable construction, and maintenance and management practices, including stream restoration. They encompass wildlife habitats and provide venues for community engagement including urban gardening and farming. Furthermore, their development and design are process-oriented and geared toward incorporating ecological and social changes over time. However, the following elaborations on Orange County Great Park in Southern California and Tempelhofer Freiheit and Johannisthal in Berlin—projects that are largely still under development—will show that while the overall goals of these park projects are often similar, the design approaches and the ideas of nature and restoration ecology on which they are based differ. Although the projects are both products of and agents in neoliberal policies and the capitalist city in general, their social and environmental sustainability depends, among other things, on the respective national and local histories, including environmental and social politics.

Tempelhofer Freiheit

In the wake of German reunification, Berlin has in the last two decades been expanding one of its airports and closing down others. While the former East Berlin airport Schönefeld is being turned into what is to become Berlin's new international airport, the city plans to turn Tegel Airport into an industrial zone and a new residential neighborhood including a park. Until 1989, Tegel functioned as the airport of West Berlin and has since then handled most of Berlin's domestic and international air travel. Johannisthal Airfield, southeast of the city center, and Tempelhof Airport, situated adjacent to the Berlin districts of Friedrichshain-Kreuzberg and Neukölln, have already been decommissioned and turned into parks. In the 1990s, one of Germany's first flying fields located in Johannisthal began to be converted into a park with an adjacent mixed-use development that is still under construction. After the U.S. Air Force vacated Tempelhof Airport in 1993, it was closed to all civilian air traffic in October 2008. Since May 2010, the landing field has been open to the public for use as a park (fig. 78). The conversion of both Johannisthal and Tempelhof into public urban parks not only illustrates city politics, but the selected park designs give expression to

FIG. 78. Runway in Tempelhofer Freiheit, July 2010. (Photograph by the author)

ideas of nature in the city that have both shaped and been shaped by local and national social and environmental policies and politics, global economic development, as well as the dominant cultural and scientific theories of the last one hundred years. As much as the park designs reflect approaches and attitudes specific to Berlin and German environmental and social politics and culture, they are also indicators of more general tendencies in contemporary Western landscape architecture, which has in the urban realm often become a handmaiden of neoliberal policies.

In April 2011, almost a year after the opening of Tempelhof to the public and the May 2010 deadline for Tempelhof's open international park design competition, the Berlin Senate Department for Urban Development accepted for realization the design of the Edinburgh landscape architecture firm Gross.Max. As one of the six firms from among seventy-eight competitors admitted to the negotiated procedure of the second round of the competition, Gross.Max. had the chance to hear and discuss the concerns and wishes of the competition jury, the Berlin Senate Department for Urban Development, and Berlin citizens and to react to these discussions in their final design.[10]

The Berlin Senate Department considered Gross.Max.'s design a successful response to the requirements voiced in the invitation to tender. Its detailed guidelines clearly revealed a framework based on the capitalist economy of Germany's self-declared "creative" capital and on local politics. To design an "urban parkland for the 21st century" as requested in this document meant to design for "social, economic, cultural and environmental sustainability." Designs were to contribute to "the integration of a multi-

FLIGHTS OF IMAGINATION

cultural, socially intermixed and ageing urban society" and of "social milieus in adjacent areas." They were to provide for a public open space that was "open for general use" while also giving certain groups the opportunity to use "parts of the parkland for their own specific purposes."[11] The invitation to tender explained that the design should offer "a unifying spatial framework for the manifold activities and needs of an increasingly diversifying society." The park design was also required to be a branding instrument that would provide the district of Tempelhof with a new public image and facilitate the entire park development process. In light of the city's financial constraints, the invitation to tender called for ideas for "new public-private areas" and "self-sustaining" areas in the park, and suggested that the design provide a framework that could accommodate do-it-yourself trends, privately organized outdoor activities, as well as activities run by charitable and not-for-profit organizations.[12] Tempelhof was identified as the site for the 2017 international garden exhibition, an event held in Germany every four years and typically used as a means to initiate the development or renewal of parts of the host city. The design concept therefore was to provide for incremental development and to be flexible so that it could respond to "changing future conditions, new actor constellations and emerging trends."[13]

While the invitation to tender asked the designers to pay special attention to the historic runways, pathways, and buildings on the site, as well as to the site's characteristic openness, flatness, and panoramic views, it also encouraged them to search for and develop "new aesthetic visions"[14] and suggested the "New Romantic style" as a source of inspiration. In addition, because the park was to be attractive as well as useful, the guidelines also encouraged entrants to consider contemporary trends of urban gardening and forestry for inclusion in the park design. The requested design called for a layered landscape in which parts could accommodate multiple uses. Only in this way, the document stated, could all the required uses be accommodated. Usefulness was also to be understood in terms of climate and habitat protection for rare animal and plant species. The conservation of the field's openness and vegetated cover was therefore requested not only for aesthetic reasons but also because Tempelhof is an important source of fresh air in a dense city housing 3.4 million inhabitants. Another challenge presented to the designers was to make Tempelhof accessible for the recreational use of Berlin's inhabitants while at the same time protecting rare and threatened species like the skylark by conserving their habitats on site and providing for the necessary ecological networks between Tempelhof and other sites.

Gross.Max. responded to the invitation to tender's various restrictive guidelines by using circular and oval-shaped paths that continue the quarter circle of the terminal apron, circumscribe the field, and substitute "belt-walks" for the taxiway (fig. 79). The runways are maintained, and their straight lines are continued into the adjacent neighborhoods as tree-lined allées and pergolas. Two additional straight pathways are suggested that run perpendicular to the east–west orientated runways to connect the new neighborhoods in the north and south of the park. A pavilion located where the north–south pathways cross the northern runway will provide exhibition space during the time of the park construction as well as space for food concessions. One of the interior circular pathways runs on an artificially created ridge that also forms a ha-ha, providing a spatial enclosure and a differentiation between the core park area near the terminal apron and the rest of the park on slightly lower ground. This protects the horizontality of the site, but uses the existing 13 to 20–foot (4 to 6–meter) elevation change of the field, which slopes down from the eastern to the western edge. The more heavily used parts of the park as well as wooded areas are located along its edge, maintaining the field's openness. Playgrounds, a skate park, and designated "pioneer areas" for the use of various citizen groups are sprinkled into the meadows along the western and southeastern edge of the park for easy access. An area between the oval pathways in the south of the field is planned to become a "pioneer woodland" that will be allowed to develop over time from beech to oak woods. Only the existing trees in the location of the 1920s terminal building—an area of high biodiversity and a habitat for a number of rare species that in Gross.Max.'s design becomes an arboretum—will obstruct open views across the field from some standpoints near it. An artificial rock with a climbing wall that doubles as a monument to Wilhelm and Alexander von Humboldt near the eastern edge of the park will offer a bird's-eye view of the field (fig. 80). The rock monument is imagined as a new vertical landmark and a counterweight to the field's 1980s radar tower in the northeast. In response to many citizens' wishes, Gross.Max. included a water basin near the terminal apron and near the circular area that is designated as event space. The designers also accommodated bird-watchers by proposing to place movable passenger boarding stairs as an observation post in the open meadows in the southern part of the field.

FLYING HIGH: TEMPELHOFER FREIHEIT AS NEW-ROMANTIC IDYLL

By demanding that the park design experiment with new design forms, explicitly mentioning the New Romanticism, the Berlin Senate Department promoted the city as cultural capital. In the 1990s, the German landscape architect Dieter Kienast had anticipated a return to romantic ideals in landscape architecture, and contemporary landscape architects themselves have recently noted the rediscovery of what they call romantic sensibilities.[15] Given the design motifs proposed for the park on the one hand, and the

FIG. 79.
Gross.Max., design
for Tempelhofer
Freiheit. (Courtesy
of Gross.Max.)

emotional and romantic portrayal of the park in perspectival renderings on the other, it appears likely that the designers followed the suggestion in the invitation to tender to study recent cultural trends and developments in the arts, including the New Romanticism.

The New Romanticism is considered a reaction to the increasing mobility of society and the lack of permanent social ties, as well as to the resulting search for security and intimacy and a result of the yearning for "a paradisiacal, beautiful and fairytale-like state." However, this does not mean that artists whose work exhibits these character traits are unaware of "the abysmal, the uncanny, and the mysterious" often present behind these idylls.[16] Although the park designers are not attempting to create the kind of emotionally disturbing landscape that is reflected in some works by the New Romanticists, they are working on and with a site that has a varied and in part disturbing history. The park project itself is the outcome of the tension created by the melancholy, nostalgia, and unease resulting from the site's historic significance and by the expectations and desires based upon its perceived potential.

FIG. 80. Gross.Max., rendering of the Rock Monument planned for Tempelhofer Freiheit. (Courtesy of Gross.Max.)

Various other connections can be drawn between the New Romanticism and nineteenth-century romanticism. Gross.Max.'s park landscape responds to the request in the invitation to tender for a combination of utility and beauty, an old trope relevant throughout garden and landscape history that was first conceptualized in Roman times during the reign of Emperor Augustus, when it was summed up in the Latin expression *dulce utili*, used to describe the integration of agricultural land and ornamental gardens in Roman villas.[17] It was subsequently prominently given expression in the first ornamented farms in eighteenth-century Britain, which consisted of country estates laid out to please the eye and accommodate agricultural lands, and in the eighteenth- and early-nineteenth-century land-embellishment schemes in some German states. Besides this old design concept, individual park features and motifs like the ha-ha reference the era of romanticism in garden design and the romantic mind-set of the eighteenth and nineteenth centuries. The rock monument is not only dedicated to two noteworthy Berlin exponents of the romantic era, the Prussian minister and philosopher Wilhelm von Humboldt, and his younger brother, the naturalist and explorer Alexander von Humboldt; it also calls to mind one of the key works of German romantic painting, the *Wanderer above the Sea of Fog* by Caspar David Friedrich. As if these references to a romantic worldview did not suffice, Gross.Max. placed the angel Damiel from Wim Wenders's 1987 film *Wings of Desire* on the top of the rock monument in one of their catchpenny renderings. Set in 1980s Berlin, Wenders's film created a counterproject to reality by establishing a world of invisible gentle angels who listen to the tortured thoughts of mortals and try to comfort them. While the film is a meditation on Berlin's past, present, and future, Gross.Max.'s phased park design for the next decades attempts to build with the past and present, to envision the future. The design turns the former airport into a modern ornamented farm.

In addition to these conceptual ideas and design motifs referencing romanticism, the visual representation of the park design in the plans and in particular in the perspectives that aim at forging an affirmative public opinion conveys a romantic atmosphere. Although existing buildings like the terminal firmly ground the illustrations in reality, many of the evocative images portray the dreamlike atmosphere of an imaginary world: A beekeeper tends to his beehives in a blossoming fruit orchard rendered in white and warm colors that evoke the heat and glistening sunlight reflected by the white petals of the flowers of the fruit trees. A slight haze apparent in certain areas of the image contributes to this atmosphere. In contrast to this rural summer idyll, two other perspectives lead the viewer to the water basin near the terminal apron in the late fall and winter. Located relatively near the city center and in the vicinity of dense residential neighborhoods in Tempelhof, Kreuzberg, and Neukölln, this park area appears populated by citizens (and waterfowl on the water and flying overhead) who are crossing the basin on a boardwalk, going for a walk, or simply spending time outdoors to enjoy the fresh air and open views across the water while sitting on the seating slabs. The dominant gray and blue tones and rose hues as well as the light used in this image transport the viewer into the late fall season, a sensation that is verified by the type of clothing worn by the people who inhabit the park in this illustration. A rendering portraying this part of the park in the winter shows an expansive frozen water surface resembling one of the many Brandenburg lakes, but populated with an urban skating crowd. The color schemes, blurry outlines, transparencies, and light make these images very evocative, suggestive, and atmospheric, transporting the viewer into the future park—a seemingly ideal world.

With their design, Gross.Max. addresses the social phenomena that are inherent in the New Romanticism, and in the firm's graphical design representation it uses techniques similar to the ones employed by artists of the New Romanticism. In atmospheric images with a dreamlike haze, produced with the help of layers and filters in computer graphic programs, the designers invoke a vast healthy new park landscape that can provide space for private contemplation and reflection and for what the art historian Martina Weinhart has described, in regard to the New Romanticism, as "perceiving the transcendent."[18] The way light, haze, and blurriness are used in some of the images recalls romantic paintings by William Turner, Thomas Cole, and Albert Bierstadt, and the landscape paintings by Gerhard Richter, and it brings to mind pictorialist photography. Before the invention of the computer and programs like Photoshop, photographic techniques used by early-twentieth-century landscape architects like Gudmund Nyeland Brandt to illustrate their designs and romantic ideas of the ideal future garden on occasion vaguely resembled the techniques and methods used by the pictorialists.

With their design for Tempelhof, the park designers, like their late-eighteenth-century and nineteenth-century romantic forebears and like the contemporary exponents of the New Romanticism,[19] strive to create "individualized counter-world[s] to [a] disillusioning reality" and attempt to build "a new relationship between the individual and nature." As in the Romantic period, the focus is on the individual and his/her emotions. Whereas the reform parks in the early twentieth century were intended to cater to the masses, Gross.Max. argues that in a society that celebrates individualism, new parks have to serve the particular and often idiosyncratic needs of the individual.[20] In keeping with the initial suggestions in the invitation to tender, Gross.Max. has tried to portray its park design as capable of attributing "the commonplace with significance, the quotidian with mystery, the familiar with the aura of the unfamiliar."[21] While creating a park imaginary that blurs high and pop culture, Gross.Max.'s design adheres to the city's aim at turning the former airport into cultural capital. In the real world, this required new planning instruments and new forms of public engagement.

A PARK FOR URBAN PIONEERS

As a postmodern project, the park design emphasizes the indefinite and the ambiguous, characteristics that have also been attributed to the New Romanticism.[22] Although it is an old toponymic description alluding to the wide, open expanse that was a parade ground in the late eighteenth century, the park's current name—Tempelhofer Freiheit (Tempelhof's Liberty)—is also programmatic. Not only does it capture the twentieth-century historical-political significance of the airport with special reference to the Berlin Airlift, but it also describes the city's intentions for the new park. Tempelhofer Freiheit and its design are the result of process-oriented urban development, and of flexible and adaptive participatory master planning that determine as little as possible and as much as necessary by integrating informal activities into a formalized design framework. The design of Tempelhofer Freiheit is the result of numerous citizen petitions and referenda, and of citizen participation through surveys, workshops, charettes, excursions, and Internet platforms that reached a climax under the social democratic government in the late 1990s and the following decade in a planning and design process that began in the early 1990s and still continues. Plans to close down commercial air traffic at Tempelhof began to be made shortly after the fall of the Berlin Wall in 1989. However, due to opposition by air carriers and various other interest groups, the closure only took effect after a final court decision and a referendum in 2008. As soon as Tempelhof was closed, the Senate Department for Urban Development could build upon the experience of the preceding two decades, during which the reconstruction efforts in the inner city had had priority.

The planning approach for the city center in the 1990s, based upon development initiatives in both East and West Berlin in the 1980s and described as "critical reconstruction" (kritische Rekonstruktion; Josef Paul Kleihues), focused on achieving a preconceived urban form based upon the image of the "historic European city," and sought to establish a long-lost historic continuity between the physical and social fabric of late-nineteenth-century Berlin and the present.[23] The evolution and development of Tempelhofer Freiheit must be understood in light of the public criticism sparked by the planning concept of "critical reconstruction," including its lack of citizen participation; the financial crisis that hit Berlin as the result of a bank scandal; and the global neoliberal economy. These events have influenced the current left-wing government to promote citizen participation and to glean development ideas from "urban pioneers," entrepreneurial citizens who through various initiatives and activities have influenced urban development since German reunification. Their temporary and often illegitimate use of leftover interstitial urban spaces have rendered parts of the city more attractive to members of the "creative" professional middle class, laying the foundations of subsequent gentrification. Because temporary urbanism often increases property values, many property owners and the city government have come to appreciate urban pioneers.

At Tempelhofer Freiheit, the Senate Department of Urban Development is using urban pioneers to aid in park development and win public

FIG. 81. A "pioneer area" used for community gardening in July 2011. (Photograph by the author)

approval (fig. 81). The realization of the park design depends on a hybrid of bottom-up and top-down processes in which the city government works with the designers to create a framework and overall vision that relies on the citizens' creative potential and entrepreneurial energy. The city government is counting on do-it-yourself initiatives and private-public partnerships for the realization of parts of the park and its programming. It considers the park a "platform enabling proactive forms of cultural engagement"[24] that can nurture an active citizenry. Less explicit is the fact that Berlin's recent left-wing government and liberal political coalitions have adopted the urban pioneer tactics to legitimize and veil the fact that the project promotes gentrification and the displacement of parts of the population, especially in the neighborhood of Schillerkiez, east of the park.

The Senate Department's call for indeterminacy and flexibility in the planning process is most visible in Gross.Max.'s phasing of its design, its accommodation of the 2017 IGA, and in the "pioneer areas," 30- to 47-acre (12- to 19- hectare) plots of land that can be used on a temporary basis by citizen groups who apply with an idea and are selected by the Tempelhof Project GmbH, a state-owned development agency. The language and rhetoric used to describe the social processes that are intended to influence the incremental park development derive from ecology. Gross.Max.'s principal, Eelco Hooftman, for example, likened Berlin's "urban pioneers" to botanical pioneer species. In 2011, he explained Berlin's development strategy as applied to Tempelhofer Freiheit as follows: "We drew a comparison with nature. Pioneer species are the first species to colonize fallow land; they are followed by successional species, and with time a stable climax vegeta-

FLIGHTS OF IMAGINATION

tion develops. Translated to urban development this means that you have to grant pioneers the opportunity to develop more complex situations so that this can finally create a stable habitat."[25] A 2007 publication issued by the Berlin Senate for Urban Development compared "urban space pioneers" to pioneer vegetation because they did not impose special requirements on the site.[26] Furthermore, it was pointed out that the initial phase of temporary urban projects provided ideal conditions for their fast "cell growth." Thus, the temporary projects and their spaces were also considered cells of a larger organism, the city. The text noted that available space and attractive experimental milieus made it easy for urban pioneers to overcome any initial inhibition, while the permanent insecurity and the collective pressure to assert oneself against the interests of the property owner led to well-organized microcommunities and networks.[27] Although the hybrid of the top-down and bottom-up planning approaches taken at Tempelhof under Berlin's social-democratic leadership differs from the 1990s conservative government's heavy-handed urban development of Berlin's inner city that made use of the organism metaphor and was based on a hierarchical conservative social model, an organicist rhetoric persists. In the 2000s, the image used is the ecosystem of which Berlin's citizens have come to be seen as integral parts. In Tempelhofer Freiheit, they can populate "pioneer areas" that are located next to zones subject to management regimens set up to protect select rare plant and animal species. However, the "pioneer areas" are not as open as they may seem. As with the protected areas for flora and fauna, an administrative unit, the state-owned development agency Tempelhof Projekt GmbH, ultimately determines who can populate them, and it may do so with the bias of promoting the "creative class."

Overall, the design strategies of Tempelhofer Freiheit reflect a global phenomenon—the loss of public funds and government control over public land and the increasing privatization of formerly public institutions—and they address a local challenge—Berlin's debt crisis—with the tool of temporary urbanism. Presenting the city with what some consider a bestowed asset and others a self-inflicted burden, Tempelhof has provided Berlin with a ground for experimenting with and testing new planning approaches and ideas. The park is designed to anticipate change and embrace the site's evolution. As a case of process-oriented urban planning, Tempelhofer Freiheit breaks with Berlin's urban planning approach of the recent past that shaped the "critical reconstruction" of Berlin's inner-city area. Current planning seeks to activate different uses of urban space and explicitly encourages community engagement and activism.[28] However, this does not mean that current planning has relinquished neoliberal ideologies. On the contrary, planners appear to have co-opted temporary urbanism as a tactic for advancing a neoliberal agenda.

THE EVOLUTION OF POSTMODERN PARK LANDSCAPES

In addition to Tempelhofer Freiheit representing both a catalyst and a laboratory of process-oriented urban development as well as flexible and collaborative master planning, the park stands alongside two other exemplary postmodern park designs of the last thirty years: Parc de la Villette (1982) on the grounds of a former meatpacking district in northeast Paris and Downsview Park (2000) on a decommissioned air base in Toronto. Like Parc de la Villette and Downsview Park, Tempelhofer Freiheit is the outcome of an international competition that requested new approaches and expressions in park design capable of contributing meaningfully to a city's image. Gross. Max.'s commissioned design and some of the other competition entries for Tempelhofer Freiheit reveal the influence of the design by the architect Bernard Tschumi for Parc de la Villette and of the design for Downsview Park by a team led by OMA and headed by Rem Koolhaas and Bruce Mau. Albeit in different ways and forms, both Tschumi at La Villette and OMA/ Bruce Mau at Downsview designed frameworks for the evolution of a variety of uses. Tschumi began to highlight strategy and process in his design, distancing it from any imposed hierarchical implications. This approach was carried forward almost twenty years later in the prize-winning design for Downsview Park, and another ten years later it became the operating mechanism for Tempelhofer Freiheit. However, whereas Tschumi's abstract overlay of three autonomous systems of points, lines, and surfaces on the site of La Villette did not exploit "the landscape's expressive power,"[29] and deliberately relied on abstract theories and systems independent from the site itself and its context, advances in this direction were made in Downsview Park and are finally playing an important role again in Tempelhofer Freiheit. Whereas the Tschumi and Koolhaas/Mau teams largely circumvented historical analysis of the sites and their contexts at La Villette and Downsview, history is again playing a central role in Tempelhof.

For Downsview Park, OMA/Bruce Mau submitted a diagram rather than a design and proposed a visionary flexible design strategy that could be implemented over a fifteen-year period. "Tree City," as their competition entry was called, used "trees rather than buildings . . . [to] serve as the catalyst of urbanization."[30] Rather than offering a design for a park as an object (albeit living), OMA/Bruce Mau provided the idea for a park as an "object-event" (Gilles Deleuze) or as a "performative catalyst subject."[31] Similarly, Gross. Max. is suggesting for Tempelhof that changing curators organize events in the park. In Toronto, "Tree City" proposed to loosen the compacted soil on the site and use a crop-rotation system during the first two years to remediate and prepare the soil for future plantings. In a second phase, a network of "1,000 paths" would be created, and playing fields and gardens established.

Finally, woods, wetlands, and open meadows would create a varied land-scape enjoyable 24/7 through active and passive recreation. While the vision and the strategy for these design phases were formulated and displayed with the help of Bruce Mau's simple iconic graphical vocabulary, no actual design features were located anywhere in the plan. Instead, the designers' intent was for the social, environmental, and economic processes to determine the ultimate design of the park. Similar to OMA's competition entry for Parc de la Villette that won second prize, its Downsview Park entry was not a designed landscape but a framework and a method that Koolhaas thought "capable of absorbing an endless series of further meanings, extensions, or intentions, without entailing compromises, redundancies or contradictions."[32] At La Vil-lette, Koolhaas had already proposed to bring the city into the park, that is, to enable and empower the public to devise their own public urban park that would consequently be characterized by constant change and debates among different interest groups. For Koolhaas, "the diverse human activities" cre-ated the park. "The more the Park works," he posited, "the more it will be in a perpetual state of revision."[33] However, whereas at La Villette OMA's emphasis was on the creation of a public sphere through civic engagement, at Downsview he determined that economic and environmental processes also should form the park.

The openness, malleability, and lack of specificity of the "design" caused the most consternation among the public, who thought that the money for the competition had been badly spent. While some professionals criticized the importance the design strategy attributed to economic processes, much professional critique was focused on the apparent lack of the design's in-tegration into the environmental context of the bioregion. As Kristina Hill noted, OMA/Bruce Mau's entry lacked references to the establishment of open space networks and existing ecologies.[34] Although Mau asserted that the "ideals of the park" should be "exported . . . beyond the park"[35] and the competition entry stated that "Tree City" could "link up with Black Creek and West Don ravines," the entry's overall character was universal and ge-neric, which was also clearly illustrated in the choice of circular—one might say global—images and dots to portray ideas, projected landscape images, and concepts. "Tree City" was therefore hardly capable of responding to site-specific ecological contexts. Revised versions and more recent plans that now appear as conventional master plans, however, have tried to add site-specificity, and despite a heavily criticized slow process, the first areas of the park are now finally beginning to take shape.

Like the competition plans for Downsview, the realization of Tempel-hof's park design is to be undertaken in phases, it depends on the input from citizens, and it provides an open framework. However, unlike OMA/ Bruce Mau at Downsview, Gross.Max. has delivered a conceptual design, rather than merely a theoretical concept and tactic. The current condition of Tempelhofer Freiheit—which was first opened to the public in more or less the condition it was found after the airport's closure, and is presently the result of constant interaction between the city and its citizens—resembles perhaps most closely what Koolhaas had intended for La Villette in the 1980s. Tempelhofer Freiheit in its current and contingent state probably gets closest to the ideal of democratic public space, which—as observed by radical democrats in the 1980s—has to be in a constant process of realization and conflict.[36] While Tempelhof's current condition can therefore be considered as a realization of some of Koolhaas's proposals for La Villette, Gross.Max.'s design for Tempelhofer Freiheit presents an evolution of OMA/Mau's proposal for Downsview.

In its design concept for Tempelhofer Freiheit, Gross.Max. uses the expressive power of the site's openness and flatness, and firmly locates "pioneer woods," "pioneer areas," a pavilion, a water basin, a rock monument, an arboretum, and all pathways on the site. In contrast to Tschumi and to a greater degree than OMA/Bruce Mau, Gross.Max. works with the site—the deposition of the land, and existing natural features—as well as with a system of pathways and "pioneer areas." In fact, following the stringent competition guidelines, all competition entries for Tempelhofer Freiheit incorporated and capitalized on the natural and existing features of the site, including the designs by the teams led by Topotek 1 and bbz landschaftsarchitekten. These clearly reveal the inspiration of La Villette and Downsview in their ideas and graphic language. Whereas bbz landschaftsarchitekten distributed differently sized "circular fields of opportunities" throughout the site that resemble OMA/Bruce Mau's undefined circles for future uses at Downsview, Topotek 1's design recalls Tschumi's overlay of systems at La Villette. In their design, which was among the six to enter the negotiated procedure, Topotek 1 added three layers to the existing one of "historic elements." The designers distributed groups of trees typical of the region across the open field, added triangulated pathways inspired by flight paths, and covered Tempelhof with a regular grid of reseau crosses to mark areas for "informal or organized events."[37] In most submitted designs, the attention paid to site-specific qualities also conditioned a greater attention paid to wildlife on and surrounding the site.

URBAN ECOLOGY

Tempelhofer Freiheit not only reveals the conflation of top-down and bottom-up government models, but it also presents itself as a hybrid expression of old and more recent ecological theories and as an evolution of the design approach taken at the airfield in Johannisthal six miles southeast of Tempelhofer Freiheit, which was turned into a park in the early 2000s.

FIG. 82. Protected area for skylarks in Tempelhofer Freiheit, July 2010. (Photograph by the author)

Given that numerous endangered and rare plant and animal species inhabit Tempelhofer Freiheit, the use of certain areas has been curtailed by law. To maintain the various grass habitats that developed during the site's use as an airfield, a management regimen has to be followed. Since the airfield's opening in 2010, areas of particular relevance for the endangered skylark have been closed to the public during the late spring and summer but are mowed once or twice yearly, after consultation with ornithologists (fig. 82).[38] The Senate Department for Urban Development has both followed and built upon the approach it took in the 1990s at Johannisthal Airfield, one of Germany's first airfields for powered flight that was established in 1909.

At Johannisthal, the 1993 framework plan for urban development, drawn up on the basis of, among other things, extensive surveys of the site's flora and fauna, determined that the 160-acre (65-hectare) core of the old airfield be maintained as park. Much of the former 1,037-acre (420-hectare) airfield had lain vacant during the Cold War era, and as at Tempelhof, the sandy open grounds had developed into a dry grass biotope that included many rare species listed as endangered flora and fauna. In an invited design competition for the park, six landscape architecture offices were selected to submit proposals, and the design by the Berlin firm Büro Kiefer (Studio Kiefer) was finally chosen (fig. 83). In accordance with the 1993 framework plan, Studio Kiefer's design combined nature preservation and recreation in an urban environment. The center of the former airfield, which was declared a nature reserve in 2002, covers 64 acres (26 hectares) and is surrounded by a 1.2 mile- (2-kilometer-) long, partly elevated walkway that provides views across the open field (fig. 84). In contrast to the nature reserve, which

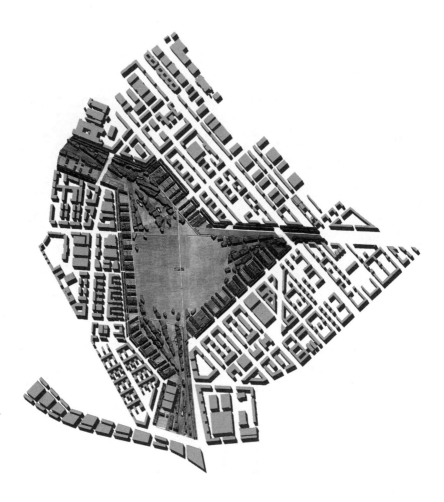

FIG. 83. Büro Kiefer, design for Johannisthal Nature and Recreation Park, 1996. (Courtesy of Büro Kiefer, Berlin)

cannot be entered, the 101 acres (41 hectares) of landscape protection area (*Landschaftsschutzgebiet*)[39] that surround the protected core are accessible. This area acts as a buffer zone between the surrounding developments and the nature reserve (fig. 85). A number of guidelines determine the use and appearance of the landscape protection area. For example, the vast open landscape character is to be protected and building activity limited to the realization of the park design that includes the construction of play and sports grounds, pedestrian and bike paths, tree plantings, and earth movement in specifically determined areas (fig. 86).[40] In contrast, the nature reserve is not accessible, its development is monitored, and flocks of sheep graze the area to ensure that the dry grass biotope is maintained. The site is therefore subject to a scientific management scheme that maintains the biotope type and landscape character, which were designated as the qualitative standard of the area in the 2002 "regulation for the protection of the landscape of the former airfield Johannisthal" (fig. 87).

FIG. 84. Viewing terrace along the beltwalk dividing the nature and landscape preservation areas, Johannisthal Nature and Recreation Park, July 2009. (Photograph by the author)

FIG. 85. Nature preservation area, Johannisthal Nature and Recreation Park, July 2009. (Photograph by the author)

Based on the state regulations for nature protection, Studio Kiefer's design attempted to provide a contemporary landscape aesthetic for the Nature and Landscape Park. In a 2004 publication of Studio Kiefer's work, park designs in general were presented as providing more or less dynamic systems that may be modeled on an ideal landscape but that cannot predict when this state will be reached.[41] Paradoxically, at Johannisthal the core

FIG. 86. Soccer field along the beltwalk, Johannisthal Nature and Recreation Park, July 2009. (Photograph by the author)

FIG. 87. Sheep grazing in the nature preservation area, Johannisthal Nature and Recreation Park, July 2009. (Photograph by the author)

area that is concerned with the ecology of the site's flora and fauna and that was also used to compensate comprehensively for the encroachment on nature and landscape caused by the urban development is the most static element in the entire design. The management of the nature reserve builds upon the idea of an anthropogenic climax. By letting sheep graze, the grassland succession is kept at bay and an endangered habitat type in this region of Germany is preserved.

In contrast, the attempt to create room for a dynamic evolution of space and its use can be seen in the design for the area of transition between the inner protected core of the park and the projected urban development surrounding it. There, Gabriele Kiefer and her team provided for what she calls park rooms: spaces that are partly enclosed by vegetation and that can provide for a variety of uses that are not programmatically determined. Although the park is supposed to be connected to the surrounding built-up areas through tree-lined roads and green corridors, the design strongly focuses inward on its core piece, which caters to nature protection. Thus, despite the programmatic declarations by Studio Kiefer that present the design as furthering dynamic processes and change, the Nature and Landscape Park Johannisthal seems to be more a product of a Berlin-specific ecological awareness and of the city's history of urban ecology, rather than the result of abstract and more recent theories that describe ecology as an open, complex, self-organizing system.

The physical isolation and enclosure of West Berlin and the lack of rural field study areas during the years of the Cold War encouraged the establishment of urban ecology as a major research area at the Technical University Berlin. At the same time, the importance that green open areas assumed for West Berlin's isolated population, the environmental movement, and their own know-how enabled urban ecologists to play an increasingly important role in urban politics and policies including city planning.[42] The work of Berlin's urban ecologists contributed to a new understanding of green open spaces in the city. While there had already been a shift in the conceptualization of green open space "from ornamental to sanitary green," as defined by the Berlin architect and planner Martin Wagner following Camillo Sitte at the beginning of the twentieth century, more than a half century later, in the 1970s, yet another function was attributed to open spaces in cities. Regardless of whether they were woods, ponds, diligently maintained gardens and parks, or urban wastelands like railway tracks, embankments, and marshaling yards, ecologists considered these open spaces biotopes, and on occasion even the habitat of endangered flora and fauna. Their work also influenced the public perception of these urban sites, encouraging an urban wilderness aesthetic, and it provided the basis for the establishment of landscape plans that in turn influenced urban land use plans.[43]

The Nature and Landscape Park Johannisthal exemplifies the culmination of this development and the understanding of public urban parks as habitats. This is displayed not only in its name but also in its physical design, the inclusion of a nature reserve in a park for recreation and aesthetic enjoyment. As much as the park is the result of the specific circumstances that developed in Berlin in these past fifty years, the idea of establishing a nature reserve in a public urban park is part of a nationwide legacy that goes back to the early German nature conservation movement at the beginning of the twentieth century. Besides promoting the establishment of large nature reserves (*Naturschutzgebiete*)[44] that were finally signed into German law in 1935, some landscape architects in early-twentieth-century Germany argued for the creation of nature reserves within public urban parks. These areas would initially be planted and managed in order to encourage the establishment of a diverse flora and fauna before being left to develop on their own and being protected against human intrusion.[45]

At Johannisthal, nature and culture remain polarized: the open, prairie-like nature of the former airport is protected on the assumption that "nature" and its ecological processes can at least to some degree be predicted, controlled, and managed. The management and maintenance concept for the nature reserve is based on the call for biodiversity and on the theory that the ecology of natural systems evolves toward a "stable" equilibrium and can be controlled, thus including humans as actors in the ecological process. Citizens and officials involved determined which species were to be protected or sacrificed, and the landscape architects provided an appropriate design. But the design of the Nature and Landscape Park Johannisthal reflects more than the particular concerns of urban ecologists in Berlin and the popular perception and policies they have generated in the last fifty years; it also reveals the influence of "critical reconstruction," the urban design paradigm used in the 1990s by the city's leading planning officials to guide much of Berlin's development. Basing their ideas on the city's urban plan and the architectural styles prevalent at the beginning of the twentieth century, the proponents of critical reconstruction promoted dense block structures, stone façades, and building heights modeled on turn-of-the-century Berlin apartment buildings. In the nineteenth and early twentieth centuries, "nature" and open space were relegated to clearly defined and confined areas that were seen as contrasting with built structure. In keeping with this idea, Johannisthal's scenery of dry grassland populated with flocks of sheep also draws on imagery that has been associated in Germany since the nineteenth century with primordial nature and an ideal cultural landscape. In his *Wanderungen durch die Mark Brandenburg* (1880), the widely read nineteenth-century German novelist Theodor Fontane highlighted the dry sandy soil, pine forests, and heathlands that are so characteristic of the Brandenburg region surrounding the Berlin. Furthered by paintings and literary works such as Fontane's, dry grass- and heathland had therefore already assumed an iconic landscape status in the German mind by the early twentieth century. It had also been promoted as quintessentially German, and as a powerful nationalist expression of the homeland by conservative and reactionary garden designers, artists, writers, and art critics, who later often sympathized with Nazi politics.[46] After World War II, the imagery of a dry grass- and heathland grazed by sheep, and the romanticism and nostalgia associated with it, were furthered by the establishment of Germany's first nature park, comprising parts of the Lüneburg Heath, in which industry and modern agriculture were forbidden in favor of traditional sheep herding.[47] Largely the result of a conservative middle-class critique of industrial society and of health concerns regarding urban life, nature parks were established to provide for controlled, "orderly" recreation like hiking, and to conserve landscape scenery for aesthetic enjoyment. As during the early nature conservation movement at the beginning of the twentieth century, the German nature park program of the 1950s and 1960s proposed the zoning of parks for different uses. Every park was to be divided into a protected core area off-limits to the general public and a belt that catered to public recreation.[48] The design for Johannisthal airfield is therefore grounded both in a national landscape aesthetic and in conceptions for nature conservation and preservation that date back to the early twentieth century.

In Tempelhofer Freiheit, valuable flora and fauna habitats are currently being conserved as at Johannisthal,[49] but the city and the park designers have declared their intent to "intensify nature," which means to increase biodiversity through human intervention and design rather than maintain the existing biodiversity through management and visitor control. Gross. Max. has rejected the contemporary practice of nature preservation and is searching for new creative ways to increase the species diversity in Tempelhofer Freiheit.[50] The designers are responding to a need for flexibility, openness, and resilience, character traits that have been part of design discussions for the last twenty years. The park's design and design process appear to be based upon a hybrid of old and recent ecological theories. On the one hand, Gross.Max. still talks of developing a stable climax vegetation, thereby expressing the old understanding that ecosystems develop toward a final, stable state. On the other hand, the firm's design does not favor nature reserves like Johannisthal, and the design process has been shaped by a hybrid bottom-up and top-down approach. Tempelhofer Freiheit's evolution so far, therefore, also reflects the more recent theory of ecosystem evolution toward a shifting steady-state mosaic and a dynamic equilibrium characterized by discontinuous and intermittent evolution and unpredictable systemic shifts and changes. The park project is an attempt at flexible management and adaptive collaborative planning, which in the last decade have been promoted as best practice for biodiversity conservation and urban development.[51] It exemplifies a design and planning approach that understands humans and their culture as part of nature, and the city as an ecosystem whose development can be shaped and formed by humans, but not entirely anticipated or controlled. In contrast to the 1990s, when urban planning rhetoric in Berlin revolved around the body-politic based on the idea of the city not as an independent but as a planned organism,[52] Berlin today is conceived by its government as an open, dynamic ecosystem of which humans are a part. How far this may be a conscious attempt to legitimize neoliberal urban-development schemes in times of financial crisis remains to be seen. The belief that humankind is an integral component of ecosystems and therewith not only responsible for but also subject to sudden changes in these systems is also apparent in the design process for Orange County Great Park on the former United States Marine Corps Air Station El Toro in Southern California.

Orange County Great Park

In contrast to Tempelhof, the Marine Corps Air Station El Toro in Southern California was never used for commercial air traffic. The air station opened in 1942 during World War II and was located near Irvine in Orange County 40.3 miles (65 kilometers) southeast of Los Angeles in a region that is today characterized by master-planned suburban neighborhoods, shopping malls, and high-rise office buildings and is one of the most popular living areas in the United States. Operations at the Air Station El Toro ceased in 1999 as a result of the U.S. Defense Base Realignment and Closure process that was begun in 1988 to reduce the expenditure on operations and maintenance of military installations.

The American landscape architect Ken Smith and his team designed the park that is currently under construction on the former base (fig. 88). A jury instated by the board of the non-profit Orange County Great Park Corporation founded in 2003 declared the Smith team the winner of an international park design competition in 2005.[53] The results of community visioning processes, focus groups, opinion polls, and a stakeholders conference held in the competition year were passed on to the seven competition semi-finalists for their incorporation in the final designs. Smith's design received wide backing by Orange County citizens, and since the time of the design's selection the Orange County Great Park Corporation has continued its efforts to forge citizen support and engagement in the park project to ensure its success. This has also been necessary as the actual conversion of the air station into a park has been very controversial from its inception.

The 1993 decision to close the base caused much discussion among citizens, politicians, and stakeholders in the region. Some wanted the base to be turned into an international airport to counter the economic downturn of the early 1990s. Others considered an international airport incompatible with their comfortable suburban lifestyle. It was not until a 2002 referendum that Orange County voters decided to turn the air station into a park. Three years later, 3,700 acres (1,497 hectares) of the 4,700-acre (1,902-hectare) site

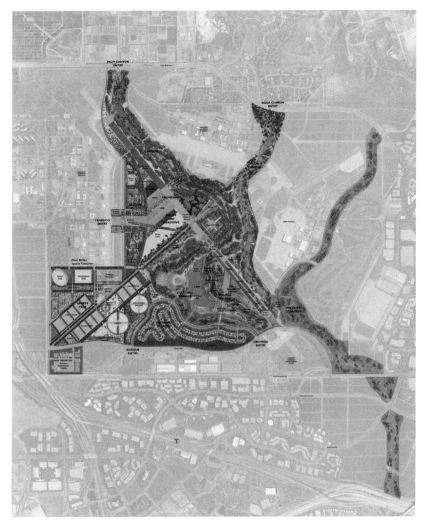

FIG. 88. WORKSHOP:
Ken Smith Landscape
Architect, Plan for
the OCGP. (Courtesy
of WORKSHOP: Ken
Smith Landscape
Architect)

were auctioned, leaving 1,000 acres (405 hectares) in federal ownership as nature reserve. The Lennar Corporation, a private developer, purchased the area by auction, agreeing to develop part of the grounds and hand over 1,347 acres (545 hectares) to the City of Irvine for the park.[54] Since the 2005 design competition the development has continued to be contentious, leading the Orange County Grand Jury in 2005–6 to point out the potential conflict of interest in the government structure of the Orange County Great Park Corporation, whose board was dominated by Irvine City Council officials and other South County members.[55]

While the government and financing of Orange County Great Park have remained contentious, the public decision makers and designers have taken into account individual citizen wishes with regards to park programming. However, the design forms and strategies rely on a selective and invented regional cultural, social, and environmental history determined by the designers besides a generally increasing environmental awareness.

INVENTED TRADITIONS

The park that is being marketed as a "metropolitan park" is situated in a postsuburban landscape characterized by a combination of urban, suburban, and rural patterns and inhabited by 3 million people.[56] Since the 1970s, homogeneous low-density suburban developments, malls, and office parks have spread across the county, decentralizing land uses. Although current demographic statistics suggest otherwise, Orange County's citizenship is still often stereotyped as white, educated, wealthy, and conservative, and social life has been generalized as occurring more inside private homes and clubs than in public streets. Until the 2008 financial crisis, Orange County had one of the highest economic growth rates in the United States, and further population increase was predicted. Although this makes it clear why a park was being developed in the first place, representatives from the northern parts of the county criticized the decision because small parks rather than "megaparks" were needed in the less wealthy and more densely populated northern neighborhoods.[57] Since the postwar years, Orange County has paid little attention to the needs of the population with lower socioeconomic status and to the provision of subsidized affordable housing.[58]

The Orange County Great Park follows in the footsteps of a development that began in the county in the 1960s, when Irvine, the biggest privately master-planned community in the United States, was built only 3.7 miles (6 kilometers) from the new park site. Fittingly, the Orange County Great Park Corporation in its 2010 annual report legitimized its preconstruction expenditures for the "Comprehensive Master Design for the Park" by referencing the region's history of master-planned communities and of Irvine in particular.[59] Home to a wealthy and homogeneous group of citizens who largely perceive it as an ordered, clean city, Irvine has become a model for other privately developed neighborhoods in the region. Critics, however, have described Irvine's regulated suburban neighborhoods, often built in a neotraditional style, as "aseptic," "faceless," and "soulless."[60] As Karen Till has shown for the nearby Rancho Santa Margarita neighborhood, private developers often assign a cultural or historical tradition to the neighborhoods they build that is for the most part invented.[61]

Similarly, the park design is based upon a narrative that intends to tell a local, regional, and national story. As with many of the nearby master-planned communities, the park's story is selective and based upon heroic western frontier myths. It deals in particular with the period immediately after the foundation of Orange County in 1889 and with the history of the Marine Corps Air Station beginning in 1942. The park itself is a testimony to the war years and the social and economic developments in California. With the conservation and adaptive reuse of buildings and parts of the base's runways, a planned military museum and veteran's memorial at the location where the two main former runways cross, the design testifies to an era when, as the historian Kevin Starr has shown, war was "an American, hence a Californian, way of life."[62] By drawing on selected parts of U.S. military history, the park design attempts to create a collective consciousness and forge a local, regional, and national identity. In a similar way, parts of the design entitled "groves" and "fields" that were inspired by orange plantations also refer to a particular period in the history of Southern California. The "groves" and "fields" situated west of an artificially built canyon are intended for urban farming and community gardening, recalling both the aesthetics and the use of the land in this region between 1890 and the 1950s. In that period, Orange County was an agricultural landscape where citrus crops dominated. The land that had been farmed initially by Native Americans, then by Spanish missionaries and colonial rulers, and finally by Mexicans was turned into orange plantations by the new Anglo-American landowners. The Irvine Ranch became one of the largest Valencia orange orchards, and the railroad helped establish a national market for California citrus fruit.[63] As various scholars have shown, "oranges in California have always been more than just fruit."[64] They were symbols for an earthly paradise, used as metaphors for health, purity, affinity with nature, entrepreneurial spirit, and for what Douglas Sackman has described as the "orange empire," an ethnically differentiated class society based upon a profit-oriented economy.[65]

In Orange County Great Park, the orange hot air balloons symbolize the oranges and orange plantations of the "orange empire." Inspired by the tethered observation balloon that took visitors for a ride while Berlin's Potsdamer Platz was being constructed in the 1990s, the park designers proposed installing three tethered orange-colored hot air balloons in Orange County Great Park (fig. 89). The proposal to use orange-colored rental bikes also alludes to this period of the county's history. Whereas oranges in the first half of the twentieth century were wrapped in tissue paper printed with images of California landscapes and virginal female beauties, today orange-colored hot air balloons brand the park with a corporate identity. They transform the park's restored seemingly virginal landscape into a product for consumption.

The park design hides parts of history by highlighting others. Although the "groves" and "fields" in Orange County Great Park are intended to represent the agricultural history of the region since the time of the Native Americans and although the designers suggest that parts of the park could be designed to call attention to the natural and cultural history of the site,

the most conspicuous design references—the hot air balloons and orange plantations—relate only to the first half of the twentieth century. The current park design therefore builds upon the two periods in the history of Orange County—the time of its military base and its citrus production—that led the region to a big economic boom. A romanticized version of the agricultural landscape at the beginning of the twentieth century, the new recreational landscape of the Great Park is intended to provide Orange County with another economic boost and to increase its national and even international esteem at the beginning of the twenty-first century.[66]

RESTORED WILDLIFE IN A "SUSTAINABLE PARK"

Orange County Great Park is advertised as a sustainable park. Besides drawing upon the site's cultural history, the designers attempt to reestablish ecological networks and mosaics, and they emphasize the reuse of building materials from the air station. The design has determined that all park architecture will be fitted with green roofs and will merge with the landscape. Buses will connect different locations in the park with other means of public transportation outside. No cars are allowed in the park, however, and ample parking space is provided amid orange groves on the park's periphery. It is assumed that the park will depend on visitors coming by car, although the park is located in the center of Orange County and relatively near the railroad connection between Los Angeles and San Diego.

In line with today's understanding of ecology based upon dynamic processes without final stable states, the designers hope to create a diverse range of new habitats that connect to existing ones in adjacent forests and coastal areas and that increase biodiversity. With their design, the park makers aim at increasing the "ecological value" of the site, which is described as "sterile plateau," and at restoring "much of the region's natural heritage."[67] In their own oxymoronic phrase, the design developed for the Great Park strives "to *restore* the El Toro Marine Airbase into a *new landscape* that reflects Orange County's rich natural heritage."[68]

The manufactured topography of an approximately 820-foot- (250-meter-) wide and 2.5-mile- (4-kilometer-) long designed canyon bisects the park running from northwest to southeast. Park visitors will be able to access the lusciously vegetated canyon that is to provide a shady, refreshing, and secluded space on a variety of hiking and biking trails. A habitat-park area east and west of the canyon, including the restored Bee Creek and its wetlands, and the day-lighted and restored Agua Chinon Creek will also be accessible to visitors. In contrast, a 178-acre (72-hectare) wildlife corridor that connects the park with the Cleveland National Forest is off-limits to park visitors. The park as a whole is envisioned as a stepping-stone within the regional system of wildlife habitats and nature reserves, connecting the Cleveland National Forest and the Santa Ana Mountains in the north with wilderness and state parks along the coast in the south. Although parts of this system are inaccessible to visitors, humankind is understood as an integral part of this system, as attested by the humorous "species account: human being" that was included in the 2009 *Orange County Great Park Ecological Guidelines.*[69] It becomes clear that the proposed restoration is not exclusively ecocentric, but that it both involves humans and acknowledges their authorship. It therefore exemplifies the recent movement in North American discussions about ecological restoration and ecology to view "humans as components of ecosystems," as the 1991 Cary Conference, an acclaimed international biannual conference series begun in 1985, was entitled.[70] To create place and establish a narrative continuity, the Orange County Great Park design adds an ecological history to its invented cultural history. The manufactured landscape and habitats like vernal pools for the endangered fairy shrimp and coastal sage scrub for the threatened California gnatcatcher in Orange County Great Park re-create a mythical Southern Californian wilderness with the help of plant seeds from similar local habitats and land formations modeled on the surrounding topography.

The Orange County Great Park therefore both resembles and contrasts with some of the early American urban public parks. Like Frederick Law Olmsted and Calvert Vaux who re-created the scenic qualities of the Catskills and Adirondacks in their 1858 Central Park design, and like Jens

Jensen, who established idealized land formations typical of the Illinois prairie in his 1916 plan for Columbus Park in Chicago, the designers of Orange County Great Park have sought to create a scenic regionalist wilderness. In contrast to Olmsted and Vaux's Central Park design and Jensen's prairie bluffs, however, the Orange County Great Park design is also informed by the habitat requirements of native plant and animal species that have been established on the basis of scientific biological research. As in Central and Columbus Parks, whose celebrations of seemingly untouched nature were intended to foster national and regional identities, identity politics also play an important role in Orange County Great Park.

The Great Park design reflects an attitude toward environmental concerns particularly prevalent in Orange County since the 1960s. There, the increased environmental consciousness that resulted from the environmental movement was not always altruistically and socially motivated. In many cases, it resulted from a fear of the loss of private property value.[71] As social scientists have observed, the political climate of large parts of Orange County have been emblematic of the New Political Culture, described simply as a social-liberal and economic-conservative attitude that embraces environmental protection on the one hand and the protection of individual interests and personal welfare on the other.[72] Fittingly and programmatically, the lead designer Ken Smith declared it as the park's objective "to make a place where the issues of our times interact directly with the private reflections and actions of the individual." At the same time, however, Smith further defined the goal as fulfilling the needs of the various citizen groups of different cultures.[73]

While the park is largely dependent on the private economy, time will tell how far individual or communal interests will determine the park development, and how far the interests of disadvantaged groups will be taken into consideration. To spark curiosity and support for the park project among the county's constituents and to render it an instrument of place-marketing, the Orange County Great Park Corporation has realized a so-called "Preview Park."

PREVIEW PARK

Since 2005, a core area of the park has been realized. In line with the film and media culture of the region, the Preview Park offers the public a preview of what they may expect once the area has been fully developed. Big, orange-colored circles painted on the approach road as markers lead the visitor to the Preview Park (fig. 90). Orange trees planted in containers organize the parking space (fig. 91). An orange hot air balloon offers views across the former air base, symbolizing the green future of the vast, still largely barren

FIG. 90.
Approach road
to the Preview
Park, OCGP, 2009.
(Photograph by
the author)

airfield. The park designers and the Orange County Great Park Corporation have made every effort to turn a visit to the Preview Park into an event. While the site hosts movie nights, art shows, concerts, and farmers markets, the design provides opportunities for nostalgic memories. Besides a visitor center and explanatory panels that inform about the future park design, a timeline painted on one of the runways offers insight into the events of the 1940s, when the air station was built and first went into operation. The idea to use the park to write history recalls Olmsted and Vaux's objectives for Central Park, which created a landscape monument to the United States, "nature's nation."

Smith's idea of complementing his plan drawings with a manga narrative and illustrations similar to film techniques fits into the regional media culture. Smith commissioned the manga artist June Kim to produce evocative black-and-white ink drawings for a storyboard of an imaginary film that narrates a day in the park from the viewpoints of a variety of fictitious park visitors. Like a manga, or a film, the park aims at providing space for desires, discoveries, and memories. The manga not only illustrates ideas for the future, but it also reflects the anticipated demographic changes in Orange County and the different attitudes of its citizens. Thus, in the manga

FIG. 91. Parking
lot at the Preview
Park, OCGP, 2009.
(Photograph by
the author)

not only Vanessa Carter and Jacob Merrick but also William Gonzales, Danny Valenzuela, Diego, Leena Kansai, and Yutako Sho tell us what they appreciate about the new park. Orange County is currently developing into a majority-minority region that is becoming home to an increasing number of Latin Americans and Asian Americans.[74] At the same time, however, the manga also reflects the pervasive critical attitude toward what was perceived by Orange County citizens up until the 1990s as the "wild" and "dilapidated Moloch" Los Angeles. The fictional manga character Hajimo Asama reflects: "This park makes me excited for the future of Orange County. It's fun for the family, ecological, historical and bold enough to distinguish us from Los Angeles. I'm going to buy a house near this park."

Like the oranges at the beginning of the twentieth century, today the Preview Park is a consumer product marketed by Orange County. While the orange once symbolized the bounty of an agricultural landscape, today it stands for a new park landscape that is advertised boisterously as the "first great metropolitan park of the twenty-first century." At the end of the nineteenth and the beginning of the twentieth centuries, economic as well as social and health concerns induced Americans to build city parks and entire park systems. Even then, American city planners and promoters realized how parks could improve a city's image. The content and presentation of

FLIGHTS OF IMAGINATION

the Smith team's design, which has won several prizes, reflect these same purposes today, and they both reflect and influence developments, policies, and concerns that have shaped in particular the central and southern parts of Orange County.[75]

GLOBALIZATION FACILITATED by aviation has enabled landscape architecture to assume an important role in the reclamation and transformation of airfields into parks. In multiple ways, however, park designs for former airport sites appear as both products and motors of capitalist economies. While the closure of airfields and airports is a result of global neoliberal developments in the first place, many landscape architectural design strategies used for the park designs both reflect and promote capitalist urban development while at the same time emphasizing locally specific site conditions and ecologies. The democratic qualities of the governance, management, and development models used in the cases presented here vary in the amount and methods of community engagement and range from directed incremental to master-planned development. In all cases, however, the designers have developed plans on the basis of the local and regional environment and ecology, which increases their potential usefulness in identity politics and in the cities' marketing and branding efforts on national and international scales.

In the designs presented here, humans are understood as part of nature and integral components of ecosystems, indicating that the designers are trying to overcome the nature-culture dichotomy. However, whereas at Orange County Great Park, ecological restoration means the creation of an environment in its "ahistoric" state—modeled on a hypothetical "pristine state" devoid of human activity and long-term historical change—at Tempelhofer Freiheit and Johannisthal, ecological restoration means the conservation of a managed ecosystem, or, one could say, the conservation of the status quo, which has obviously been influenced by humans.

It is true that the sociospatial and geographical context of these projects differs in significant ways: While Orange County Great Park is surrounded by suburban residential neighborhoods in a Mediterranean climate, Tempelhofer Freiheit and Johannisthal are located amid mostly four- to five-story urban fabric in the mid-European temperate climate zone. However, besides these factors, the different approaches to ecological restoration that have informed the park designs also depend on the different histories of ecological restoration in these two locations. Whereas in the United States, ahistoric ecology has a long tradition and has only recently been modified to include humans as components of ecosystems and to acknowledge the various human-induced changes of ecosystems over time, in Germany, ecologists have considered ecosystems to be influenced by human activity since the early twentieth century. Thus, the new landscape and habitat conditions that were created at Tempelhof and Johannisthal when the airfields were first laid out and that have developed with their use since then have been recognized as unique and worthy of conservation. In contrast, the land of the Marine Corps Air Station El Toro has been described as a "sterile plateau" whose ecological value needed to be increased. Despite these differences in perception and approach, in all parks areas have been set aside for wildlife conservation, and traces of human history are being preserved. Special design features like the hot air balloon in Orange County Great Park and the rock monument in Tempelhofer Freiheit recall local or specific periods of the site's history, thereby forging identity and providing a design narrative. Furthermore, despite the different landscape ideals that have been used as models, nostalgia and romanticism associated with previous site conditions play a role in the park designs.

With projects like Orange County Great Park, Tempelhofer Freiheit, and Johannisthal, airports have come full circle. As the authors of the *Regional Plan of New York and Its Environs* suggested in the 1920s, undesirable airfields are being turned into permanent public open space and wildlife habitats. What Sydney E. Veale described in 1945 as "man-made" technological infrastructure on which "the frugalities of nature" had been "rectif[ied]"[76] with machines is today being returned to nature, a nature that has come to be understood, however, as including humans and their culture, and as a manufactured commodity.

AS MUCH AS THE history of airports and powered flight, which now spans a century, is a history of technological progress, it is also a history of the landscape that can reveal the recent evolution of our changeable relationship with our environment. This history is not one of exclusive unmediated change and powerful subordination of nature; rather, it is the history of nature's transformation characterized by the ambivalence and ambiguities of modernity.

The effects that powered flight and the related view from above have had on the design and perception of the land, and, conversely, the effects that our designs, use, and perception of the land have had on the formation of flight and the ways of seeing from above, have varied. Landscapes have been designed, built, and transformed for and against the aerial view, depending on the circumstances. Land has been exploited and conserved with the help of the aerial view. Landscapes have been designed, built, transformed, destroyed, and reconstructed as a result of powered aviation, and with the use of the aerial view. And while powered aviation has created some of the most modern environments, airports in particular have often also tended to be expressions of a vernacular modernism. At the same time, the landscape and events on the ground such as the industrialization and urbanization of large parts of the world, archaeological exploration, colonial expansion, and warfare have influenced the development of powered aviation and of the ways we see our world from above. Furthermore, powered aviation and the aerial view have redirected design professionals' attention to the ground, and to the horizontal view. Despite our life-sustaining flights of imagination, not only the human body, but also human consciousness must return to the earth.

Notes

Introduction

1. Malewitsch, *Die gegenstandslose Welt*, 16. Malevich was echoed some decades later by the Austrian-born avant-garde architect Richard Neutra: "To gain height against the eternal pull of gravity is the supreme triumph of the living; only the dead must lie level. . . . Flatness is the prototype of forced and final relaxation . . . of resigned vertical aspiration" (Neutra, *Survival*, 166ff.).

2. See Lokaj, *Petrarch's Ascent*, 105. See also Clark, *Landscape*, 10.

3. See Stilgoe, "The Railroad Beautiful."

4. See Robinson, "A Railroad Beautiful," 570.

5. See Stilgoe, "The Railroad Beautiful," 57–58.

6. See Freytag, "When the Railway Conquered the Garden," 233.

7. Eliot, "Influence of the Automobile," 31–32.

8. Ibid., 37.

9. Turner, *Aerial Navigation*, 277–78.

10. See Deutsche Lufthansa A.G., *Going to Europe? Time Flies! Save Time! Look It Over! Fly!* (Frankfurt a.M.: Hellerdruck A.G., n.d.), unpaginated.

11. Stein, *Picasso*, 49.

12. Colvin, *Land and Landscape* (1948), 9.

13. See ibid., 252–53.

14. Gutkind, *World from the Air*, opposite figs. 396 and 397.

15. See, for example, the direct reference to Charles Lindbergh in an article by the German architect Franz Schuster, "Die neue Wohnung und ihr Garten," *Die Gartenkunst* 40, no. 9 (1927): 142.

16. Wood, *Airports*, 8.

17. In the 1930s, Lufthansa's cartographic flight schedules included more and increasingly diverse information reflecting the greater number of planes in the sky. By 1934, the plans included information on different route types (i.e., passenger, mail, and cargo routes), prices, and the routes and schedules of foreign air carriers serving German cities.

18. See Bradshaw's *Continental Railway Guide and General Handbook Illustrated*, with local and other maps, special edition 3/6 (1905); and *Deutsche Lufthansa Nachrichten* 7, no. 3–4 (1932): title page.

19. See Fischer von Poturzyn, *Lufthansa*, 31.

20. Aronovici, "Space-Time Planning."

21. For vernacular modernism and the ambivalence of modernity, see Hüppauf and Umbach, "Introduction," 14.

22. Ibid., 4.

23. For children's recognition of aerial photographs as map space and cognitive mapping in childhood, see Freudenschuh, "Micro- and Macro-Scale Environments"; and Uttal and Tan, "Cognitive Mapping." For the Australian Aborigines, see Cosgrove and Fox, *Photography*, 11.

24. In 1930, a class in city planning at the Department of City Planning and Landscape Architecture in the College of Fine and Applied Arts of the University of Illinois took to the air "for a view of the Chicago region." The department chair, Karl B. Lohmann, later reported that it was, "so far as is known, the first time any class in City Planning as such (and perhaps in any other subject as well) had included an air trip in its itinerary" (Karl B. Lohmann, "City Planning and Landscape Architecture at the University of Illinois: An Historical Record [1868–1954]," 6. RS 12/4/805, box 1: "An Historical Record, 1868–1954," 1954, University of Illinois Archives).

25. Hitchcock, "Gardens," 19.

26. Gropius, *Bauhausbauten*, 8–9, 11.

27. Moholy-Nagy, *Material*, 195.

28. Hayler, "Aeroplane and City Planning," 576, 578.

29. See, for example, Laser, Naumann, and Wöll-ner, *Plauen und Umgebung von oben.* See also Boemi and Travaglini, *Roma,* for a recent work that uses aerial photographs from a variety of sources and years to illustrate the changes of Roman urban development throughout the late nineteenth and twentieth centuries.

30. Hüppauf and Umbach, "Introduction," 7.

31. See http://terra-x.zdf.de/ZDFde/inhalt/30 /0,1872,8238398,00.

32. See http://terra-x.zdf.de/ZDFde/inhalt/13 /0,1872,8238125,00.html.

33. Le Corbusier, *Towards a New Architecture,* 13.

34. Friedland and Boden, "NowHere," 36.

35. Arnheim, "Order and Complexity," 160.

36. Wray et al., "Photo Interpretation," 668.

37. Merleau-Ponty, "Eye and Mind," 160–61.

38. Lister, "Sustainable Large Parks," 36.

39. Jordan and Lubick, *Making the Nature Whole,* 178–79.

40. For aircraft numbers, see Weir, "Airport," 119; and McGregor, *Kansas City,* 10.

41. The American Society of Landscape Architects was founded in 1899. The Society of German Garden Artists (VdG; Verein Deutscher Gartenkünstler) was founded in 1887; and in 1913, the Association of German Garden Architects (BDGA; Bund Deutscher Gartenarchitekten) was established, a forerunner of what finally became today's German Association of Landscape Architects (BDLA; Bund Deutscher Landschaftsarchitekten). In Britain, the Institute of Landscape Architects was founded in 1929 (today's Landscape Institute), followed by the Danish Association of Garden Architects (today's DL; Danske Landskabsarkitekter) in 1931, the Association Belge des Architectes de Jardin et Paysagistes (ABAJP) in 1935, and the Associazione Italiana di Architettura del Paesaggio (AIAPP; Italian Association of Landscape Architecture) in 1950, to name a few.

42. John Dixon Hunt characterized landscape architecture as having a "fuzzy profile" (see Hunt, *Greater Perfections,* 3).

One | Plans in the Air

1. See Hallion, *Taking Flight,* 59.

2. Jeffries, *Aerial Voyages,* 29.

3. A. Black, *Civil Airports,* 29–30; see also A. Black, "Air Terminal." The word "airport" only began to be

commonly used at the end of the 1920s, when terminal buildings marked the advent of commercial aviation (see Douglas, "Who Designs Airports?," 303). For the use of the words "airfield," "airport," "aerodrome," "airdrome," etc., see also Voigt, "Hippodrome to the Aerodrome," 27).

4. Veale, *To-morrow's Airliners,* 247.

5. Ibid., 295.

6. See Fischer von Poturzyn, *Lufthansa,* 73. *The Future of Aviation Is on the Ground,* brochure (F. A. Inc., 1929).

7. See Reade, "Aeroplanes," 265.

8. Mitchell, *Skyways,* 94.

9. Meisch, "Architecture and Air Transportation," 38.

10. Mitchell, *Skyways,* 108, 92–93.

11. See ibid.

12. Le Corbusier, *City of Tomorrow,* 187–88.

13. See Brock, "Giving Thought." For Keally's airport projects, see also A. Lee, "Francis Keally."

14. See Low, "Future of Flying," 112; and Beaulieu, *London,* 94.

15. See Norman, "London," 328; "A Central London Airport," *Air and Airways* (July 1931): 109–10.

16. Wenneman, *Municipal Airports,* 796.

17. See Lurçat, "Projet pour un aéroport-relais"; Cohen, *André Lurçat,* 136–40.

18. See Reade, "Aeroplanes."

19. See Andriello, *Aerourbanistica,* 60.

20. Kaempffert, Patterson, and Wirth, *Airplane,* 18.

21. Ogburn, *Social Effects,* 341; Andriello, *Aerourbanistica,* 60. For the vision of the use of mass-produced helicopters, see also Kaempffert, *Airplane,* 18.

22. Ogburn, *Social Effects,* 341–43, 362.

23. For the development of different airport types, see Arthur, "Airports," 301; and Karl W. Wittmann, "Flughafenbau," 190. This idea continued to be supported into the 1940s (see Meisch, "Architecture and Air Transportation," 42; and Ogburn, *Social Effects,* 210).

24. Neutra, "Terminals?—Transfer!" 100, 104; Bel Geddes, *Horizons,* 79–108.

25. Goodrich, "Airports as a Factor in City Planning," 190.

26. See Migge, *Gartenkultur,* 7, 35.

27. See Aerodromes Committee, *Town Planning,* 7; and Onosaki, *Airport.* In his short treatise, Onosaki made use of the diagrams representing prototypical design schemes that the American consulting

engineer E. P. Goodrich had developed and published in the same year. In these layouts for airfields, Goodrich assumed a circular landing area covering 1,000 acres (405 hectares) that enclosed a circular space for all necessary buildings like hangars, administrative buildings, hotels, signal towers, and machine shops. A mooring mast for dirigibles marked the center. In his schemes, Goodrich showed how multiples of one module, or unit, could be put together to form a circular landing area. At its full extension, the airfield would, according to Goodrich, accommodate the landing and departure of forty-four airplanes simultaneously regardless of wind direction (see Goodrich, "Airports as a Factor in City Planning").

28. Sudell, *Landscape Gardening*, 418.

29. Norman, "London," 329.

30. See A. Black, "Air Terminal."

31. Ibid., 225.

32. U.S. Department of Commerce, Aeronautics Branch, *Aviation Training*, 1.

33. Wirth, "Municipal Airport," 13–14. Wirth was successful with his argumentation in Minneapolis. The Wold-Chamberlain Field, the Minneapolis Municipal Airport, which had been built on the former Twin City Motor Speedway, was supervised by the Board of Park Commissioners until 1943, when it was turned over to the Metropolitan Airports Commission (see Wenneman, *Municipal Airports*).

34. Wirth, "Municipal Airport," 11.

35. See Grant, "Airports," 189–91.

36. Weir, "Airport," 120.

37. Clarke, "Airport." See also Nolen, "Public Airports," 127.

38. "Editorial," 29.

39. See Hubbard, McClintock, and Williams, *Airports*, 22, 58, 166, 169.

40. See Whitbeck, "Airports," 107; Harland Bartholomew and Associates, "A Proposed Parkway System for Lucas County, Ohio," *Parks & Recreation* 13, no. 5 (May–June 1930): 267; and Harland Bartholomew and Associates, *A Comprehensive Report on a Proposed System of Major Highways and Parkways for Lucas County, Ohio* (1928), 70–73.

41. Brock, "Giving Thought."

42. Wagner, *Modern Airport*, 107.

43. Aronovici, "Space-Time Planning."

44. Walsh, "Architectural Principles," 35; Douglas, "Who Designs Airports?," 312.

45. Le Corbusier, *Towards a New Architecture*, 11, 19.

46. Pirath, *Flughäfen*, 7.

47. See Brock, "Giving Thought"; Voigt, "Hippodrome to the Aerodrome," 43; "R.I.B.A. Aerodrome Competition," *Architects' Journal* (January 30, 1929): 208–11; "R.I.B.A. Competition for a Design for an Aerodrome," *Journal of the Royal Institute of British Architects* (February 23, 1929): 325–26; Thomas Mitchell, "British Architects Competition for a London Aerodrome," *Airports* (April 1929): 19–20; and "Future London Air Ports," *Flight* 21 (February 1929): 117.

48. See Lewis-Dale, *Aviation*, 4–5; and Aerodromes Committee, *Town Planning*, 3.

49. For the Schinkel Competition and the first airport competitions for Hamburg, Munich, and Berlin, see Gärtner, "Flughafenarchitektur," 53, 70–102. For the American student competition for airport design at the Beaux Arts Institute of Design, see Menhinick, "Municipal Airports," 280.

50. Hubbard, McClintock, and Williams, *Airports*, 36.

51. Wood, *Airports*, 306. For the vision of airports as civic center and the combination of utility and beauty in their planning and design, see, for example, Keally, "Architectural Treatment," 40, 47.

52. See Wood, *Airports*, 11–12. See also Douglas, "Who Designs Airports?" Wood did not mention landscape architects, although together with engineers they were among the first city planners in his country and although their training also allowed them to fulfill many of the tasks mentioned above assigned to engineers and architects.

53. *Lehigh Airports Competition*, first page.

54. Lehigh Portland Cement Company, *Airport Designs*, 12.

55. Ibid. While cement runways improved airplane takeoff because they enabled higher speeds, until airplanes were outfitted with better break systems, grass landing strips were preferred because they were softer and more elastic and facilitated slowing down the airplane once it had touched down.

56. See, for example, Arthur, "Airports," 300–301; A. Black, *Civil Airports*, 1; Whitbeck, "Airports," 107; and Froesch and Prokosch, *Airport Planning*, 6.

57. Wagner, *Modern Airport*, 70.

58. See Wenneman, *Municipal Airports*, 771–73.

59. Stratton Coyner, "The Job of the Airport

Manager," *American City* 42 (March 1930): 128; Wagner, *Modern Airport*, 83.

60. Francis Keally quoted in A. Lee, "Francis Keally," 47.

61. See U.S. Department of Commerce, Aeronautics Branch, Regional Airport Advisor—CWA, "Airparks," in Miscellaneous Records of Colonel Sumpter Smith, 1935–46, box 3, Federal Aviation Administration, Civil Aeronautics Administration, RG 237, National Archives and Records Administration. On the role of airparks in the WPA, see also the 1937 brochure by the Works Progress Administration and Federal Works Program entitled *America Spreads Her Wings.*

62. See U.S. Department of Commerce and Civil Aeronautics Administration, *Small Airports;* and Strohmeier, "More Fun."

63. See Hines, *Richard Neutra,* 73; and Ogburn, *Social Effects,* 411–12.

64. See "Airports for Private Flying," undated manuscript, NASMA F3-610000-03; and Ogburn, *Social Effects,* 549–50.

65. Oertel, *Community Airports.* See also Froesch and Prokosch, *Airport Planning,* 6.

66. John Softness, "The City Called Idlewild," *Shell Aviation News* 275 (May 1961): 7.

67. See "Airport Cities: Gateways to the Jet Age," *Time,* August 15, 1960; Fuller and Harley, *Aviopolis,* 48; Kasarda and Lindsay, *Aerotropolis;* and Kasarda, "Airport City."

68. Soleri, "City," 11–13.

69. See Urry, "Aeromobilities," 35; and Sheller and Urry, "Introduction," 14–15.

70. The "A" rating referred to the best and most extensively equipped airport (see U.S. Department of Commerce, Aeronautics Branch, *Airport Rating Regulations*).

71. Steele, "Modern Landscape Architecture," 23.

72. Ibid., 24.

73. See Gothein, *Geschichte,* 132.

74. Hubbard and Kimball, *Introduction,* 43.

75. See the aerial photographs of Les Miroirs, Les Tuileries, the Luxembourg Gardens, Champs, Maintenon, Sassy, Chenonceaux, and Villandry in Gromort, *L'art des jardins.*

76. See Le Corbusier, *Towards a New Architecture,* 47–64.

77. See ibid., 51–52.

78. Brock, "Giving Thought." For a comparison of airports to André Le Nôtre's gardens of Versailles, see also Keally, "Architectural Treatment," 40.

79. Brock, "Giving Thought."

80. See Davison, "Airport Design," 509.

81. Wagner, *Modern Airport,* 73.

82. See L. Magnus Austin, "Air Park at Heston," *Architects' Journal* 70, no. 7 (August 1929): 199–204.

83. Nolen, *Airports and Airways.*

84. See Karl W. Wittmann, "Flughafenbau," 189.

85. See Meisch, "Architecture and Air Transportation," 41. Once the Jet Age had begun with the certification of the Boeing 707 in 1958, it was believed that airplane design characteristics would no longer determine the airport size and layout but that the growth in airport transportation would enable the airport designer to freely search for solutions that could accommodate this growth outside of the current boundaries (see Oscar Bakke, "The Aviation World of Tomorrow," in *Master Planning the Aviation Environment,* ed. Angelo Cherchione et al. [Tucson: University of Arizona Press, 1970], 3–5).

86. See Ogburn, *Social Effects,* 192; Fischer von Poturzyn, *Lufthansa,* 56; and Kaempffert, *Airplane,* 18.

87. Brock, "Giving Thought."

88. See Keally, "Architectural Treatment," 115–16.

89. Brock, "Giving Thought."

90. Spoon, "Landscape Design," 34. Spoon exhibited the landscape design for a proposed airport at the eleventh annual exhibition of the New York Chapter of the American Society of Landscape Architects in May 1934 (see "Landscape Plans Put on Exhibition," *New York Times,* March 21, 1934, 19). As options for airport planting in the New York and New Jersey regions, he noted sumac, bush blueberry, bayberry, and beach grass (see Spoon, "Artistic Design?," 33).

91. Herminghaus, "Landscape Art," 15, 17.

92. Keally quoted in Lee, "Francis Keally," 47.

93. Herminghaus, "Landscape Art," 15.

94. Ibid., 15, 18.

95. McGregor, *Kansas City,* 12–13.

96. "Aviation clip," 629.13 clipp. v. 1, p. 303, Kansas Historical Society.

97. "Topeka Daily Capital 50th Anniversary Edition," 978.1-Sh/T62, pp. 40–42, Kansas Historical Society.

98. See McGregor, *Kansas City,* 28–29.

99. *The Future of Aviation Is on the Ground,* brochure (F. A. Inc., 1929).

100. Wagner, *Modern Airport,* 73.

101. Hall, "Basic Principles," 50.

102. Le Corbusier quoted in Boesiger, *Le Corbusier,* 199.

103. See Dittrich, *Ernst Sagebiel,* 198–205.

104. In the United States, the architect Francis Keally proposed that the airport color scheme should be determined by the surrounding landscape (see Keally, "Architectural Treatment," 49).

105. Early height regulations on land adjacent to airports varied from country to country as a result of the motor power and mechanical capabilities of the airplanes. For example, whereas German manuals required a distance between runway and vertical feature fifteen times its height, in the United States the required distance was only seven times its height (see Karl W. Wittmann, "Flughafenbau," 190).

106. See Onosaki, *Airport.* For the reception of Western ideas regarding landscape architecture and urban public parks during the Meiji Restoration that preceded the period discussed here, see Aya Sakai, "The Hybridization of Ideas on Public Parks: Introduction of Western Thought and Practice into Nineteenth-Century Japan," *Planning Perspectives* 26, no. 3 (2011): 347–71. Besides the landscape design elements suggested by Onosaki that derived from Western precedents, the use of the airport as park and public open space is a result of the new ideas that were introduced into Japanese city planning in the second half of the nineteenth century. Landscaped areas had until then only existed in the private sphere as gardens of the emperor and other social elites and had not been publicly accessible areas.

107. F. Robinson, *Landscape Planting,* 6–7, 10, 11.

108. Ibid., 8–9.

109. U.S. Department of Commerce and Civil Aeronautics Administration, *Airport Landscape Planting,* 1, 4–5.

110. See *Report of the Airway Marking Committee,* January 23, 1929 (Washington, D.C.: U.S. Department of Commerce, 1929), 2; U.S. Department of Commerce, *Air Marking.*

111. Turner, *Aerial Navigation,* 185.

112. Le Corbusier, *Towards a New Architecture,* 110.

113. Hüppauf and Umbach, "Introduction," 2.

114. Umbach, "Deutscher Werkbund," 140.

115. For the importance attributed to the existing rows of poplars in the design competition and the final design, see "Ernstes und Weniger Ernstes: Berliner Flughafen-Wettbewerb," *Wasmuths Monatshefte für Baukunst und Städtebau* 9, no. 10 (1925): 447–53.

116. See *Civil Aviation in Brazil,* 22.

117. Interdepartmental Engineering Commission, *Washington.*

118. Undated sheet entitled "Washington National Airport," box 200, Project Files, 1910–1952, Commission of Fine Arts, RG 66, National Archives.

119. Interdepartmental Engineering Commission, *Washington.*

120. Augé, *Non-Places,* 77–78.

121. See Cresswell, *On the Move,* 221.

122. Neil Brenner quoted in Kesselring, "Global Transfer Points," 41.

123. Kesselring, "Global Transfer Points," 41.

124. See ibid., 47–48.

125. Cresswell, *On the Move,* 225.

126. Banham, "Obsolescent Airport," 252.

127. *Aerial Gateway to the United States,* brochure published on occasion of the dedication of the International Arrival and Airline Wing Buildings, 1957, Idlewild IAP, NYC, New York, F4-613385-01, Technical files, NASMA; see plans and photographs in *Architectural Record* 130, no. 9 (1961): 151–90. The colored piping systems inside the heating and refrigeration plant were reflected in the Fountain plaza pool, providing what *Life* termed "The Dazzle of Idlewild" in 1961 (see "Phenomenon of the Jet Age," *Life,* September 22, 1961, 70–86).

128. "New Aerial Gateway to America," *Architectural Forum* 108, no. 2 (1958): 79–87; "Idlewild Airport," *Architect and Building News* 213, no. 4 (1958): 567–73; *Aerial Gateway to the United States,* brochure published on occasion of the dedication of the International Arrival and Airline Wing Buildings, 1957, Idlewild IAP, NYC, New York, F4-613385-01, Technical files, NASMA.

129. Kiley and Amidon, *Dan Kiley,* 41.

130. See *Landscape Report for Dulles International Airport, Prepared by Office of Dan Kiley, Site and Landscape Consultant,* March 10, 1960. Courtesy Metropolitan Washington Airports Authority.

131. *O'Hare Airport,* 24, 20.

132. Colvin, *Land and Landscape: Evolution, Design and Control* (1970), 377.

133. See Krauss, "Investigations," 12–19.

134. Aronson, "Ben Gurion International Airport."

135. The width of water canals during summertime was not to exceed 66 feet (20 meters), and within a 984-foot (300-meter) diameter of buildings no water canals could exceed a width of 49 feet (15 meters). In contrast, ponds were not to exceed 7.4 acres (three hectares), but were to be built as large as possible within this limit so as to limit border habitats that would attract birds. Planting water lilies also made water bodies less attractive to birds (see West 8, "Schiphol Leidraad Buitenruimte Januari 2011," 32, Courtesy West 8).

136. Ibid., 23.

137. See U.S. Department of the Interior, *Environmental Impact of the Big Cypress Swamp Jetport* (1969).

Two | Air-Minded Visions

1. See Moholy-Nagy, *Material*, 222–23.

2. See ibid., 37.

3. Lefebvre, *Production of Space*, 124.

4. Wertheimer, "On Truth," 135.

5. Harrington, *Reenchanted Science*, 134.

6. Ibid.; Wertheimer, "On Truth," 137.

7. Baldwin, *Airopaidia*, 38.

8. Jeffries, *Aerial Voyages*, 19.

9. Pückler-Muskau, *Tutti frutti*, 313–15. For the relief by Pfyffer, see entry "Kummer, Karl Wilhelm," in *Allgemeine deutsche Real-Enzyklopädie für die gebildeten Stände* (Leipzig: Brockhaus, 1825), 56; and Bürgi, *Relief der Urschweiz*.

10. Ives, *Airplane Photography*, 30.

11. Mitchell, *Skyways*, 158.

12. Lunardi, *First Aërial Voyage*, 35.

13. Nadar, *Quand j'étais photographe*, 77–78.

14. High oblique views include the horizon and show portions of the land and the sky. Low oblique views only show parts of the land.

15. Leatherbarrow, *Uncommon Ground*, 171–72, 173.

16. Casey, "Borders and Boundaries," 69.

17. See Oettermann, *Panorama*, 9.

18. See ibid.

19. Le Corbusier, *Precisions*, 4.

20. Ibid.; Stein, *Autobiography*, 191. See also Stein, *Picasso*, 50.

21. Piper, "Prehistory," 5.

22. Lunardi, *First Aërial Voyage*, 32–34.

23. Baldwin, *Airopaidia*, 38; Garrick Mallery quoted in Jaeger and Luritzen, *Memoirs*, 29–30.

24. Oettermann, *Panorama*; Oleksijczuk, *First Panoramas*.

25. Huhtamo, "Aeronautikon!"

26. Brock, "Travel by Air."

27. Nolen, "Civic Planning," 412.

28. Hubbard, McClintock, and Williams, *Airports*, 36.

29. Aerodromes Committee, *Town Planning*, 6.

30. Brock, "Travel by Air," 18.

31. Moholy-Nagy, *Material*, 223. Numerous authors in the 1920s and 1930s commented on the public's unfamiliarity with the aerial view. For example, in 1924 Francis L. Wills, the British World War I veteran and cofounder of the first British aerial photography company, Aerofilms Ltd., noted that aerial photography accustomed the public to looking at the world from above and could thereby popularize air travel (Wills, "Aerial Camera Man," 100).

32. See Turner, *Aerial Navigation*, 185.

33. Amelia Earhart quoted in Duke and Lanchbery, *The Saga of Flight*, 324. In 1943, H. T. U. Smith, assistant professor of geology at the University of Kansas, could still argue that "vertical photos present the land surface from a comparatively unfamiliar angle. The appearance is that of a pictorial map. Unless shadows are present to accentuate relief features, the picture looks flat." He wrote that "unless one has traveled extensively by air, some practice is required to adjust the mind's eye to the new viewpoint" (Smith, *Aerial Photographs*, 31, 55).

34. See Ehrenberg, "Up in the Air," 212; and Lloyd-Williams, "Re-Marking the Air Route," 350, 359.

35. Mitchell, *Skyways*, 159.

36. Sontag, *On Photography*, 3.

37. See Nuti, *Ritratti*, 133–63; Nuti, "Perspective Plan," 107–9; and Nuti, "Mapping Places," 94.

38. Nuti, "Mapping Places," 100–101; Nuti, *Ritratti*, 155.

39. Nuti, *Ritratti*, 154–56; Deborah Howard, "Venice as a Dolphin: Further Investigations into Jacopo de' Barbari's View," *Artibus et Historiae* 35 (1997): 101–11; Juergen Schulz, "Jacopo de' Barbari's View of Venice: Map Making, City Views, and Moralized Geography before the Year 1500," *Art Bulletin* 60, no. 3 (September 1978): 425–74; Terisio Pignatti, "La pianta di Venezia di Jacopo de' Barbari," *Bolletino dei Musei Civici Veneziani* 9 (1964): 9–49.

40. See Reps, *Views and Viewmakers of Urban America*, 3, 17; and Reps, *Bird's Eye Views*, 7–15.

41. See Baker, "San Francisco in Ruins"; and Hales, *Silver Cities*, 173–78.

42. See Hales, *Silver Cities*, 132–78.

43. Kahle, "Luftschiffahrt," 57–62; "Der Kgl. Botanische Garten in Dahlem bei Berlin aus der Vogelschau," *Die Gartenwelt* 17, no. 18 (1913): 249.

44. Ives, *Airplane Photography*, 320.

45. H. Smith, *Aerial Photographs*, 31.

46. Mitchell, *Skyways*, 166.

47. Crawford and Keiller, *Wessex*, 6.

48. See Crawford, "Luftbildaufnahmen," 16–17.

49. Lt. Henry Reed, *Photography*, 64.

50. See the brochure in folder "Historical Fairchild Aerial Surveys," box 6, Sherman Fairchild Collection of the Manuscript Division, Library of Congress.

51. See www.pictometry.com/government/economic.shtml.

52. See Nagel, *The View from Nowhere*; Merleau-Ponty, *Visible*, 73; and Merleau-Ponty, "Eye and Mind," 160–61.

53. Abendroth, "Förderung der räumlichen Auffassung," 29.

54. Rorty, *Philosophy*, 334.

55. See Daston and Galison, *Objectivity*, 17. For the nineteenth-century distinctions made between photography and art and the use of photography in science, see ibid., 125–73; and Snyder, "Res ipsa loquitur."

56. Steichen, "American Aerial Photography," 38. In the same article, Steichen also attributed aesthetic value to aerial photographs, especially to oblique views.

57. Gutkind, "Author's Preface," in *World from the Air*.

58. Wright, "Application of Aerial Photography," 357.

59. Mitchell, *Skyways*, 159.

60. Ibid., 158.

61. Hayler, "Aeroplane and City Planning," 576, 578.

62. "Mosaic Maps," 253.

63. See Steinberg, "Mapping," 364; and Mitchell, *Skyways*, 160.

64. The term "photogrammetry" was coined by the German architect Albrecht Meydenbauer in 1893 to describe the general use of photography in the surveying and measurement of spatial objects and topography.

65. See advertisement in *City Planning* 2, no. 4 (October 1926).

66. "Mosaic Maps," 253; Steinberg, "Mapping," 365–66.

67. Winchester and Wills, *Aerial Photography*, 216.

68. See Charles E. Emerson, "Surveying with Eagle Eye," *Open Road* (October 1924): 13.

69. Brittenden, "Surveying," 88.

70. R. Black, "Air Maps," 22–23.

71. Berger, *About Looking*, 59.

72. See Cret, "Aerial Photography," 8.

73. Kahle, "Luftschiffahrt," 58.

74. For the history of the stereoscope, see Crary, *Techniques of the Observer*, 97–136.

75. Berleant, *Art and Engagement*, 62–75.

76. Abendroth, "Förderung der räumlichen Auffassung," 29–30.

77. Piper, "Prehistory."

78. Abendroth, "Bedeutung des Luftbildes," 49.

79. Kahle, "Luftschiffahrt," 58.

80. Le Corbusier, *Towards a New Architecture*, 48.

81. Gibson, *Ecological Approach*, 35.

82. F. Smith, "Aerial Photography," 40.

83. See Committee on Regional Plan of New York and Its Environs, *Regional Plan*, 2:272, 486, 489.

84. Poggi, *Defiance*, xii.

85. Stein, *Picasso*, 12.

86. See Ehrenfels, "Gestaltqualitäten"; Clements, *Research Methods*; Clements, *Plant Succession*; and J. Phillips, "Biotic Community," 20. For the use of holism in ecology, see Golley, *History of the Ecosystem Concept in Ecology*, 25–29, 222.

87. See Smuts, *Holism*, 89.

88. Ibid., 103.

89. Ibid., 104.

90. See ibid., 108–10.

91. Köhler, "Max Wertheimer," 143.

92. See Wertheimer, "Untersuchungen."

93. See Moholy-Nagy, *Material*, 198–99.

94. See Tobey, *Saving the Prairies*, 155–90; and Hagen, *An Entangled Bank*, 84–87, 136.

95. Clements, *Research Methods*, 7, 188; see also 183, 185–96.

96. See *Berliner Tageblatt*, September 10, 1887, 2.

97. See Winchester and Wills, *Aerial Photography,* 150; and Robbins, "Northern Rhodesia."

98. Troll, "Landscape Ecology," 44. Troll's Dutch colleague Isak Zonneveld pointed out in 1971 that "landscape has received considerable stimulation from aerial photo interpretation, as the photographic image is suggestive of the holistic approach" and that "the bird's-eye view of the land surface leads naturally to a holistic approach for the simple reason that the photo-image gives a kind of holistic impression of the land" (Zonneveld, *Land Evaluation,* 21, 60).

99. Carl Troll in a typescript entitled "Landscape Ecology: Summary," p. 1, NL Troll 284, Geographisches Institut Universität Bonn. See also Troll, *Landscape Ecology,* 5.

100. Troll, typescript, p. 1.

101. Ibid. See also Troll, "Landscape Ecology."

102. Gray, *About Face,* 180.

103. Willy Lange, Gartengestaltung der Neuzeit (Leipzig: Verlagsbuchhandlung von J. J. Weber), 151.

104. Troll, "Landscape Ecology," 43. See also Troll, "Luftbild."

105. Troll, *Landscape Ecology,* 5.

106. Troll, "Landscape Ecology," 43.

107. Troll, *Landscape Ecology,* 7.

108. See, for example, Troll, "Fortschritte," 284–89. In the 1930s, Russian geographers used the term translated into English as "aero-landscape" to describe the landscape units identifiable in aerial photographs.

109. Schreiber, "History of Landscape Ecology," 25.

110. Troll, typescript, p. 2.

111. Jenny, "Role of Plant Factor."

112. Zonneveld, *Land Evaluation,* 60–61.

113. Carl Troll in letters to his mother, NL Troll 295, 7537–7540 [7540] and [7543], Geographisches Institut Universität Bonn.

114. Wray et al., "Photo Interpretation," 668.

115. Matless, "Uses of Cartographic Literacy," 211–12.

116. Ibid.; Branford and Geddes, *Coming Polity,* 90–91.

117. Matless, "Regional Surveys," 474.

118. Zueblin, "World's First Sociological Laboratory," 585.

119. Welter, *Biopolis,* 76.

120. See ibid., 78.

121. See ibid., 131.

122. Geddes in a lecture at the 1904 meeting of the Sociological Society in London, quoted in Tyrwhitt, "Valley Section," 63.

123. For Geddes and Flahault, and the analogy between early phytosociology and the Valley Section, see Welter, *Biopolis,* 61; and Meller, *Patrick Geddes,* 130–31.

124. Odum, "Patrick Geddes."

125. See Geddes, "Naturalists' Society," 95; and Matless, "Regional Surveys," 467, 472.

126. Geddes quoted in Tyrwhitt, "Valley Section," 63.

127. See Fairchild Aerial Camera Corporation, "Aerial Surveying and Its Relation to City Planning" (1923), typescript held in the Francis Loeb Library, Harvard Graduate School of Design; and Fairchild, "Aerial Photography," 50.

128. See Desha, "Aerial Photography," 42; and Fairchild, "Aerial Mapping."

129. See Fairchild, "Aerial Photography," 51.

130. See Fishman, "Death and Life."

131. See Committee on Regional Plan of New York and Its Environs, *Regional Plan,* vol. 1; King, *King's Views,* 8–9.

132. Lewis, *Planning,* 356.

133. Abercrombie, "Regional Planning," 111.

134. Lewis, *Planning,* 356.

135. See Duffus, *Mastering a Metropolis,* between pages 32 and 33.

136. Nolen quoted in Fairchild Aerial Camera Corporation, *Sky Pictures* (New York), 6, folder "Historical Fairchild Aerial Survey," box 6. Sherman Fairchild Collection of the Manuscript Division, Library of Congress.

137. Theodora Kimball cited ibid., 7.

138. Lewis, *Planning,* 365–66.

139. Ibid., 366.

140. Desha, "Aerial Photography," 43.

141. See Hayler, "Aeroplane and City Planning," 575–79.

142. Bacon, *Record of an Aeronaut,* 160.

143. See Gropius, *Die neue Architektur,* 14; and the English translation by P. Morton Shand, *The New Architecture,* 27.

144. Hilberseimer, *Regional Pattern,* 89.

145. Barthes, "The Eiffel Tower," 241–42. Jennifer S. Light has shown that the interest of urban professionals in drawing analogies with ecosystem science declined in the 1960s and that their interest shifted

instead toward the new theories and concepts of the systems sciences, cybernetics, and "systems-inspired military planning" (Light, *Nature of Cities*, 169–71). However, in recent years, organicist and biologistic rhetoric has again played an important role in the discourse about cities, as the project "Shrinking Cities" attests. This project directed by Philipp Oswalt deals with the phenomenon of population loss in many post-fordist cities in east European countries and in the Rust Belt of the United States.

146. G. W. P., "Physiognomy of Cities." I thank Suleiman Osman for this reference.

147. See Sennett, *Flesh and Stone*, 255–70.

148. Hayler, "Aeroplane and City Planning," 577.

149. Barthes, "Eiffel Tower," 241–42.

150. Hayler, "Aeroplane and City Planning," 575.

151. *First Interallied Town Planning Conference*, 20.

152. See Pick, "Aerial Photography"; Brittenden, "Surveying"; Abendroth, "Förderung der räumlichen Auffassung"; Abendroth, "Bedeutung des Luftbildes"; Abendroth, "Städtebau und Luftbild"; and Balleyguier, "L'aviation au travail," 184.

153. For the description of the war landscape by Kurt Lewin, see Lewin quoted in Dünne and Günzel, *Raumtheorie*, 139.

154. See Gropius, *Die neue Architektur*, 73, and the English translation, *The New Architecture*, 77.

155. *First Interallied Town Planning Conference*, 22.

Three | "Cultivating Beautiful Air Views"

1. See Brock, "City."

2. See Nolen, "Civic Planning," 412; and Wichert, "Luftschiffahrt," 2. For Wichert, see also Asendorf, *Super Constellation*, 1–2; and "Provisions to be Made in City Planning to Facilitate Aerial Transportation: Address Delivered by Henry Woodhouse, Appointed by Governor Charles S. Whitman as Delegate to the American Civic Association's Convention, Held at Washington, D.C., December 13, 14, 15, 1916," *Flying* 5 (January 1917): 491. In 1930, Walter Gropius argued, like Nolen, that the new aviation routes challenged architects and city planners to build and plan also for the bird's-eye view (see Gropius, *Bauhausbauten*, 16).

3. See Wohl, *Spectacle of Flight;* and Wohl, *Passion for Wings*.

4. Le Corbusier, *Four Routes*, 108.

5. Le Corbusier, *Aircraft*, 12.

6. Le Corbusier, *City of Tomorrow*, 280.

7. "Mosaic Maps," 209–12.

8. Brunner, *Weisungen der Vogelschau*, 121.

9. Ibid., 9, 99.

10. See ibid., 9–11, 21–22 59–60, 97, 108.

11. Brunner, "Ziele der Architektenschulung," 333. See also Hofer, "Latin American City and Its Viennese Planning Approach."

12. Brunner, *Weisungen der Vogelschau*, 108. For a description of technological romanticism, see Thomas Mann, *Deutschland und die Deutschen* (Stockholm: Bermann-Fischer Verlag, 1947), 33.

13. Ewald, "Luftbild," 6, 28.

14. Ewald, *Flugzeug*, 19, 21, 26–27.

15. Ewald, *Deutschland*, 11, 12.

16. For an analysis of Le Corbusier's use of the aerial perspective, see Boyer, "Aviation and the Aerial View," 93–116; Morshed, "Cultural Politics of Aerial Vision"; and Morshed, "Architecture of Ascension."

17. Boyer, "Aviation and the Aerial View," 96.

18. Le Corbusier, *Radiant City*, 341.

19. See Le Corbusier, *City of Tomorrow*, 6. For a contemporary critique of Camillo Sitte and Le Corbusier, see Adshead, "Camillo Sitte."

20. Le Corbusier, *Four Routes*, 108, 110, 111.

21. Hans Schmidt, "Das Chaos im Städtebau" (1924), in Schmidt, *Beiträge*, 17; Shelmerdine, *Airports and Airways*, 69–70.

22. Jencks, *Le Corbusier*, 125.

23. Le Corbusier, *Radiant City*, 223.

24. Le Corbusier, *Precisions*, 3.

25. Ibid., 244.

26. Ibid., 241.

27. Morshed, "Cultural Politics of Aerial Vision," 203.

28. Le Corbusier, *Precisions*, 245.

29. Ibid., 241–42.

30. Ibid., 5.

31. Ibid., 6–7.

32. Le Corbusier, *Radiant City*, 79.

33. Morshed, "Cultural Politics of Aerial Vision," 205.

34. See Marchant, "Aviation," 1–2.

35. See Hofer, "Latin American City and Its Viennese Planning Approach," 215–16; and Brunner, "La vista aerea."

36. See Brunner, *Manual de urbanismo*, 37; and Hofer, "Latin American City and Its Viennese Planning Approach," 215–17.

37. See Hegemann, "Als Städtebauer in Südamerika," 144.

38. For Hegemann in South America, see Crasemann Collins, "Urban Interchange"; and Gutiérrez, "Buenos Aires," 67–68. For Brunner's and Hegemann's planning paradigm for South American cities, see Pérez Oyarzun and Rosas Vera, "Cities within the City."

39. Lee, *The Face of the Earth*, 11–12.

40. Cret, "Aerial Photography," 9.

41. Cautley, "New Horizons," 18; I thank Thaïsa Way for this reference. Steele, "New Styles," 353.

42. See Steele, "New Styles," 353; Steele, "New Pioneering"; and Imbert, "Unnatural Acts," 177.

43. Steele, "New Styles," 353.

44. Steele, "Modern Landscape Architecture," 25.

45. Spoon, "Modern Landscape Art," 30, 39.

46. Vera, *Les jardins,* 131; Imbert, *Modernist Garden,* 77.

47. Vera, *Les jardins,* 134–35.

48. Vera, *Le nouveau jardin,* 9.

49. See Frange, *Le style Duchêne.*

50. See Andersson and Høyer, *C. Th. Sørensen.* For Malevich, suprematism, and the aerial view, see Lodder, "Malevich."

51. Kassler, *Modern Gardens,* 47.

52. See Alberti, *Ten Books of Architecture,* II, chap. 1, 22; Nuti, "Mapping Places," 91–92; and Andersson and Høyer, *C. Th. Sørensen.*

53. For an account of axonometric representation in architectural history, see Bois, "Metamorphosis of Axonometry." For the use of axonometry in representing garden designs by the landscape architect Jean Canneel-Claes, see Imbert, *Between Garden and City,* 57–63.

54. See Gropius, *Die neue Architektur,* 35.

55. See, for example, the model photograph and its juxtaposition with an axonometric drawing on two facing pages in Gropius, *Internationale Architektur,* 58.

56. For aerial views of Dutch gardens, see Jong, *Nature and Art.*

57. Valentien, "Mehr bodenständige Gartengestaltung."

58. Burle Marx, "Garden Style in Brazil," 202.

59. The work of Rossana Vaccarino provides an interesting twist in the search for the relevance of the aerial view in Burle Marx's designs. In order to develop garden plans and three-dimensional models that illustrate volumes, spatial qualities, and seasonal color change for the poorly documented gardens at Fazenda Marambaia and Fazenda Vargem Grande, Vaccarino used high-level stereoscopic aerial photographs and low-level color photographs taken from a helicopter (see Vaccarino, "Correspondence of Time and Instability," 43).

60. Jellicoe, *Studies,* 1:106.

61. Le Corbusier, *Precisions,* 6.

62. Fraser, "Cannibalizing Le Corbusier," 185.

63. Ibid., 184.

64. Ibid., 189–90.

65. Giedion, preface, ix.

66. See Aalto, "Finland." For Aalto's architecture, Finnish nature, nationalism, and geopolitics, see Pelkonen, *Alvar Aalto,* esp. 1, 43, 136, 143–79.

67. Giedion, *Space,* 640.

68. See Eskola, *Water Lilies.*

69. See ibid., 77.

70. See Giedion, *Space,* 635, 665. For a nuanced elaboration on the origins of the curvilinear form in Aalto's work, see Pelkonen, *Alvar Aalto,* 143–57.

71. Editorial in *New York Sun,* October 20, 1928, quoted in Harry B. Brainerd, "Uses of Roofs and Terraces for Recreation," *City Planning* 5, no. 7 (1929): 174.

72. See Gropius, *Die neue Architektur,* my translation.

73. Le Corbusier, *City of Tomorrow,* 280.

74. Sudell, *Landscape Gardening,* 373.

75. Hurtwood, "Roof-Gardens," 46. See also Betts, "Gardens"; and Waters, "Roof-Dwellers."

76. Wigoder, "The 'Solar Eye' of Vision," 159; Nye, *American Technological Sublime,* 96–97.

77. Weisman, "First Landscaped Skyscraper," 57–58. In 1933, when the idea of roof gardens was discussed by the architects and John D. Rockefeller Jr., the architects and landscape architects Frederick Law Olmsted Jr., Arthur Shurtleff, Jacques Greber, and Fletcher Steele were seen as potential designers for the gardens (see letters from 1933 between John R. Todd and John D. Rockefeller Jr., in "Rockefeller Center, Inc.–Todd Robertson [Brown]"), folder 581, box 78, Business Interests, RG2, Rockefeller Family Collection, Rockefeller Archive Center.

78. *Sky Garden Tour,* brochure, 1937, 2, Rockefeller Center.

79. Ibid. See also F. F. Rockwell, "Gardens of the World Atop Radio City," *New York Times,* September 2, 1934, X8; and H. I. Brock, "Nature Garlands

a Skyscraper," *New York Times Sunday Magazine,* April 14, 1935, 12. Letters between Hancock and executives of the Rockefeller Center, Inc., reveal that Hancock complained about the upkeep of the gardens as early as July 1935 despite the fact that John D. Rockefeller Jr. and his wife were reported to have been enthusiastic in their praise of the gardens (see letters between Hancock, William J. Hoffmann, and Hugh S. Robertson dated July 12, 13, 16, 1935, in "RCI-Planting and Roof Garden," folder 745, box 99, Business Interests, Rockefeller Family Collection, Rockefeller Archive Center).

80. *Gardens of the Nations,* undated brochure, 2, Rockefeller Center. Available as pdf-document at www.ralphhancock.com/gardenofthenations.

81. Fletcher Steele to W. B. Todd, June 20, 1933, Rockefeller Center Archives, © 2008 Rockefeller Group Inc.

82. Leopold Arneaud, "Greetings," in "Protective Obscurement: Notes from Classes in Protective Obscurement," mimeograph (New York: School of Architecture, Columbia University, 1943), 1; available at Loeb Library, Harvard University.

Four | Concealing the Land

1. See the British aerial photograph of Munich's city center with painted fake urban fabric in *Evidence in Camera* 1, no. 5 (November 16, 1942): 183.

2. Root, *Camouflage,* 29.

3. Ibid., 35.

4. Casson, "Aesthetics of Camouflage," 66.

5. Kern, "Cubism, Camouflage, Silence, and Democracy," 166.

6. Ibid.

7. Stein, *Picasso,* 11.

8. Kahn, *Neglected Majority;* Behrens, "Iowa's Contribution," 100; Kern, "Cubism, Camouflage, Silence, and Democracy," 166; Goff, "Camouflage," 27.

9. Saint-Gaudens, "Camouflage and Art," 322.

10. Homer Saint-Gaudens quoted in *Christian Science Monitor,* quoted in Edward Alden Jewell, "Art in a Practical Service to War," *New York Times,* December 14, 1941, X11.

11. "Progress of Camouflage in the U.S. Army during World War I," box 1, Edward Farmer Papers, Hoover Institution Archives, Stanford University. See also Hartcup, *Camouflage,* 28–29.

12. H. Ledyard Towle, "What the American 'Camouflage' Signifies," *New York Times,* June 3, 1917,

62; "Our Industrial Art Needs Co-ordination," *New York Times,* June 10, 1917, 68; "Faking as an Art in Conducting War," *New York Times,* June 24, 1917, 35; "Camouflage Course for N.Y. Soldiers," *New York Times,* May 19, 1918, 50; "Camouflage Now a Regimental Essential," *New York Times Sunday Magazine,* May 26, 1918, 4.

13. McCabe, "Camouflage," 316.

14. Virilio, *Vision Machine,* 48–49.

15. See Kahn, *Neglected Majority,* 19.

16. Schlemmer, *Letters,* 381; see also 389–90.

17. Welchman, "Here, There & Otherwise," 18.

18. Demuth, *Practical Camouflage,* 43.

19. See Virilio, *Vision Machine,* 48–49; and Welchman, "Here, There & Otherwise."

20. Herbert Friedmann, *Natural-History Background;* see also Behrens, "Iowa's Contribution," 99.

21. "Call for 'Fakers' to Fool Germans," *New York Times,* September 4, 1917, 7. See also "Wants Camouflage Force," *New York Times,* August 30, 1917, 3.

22. Solomon, *Strategic Camouflage,* 9.

23. "Urge Dyeing Horses as War Camouflage," *New York Times,* September 8, 1927, 20.

24. Luckiesh, *Visual Illusions,* 215, 293, 214.

25. Köhler, *Gestalt Psychology,* 201, 172; for the line drawings exemplifying visual illusions, see 184–85, 200, 210. Very similar drawings were used in several articles on camouflage published in the United States during World War II (see, for example, U.S. Office of Civil Defense, *Precautionary Camouflage,* 7, 55–57). For the line drawings used in camouflage publications, see also the precedents in Luckiesh, *Visual Illusions,* 44–101.

26. See, for example, Dee, "Camouflage"; United States Office of Civilian Defense, *Precautionary Camouflage.*

27. See Hartcup, *Camouflage,* 56.

28. See *Science in War,* 42–46; and "Camouflage in Modern Warfare."

29. Saint-Gaudens quoted in Fox, "Camouflage and the Artist," 156.

30. E. Walker, "Camouflage Planning," 240.

31. Breckenridge, *Camouflage.*

32. For Moholy-Nagy's involvement in camouflage, see Engelbrecht, "Moholy-Nagy," 60.

33. Root, *Camouflage,* 12.

34. Clausewitz, *On War,* 2.

35. Wheeler, *Elements of the Art and Science of War,* 12.

36. A. Smith, "Notes on Camouflage," 469.

37. For dummy trees, see, for example, Kirby, *Manual of Camouflage,* 50.

38. "Cooper Union Starts Camouflage Course," *New York Times,* November 18, 1942, 29.

39. Konrad F. Wittmann, *Camouflage Manual,* 43.

40. Goff, "Camouflage," 27.

41. See, for example, Hornbeck, "Camouflage," 4.

42. See Goodden, *Camouflage and Art,* 50.

43. See Pearson, "Model Making"; Harrison Reed, "Terrain Model"; Spooner, "Use of Aerial Photographs"; U.S. Bureau of Aeronautics, *Photo Surface Modeling;* and Reagan, "Shaded-Relief Maps."

44. See Schmal and Selke, *Bunker-Luftschutz,* 35.

45. See Konrad F. Wittmann, *Camouflage Manual,* 120.

46. Stanley, *Glass Eye,* 176.

47. "Big R.A.F. Damage in Hamburg Listed," *New York Times,* June 29, 1941, 7.

48. See *Secret Report,* 92, 22–23.

49. See Captain G. M. Leet, 91/21, Department of Documents, Imperial War Museum, London.

50. See Berlin District Target Map, box 14, RG 243, IIIA (257)-21-III (271), United States National Archives and Records Administration.

51. See Landesarchiv Berlin, A Rep. 037-08 Nr. 364, p. 85.

52. Ibid., pp. 94, 97.

53. *Evidence in Camera* 7, no. 5 (May 1, 1944): 93.

54. Nye, *When the Lights Went Out,* 58.

55. On blackouts, see U.S. War Department radiogram dated January 13, 1942, sent as copy to Headquarters Third Corps Area, United States Army, Baltimore, Maryland, on January 14, 1942, box 1, Edward Farmer Papers, Hoover Institution Archives, Stanford University.

56. "Blackout," 6.

57. "Plane over Newark Provides Vivid View of Sudden Darkness and Return of Lights," special to *New York Times,* May 26, 1941, 21.

58. "Washington Tests Blackout System," special to *New York Times,* December 31, 1941, 13.

59. Informational Memorandum issued by the Office of Civilian Defense Washington, D.C., May 21, 1942: paper delivered by Creville Rickard to the Conference on Aerial Bombardment Protection sponsored by Harvard University, Massachusetts Institute of Technology, and Northeastern University at Boston, Massachusetts, April 19, 1942, p. 9, box 1, Edward Farmer Papers, Hoover Institution Archives, Stanford University.

60. See U.S. War Department, *Blackouts,* 45.

61. See Breckenridge, *Camouflage,* 189.

62. See Hartcup, *Camouflage,* 71.

63. See "Nightly Blackout Ordered by Swiss," *New York Times,* November 7, 1940, 3.

64. See Knothe, *Tarnung,* 6.

65. Konrad F. Wittmann, *Camouflage Manual,* 27.

66. See Le Corbusier, *Radiant City,* 60–61, 171; and Le Corbusier references in Lt. Col. Paul Vauthier's *Le danger aérien et l'avenir du pays* (1930) and Hans Schossberger's *Bautechnischer Luftschutz* (1934).

67. See Sert, *Can Our Cities Survive?,* 66–68.

68. See Berg, "Luftschutz," 96.

69. See Düwel and Gutschow, *Städtebau,* 90–136; Durth and Gutschow, *Träume,* 174–96; and Mantziaras, "Rudolf Schwarz."

70. See Hammerling, "Luftschutz und Städtebau."

71. See Reichsstatthalter der Stadt Hamburg, *Luftschutzbauten.* See also Foedrowitz, *Bunkerwelten;* and Schmal and Selke, *Bunker-Luftschutz.*

72. See Speer, *Erinnerungen,* 92.

73. See documents in Bundesarchiv Berlin, R 4606, 1601; and Bundesarchiv Berlin, R 4606, 1592.

74. See Morshed, "Aesthetics of Ascension"; and K. Jackson, *Crabgrass Frontier,* 248–51.

75. U.S. Office of Civilian Defense, *Precautionary Camouflage,* 49.

76. For the use of aerial photographs in civil defense planning in the United States, see Wittenstein, "Aerial Photography," 572.

77. See Augur, "Dispersal of Cities," 133; Light, *Warfare to Welfare,* 10–31; Tobin, "Reduction of Urban Vulnerability"; and Dudley, "Sprawl as Strategy."

78. See Augur, "Dispersal of Cities," 134.

79. See Düwel and Gutschow, *Städtebau,* 128–29; Gröning, "Teutonic Myth, Rubble, and Recovery," 132.

80. See "How U.S. Cities." For a discussion of Wiener's plan, see Kargon and Molella, "City as Communications Net"; Macy and Bonnemaison, *Architecture and Nature,* 264–65; and Dudley, "Sprawl as Strategy," 55.

81. See Eckbo, "H-Bomb," 68, 72; Tobin, "Reduction of Urban Vulnerability"; and Dudley, "Sprawl as Strategy."

82. See Andriello, *Aerourbanistica,* 9–10, 32, 26–29.

83. See Dräger, *Schnellbahnstadt*, 9–43; and Durth and Gutschow, *Träume*, 214–19.

84. See documents in Landesarchiv Berlin A Rep. 230-02 Nr. 242. See also Berg, "Luftschutz."

85. See "The Artist Goes to War," *PM*, Monday, December 29, 1941, 14.

86. Konrad F. Wittmann, *Camouflage Manual*, 7.

87. See "Pratt Pushes Tests in Camouflage Work," *New York Times*, June 7, 1942, D6; "Camouflage Data," 83; and "Cooper Union Starts Camouflage Course," *New York Times*, November 18, 1942, 29.

88. Konrad F. Wittmann, *Camouflage Manual*, 30.

89. Ibid.

90. Ibid., 14, 23, 33, 40, 67, 81, 44–47. For the use of Spanish moss, see also U.S. Corps of Engineers, *Camouflage Materials*, 84–85.

91. See Breckenridge, *Camouflage*, 195.

92. See Stanley, *Glass Eye*, 171–75; Reit, *Masquerade*, 88–89; and Goff, "Camouflage," 27.

93. See Shirer, *Berlin Diary*, 469, 477–78; and De Longe, *Airfield Planning*, 11, 125–26.

94. De Longe, *Airfield Planning*, 134, 59.

95. See Hartcup, *Camouflage*, 58–59; box 1, Edward Farmer Papers, Hoover Institution Archives, Stanford University.

96. See "Report on Camouflage for Windsor Locks Airbase Connecticut" November 24, 1941, Camouflage Section The Engineer Board, Fort Belvoir, Virginia, box 1, Edward Farmer Papers, Hoover Institution Archives, Stanford University; "Work Begins on First Camouflaged Airfield," *Engineering News-Record* 126 (May 1, 1941): 1; and Reit, *Masquerade*, 67–69.

97. Sloane, *Camouflage*, 60.

98. Edward Alden Jewell, "Art in a Practical Service to War," *New York Times*, December 14, 1941, X11.

99. Fitzhugh, "Camouflage," 119.

100. Ibid., 120.

101. Ibid.

102. Ibid., 121.

103. Ibid., 122.

104. Casson, "Aesthetics of Camouflage," 67.

105. Burke, *Philosophical Enquiry*, 28–30.

106. Ibid., 59.

107. Whately, *Observations*.

108. U.S. Office of Civilian Defense, *Precautionary Camouflage*, 20.

109. The program (Reichsamt "Schönheit der Arbeit" in der Deutschen Arbeitsfront) "Schönheit der Arbeit" was begun in 1934 under the supervision of Albert Speer. It was a program that encouraged the beautification of the working environment and therefore led factory owners to commission landscape architects with the design of parks and gardens adjacent to their factories.

110. Urhammer, "Neue Aufgaben," 3.

111. Walter Berkowski, "Gartenbau und Landschaftspflege bei der Reichsbahn," *Die Gartenkunst* 48, no. 10 (1935): 180–88.

112. See *Kraft durch Freude*, pamphlet in Major D A J Pavitt, 86/50/3, Department of Documents at the Imperial War Museum, London.

113. See Mappes, "Schönheit der Arbeit," *Die Gartenkunst* 55, no. 11 (1942): 149–51; G. Gunder, "Soziale Grünanlagen," *Die Gartenkunst* 55, no. 11 (1942): 151–53; and Franz Kolbrand, "Grün und Blumen im Fabrikgelände," *Die Gartenkunst* 55, no. 11 (1942): 153–62.

114. See Löftken, "Luftschutz und Städtebau," 7.

115. See Zeller, "Molding the Landscape of Nazi Environmentalism," 158.

116. Wiepking-Jürgensmann, *Landschaftsfibel*, 323, 327.

117. Becker, *Wehrtechnischer Einsatz*, 4, 9, 14, 13, 25.

118. See documents in NL Troll 197, Geographisches Institut Universität Bonn; and Troll, "Luftbildinterpretation," 121–23. For Troll's relationship to Nazi politics, see Böhm, "Annäherungen," 74–76.

119. See Hiller, *Herman Göritz*, 107–8; Boehm, Brucklacher, and Pillewitzer, "Luftbildinterpretation." For the special research unit of the German Army High Command, see T. Smith and Black, "German Geography."

120. See Parpagliolo, "Le zone verdi," 37; Matteini, *Pietro Porcinai*, 43; and Boesiger, *Le Corbusier*, 76–79.

121. Major D A J Pavitt, 86/50/3, Department of Documents at the Imperial War Museum, London.

122. Major D A J Pavitt, 86/05/2, Department of Documents at the Imperial War Museum, London; and Major D A J Pavitt, 86/50/3, Department of Documents at the Imperial War Museum, London.

123. See National Archives, Kew, HO 217/3, TMM 23 Watson's Pots; Hartcup, *Camouflage*, 55.

124. Lecture by J. K. Doliva, "The Assembly of Reference, Source Material and Data in Camouflage Design," February 2, 1942, box 1, Edward Farmer Papers, Hoover Institution Archives, Stanford University; Informational Memorandum issued by the

Office of Civilian Defense Washington, D.C., May 21, 1942; paper delivered by Creville Rickard to the Conference on Aerial Bombardment Protection sponsored by Harvard University, Massachusetts Institute of Technology, and Northeastern University at Boston, Massachusetts, April 19, 1942, p. 7, box 1, Edward Farmer Papers, Hoover Institution Archives, Stanford University; U.S. Office of Civilian Defense, *Precautionary Camouflage*, 20.

125. Information Concerning the National Defense Program, March 15, 1941, Circular No. 6, box 9, ASLA Records, Library of Congress.

126. Armistead Fitzhugh quoted in "ASLA Survey," 201.

127. *Landscape Architecture* 31, no. 2 (January 1941): 83. See also plan in box 1, Edward Farmer Papers, Hoover Institution Archives, Stanford University; Forbes to Colonel Godfrey, Chief of the Operations and Training Section in the Office of the Chief of Engineers, Washington, D.C. September 24, 1940, folder 317, box 13, Forbes Papers, Harvard Art Museum Archives; Edward W. Forbes to President Karl T. Compton at MIT, December 26, 1940, folder 316, box 13, Forbes Papers, Harvard Art Museum Archives.

128. "Judkins, Winthrop O.," folder 1034, box 52, HC3, Paul J. Sachs Papers, Harvard Art Museum Archives.

129. See Merrill, "Camouflage and Landscape Architecture," 15, 16.

130. Root, *Camouflage*, 59.

131. Root, *Contourscaping*, 15.

132. Ibid., 55–56.

133. Root, *Camouflage*, 37.

134. See U.S. Corps of Engineers, *Camouflage Materials*, 6–7.

135. See Root, *Camouflage*, 64.

136. "Recent References."

137. For the participation of landscape architects at the camouflage courses at Fort Belvoir, see also box 9, ASLA Records, Library of Congress. In response to numerous requests from universities and other institutions throughout the United States, the OCD organized special two-week training courses for faculty and selected individuals from professional engineering, architectural, and landscape architectural societies at Fort Belvoir in July 1942. Many more landscape architects were employed in the site planning group and construction division of the Office of

the Quartermaster General of the War Department. See listings in *Landscape Architecture*, October 1941.

138. Recommendations to the Office of Civilian Defense on Industrial Camouflage courses at universities, June 1942, box 1, Edward Farmer Papers, Hoover Institution Archives, Stanford University. Landscape architects trained in camouflage courses at Fort Belvoir included Alfred Edwards from Alabama Polytechnic Institute in Auburn; Mark Shoemaker from the University of Maryland at College Park; Morris E. Trotter from Ohio State University; Stanley H. White from the University of Illinois in Urbana; and Harlow O. Whittmore from the University of Michigan in Ann Arbor. See Hornbeck, "Camouflage"; and "A-B-C" (Association of Belvoir Civilians), "Garnishings," typescript, November 1942, box 1, Edward Farmer Papers, Hoover Institution Archives, Stanford University.

139. "Course in Camouflage."

140. See "A-B-C" (Association of Belvoir Civilians), "IV Garnishings IV," typescript, 7 Water Street, Boston, February, 1943, box 1, Edward Farmer Papers, Hoover Institution Archives, Stanford University.

141. "Camouflage Plants," *New York Times,* March 5, 1944, E9.

142. See Harvard Camouflage Committee, *Cut Foliage;* and Harvard Camouflage Committee, *Cut Foliage, Supplement.*

143. "Aid to Florist Seen in Research by Army," *New York Times,* February 9, 1969, 22.

144. See Neale, "Trees."

145. Cynthia Westcott, "Protection of Our Shade Trees Is Urged as a Defense Measure," *New York Times,* May 24, 1942, D9.

146. U.S. Army Corps of Engineers, *Camouflage Materials,* 84–85.

147. See Fox, *Camouflage,* 2.

148. Breckenridge, *Camouflage,* 264–65.

149. Ibid., 268.

150. Sloane, *Camouflage,* 59–60.

151. Keally, Introduction to "Protective Obscurement," 1; Casson, "Aesthetics of Camouflage," 67–68.

152. Hackett, "Restoration," 11.

153. Ibid., 11–12.

154. Ibid., 13–14.

155. Crowe, *Landscape of Power,* 100, 101, 102.

156. Ibid, 99.

157. Ibid., 110. Sylvia Crowe was one of a number

of landscape architects who consulted for the Central Electricity Generating Board in the late 1950s and early 1960s. In 1958–59, 1959–60, and 1960–61, the consulting landscape architects were: Sylvia Crowe, F. Gibbert, Sheila Haywood, Geoffrey Jellicoe, Milner White, D. Lovejoy, and Peter Youngman (see Central Electricity Generating Board, *First Report and Accounts, 1st January 1958–31st March 1959* [London: Her Majesty's Stationary Office, 1959], 186; Central Electricity Generating Board, *Annual Report and Accounts, 1959–60* [London: Her Majesty's Stationary Office, 1960], 168; and Central Electricity Generating Board, *Annual Report and Accounts, 1960–61* [London: Her Majesty's Stationary Office, 1961], 178).

158. Strang, "Power Production"; Deedes quoted in *The Architecture of Power*, exhibition brochure, Central Electricity Generating Board, 1963, unpaginated.

159. See Jellicoe, "Collaboration," 6.

160. See Crowe, *Tomorrow's Landscape*, 154–55.

161. Crowe, *Landscape of Power*, 17.

162. Crowe, "Presidential Address," 4.

163. Crowe, *Landscape of Power*, 18.

164. Ibid.

165. Ibid., 24.

166. See ibid., 20.

167. See Eckbo, "New Landscape."

168. See Kepes, "Die technische Landschaft," 65.

169. See Crowe, *Landscape of Power*, 87–88.

170. See Crowe, *Tomorrow's Landscape*, 154–55, 75.

171. Crowe, *Landscape of Power*, 50. See also Central Electricity Generating Board, *Design Memorandum*.

172. See Crowe, *Landscape of Power*, 37; Crowe, "Power and the Landscape," 6, 4.

173. Sylvia Crowe & Associates, "Trawsfynydd Nuclear Power Station," 2, Sylvia Crowe Collection, Landscape Institute. See also Central Electricity Generating Board, *Trawsfynydd*, unpaginated; and Crowe, "Power and the Landscape," 6.

174. See Jellicoe, "Power Stations"; Thirkettle, "Ground Modelling," 14; and Jellicoe, *Studies*, 2:9–11.

175. Crowe, *Landscape of Power*, 41.

176. Quoted in Ortolano, *Two Cultures Controversy*, 5.

177. Snow, *Two Cultures*, 48–49. For a similar interest in bringing together the "visual arts and the

sciences" expressed after World War II, see Kepes, "Visual Arts."

178. Crowe, *Landscape of Power*, 41. See also Crowe, "Presidential Address," 4.

Five | Conserving the Land

1. Geddes had been one of the founders of the Sociological Society that in 1930 merged with the Le Play House organization to form the Institute of Sociology.

2. Gutkind, "Our World from the Air: Conflict," 5–6. What Gutkind called "social ecology" was described by American sociologists as human ecology.

3. Ibid., 5–6, 38–39, figure caption.

4. See, for example, Light, *Nature of Cities*, 22–27, 39, 43–45.

5. Chombart de Lauwe, *Photographies aériennes*, 134. Chombart de Lauwe, who had also published on aerial photography and its use for research in sociology and human ecology a few years earlier, claimed that his 1951 manual on aerial photography was the first to promote and employ aerial photography in sociological research in France (see Chombart de Lauwe, *Photographies aériennes*, 7; see also Chombart de Lauwe, *La découverte aérienne*, 11–17 [introduction], 327–70, 402–6).

6. Chombart de Lauwe, *Photographies aériennes*, 2.

7. *An Opportunity for Private and Public Investment in Rebuilding Chicago*, published in 1947 by the Illinois Institute of Technology, Michael Reese Hospital, the South Side Planning Board, the Metropolitan Housing Council, Pace Associates, Architects, and the Chicago Housing Authority, included a schematic drawing of Chicago showing the major land uses like transportation hubs (airports, freight stations, main railway, and highway), the central business district, major heavy and light industrial areas, parks, and the greenbelt. The diagram was entitled *Natural Form of Chicago*. In 1954, the Chicago Plan Commission published *Recommended Policies for Redevelopment in Chicago*, including a diagram entitled *Geographic Pattern of Redevelopment* that built upon the 1925 concentric zonal model of the city developed by Ernest Burgess. As Jennifer S. Light has pointed out, the Chicago Plan Commission collaborated closely with faculty at the University of Chicago (see Light, *Nature of Cities*, 108).

8. *An Opportunity for Private and Public Investment in Rebuilding Chicago*, 24.

9. Branch, *City Planning*, 35.

10. Ibid., 90.

11. As Hillel Schwartz has pointed out in the context of late-nineteenth-century medical microscopy, "the microscopist was engaged in looking *down-and-in*," an act that was believed to be able to reveal the inner truth of the object under study, detecting disease (see Schwartz, *Culture of the Copy*, 184).

12. See Colean, *Renewing Our Cities*. The verb "renew" was already in use in the 1940s in the context of urban planning (see Light, *Nature of Cities*, 136–37).

13. *Chicago's Face Lifting Program*, pamphlet, Chicago Land Clearance Commission, 1952[?].

14. *Action*, brochure, American Council to Improve Our Neighborhoods, 1954.

15. Tracy Augur, "Urban Renewal and Community Development," remarks at the Jaycee Community Development Seminar held in Detroit, Michigan on July 14–15, 1959.

16. A brochure entitled *A B C's of Urban Renewal*, published by the Urban Renewal Division of Sears, Roebuck and Co., Chicago, Illinois, proclaimed that "a common pattern of growth in American cities" led to "blight or outright slums" in "the older, central sections, because of lack of planning, inadequate regulatory controls and deficient municipal services." It argued that "surgery must be applied and municipal processes set in motion to re-create soundness out of waste" (14).

17. "Harvester's Ed Stokes and His Land-Clearance Colleagues Prescribe Surgery for a City," *Harvester World*, October 1954, 12.

18. Le Corbusier, *City of Tomorrow*, 251–52.

19. The American planner Tracy Augur considered a city's "life cycle" to be between thirty and sixty years (see Tracy Augur, "Urban Renewal and Community Development," remarks at the Jaycee Community Development Seminar held in Detroit, Michigan, on July 14–15, 1959). In a brochure issued by the Chicago Land Clearance Commission entitled *Chicago's Face Lifting Program*, cities were compared to people: "Cities like people, grow old, weary and worn out. Sometimes their houses become so weak that they topple over. They age and wear by years of service, excessive use, neglect and abuse."

20. Bill, "Use of Aerial Photography."

21. On the use of militaristic rhetoric in city planning, see Light, *Warfare to Welfare*, 65.

22. See Branch, *City Planning*, 96.

23. See Light, *Warfare to Welfare*.

24. Branch, *Aerial Photography*, 1.

25. Ibid., 8.

26. See ibid., 9.

27. Ibid., 8.

28. Ibid., 12.

29. See Branch, *City Planning*, 127–28.

30. See the studies undertaken by Paul Henry Chombart de Lauwe and his colleagues at the Centre d'Études Sociologiques in Paris and published in two volumes on *Paris et l'agglomération parisienne* (1952).

31. Green and Monier, "Aerial Photographic Interpretation," 770.

32. Green, "Aerial Photography," 249.

33. Ibid., 218.

34. Ibid., 249.

35. Ibid., 218.

36. Ibid., 249.

37. Green and Monier, *Reliability and Validity*, 1.

38. See ibid., 2.

39. See ibid., 4.

40. Green and Monier based their studies on the work of the urban sociologists Robert Park, Louis Wirth, Robert E. L. Faris, and H. Warren Dunham (see Green, "Aerial Photographic Interpretation," 90–91). For theories regarding the relationship between social and spatial relations, see Robert E. Park, "Urban Community."

41. Green, "Aerial Photographic Interpretation," 94. See also Green, "Photographic Analysis."

42. Green, "Photographic Analysis," 147. See also Green, "Scale Analysis." Green did point out, however, that his studies also suggested that sociophysical relationships existed in varying forms depending on the culture and geography of the region that the respective urban complex was located in (see Green and Monier, "Photographic Interpretation," 773).

43. See Wray et al., "Photo Interpretation," 668.

44. "Aerial Slum-Spotting," 25.

45. Mumbower and Donoghue, "Urban Poverty Study," 616.

46. Ibid., 617–18.

47. Ibid.

48. See "Aerial Slum-Spotting," 25.

49. See Branch, *Aerial Photography*, 15.

50. Planning from the air has continued ever since

aerial photographs became more readily available to planners, developers, and municipalities in the 1930s. Pictometry, a company founded in 2000 that sells—to private, state, and federal agencies— vertical and oblique aerial photographs and related software that enables the images' incorporation into a number of computer-aided design programs and geographical information systems, advertises its services with the trademarked slogan *See Everywhere, Measure Anything, Plan Everything*. While suggesting an omniscient and omnipotent system and service, Pictometry also proudly presents this service as enabling the view and analysis of a "location, structure, building, obstacle . . . from up to 12 different directions from the convenience of the . . . laptop or computer workstation." The fact that Pictometry's images and software can be used "remotely via a wireless connection or from the convenience of an office desktop" is stressed, thus further promoting "planning from the air" and facilitating design and planning decisions based upon detached and disembodied observations rather than the actual experience on the ground. This heavy-handed approach to planning and development decisions is also reflected in the company's list of "planning and development solutions" that includes the seeming benefit of "easily mov[ing] buildings in and out of a [computer] model" (see www.pictometry.com/government/economic.shtml).

51. Max Lock quoted in "Application of Air Photography," 322.

52. Rolf Hellberg quoted ibid., 323.

53. Branch, *City Planning*, 91. Infrared film was considered by many planners at the time particularly useful because of the color contrast it offered between built-up areas and open green space and vegetation that appeared bright red. Because lawns and landscaping in lower-income neighborhoods were generally sparser and less well kept than in more prosperous parts of a city, these areas would appear darker with fewer bright-red patches.

54. Branch, *City Planning*, 122–23.

55. Berger, *About Looking*, 65.

56. Ibid., 64.

57. Urry, "Aeromobilities."

58. Kahle, "Luftschiffahrt," 60–61.

59. Branch, *City Planning*, 20.

60. Ibid., 19.

61. See ibid., 20.

62. See Branch, "Planning and Operations Research," 172.

63. The terms landscape planning, environmental planning, environmental design, and ecological planning were often used interchangeably in contemporary literature. They were parts of regional planning. In this work, the term (regional) landscape planning will be used predominantly. Landscape planning analyzed the impact of land uses and humankind's specific utilitarian requirements of the open landscape, and developed plans for the development and conservation of natural and cultural resources.

64. Anker, *From Bauhaus to Ecohaus*, 108.

65. See also Hills, "Philosophical Approach"; and Eckbo, "Ecology and Design," 130.

66. See documents in NL Troll 280. See also Troll, "Luftbildinterpretation," 121–23. The use of aerial photography in planning was a recurring topic in publications and conferences of the time, for example, at the 1962 symposium for photo interpretation held in Delft, Holland, where the International Training Centre for Aerial Survey was founded in 1951. The later Franco-American-Canadian school of landscape ecology that began to define its theory and methods in the 1980s, like Troll, also emphasized the spatial distribution of ecosystems within the larger landscape unit, paying particular attention to the interrelationships and distribution of matter between the individual spatial units. For the Franco-American-Canadian school of landscape ecology, see Bergandi and Blandin, "Holism vs. Reductionism," 193–96. In the United States, the Harvard Graduate School of Design (GSD) recognized the need for landscape ecology to contribute to its landscape architecture and regional planning programs. The GSD established an endowed professorship, the Professor of Advanced Environmental Studies in Ecology, in 1969, and the landscape architecture programs at Harvard and the University of Pennsylvania incorporated ecological matters into their curricula. For the development of the studies in landscape architecture at Harvard, see Simo, *The Coalescing of Different Forces and Ideas*, 54. Landscape ecology became a subdiscipline of ecology in the United States in 1983, and in 1987 the U.S. International Association of Landscape Ecology was established.

67. Zonneveld, "Land(scape) Ecology," 15.

68. Naveh and Lieberman, *Landscape Ecology*, xi.

69. Zonneveld, "Land(scape) Ecology," 15. For the holistic approach in land classification and evaluation for planning the development of natural resources, see Zonneveld, *Land Evaluation*.

70. For the role of general systems theory and cybernetics in ecology, see Bakuzis, *Foundations of Forest Ecosystems*, chaps. 1 and 4.

71. See Steinitz et al., *Comparative Study*, 19, 294.

72. William Anders cited in Kepes, "Art and Ecological Consciousness," 10.

73. See Cosgrove and Fox, *Photography*, 63.

74. See Gaarb, "Use and Misuse"; and Cosgrove, "One-World."

75. The photograph's caption in the 1968 *Time* issue was "Dawn." See Cosgrove, "One-World," 284.

76. Ibid., 284–85.

77. See Ingold, "Globes and Spheres," 31–42; and Gaarb, "Use and Misuse."

78. See Adams and Newhall, *American Earth*, 36–38, quotation on 36; and Cosgrove and Fox, *Photography and Flight*, 66.

79. See, for example, Blake, *God's Own Junkyard*, 106–7; Rome, *Bulldozer in the Countryside*, 151–54; and Cosgrove, "Images and Imagination in 20th-Century Environmentalism," 1869–71.

80. See Sørensen, *39 Haveplaner*; and McHarg, *Design with Nature*, 19–23.

81. See McHarg, *Quest for Life*, 43, 95, 197, 201. See also Anker, *From Bauhaus to Ecohaus*, 103–8.

82. McHarg, "Ecology," 66.

83. McHarg, *Design with Nature*, 5.

84. Ibid., 151.

85. McHarg, "Ecological Method," 105.

86. See ibid., 106.

87. Anker, *From Bauhaus to Ecohaus*, 128.

88. See ibid., 129.

89. As Joel Hagen has pointed out, "the ecosystem concept did become closely identified with the rational management of nature for human benefit" (Hagen, *An Entangled Bank*, 139).

90. McHarg, "Regional Landscape Planning," 35; McHarg, *Quest for Life*, 191–93.

91. For a contemporary view of Lewis and McHarg, see William H. Whyte, *Last Landscape*, 182–95; Harvard University Landscape Architecture Research Office, *Environmental Resource Analysis*; and P. Lewis, "Quality Corridors."

92. P. Lewis, "Nature in Our Cities," 24, 27.

93. See McHarg, "Ecological Method," 105–6.

94. P. Lewis, "Nature in Our Cities," 25.

95. P. Lewis, *Tomorrow by Design*, 183.

96. P. Lewis, "Nature in Our Cities," 27.

97. Ibid.

98. Hills, "Philosophical Approach," 345.

99. McHarg, "Ecological Planning," 10. For McHarg's comments with regard to creativity and creative evolution, see ibid., 8–9.

100. Hills, "Philosophical Approach," 365.

101. Ibid., 346.

102. Naveh and Lieberman, *Landscape Ecology*, 112.

103. Hills, "Philosophical Approach," 365.

104. Eckbo, "Ecology and Design," 131.

105. See P. Lewis, "Nature in Our Cities," 24.

106. For the "metropolitanist" and "regionalist" approaches in regional planning, see Fishman, "Death and Life."

107. See P. Lewis, "Nature in Our Cities," 24; and P. Lewis, "Landscape Inventory," 125.

108. P. Lewis, "Quality Corridors"; P. Lewis, "Nature in Our Cities," 25.

109. Hills, "Philosophical Approach," 360.

110. See Herrington, "Nature of Ian McHarg's Science"; and Steinitz, Parker, and Jordan, "Hand-Drawn Overlays."

111. See P. Lewis, "Landscape Inventory," 115.

112. Ibid., 122.

113. See ibid., 122, 128.

114. Way, *Air Photo Interpretation*, 1.

115. See Way, *Terrain Analysis*, 1–2; and "Douglas Way Employs Remotely Sensed Imagery for Innovative Landscape Analysis," *Harvard Graduate School of Design News* 11, no. 2 (1982): 8.

116. On the identification of regional patterns and distinct patches within these regions in early ecology, see Golley, *History of the Ecosystem Concept in Ecology*, 22–24.

117. Troll, "Landscape Ecology," 43.

118. Zonneveld, *Land Evaluation*, 21.

119. Forman, *Urban Regions*, 16–17; see also 11, 13, 18.

120. See Spirn, "Ian McHarg," 105; P. Lewis, *Tomorrow by Design*, 33; and Eckbo, "Ecology and Design," 130.

121. Hackett, "Landscape Contribution," 207.

122. Hackett, "Landscape Design," 211.

123. Eckbo, "Ecology and Design," 131.

124. Press release from Charles H. Gale, Fairchild Aviation Corporation, box 51, folder "Fairchild Aerial Surveys, 1935,"
Sherman Fairchild Collection of the Manuscript Division, Library of Congress.

125. Chombart de Lauwe, *La découverte aérienne*, 19.

126. Kepes, *New Landscape,* 69.

127. Ibid., 21.

128. Ibid., 74.

129. Ibid., 104. The World War II camouflage landscapes of Kepes's Bauhaus colleague Oskar Schlemmer already had been "inspired by what appear to be microscopic photographs of natural objects such as sponges, bark, etc." (see Schlemmer, *Letters,* 389).

130. Oeser, *Wunder,* 7.

131. Ibid., 7–8.

132. See ibid., 8, 15–16.

133. For the use of photography in science and the discussions about its objective and artistic nature, see Daston and Galison, *Objectivity,* 125–73.

134. See Schrader, "Poetry of Ideas," 10–11.

135. Arendt, "Man's Conquest of Space," 528.

136. Stephan L. Chorover to the Office of Charles and Ray Eames, October 25, 1978, box 208, folder 4, Charles and Ray Eames Collection, Manuscript Division, Library of Congress.

137. Arthur Drexler, "Man and Nature," in *Modern Gardens and the Landscape,* ed. Elizabeth Kessler, 4–15 (New York: Museum of Modern Art, 1964), 15.

138. Smithson, "Aerial Art."

139. Smithson's projects were predated by Herbert Bayer's site-specific earth sculpture created in Aspen, Colorado, in 1955.

140. Smithson, "Aerial Art," 180.

141. Robert Smithson at a symposium on earth art held at Cornell University, February 6, 1969, in Flam, *Robert Smithson,* 177. For Smithson's "aerial art" and the first earth works, see Boettger, *Earthworks,* 45–101.

142. Wagstaff, "Tony Smith."

143. See Boettger, *Earthworks,* 56–57.

144. Dennis Oppenheim at a symposium on earth art held at Cornell University, February 6, 1969, in Flam, *Robert Smithson,* 177.

145. At the same time the aerial view also began to fascinate and inspire artists who worked with more traditional media, like painting. Aerial landscape art that used the aerial perspective in the depiction or evocation of landscapes developed as a genre in the 1970s. Work by the artists Jane Frank, Georgia O'Keeffe, Susan Crile, Yvonne Jacquette, Nancy Graves, and Richard Diebenkorn can be assigned to this genre (see Dreikausen, *Aerial Perception*).

146. Smithson, "Aerial Art," 180.

147. Ibid.

148. Robert Smithson, "Proposal for Earthworks and Landmarks to be Built on the Fringes of the Fort Worth–Dallas Regional Air Terminal Site (1966–67)," in Flam, *Robert Smithson,* 354.

149. To make his aerial art accessible also to passengers and visitors in the terminal, Smithson planned to set up TV cameras that would transmit images of the aerial art outdoors to the inside of the terminal.

150. Smithson, "Aerial Art," 180.

151. On the role of photography for conceptual art and earthworks, see Foote, "The Anti-Photographers."

152. See Kepes, "Artist as Environmentalist; Kepes, "Artist's Role"; and Kepes, "Art and Ecological Consciousness."

153. Robert Smithson to Gyorgy Kepes, July 3, 1969, in Flam, *Robert Smithson,* 369. Kepes later canceled the entire show. For communication between Kepes and Smithson, and their different approaches to environmental art, see Martin, "Organicism's Other."

154. See Robert Smithson (1971), in Flam, *Robert Smithson,* 376.

155. Environmental and site artists who have been particularly influential in landscape architectural practice include Michael Heizer, Walter De Maria, Mary Miss, and Robert Irwin. Smithson developed two works, *Broken Circle* and *Spiral Hill,* to reclaim an industrially devastated landscape on the occasion of his participation at the 1971 international exhibition *Sonsbeek 71* in Holland.

156. Robert Smithson died tragically in an airplane crash during an inspection flight of a site he was working on at a ranch in West Texas.

157. See Irwin, *Being and Circumstance,* 27.

158. Meyer, "Post–Earth Day Conundrum," 196.

159. Hargreaves talks about the inspiration provided by various works by Robert Smithson in

Hargreaves, "Postmodernism"; and Hargreaves, "Most Influential Landscapes."

160. Like many earthworks and landscape architectural works that use sculptural forms and different surface textures, the keyhole recalls the prehistoric traces that were first identified by archaeologists through the aerial view and aerial photography at the beginning of the twentieth century.

161. For accounts of Byxbee Park, see Engler, *Designing America's Waste Landscapes,* 110–12; Rainey, "Environmental Ethics and Park Design; and Beardsley, "Entropy."

162. Merleau-Ponty, *Visible,* 73.

163. Merleau-Ponty, "Eye and Mind," 160–61.

164. Dodge and Perkins, "View from Nowhere?," 497.

165. Farman, "Mapping the Digital Empire," 869.

166. On the subversion of Google Earth™ within its own media, see ibid.; and Kingsbury and Jones, "Walter Benjamin's Dionysian Adventures."

167. For the Coronado Air Base, see Tony Perry, "Navy to Mask Barracks Shaped Like Swastica," *Los Angeles Times,* September 26, 2007; and Carolyn Marshall, "Navy to Mask Swastika Look of Barracks in California," *New York Times,* September 27, 2007. For the German cases, see Benedikt Weyerer, *München 1933–1949: Stadtrundgänge zur politischen Geschichte* (Munich: Buchendorfer Verlag, 1996), 288–89; and Claus-Dieter Steyer, "'Hakenkreuzwald': Holzfäller im Forst bei Zernikow," *Der Tagesspiegel,* December 4, 2000.

168. See Sheppard and Cizek, "Ethics of Google Earth."

169. For the affective value of virtual globes like Google Earth™ and its risk, see ibid., 2108.

170. See www.lippeplus.de/.

171. Mitchell, *Skyways,* 158.

Six | From Airfields to Green Fields

1. See Blackwell, DeVault, Fernández-Juricic, and Dolbeer, "Wildlife Collisions with Aircraft."

2. Smithson, "Aerial Art," 180.

3. Cosgrove, "Airport/Landscape," 231.

4. Ibid.

5. Banham, "Obsolescent Airport," 252.

6. Ibid.

7. See Committee on Regional Plan of New York and Its Environs, *Regional Plan,* 1:371.

8. See Hooftman in "Urban Agriculture," 34.

9. The nineteenth-century American park designer and advocate Andrew Jackson Downing described 500 acres (202 hectares) as the ideal size of parks (see Czerniak, "Introduction/Speculating on Size," 23; and Cranz and Boland, "Defining the Sustainable Park").

10. For the competition entries, see Senatsverwaltung für Stadtentwicklung, *Parklandschaft Tempelhof.*

11. Senate Department for Urban Development, *Tempelhof Parkland,* 8.

12. Ibid., 25.

13. Ibid., 29.

14. Ibid., 25.

15. For Kienast, see Weilacher, *Zwischen Landschaftsarchitektur,* 150. For statements by German contemporary landscape architects, see Franke and Kühne, "Wiederentdeckung der Romantik."

16. See Hollein, preface, 17.

17. See Quintus Horatius Flaccus: Liber prior, epistulae XVI. For an English translation, see Horace, *Complete Works,* trans. Passage, 286–87.

18. Weinhart, "World Must Be Made Romantic," 35–36.

19. See, for example, the artists Catherine Opie, David Thorpe, and Laura Owens.

20. See A. J. Goldman, "Repurposing Tempelhof," *Wall Street Journal,* August 25, 2011; and "Urban Agriculture," 34.

21. Senate Department for Urban Development, *Tempelhof Parkland,* 33.

22. For a characterization of the New Romanticism, see Hollein, preface, 19.

23. For Berlin's "critical reconstruction," see Ladd, *Ghosts of Berlin,* 108–10, 217–35; and Bodenschatz, "Es gab 1989/90 keine Stunde Null im Städtebau."

24. Senate Department for Urban Development, *Tempelhof Parkland,* 120–21.

25. Hooftman in "Urban Agriculture," 30.

26. "Raumpioniere," in Senatsverwaltung für Stadtentwicklung Berlin, *Urban Pioneers,* 36.

27. Ibid., 38.

28. For Berlin's flexible master planning, see Misselwitz, Oswalt, and Overmeyer, "Stadtentwicklung."

29. Meyer, "Public Park as Avante-Garde (Landscape) Architecture," 25.

30. First board of competition entry by OMA, 2000.

31. Klingmann, *Brandscapes,* 114.

32. Koolhaas and Mau, "Congestion without Matter," 934. On Koolhaas and his design for La Villette see Constant, *Modern Architectural Landscape,* chap. 9.

33. Koolhaas and Mau, "Congestion without Matter," 921.

34. Hill, "Urban Ecologies."

35. Mau quoted in Blum, "Play."

36. See Deutsche, *Evictions,* xiii, 269–327; and Mouffe, *Democratic Paradox,* 80–107.

37. Senate Department for Urban Development, *Tempelhof Parkland,* 62–63.

38. To provide citizens with lawns that can be used for various recreational purposes, a part of the meadows in Tempelhof is mowed up to twelve times per year, depending on the weather. A 15-meter- (49.21 feet-) wide strip parallel to the runways is mowed approximately six times per year to act as an optical boundary surrounding the park areas that provide the endangered skylarks with breeding grounds. I thank Michael Krebs, park manager of Tempelhofer Freiheit, for this information.

39. Landscape protection areas are areas that are established and protected under German law for the conservation, development, or restoration of natural processes, habitats, and wildlife; and for the conservation of an area's landscape character, aesthetic, and/or recreational value. They are protected against any influences that would change their character, such as development and unregulated waste dumping. Individual by-laws specify the use and prohibitions regarding the respective landscape protection area (Bundesnaturschutzgesetz [2 G v. 6.12.2011 I 2557], § 26).

40. Verordnung zum Schutz der Landschaft des ehemaligen Flugfeldes Johannisthal und über das Naturschutzgebiet ehemaliges Flugfeld Johannisthal im Bezirk Treptow-Köpenick von Berlin. Vom 4. September 2002.

41. See Schröder, *Rekombinationen,* 115.

42. For the development of urban ecology in Berlin, see Lachmund, "Ecology in a Walled City"; Lachmund, "The Making of an Urban Ecology"; and Lachmund, "Exploring the City of Rubble."

43. Lachmund, "Making of an Urban Ecology."

44. Nature reserves are legally established areas in which nature and landscape are strictly protected as a whole or in parts to preserve wildlife habitats; for scientific research of wild plant or animal species; for scientific, cultural, natural-historic, or regional reasons; or/and because of their uniqueness, significant character and beauty. All acts that may lead to the destruction, damage, or change of a nature reserve or its elements, are prohibited (Bundesnaturschutzgesetz [2 G v. 6.12.2011 I 2557], § 23).

45. Heick, "Naturschutzpark," 226.

46. For the use of heathland in nineteenth- and twentieth-century German gardens and art, and its perception and meaning, see Gröning and Schneider, *Heide.*

47. For the first German nature park, the Heidepark, see Engels, *Naturpolitik,* 102–3.

48. For the history of nature conservation and nature parks in postwar Germany, see ibid. On nature parks, see, in particular, 93–154; and Chaney, *Nature of the Miracle Years,* 114–47.

49. Since 2010, the city has monitored the impact of human use on the plant and animal species living on the site. While the designers in collaboration with the Senate Department of Urban Development have argued that the site's biodiversity should be increased further, the current (2012) objective is to maintain the status quo. Species monitoring that includes surveys of plants, grasshoppers, butterflies and moths, has shown that the protective measurements through signage, fences, and design have succeeded in maintaining, for example, the previously existing number of skylarks on site.

50. See "Urban Agriculture," 33.

51. For adaptive planning in the context of biodiversity conservation, see Lister, "Systems Approach"; and Lister and Kay, "Celebrating Diversity."

52. On the organism metaphor in Berlin city politics of the 1990s, see Hennecke, "Berlin soll wachsen"; and Hennecke, "ParZellen."

53. Forty designers were invited to participate in the competition, and twenty-four accepted the invitation. Besides Ken Smith, who had partnered with Ten-Arquitectos of Mexico City, Mary Miss Studio of New York, and Mia Lehrer and Associates of Los Angeles, the following six firms were then chosen by the jury as semifinalists: Abalos & Herreros of Madrid, Spain; Miralles/Tagliabue of Barcelona,

Spain; Richard Haag Associates of Seattle, Washington; Hargreaves Associates of San Francisco, California; Olin Patnership of Philadelphia, Pennsylvania; Royston Hanamoto Alley & Abbey of Mill Valley, California. See Orange County Great Park Corporation, *From Concept to Production*, 19–25.

54. For the developments in the creation of the park, see Orange County Grand Jury 2005–2006, "The Orange County Great Park: Whose Park Is It?," 3–5; Orange County Great Park Corporation, *From Concept to Production*; Larry Agran, "Grand Plans for the Great Park," *American City and County* 124, no. 6 (June 1, 2009); "Great Park's Finishing Touches Are Done—On Paper, Anyway; Building Is Another Matter, as Schedule and Budget Are Undecided," *Los Angeles Times*, February 10, 2009, "Metro Desk," B1; Fred A. Bernstein, "From Old Air Base to Residential Amenity," *New York Times*, February 4, 2007; and Morris Newman, "El Toro Airport: In the War Zone," *Planning* (June 2000): 4–9.

55. The grand jury queried whether the Orange County Great Park Corporation would be able to represent the interests of the county as a whole, raised concerns over the award of no-bid contracts by the City of Irvine, and suggested that the Great Park project, intended for the entire county, had been hijacked by the city (see Orange County Grand Jury 2005–2006, "The Orange County Great Park: Whose Park Is It?").

56. Kling, Olin, and Poster "Emergence of Postsuburbia," 5–11.

57. See James Sterngold, "California Officials Wrangle over Plans for Great Park," *New York Times*, July 1, 2002, A8.

58. See Forsyth, *Reforming Suburbia*, 78, 80, 87–88, 261–362; and Baldassare, *California in the New Millennium*, 148.

59. Orange County Great Park Corporation, *From Concept to Production*, 27–28.

60. Forsyth, *Reforming Suburbia*, 98.

61. Till, "Neotraditional Towns and Urban Villages."

62. Starr, *Embattled Dreams*, x.

63. See Gonzalez, *Labor and Community*, 19.

64. Starrs, "The Navel of California and Other Oranges," 1; Sackman, *Orange Empire*; Gonzalez, *Labor and Community*, 43–54.

65. See Sackman, *Orange Empire*, 7, 10–11.

66. See Larry Agran, "Let's Put Some Green into Our Parks," *Los Angeles Times*, March 19, 2009, A29; Larry Agran, "Grand Plans for the Great Park," *American City and County* 124, no. 6 (June 1, 2009).

67. Handel et al., *Orange County Great Park*, 3.

68. Ibid., 1, emphasis added.

69. Handel et al., *Orange County Great Park*, 146–51.

70. See McDonnell and Pickett, *Humans as Components of Ecosystems*.

71. See Forsyth, *Reforming Suburbia*, 100–101.

72. See Baldassare, *California in the New Millennium*, 168–70.

73. See K. Smith, "Orange County Great Park."

74. See Baldassare, *California in the New Millennium*, 24, 143.

75. The park project was awarded three prizes from the American Society of Landscape Architects (2008, 2009), one prize from the American Planning Association (2009), and one prize from the American Institute of Architects (2009).

76. Veale, *To-morrow's Airliners*, 247.

Bibliography

Aalto, Alvar "Finland." *Architectural Forum* 75, no. 6 (1940): 399–412.

Abendroth, Alfred. "Die Bedeutung des Luftbildes für die Erschliessung der Landschaft." *Der Städtebau* 17, no. 5/6 (1920): 46–50.

———. "Die Förderung der räumlichen Auffassung im Städtebau durch das Luftbild," *Der Städtebau* 16, no. 3/4 (1919): 28–32.

———. "Städtebau und Luftbild." *Städtebau* 24, no. 7 (1929): 201–6.

Abercrombie, Patrick. "Regional Planning." *Town Planning Review* 10, no. 2 (1923): 109–18.

Adams, Ansel, and Nancy Newhall. *This Is the American Earth*. San Francisco: Sierra Club, 1960.

Adey, Peter. *Aerial Life: Spaces, Mobilities, Affects*. Chichester, U.K., and Malden, Mass.: Wiley-Blackwell, 2010.

———. *Mobility*. London and New York: Routledge, 2010.

Adshead, S. D. "Camillo Sitte and Le Corbusier." *Town Planning Review* 14, no. 2 (1930): 85–94.

"Aerial Slum-Spotting." *Engineering News-Record*, November 2, 1967, 25.

Aerodromes Committee Royal Institute of British Architects. First (Interim) Report: *Town Planning & Aviation*. London, March 1931.

Alberti, Leon Battista. *The Ten Books of Architecture: The 1755 Leoni Edition*. Translated into Italian by Cosimo Bartoli; translated into English by James Leoni. New York: Dover, 1986.

Andersson, Sven-Ingvar, and Steen Høyer. *C. Th. Sørensen Landscape Modernist*. Copenhagen: Danish Architectural Press, 2001.

Andriello, Domenico. *Aerourbanistica*. Naples: Arti Grafiche 'La Nuovissima,' 1947.

Anker, Peder. *From Bauhaus to Ecohaus: A History of Ecological Design*. Baton Rouge: Louisiana State University Press, 2010.

"The Application of Air Photography to Architecture and Town Planning." *Journal of the Royal Institute of British Architects* 53 (June 1946): 319–23.

Arendt, Hannah. "Man's Conquest of Space." *American Scholar* 32, no. 4 (1963): 527–40.

Arnheim, Rudolf. "Order and Complexity in Landscape Design." In *The Concept of Order*, edited by Paul G. Kuntz, 153–66. Seattle: University of Washington Press, 1968.

Aronovici, Carol. "Space-Time Planning and Air-mindedness." *American City* 42, no. 4 (1920): 104–6.

Aronson, Shlomo. "Ben Gurion International Airport in Lod." *Topos*, no. 53 (2005): 60–64.

Arthur, William E. "How Shall We Design Our Airports?" *Scientific American* 141 (October 1929), 298–301.

Asendorf, Christoph. *Super Constellation—Flugzeug und Raumrevolution: Die Wirkung der Luftfahrt auf Kunst und Kultur der Moderne*. Vienna and New York: Springer-Verlag, 1997.

"ASLA Survey of Defense Activities." *Landscape Architecture* 31, no. 4 (1941): 200–206.

Augé, Marc. *Non-Places: Introduction to an Anthropology of Supermodernity*. London and New York: Verso, 1995.

Augur, Tracy. "The Dispersal of Cities as a Defense Measure." *Bulletin of the Atomic Scientists* 4, no. 5 (May 1948): 131–34.

Bacon, Gertrude. *The Record of an Aeronaut, Being the Life of John M. Bacon*. London: J. Long, 1907.

Baker, Simon. "San Francisco in Ruins: The 1906

Aerial Photographs of George R. Lawrence." *Landscape* 30 (1989): 9–14.

Bakuzis, Egolfs v. *Foundations of Forest Ecosystems: Lecture and Research Notes.* St. Paul: College of Forestry, University of Minnesota, 1974.

Baldassare, Mark. *California in the New Millennium: The Changing Social and Political Landscape.* Berkeley, Los Angeles, and London: University of California Press, 2000.

Baldwin, Thomas. *Airopaidia.* Chester: J. Fletcher, 1786.

Balfour, Alan. *Rockefeller Center: Architecture as Theater.* New York: McGraw-Hill, 1978.

Balleyguier, Henri. "L'aviation au travail." *L'Architecture* 33 (1920): 182–86, 195–98.

Banham, Reyner. "The Obsolescent Airport." *Architectural Review* 132, no. 788 (1962): 252–53.

Barber, Martyn, and Helen Wickstead. "'One Immense Black Spot': Aerial Views of London 1784–1918." *London Journal* 35, no. 3 (2010): 236–54.

Barthes, Roland. *Camera Lucida: Reflections on Photography.* Translated by Richard Howard. New York: Hill and Wang, 1981.

———. "The Eiffel Tower." In *A Roland Barthes Reader,* edited by Susan Sontag, 236–50. London: Vintage, 1993.

Beardsley, John. "Entropy and the New Landscapes." In "Hargreaves, Landscape Works," special issue, *Process Architecture,* no. 128 (1996): 14–25.

Beaulieu, Lord Montagu of. *London of the Future.* London: T. F. Unwin, 1921.

Becker, Alfred. *Wehrtechnischer Einsatz der Ingenieurbiologie: Schriften des Frontingenieurs.* Berlin: Volk und Reich Verlag, 1944.

Bednarek, Janet R. Daly. *America's Airports: Airfield Development, 1918–1947.* College Station: Texas A&M University Press, 2001.

Bednarek, Janet Rose Daly, and Michael H. Bednarek. *Dreams of Flight: General Aviation in the United States.* College Station: Texas A&M University Press, 2003.

———. "The Flying Machine in the Garden: Parks and Airports, (1918–1938)." *Technology & Culture* 46, no. 2 (2005): 350–73.

Behrens, Roy R. "Art, Design and Gestalt Theory." *Leonardo* 31, no. 4 (1998): 299–303.

———. *False Colors: Art, Design, and Modern Camouflage.* Dysart, Iowa: Bobolink, 2002.

———. "Iowa's Contribution to Camouflage." *Iowa Heritage Illustrated* 78, no. 322 (1997): 98–109.

Bel Geddes, Norman. *Horizons.* Boston: Little, Brown, 1932.

Berg, Kurt. "Luftschutz im Städtebau der Neuzeit." Diploma thesis, Berlin, 1933. Landesarchiv Berlin, B Rep. 009 Nr. 84.

Bergandi, Donato, and Patrick Blandin. "Holism vs. Reductionism: Do Ecosystem Ecology and Landscape Ecology Clarify the Debate?" *Acta Biotheoretica* 46, no. 3 (1998): 185–206.

Berger, John. *About Looking.* New York: Vintage, 1991.

Berleant, Arnold. *Art and Engagement.* Philadelphia: Temple University Press, 1991.

Betts, Benjamin. "Gardens on the Roofs of Radio City." *American Architect* 140, no. 2601 (1931): 34–35, 74–76.

Bill, Joseph T. "Use of Aerial Photography in Urban Planning." *Photogrammetric Engineering* 18, no. 4 (1952): 760–61.

Black, Archibald. "Air Terminal Engineering." *Landscape Architecture* 13, no. 4 (1923): 225–38.

———. *Civil Airports and Airways.* New York: Simmons-Boardman, 1929.

Black, Russell Van Nest. "Air Maps and Photographs in City, County and Regional Planning." *Pennsylvania Planning* 9, no. 3 (1944): 21–24.

"Blackout." *Architectural Forum* (January 1942), 6–15, 42–43.

Blackwell, Bradley F., Travis L. DeVault, Esteban Fernández-Juricic, and Richard A. Dolbeer. "Wildlife Collisions with Aircraft: A Missing Component of Land-Use Planning for Airports." *Landscape and Urban Planning* 93, no. 1 (2009): 1–9.

Blake, Peter. *God's Own Junkyard: The Planned Deterioration of America's Landscape.* New York: Holt, Rinehart and Winston, 1964.

Blum, Andrew. "Play: Toronto Reinvents the Park as a Flexible Landscape for a Changing Community." *Metropolis* 23, no. 5 (2004): 79.

Bodenschatz, Harald. "Es gab 1989/90 keine Stunde Null im Städtebau." In *Berlin plant: Plädoyer für ein Planwerk Innenstadt Berlin 2.0,* edited by Harald Bodenschatz and Thomas Flierl, 74–97. Berlin: Theater der Zeit, 2010.

Boehm, E., W. Brucklacher, and W. Pillewitzer. "Luftbildinterpretation und Geländevergleich—

die Tätigkeit der Forschungsstaffel von 1943–
1945." In *Berichte und Informationen Nr. 8*, edited
by Österreichische Akademie der Wissenschaften,
Institut für Kartographie. Vienna, 1989.

Boemi, Maria Filomena, and Carlo M. Travaglini,
eds. *Roma dall'alto*. Rome: Università degli studi,
Roma Tre: CROMA, Centro di ateneo per lo studio di Roma, 2006.

Boesiger, W., ed. *Le Corbusier: Œuvre complète 1938–
1946*. Zürich: Verlag für Architektur, 1946.

———. *Richard Neutra: Buildings and Projects*.
Zürich: Editions Girsberger, 1951.

Boettger, Suzaan. *Earthworks: Art and the Landscape
of the Sixties*. Berkeley, Los Angeles, and London:
University of California Press, 2002.

Böhm, Hans. "Annäherungen: Carl Troll (1899–
1975)—Wissenschaftler in der NS-Zeit." In *Carl
Troll: Zeitumstände und Forschungsperspektiven*,
Colloquium Geographicum, vol. 26, edited
by Matthias Winiger, 1–77. Sankt Augustin:
Asgard-Verlag, 2003.

Bois, Yve-Alain. "Metamorphosis of Axonometry."
Daidalos 1, no. 1 (1981): 41–58.

Bouman, Mark J. "Cities of the Plane: Airports in
the Networked City." In *Building for Air Travel*,
edited by John Zukowsky, 177–93. Chicago, Munich, and New York: Prestel and Art Institute of
Chicago, 1996.

Boyer, M. Christine. "Aviation and the Aerial View:
Le Corbusier's Spatial Transformations in the
1930s and 1940s." *Diacritics* 33, no. 3/4 (2003):
93–116.

Brainerd, Harry B. "Uses of Roofs and Terraces for
Recreation." *City Planning* 5, no. 7 (1929): 168–76.

Branch, Melville C. *Aerial Photography in Urban Planning and Research*. Harvard City Planning Studies
14. Cambridge: Harvard University Press, 1948.

———. *City Planning and Aerial Information*. Cambridge: Harvard University Press, 1971.

———. "Planning and Operations Research." *Journal of the American Institute of Planners* 23, no. 4
(1957): 168–75.

Branford, Victor, and Patrick Geddes. *The Coming
Polity*. London: Williams and Norgate, 1917.

Breckenridge, Robert P. *Modern Camouflage: The
New Science of Protective Concealment*. New York
and Toronto: Farrar and Rinehart, 1942.

Brittenden, J. E. "Surveying for Town Planning by
the Use of Aerial Photographs." *Garden Cities and
Town Planning* 10, no. 1 (1920): 87–89.

Brock, H. I. "The City That the Air Traveler Sees."
New York Times Sunday Magazine, March 11, 1928,
14–15, 27.

———. "Giving Thought to Our New Airports." *New
York Times*, December 30, 1928, 64.

———. "Travel by Air Creates a New Scenery." *New
York Times Sunday Magazine*, October 31, 1926,
9, 18.

Brunner, Karl H. *Manual de urbanismo*. Vol. 1.
Bogotá: Imprenta Municipal, 1939.

———. "La vista aerea y el urbanismo." *Registro
Municipal* 56, no. 31 (April 15, 1934): 221–23.

———. *Weisungen der Vogelschau: Flugbilder aus
Deutschland und Österreich und ihre Lehren für
Kultur, Siedlung und Städtebau*. Munich: Georg
Callwey, 1928.

———. "Ziele der Architektenschulung." *Die Bau-
zeitung* 31 (August 1929): 331–35.

Burchfield, Jerry, ed. *The Edge of Air: The Legacy
Project*. Laguna Beach, Calif.: Laguna Wilderness
Press; Irvine, Calif.: Irvine Fine Arts Center,
2005.

Burden, William A. M. *The Struggle for Airways in
Latin America*. New York: New York Times Company, 1977.

Bürgi, Andreas. *Relief der Urschweiz: Entstehung
und Bedeutung des Landschaftsmodells von Franz
Ludwig Pfyffer*. Zürich: Verlag Neue Züricher
Zeitung, 2007.

Burke, Edmund. *A Philosophical Enquiry into the
Origin of our Ideas of the Sublime and Beautiful*.
London: R. and J. Dodsley, 1757.

Burle Marx, Roberto. "A Garden Style in Brazil to
Meet Contemporary Needs." *Landscape Architecture* 44, no. 4 (1954): 200–208.

"Camouflage Data Is Correlated: Pratt Institute to
Publish Results of Studies." *Pencil Points* 23 (February 1942): 83–89.

"Camouflage in Modern Warfare." *Nature* 145, no.
3686 (June 22, 1940): 949–51.

Campanella, Thomas J. *Cities from the Sky: An Aerial
Portrait of America*. New York: Princeton Architectural Press, 2001.

Carr, Ethan. *Wilderness by Design*. Lincoln: University of Nebraska Press, 1998.

Casey, Edward S. "Borders and Boundaries: Edging

into the Environment." In *Merleau-Ponty and Environmental Philosophy,* edited by Suzanne L. Cataldi and William S. Hamrick, 67–92. Albany: State University of New York Press, 2007.

Casson, Hugh. "The Aesthetics of Camouflage." *Architectural Review* 96, no. 9 (1944): 62–68.

Cautley, Marjorie. "New Horizons from Aloft." *American Landscape Architect* 3, no. 12 (1930): 17–19.

Central Electricity Generating Board. *Design Memorandum on the Use of Fences.* 1965. London: George Berridge, 1966.

———. *Trawsfynydd Nuclear Power Station.* London: Pulman and Sons, 1961.

Chaney, Sandra. *Nature of the Miracle Years.* New York and Oxford: Berghahn, 2008.

Chase, John, Margaret Crawford, and John Kaliski, eds. *Everyday Urbanism.* New York: Monacelli Press, 1999.

Chombart de Lauwe, Paul Henry, ed. *La découverte aérienne du monde.* Paris: Horizons de France, 1948.

———. *Paris et l'agglomération parisienne.* Paris: Presses universitaires de France, 1952.

———. *Photographies aériennes.* Paris: Librairie Armand Colin, 1951.

Civil Aviation in Brazil: Its Beginning, Growth, Present State. S. Paulo: "Graphicars," Romiti and Lanzara, 1939.

Clark, Kenneth. *Landscape into Art.* New York: Harper and Row, 1976.

Clarke, Gilmore D. "The Airport Is Specialized Commercial Space." *City Planning* 6, no. 2 (1930): 123–24.

Clausewitz, Gen. Carl von. *On War.* Vol. 2. Translated by Colonel J. J. Graham. London: Kegan Paul, Trench, Trubner, 1918.

Clements, Frederic E. *Plant Succession: An Analysis of the Development of Vegetation.* Washington, D.C.: Carnegie Institution, 1916.

———. *Research Methods in Ecology.* Lincoln, Neb.: University Publishing, 1905.

Cohen, Jean-Louis. *André Lurçat 1894–1970.* Liège: Mardaga, 1995.

———. *Architecture in Uniform: Designing and Building for the Second World War.* New Haven, Conn.: Yale University Press, 2011.

Colean, Miles. *Renewing Our Cities.* New York: Twentieth Century Fund, 1953.

Collins, Christiane Crasemann. "Urban Interchange in the Southern Cone: Le Corbusier (1929) and Werner Hegemann (1931) in Argentina." *Journal of the Society of Architectural Historians* 54, no. 2 (1995): 208–27.

Colvin, Brenda. *Land and Landscape.* London: John Murray, 1948.

———. *Land and Landscape: Evolution, Design and Control.* London: John Murray, 1970.

Colwell, Robert N., ed. *Manual of Photographic Interpretation.* Washington D.C.: American Society of Photogrammetry, 1960.

Committee on Regional Plan of New York and Its Environs. *Regional Plan of New York and Its Environs.* Vol. 1, *Atlas and Description.* Philadelphia: Wm. F. Fell Co. Printers, 1929.

———. *Regional Plan of New York and Its Environs.* Vol. 2, *The Building of the City.* Philadelphia: Wm. F. Fell Co. Printers, 1931.

Constant, Caroline. *The Modern Architectural Landscape.* Minneapolis and London: University of Minnesota Press, 2012.

Corner, James. *Taking Measures: Across the American Landscape.* New Haven, Conn.: Yale University Press, 1996.

Cosgrove, Denis. "Airport/Landscape." In *Recovering Landscape: Essays in Contemporary Landscape Architecture,* edited by James Corner, 221–31. New York: Princeton Architectural Press, 1999.

———. "Images and Imagination in 20th-Century Environmentalism: From the Sierras to the Poles." *Environment and Planning A,* 40, no. 8 (2008): 1862–80.

———. "One-World, Whole-Earth, and the Apollo Space Photographs." *Annals of the Association of American Geographers* 84, no. 2 (1994): 270–94.

Cosgrove, Denis, and William L. Fox. *Photography and Flight.* London: Reaktion, 2010.

"Course in Camouflage." *American Nurseryman* 72 (December 15, 1940): 23.

Cranz, Galen, and Michael Boland. "Defining the Sustainable Park: A Fifth Model for Urban Parks." *Landscape Journal* 23, no. 2 (2004): 102–20.

Crary, Jonathan. *Techniques of the Observer: On Vision and Modernity in the Nineteenth Century.* Cambridge: MIT Press, 1990.

Crawford, O. G. S. "Luftbildaufnahmen von archäologischen Bodendenkmälern in England." In "Luftbild und Vorgeschichte," edited by Lilienthal-

Gesellschaft für Luftfahrtforschung, special issue, *Luftbild und Luftbildmessung* 16 (1938): 9–22.

Crawford, O. G. S., and Alexander Keiller. *Wessex from the Air.* Oxford: Clarendon Press, 1928.

Cresswell, Tim. *On the Move: Mobility in the Modern Western World.* New York: Routledge, 2006.

Cresswell, Tim, and Peter Merriman, eds. *Geographies of Mobilities: Practices, Spaces, Subjects.* Farnham, Surrey, and Burlington, Vt.: Ashgate, 2011.

Cret, Paul P. "Aerial Photography and Architecture." *Journal of the American Institute of Architects* 9 (January 1921): 8–12.

Crowe, Simon. "The Early Years." In *Sylvia Crowe,* edited by Geoffrey Collins and Wendy Powell. Reigate: LDT Monographs, 1999.

Crowe, Sylvia. *The Landscape of Power.* London: Architectural Press, 1958.

———. "Power and the Landscape." *Journal of the Institute of Landscape Architects,* no. 52 (November 1960): 3–7.

———. "Presidential Address." *Journal of the Institute of Landscape Architects,* no. 40 (November 1957): 3–5, 20.

———. *Tomorrow's Landscape.* London: Architectural Press, 1956.

Czerniak, Julia. "Introduction/Speculating on Size." In *Large Parks,* edited by Czerniak and George Hargreaves, 19–33. New York: Princeton Architectural Press, 2007.

Czerniak, Julia, and George Hargreaves, eds. *Large Parks.* New York: Princeton Architectural Press, 2007.

Daston, Lorraine, and Peter Galison. *Objectivity.* New York: Zone, 2007.

Davison, Robert L. "Airport Design and Construction." *Architectural Record* 65 (May 1929): 490–515.

Dee, Hy. "Camouflage Ground Patterns." *Design* 43, no. 9 (1942): 16–19.

De Longe, Merrill E. *Modern Airfield Planning and Concealment.* New York and Chicago: Pitman, 1943.

Demuth, Norman. *Practical Camouflage or The Art of Guile.* Bognor Regis, Sussex, U.K.: John Crowther, 1942.

Deriu, Davide. "The Ascent of the Modern *Planeur:* Aerial Images and Urban Imaginary in the 1920s." In *Imagining the City,* edited by Christian Emden, Catherine Keen, and David Midgley, 189–211. Oxford and New York: Peter Lang, 2006.

———. "Between Veiling and Unveiling: Modern Camouflage and the City as a Theater of War." In *Endangered Cities: Military Power and Urban Societies in the Era of the World Wars,* edited by Marcus Funck and Roger Chickering, 15–34. Boston: Brill, 2004.

———. "Capital Views; Interwar London in the Photographs of Aerofilms Ltd." *London Journal* 35, no. 3 (2010): 255–76.

Desha, J. D. "Aerial Photography—An Aid to the Municipal Engineer in City Planning." *Municipal Engineers Journal* 1, no. 1 (1923): 32–44.

Deutsche, Rosalyn. *Evictions: Art and Spatial Politics.* Cambridge: MIT Press, 1996.

Dittrich, Elke. *Ernst Sagebiel: Leben und Werk (1892–1970).* Berlin: Lukas Verlag, 2003.

Dodge, Martin, and Chris Perkins. "The 'View from Nowhere'? Spatial Politics and Cultural Significance of High-Resolution Satellite Imagery." *Geoforum* 40, no. 4 (2009): 497–501.

Dorrian, Mark. "The Aerial View: Notes for a Cultural History." *Strates* 13 (2007): 2–19.

Douglas, Deborah G. "Who Designs Airports . . . Engineers, Architects, or City Planners? Aspects of American Airport Design before World War II." In *Atmospheric Flight in the Twentieth Century,* edited by P. Galison and A. Roland, 301–22. Dordrecht and Boston: Kluwer, 2000.

"Douglas Way Employs Remotely Sensed Imagery for Innovative Landscape Analysis." *Harvard Graduate School of Design News* 11, no. 2 (1982): 8.

Dräger, Heinrich. *Die Schnellbahnstadt.* Koblenz: Verlag Gasschutz und Luftschutz Dr. Ebeling, 1956.

Dreikausen, Margret. *Aerial Perception: The Earth as Seen from Aircraft and Spacecraft and Its Influence on Contemporary Art.* Philadelphia: Art Alliance Press, 1985.

Drexler, Arthur. "Man and Nature." In *Modern Gardens and the Landscape,* edited by Elizabeth Kessler, 4–15. New York: Museum of Modern Art, 1964.

Dudley, Michael Quinn. "Sprawl as Strategy: City Planners Face the Bomb." *Journal of Planning Education and Research* 21 (2001): 52–63.

Duempelmann, Sonja. "Taking Turns: Landscape and Environmental History at the Crossroads." *Landscape Research* 36, no. 6 (2011): 625–40.

Duffus, R. L. *Mastering a Metropolis: Planning the Future of the New York Region.* New York and London: Harper and Brothers, 1930.

Duke, Neville, and Edward Lanchbery. *The Saga of Flight.* New York: John Day, 1961.

Dünne, Jörg, and Stephan Günzel, eds. *Raumtheorie.* Frankfurt am Main: Suhrkamp, 2006.

Durth, Werner, and Niels Gutschow. *Träume in Trümmern.* Vol. 1. Braunschweig and Wiesbaden: Friedrich Viehweg and Sohn, 1988.

Düwel, Jörn, and Niels Gutschow. *Städtebau in Deutschland im 20. Jahrhundert.* Stuttgart, Leipzig, and Wiesbaden: Teubner, 1965.

Eckbo, Garrett. "Ecology and Design." *Journal of Soil and Water Conservation* 26 (July/August 1971): 130–31.

———. "H-Bomb and City Planning." *Architectural Forum* 101, no. 1 (1954): 68, 72, 76, 78, 80, 87.

———. "The New Landscape in Art and Science." *Landscape Architecture* 48, no. 3 (1958): 197.

"Editorial: Airports." *City Planning* 6, no. 1 (January 1930): 28–29.

Edwards, Sam. "Ruins, Relics and Restoration: The Afterlife of World War Two American Airfields in England, 1945–2005." In *Militarized Landscapes: From Gettysburg to Salisbury Plain,* edited by Chris Pearson, Peter Coates, and Tim Cole, 209–28. London and New York: Continuum, 2010.

Ehrenberg, Ralph E. "'Up in the Air in More Ways Than One': The Emergence of Aeronautical Charts in the United States." In *Cartographies of Travel and Navigation,* edited by James R. Akerman, 207–59. Chicago: University of Chicago Press, 2006.

Ehrenfels, Christian von. "Über Gestaltqualitäten." *Vierteljahresschrift für Wissenschaftliche Philosophie* 14 (1890): 249–92.

Eliot, Charles W. "The Influence of the Automobile on the Design of Park Roads." *Landscape Architecture* 13, no. 1 (1922): 27–37.

Emerson, Charles E. "Surveying With Eagle Eye." *Open Road* 6 (October 1924), 12–15.

Engelbrecht, Lloyd C. "Moholy-Nagy und Chermayeff in Chicago." In *50 Jahre New Bauhaus,* edited by Peter Hahn, 51–68. Berlin: Bauhaus Archiv, Argon, 1987.

Engels, Jens Ivo. *Naturpolitik in der Bundesrepublik.* Munich: Schöningh, 2005.

Engler, Mira. *Designing America's Waste Landscapes.* Baltimore and London: Johns Hopkins University Press, 2004.

Enoch, Kurt, ed. *Flugkarte von Hamburg und Umgebung.* Hamburg: Kurt Enoch, 1925.

Eskola, Tanelli. *Water Lilies and Wings of Steel.* Helsinki: University of Art and Design Helsinki UIAH, 1997.

Ewald, Erich. *Deutschland aus der Vogelschau.* Berlin: Otto Stollberg, 1925.

———. *Im Flugzeug über Berlin.* Marburg: Elwert'sche Verlagsbuchhandlung, 1928.

———. "Das Luftbild im Dienste des Städtebaues und Siedlungswesens." Ph.D. diss., Technische Hochschule zu Berlin, 1922.

Farman, Jason "Mapping the Digital Empire: Google Earth and the Process of Postmodern Cartography." *New Media & Society* 12, no. 6 (2010): 869–88.

Fairchild, Sherman M. "Aerial Mapping of New York City." *American City* 30, no. 1 (January 1924): 74–75.

———. "Aerial Photography: Its Development and Future." *Annals of the American Academy of Political and Social Science* 131 (May 1927): 49–55.

First Interallied Town Planning Conference. Paris: La Bibliothèque de la Renaissance des Cités, 1919.

Fischer von Poturzyn, Friedrich Andreas. *Lufthansa: Luftpolitische Möglichkeiten.* Leipzig: Werner Lehmann Verlag, 1925.

Fishman, Robert. "The Death and Life of American Regional Planning." In *Reflections on Regionalism,* edited by Bruce Katz, 107–21. Washington, D.C.: Brookings Institution Press, 2000.

Fitzhugh, Armistead. "Camouflage: Adaptation of Basic Principles of Landscape Architecture." *Landscape Architecture* 33, no. 4 (July 1943): 119–24.

Flam, Jack, ed. *Robert Smithson: The Collected Writings.* Berkeley and Los Angeles: University of California Press, 1996.

Foedrowitz, Michael. *Bunkerwelten, Luftschutzanlagen in Norddeutschland.* Eggolsheim: Ed. Dörfler im Nebel-Verl., 2002.

Foote, Nancy. "The Anti-Photographers." *Artforum* 15, no. 1 (September 1976): 46–54.

Ford, George B. "The Design of Airports." *American Architect* 82, no. 2532 (November 5, 1927): 561–68.

Forman, Richard T. T. *Urban Regions: Ecology and*

Planning Beyond the City. Cambridge: Cambridge University Press, 2008.

Forsyth, Ann. *Reforming Suburbia: The Planned Communities of Irvine, Columbia, and the Woodlands.* Berkeley, Los Angeles, and London: University of California Press, 2005.

Fox, Milton S. "Camouflage and the Artist." *Magazine of Art* 35, no. 4 (1942): 136–37, 154, 156.

———. *Camouflage, Theory and Practice: A Summary.* Cleveland: Cleveland Museum of Art, 1943.

Frange, Calire. *Le style Duchêne: Henri & Achille Duchêne: Architectes paysagistes, 1841–1947.* Neuilly: Editions du Labyrinthe, 1998.

Franke, Ulrich, and Olaf Kühne. "Die Wiederentdeckung der Romantik." *Stadt und Grün* 12 (2010): 48–55.

Fraser, Valerie. "Cannibalizing Le Corbusier." *Journal of the Society of Architectural Historians* 59, no. 2 (2000): 180–93.

Freudenschuh, Scott. "Micro- and Macro-Scale Environments." In *Cognitive Mapping: Past, Present and Future,* edited by Rob Kitchin and Freudenschuh, 125–46. London and New York: Routledge, 2000.

Freytag, Anette. "When the Railway Conquered the Garden: Velocity in Parisian and Viennese Parks." In *Landscape Design and the Experience of Motion,* edited by Michel Conan, 215–42. Washington, D.C.: Dumbarton Oaks Trustees for Harvard University, 2003.

Friedland, Roger, and Deirdre Boden, "NowHere: An Introduction to Space, Time and Modernity." In *NowHere: Space, Time and Modernity,* edited by Friedland and Boden, 1–60. Berkeley, Los Angeles, and London: University of California Press, 1994.

Friedmann, Herbert. *The Natural-History Background of Camouflage.* Smithsonian Institution War Background Studies no. 5. Washington, D.C.: Lord Baltimore Press, Smithsonian Institution, 1942.

Froesch, Charles, and Walther Prokosch. *Airport Planning.* New York: Wiley and Sons, 1946.

Fuller, G., and R. Harley, *Aviopolis: A Book about Airports.* London: Black Dog, 2005.

Gaarb, Y. J. "The Use and Misuse of the Whole Earth Image." *Whole Earth Review,* March 1985, 18–25.

Gärtner, Ulrike. "Flughafenarchitektur der 20er und 30er Jahre in Deutschland." Ph.D. diss., Marburg University, 1990.

Geddes, Patrick. "A Naturalists' Society and its Work." *Scottish Geographical Magazine* 19 (1903): 89–95, 141–47.

Gibson, James. *The Ecological Approach to Visual Perception.* Boston: Houghton Mifflin, 1979.

Giedion, Sigfried. Preface to *Brazil and Contemporary Architecture,* edited by Henrique E. Mindlin, ix–xii. New York: Reinhold, 1956.

———. *Space, Time and Architecture.* 5th ed. Cambridge: Harvard University Press, 1967.

Gilbert, David. "The Three Ages of Aerial Vision: London's Aerial Iconography from Wenceslaus Hollar to Google Earth." *London Journal* 35, no. 3 (2010): 289–99.

Goff, Harper. "Camouflage in America Is More Than a Science: It Is an Art with a Definite Technique." *Architect and Engineer* 152 (January 1943): 26–36.

Golley, Frank Benjamin. *A History of the Ecosystem Concept in Ecology: More Than the Sum of Its Parts.* New Haven, Conn., and London: Yale University Press, 1993.

Gonzalez, Gilbert G. *Labor and Community: Mexican Citrus Worker Villages in a Southern California County 1900–1950.* Urbana and Chicago: University of Illinois Press, 1994.

Goodden, Henrietta. *Camouflage and Art: Design for Deception in World War 2.* London: Unicorn Press, 2007.

Goodrich, E. P. "Airports as a Factor in City Planning." Supplement to the *National Municipal Review* 17, no. 3 (1928): 181–94.

Gordon, Alastair. *Naked Airport: A Cultural History of the World's Most Revolutionary Structure.* New York: Metropolitan Books and H. Holt, 2004.

Gothein, Marie Luise. *Geschichte der Gartenkunst.* Vol. 2. Jena: Diederichs, 1914.

Grant, Lieut. Colonel U. S. "Airports and Public Parks." *Parks & Recreation* 13, no. 4 (1930): 188–91.

Gray, Richard T. *About Face: German Physiognomic Thought from Lavater to Auschwitz.* Detroit: Wayne State University Press, 2004.

Green, Norman E. "Aerial Photographic Analysis of Residential Neighborhoods: An Evaluation of Data Accuracy." *Social Forces* 35, no. 2 (1956): 142–47.

———. "Aerial Photographic Interpretation and the Social Structure of the City." *Photogrammetric Engineering* 23, no. 1 (1957): 89–96.

———. "Aerial Photography in the Analysis of Urban Structures. Sociological and Social." Ph.D. diss., University of North Carolina, Chapel Hill, 1955.

———. "Scale Analysis of Urban Structures: A Study of Birmingham, Alabama." *American Sociological Review* 21, no. 1 (February 1956): 8–13.

Green, Norman E., and Robert B. Monier. "Aerial Photographic Interpretation and the Human Ecology of the City." *Photogrammetric Engineering* 25, no. 5 (1959): 770–73.

———. *Reliability and Validity of Air Reconnaissance as a Collection Method for Urban Demographic & Sociological Information.* Vol. 11 of [U.S.] Human Resources Research Institute. Technical Research Report. Air University, Maxwell Air Force Base, 1953.

Gromort, Georges. *L'art des jardins: Une courte étude d'ensemble sur l'art de la composition des jardins.* Paris: Vincent, Fréal et cie, 1934.

Gröning, Gert. "Teutonic Myth, Rubble, and Recovery: Landscape Architecture in Germany." In *The Architecture of Landscape 1940–1960,* edited by Marc Treib, 120–53. Philadelphia: University of Pennsylvania Press, 2002.

Gröning, Gert, and Uwe Schneider. *Die Heide in Park und Garten.* Worms: Wernersche Verlagsgesellschaft, 1999.

Gropius, Walter. *Bauhausbauten Dessau.* Munich: Albert Langen Verlag, 1930.

———. *Internationale Architektur.* 1927. Mainz and Berlin: Florian Kupferberg, 1981.

———. *Die neue Architektur und das Bauhaus.* Mainz and Berlin: Kupferberg, 1965.

———. *The New Architecture and the Bauhaus.* Translated by P. Morton Shand. London: Faber and Faber, 1935.

Gutiérrez, Ramón. "Buenos Aires, A Great European City." In *Planning Latin America's Capital Cities, 1850–1950,* edited by Arturo Almandoz, 45–74. London: Routledge, 2002.

Gutkind, E. A. *Our World from the Air.* London: Chatto and Windus, 1952.

———. "Our World from the Air: Conflict and Adaptation." In *Man's Role in Changing the Face of the Earth,* edited by William L. Thomas Jr., 1–48. Chicago: University of Chicago Press, 1956.

G. W. P. "The Physiognomy of Cities." *American Review* 6, no. 3 (September 1847): 233–42.

Hackett, Brian. "The Landscape Contribution to Town and Country Planning." *Journal of the Town Planning Institute* 35, no.7 (1949): 203–11.

———. "Landscape Design in the Present Economy." *Landscape Architecture* 45, no. 4 (1955): 211–14.

———. "The Restoration of the Landscape Affected by War-Time Airfields." *Journal of the Institute of Landscape Architects,* no. 8 (October 1945): 10–14.

Hagen, Joel B. *An Entangled Bank: The Origins of Ecosystem Ecology.* New Brunswick, N.J.: Rutgers University Press, 1992.

Hales, Peter Bacon. *Silver Cities: Photographing American Urbanization, 1839–1939.* Albuquerque: University of New Mexico Press, 2005.

Hall, Glenn L. "Basic Principles of Landscaping Parks and Other Public Grounds." *Parks & Recreation* 12, no. 2 (November-December 1928): 44–50.

Hallion, Richard P. *Taking Flight: Inventing the Aerial Age from Antiquity through the First World War.* London: Oxford University Press, 2003.

Hammerling, Rudolf. "Luftschutz und Städtebau." Ph.D. diss., Technische Hochschule zu Breslau, 1941.

Handel, Steven N., Milan J. Mitrovich, Elizabeth Hook, and Rebecca Aicher. *Orange County Great Park Ecological Guidelines.* Green Shield Ecology, Inc., 2009.

Hargreaves, George. "Most Influential Landscapes." *Landscape Journal* 12, no. 2 (1993): 177.

———. "Postmodernism Looks beyond Itself." *Landscape Architecture* 73, no. 4 (1983): 60–65.

Harrington, Anne. *Reenchanted Science: Holism in German Culture from Wilhelm II to Hitler.* Princeton: Princeton University Press, 1996.

Harris, Dianne, and D. Fairchild Ruggles. *Sites Unseen: Landscape and Vision.* Pittsburgh, Pa.: University of Pittsburgh Press, 2007.

Hartcup, Guy. *Camouflage: A History of Concealment and Deception in War.* New York: Charles Scribner's Sons, 1980.

Harvard Camouflage Committee. *Using Cut Foliage for Camouflage.* Technical manual. Harvard University, August 1943.

———. *Using Cut Foliage for Camouflage: Supplement on Tropical Pacific Islands.* Technical manual. Harvard University, November 1943.

Harvard University Landscape Architecture Research Office. *Three Approaches to Environmental Resource Analysis.* Washington, D.C.: Conservation Foundation, 1967.

"Harvester's Ed Stokes and His Land-Clearance Colleagues Prescribe Surgery for a City." *Harvester World,* October 1954, 12–17.

Hauser, Kitty. *Bloody Old Britain: O. G. S. Crawford and the Archaeology of Modern Life.* London: Granta, 2008.

Hayler, Guy Wilfrid. "The Aeroplane and City Planning: The Advantage of Seeing Cities from Above." *American City* 23, no. 6 (1920): 575–79.

Hegemann, Werner. "Als Städtebauer in Südamerika." *Wasmuths Monatshefte für Baukunst und Städtebau* 16, no. 3 (1932): 141–48.

Hegemann, Werner, and Elbert Peets. *The American Vitruvius: An Architects' Handbook of Civic Art.* 1922. New York: Princeton Architectural Press, 1988.

Heick, G. "Der Naturschutzpark in den Parkanlagen." *Die Gartenkunst* 13, no. 12 (1913): 223–27.

Hennecke, Stefanie. "Aus ParZellen keimt die Stadt." In *Landschaftlichkeit: Zwischen Kunst, Architektur und Theorie,* edited by Irene Nierhaus, Josch Hoenes, and Anette Urban, 91–101. Berlin: Reimer, 2010.

———. "'Berlin soll wachsen'—Kritik an einem organischen Stadtmodell." In *Spielarten des Organischen in Architektur, Design und Kunst,* edited by Anette Geiger, Hennecke, and Christin Kempf, 149–63. Berlin: Reimer, 2005.

Hergesell, Hugo, C. von Bassus, and Hugo Eckener. *Graf Zeppelins Fernfahrten: Schilderungen in Wort und Bild.* Stuttgart: Graphische Kunstanstalt E. Schreiber, 1908.

Herminghaus, Ernst. "Landscape Art in Airport Design." *American Landscape Architect* 3, no. 1 (1930): 15–18.

Herrington, Susan. "The Nature of Ian McHarg's Science." *Landscape Journal* 29, no. 1 (2010): 1–20.

Hilberseimer, Ludwig. *The Regional Pattern: Industries and Gardens, Workshops and Farms.* Chicago: Paul Theobald, 1949.

Hill, Kristina. "Urban Ecologies: Biodiversity and Urban Design." In *Downsview Park Toronto,* edited by Julia Czerniak, 91–101. New York: Harvard Graduate School of Design and Prestel Verlag, 2001.

Hiller, Olaf. *Herman Göritz: Eine biographische Studie als Beitrag zur Fachgeschicht der Garten- und Landschaftsarchitektur im 20. Jahrhundert.* Materialien zur Geschichte der Gartenkunst 1, edited by Johannes Küchler. Berlin: Technische Universität Berlin, 1997.

Hills, Angus. "A Philosophical Approach to Landscape Planning." *Landscape Planning* 1 (1974): 339–71.

Hinchcliffe, Tanis. "Aerial Photography and the Postwar Urban Planner." *London Journal* 35, no. 3 (2010): 277–88.

Hines, Thomas S. *Richard Neutra and the Search for Modern Architecture.* 1982. New York: Rizzoli, 2005.

Hitchcock, Henry-Russell, Jr. "Gardens in Relation to Modern Architecture." In *Contemporary Landscape Architecture and Its Sources,* 15–19. San Francisco: San Francisco Museum of Art, 1937.

Hofer, Andreas. *Karl Brunner und der europäische Städtebau in Lateinamerika.* Vienna: Lit., 2010.

———. "The Latin American City and Its Viennese Planning Approach: Karl Brunner in Chile and Colombia (1929–1948)." In *Sitte, Hegemann and the Metropolis,* edited by Charles C. Bohl and Jean-François Lejeune, 211–25. London and New York: Routledge, 2009.

Hollein, Max. Preface to *Wunschwelten: Neue Romantik in der Kunst der Gegenwart,* 17–21. Frankfurt: Kunsthalle Schirn Hatje Cantz, 2005.

Horace. *The Complete Works of Horace.* Translated by Charles E. Passage. New York: Ungar, 1983.

Hornbeck, Henry L. "Camouflage—Here and Now." *Landscape Architecture* 33, no. 1 (1942): 1–7.

Howard, Deborah. "Venice as a Dolphin: Further Investigations into Jacopo de' Barbari's View." *Artibus et Historiae* 18, no. 35 (1997): 101–11.

Howard, Richard A. "The Role of Botanists during World War II in the Pacific Theatre." *Botanical Review* 60, no. 2 (1994): 197–257.

Howett, Catherine. "Systems, Signs, Sensibilities: Sources for a New Landscape Aesthetic." *Landscape Journal* 6, no. 1 (1987): 1–12.

"How U.S. Cities Can Prepare for Atomic War." *Life,* December 18, 1950, 77–86.

Hubbard, Henry Vincent, and Theodora Kimball. *An Introduction to the Study of Landscape Design.* New York: Macmillan, 1917.

Hubbard, Henry V., Miller McClintock, and Frank B.

Williams. *Airports: Their Location, Administration and Legal Basis*. Cambridge: Harvard University Press, 1930.

Huhtamo, Erkki. "Aeronautikon! Or, the Journey of the Balloon Panorama." *Early Popular Visual Culture* 7, no. 3 (2009): 295–306.

Hunt, John Dixon. *Greater Perfections: The Practice of Garden Theory*. Philadelphia: University of Pennsylvania Press, 2000.

Hüppauf, Bernd, and Maiken Umbach. "Introduction: Vernacular Modernism." In *Vernacular Modernism*, edited by Hüppauf and Umbach, 1–23. Stanford, Calif.: Stanford University Press, 2005.

Hurtwood, Lady Allen of. "Roof-Gardens: Lungs of the Future." *Landscape and Garden* 1, no. 1 (1934): 43–46.

Imbert, Dorothée. *Between Garden and City: Jean Canneel-Claes and Landscape Modernism*. Pittsburgh: University of Pittsburgh Press, 2009.

———. *The Modernist Garden in France*. New Haven, Conn.: Yale University Press, 1993.

———. "Unnatural Acts: Propositions for a New French Garden, 1920–1930." In *Architecture and Cubism*, edited by Eve Blau and Nancy J. Troy, 167–85. Montréal: Canadian Centre for Architecture; Cambridge: MIT Press, 1997.

Ingold, Tim. "Globes and Spheres: The Topology of Environmentalism." In *Environmentalism: The View from Anthropology*, 31–42. London and New York: Routledge, 1993.

Interdepartmental Engineering Commission. *Washington International Airport*. Washington, D.C.: U.S. Government Printing Office, 1941.

Irwin, Robert. *Being and Circumstance*. Larkspur Landing, Calif.: Lapis Press in conjunction with the Pace Gallery and the San Francisco Museum of Modern Art, 1985.

Ives, Herbert E. *Airplane Photography*. Philadelphia and London: Lippincott, 1920.

Jackson, John Brinckerhoff. *The Necessity for Ruins, and Other Topics*. Amherst: University of Massachusetts Press, 1980.

Jackson, Kenneth T. *Crabgrass Frontier*. New York and Oxford: Oxford University Press, 1985.

Jaeger, Michael, and Carol Luritzen, eds. *Memoirs of Thaddeus S.C. Lowe, Chief of the Aeronautic Corps of the Army of the United States during the Civil War: My Balloons in Peace and War*. Studies in American History, vol. 53. Lewiston, Queenston, and Lampeter: Edwin Mellen Press, 2004.

Jay, Martin. "Scopic Regimes of Modernity." In *Vision and Visuality*, edited by Hal Foster, 3–27. New York: New Press, 1988.

Jeffries, John. *A Narrative of the Two Aerial Voyages of Doctor Jeffries with Mons. Blanchard*. London: Printed for the author and sold by J. Robson, 1786.

Jellicoe, G. A. "The Collaboration of Civil Engineering and Landscape Architecture." *Journal of the Institute of Landscape Architects* 54 (May 1961): 3–6.

———. "Power Stations in the Landscape." *Architectural Review* 57, no. 580 (1945): 114–16.

———. *Studies in Landscape Design*. Vol. 1. London: Oxford University Press, 1960.

———. *Studies in Landscape Design*. Vol. 2. London: Oxford University Press, 1966.

Jencks, Charles. *Le Corbusier and the Tragic View of Architecture*. Cambridge: Harvard University Press, 1973.

Jenny, Hans. "Role of Plant Factor in the Pedogenic Function." *Ecology* 39, no. 1 (1958): 5–16.

Jester, G. A. "Architectural Models." *Industrial Arts and Vocational Education* 29 (October 1940): 340–42.

Jong, Erik de. *Nature and Art: Dutch Garden and Landscape Architecture, 1650–1740*. 1993. Philadelphia: University of Pennsylvania Press, 2000.

Jordan, William R., and George M. Lubick. *Making Nature Whole: A History of Ecological Restoration*. Washington, D.C.: Island Press, 2011.

Kaempffert, Waldemar. *The Airplane and Tomorrow's World*. Public Affairs Pamphlet 78. New York: Public Affairs Committee, 1943.

Kaempffert, Waldemar, William Patterson, and Louis Wirth. *The Airplane and the Future*. The University of Chicago Round Table 258. Chicago: University of Chicago and National Broadcasting Company, 1943.

Kahle, P. "Die Bedeutung der Luftschiffahrt mit lenkbaren Flugzeugen für Städtebau, Kartographie und Erdkunde." *Zeitschrift für Vermessungswesen* 38, no. 3 (1909): 57–62.

Kahn, Elizabeth Louise. *The Neglected Majority: "Les Camoufleurs," Art History, and World War I*. Lanham, N.Y., and London: University Press of America, 1984.

Kargon, Robert, and Arthur Molella. "The City as

Communications Net: Nobert Wiener, the Atomic Bomb, and Urban Dispersal." *Technology and Culture* 45, no. 4 (October 2004): 764–77.

Kasarda, John D. "From Airport City to Aerotropolis." *Airport World* 6, no. 4 (2001): 42–47.

Kasarda, John D., and Greg Lindsay. *Aerotropolis: The Way We'll Live Next*. New York: Farrar, Straus and Giroux, 2011.

Kassler, Elizabeth. *Modern Gardens and the Landscape*. New York: Museum of Modern Art, 1964.

Keally, Francis. "Architectural Treatment of Airports." *Journal of the Society of Automotive Engineers* 25 (August 1929): 115–19.

———. "Architectural Treatment of the Modern Airport." *Airports* 2 (June 1929): 39–40, 47.

———. Introduction to "Protective Obscurement: Notes from Classes in Protective Obscurement." Mimeograph. New York City: School of Architecture, Columbia University, 1943, 1. Available in Loeb Library, Harvard University.

Kepes, Gyorgy. "Art and Ecological Consciousness." In *Arts of the Environment*, edited by Kepes, 1–12. New York: George Braziller, 1972.

———. "The Artist as Environmentalist: A Proposal." *Ekistics* 34, no. 204 (1972): 372–74.

———. "The Artist's Role in Environmental Self-Regulation." In *Arts of the Environment*, edited by Kepes, 167–97. New York: George Braziller, 1972.

———. "Die neue und die technische Landschaft." *Der Aufbau* 10, no. 2/3 (1955): 60–65.

———. *The New Landscape in Art and Science*. Chicago: Paul Theobald, 1956.

———. "The Visual Arts and the Sciences." *Daedalus* 94 (Winter 1965): 117–34.

Kern, Stephen. "Cubism, Camouflage, Silence, and Democracy: A Phenomenological Approach." In *NowHere: Space, Time and Modernity*, edited by Roger Friedland and Deirdre Boden, 163–80. Berkeley and Los Angeles: University of California Press, 1994.

———. *The Culture of Time and Space 1880–1918*. Cambridge: Harvard University Press, 1983.

Kesselring, Sven. "Global Transfer Points." In *Aeromobilities*, edited by Saulo Cwerner, 39–59. Abingdon: Routledge, 2009.

Kiley, Dan, and Jane Amidon. *Dan Kiley in His Own Words*. London: Thames and Hudson, 1999.

King, Moses. *King's Views of New York*. New York: Moses King, 1908.

Kingsbury, Paul, and John Paul Jones III. "Walter Benjamin's Dionysian Adventures on Google Earth." *Geoforum* 40, no. 4 (2009): 502–13.

Kingsland, Sharon E. *The Evolution of American Ecology, 1890–2000*. Baltimore: Johns Hopkins University Press, 2005.

Kirby, Major William. *Manual of Camouflage, Concealment and Cover of Troops*. New York: Edwin Appleton, 1917.

Kling, Rob, Spencer Olin, and Mark Poster. "The Emergence of Postsuburbia: An Introduction." In *Postsuburban California: The Transformation of Orange County since World War II*, edited by Kling, Olin, and Poster, 1–30. Berkeley and Los Angeles: University of California Press, 1991.

Klingmann, Anna. *Brandscapes: Architecture in the Experience Economy*. Cambridge: MIT Press, 2007.

Knothe, Herbert. *Tarnung und Verdunkelung als Schutz gegen Luftangriffe*. Berlin: Verlag von Wilhelm Erst and Sohn, 1936.

Köhler, Wolfgang. *Gestalt Psychology*. New York: Horace Liveright, 1929.

———. "Max Wertheimer." *Psychological Review* 51, no. 3 (1944): 143–46.

Koolhaas, Rem, and Bruce Mau. "Congestion without Matter." In *S, M, L, XL* [Small, Medium, Large, Extra-Large], edited by Jennifer Sigler, 894–993. New York: Monacelli Press, 1995.

Krauss, Eberhard. "Investigations of Regional Structure." In *Munich Airport: Landscape Visual Design Architecture*, edited by Jan Uhrich, 12–20. Munich: Flughafen München GmbH, 1992.

Krinsky, Carol Herselle. *Rockefeller Center*. New York: Oxford University Press, 1978.

Krusen, William A. *Flying the Andes*. Tampa: University of Tampa Press, 1997.

Lachmund, Jens. "Ecology in a Walled City: Researching Urban Wildlife in Post-War Berlin." *Endeavor* 31, no. 2 (2007): 78–82.

———. "Exploring the City of Rubble: Botanical Fieldwork in Bombed Cities in Germany after World War II." *Osiris* 18 (2003): 234–54.

———. "The Making of an Urban Ecology: Biological Expertise and Wildlife Preservation in West Berlin." In *Greening the City: Urban Landscapes in* the Twentieth Century, edited by Dorothee Brantz and Sonja Dümpelmann, 204–26. Charlottesville: University of Virginia Press, 2011.

Ladd, Brian. *The Ghosts of Berlin: Confronting German History in the Urban Landscape.* Chicago: University of Chicago Press, 1997.

Laser, Rudolf, Gerd Naumann, and Thomas Wöllner. *Plauen und Umgebung von oben: Historische Luftaufnahmen von 1928.* Lappersdorf: Kerschensteiner, 2005.

Leatherbarrow, David. *Uncommon Ground: Architecture, Technology, and Topography.* Cambridge: MIT Press, 2000.

Leberecht, Gerd Fritz. *Luftfahrten im Frieden und im Kriege.* Berlin: Verlag von Leonhard Simion Nf., 1913.

Le Corbusier. *Aircraft.* New York: Universe, 1935.

———. *The City of Tomorrow and Its Planning.* London: John Rodker, 1929.

———. *The Four Routes.* London: Dennis Dobson, 1941.

———. *Precisions on the Present State of Architecture and City Planning.* 1930. Cambridge: MIT Press, 1991.

———. *The Radiant City.* New York: Orion Press, 1933.

———. *Towards a New Architecture.* New York: Payson and Clarke, 1927.

Lee, A. "Francis Keally Discusses Airports." *The Western Architect* 39 (March 1930), 45–48.

Lee, Willis T. *The Face of the Earth as Seen from the Air.* American Geographical Society Special Publication No. 4. New York: American Geographical Society, 1922.

Lefebvre, Henri. *The Production of Space.* 1974. Translated by Donald Nicholson-Smith. Oxford: Blackwell, 1991.

Lehigh Airports Competition: Announcement and Program. New York: Taylor, Rogers and Bliss, 1929.

Lehigh Portland Cement Company, ed. *American Airport Designs.* New York: Taylor, Rogers and Bliss, 1930.

Lemke, Bernd, *Luft- und Zivilschutz in Deutschland im 20. Jahrhundert.* Potsdam: Militärgeschichtliches Forschungsamt, 2007.

Leslie, S. W. *The Cold War and American Science: The Military-Industrial-Academic Complex at MIT and Stanford.* New York: Columbia University Press, 1992.

Lewis, Nelson P. *The Planning of the Modern City.* New York: John Wiley and Sons, 1923.

Lewis, Philip H. "Kriterien für die Landschaftsplanung." *Garten und Landschaft* 78, no. 11 (1968): 365–74.

———. "Nature in Our Cities." In *Man and Nature in the City,* 22–29. Washington, D.C.: U.S. Government Printing Office [U.S. Bureau of Sport Fisheries and Wildlife], 1969.

———. "Quality Corridors for Wisconsin." *Landscape Architecture* 54, no. 2 (1964): 100–107.

———. "Regional Landscape Inventory and Design." In *Regional Planning, Challenge and Prospects,* edited by Maynard M. Hufschmidt, 115–31. New York: Praeger, 1969.

———. *Tomorrow by Design: A Regional Design Process for Sustainability.* New York: John Wiley and Sons, 1996.

Lewis-Dale, H. Angley. *Aviation and the Aerodrome.* Philadelphia: Lippincott, 1932.

Light, Jennifer S. *From Warfare to Welfare: Defense Intellectuals and Urban Problems in Cold War America.* Baltimore: Johns Hopkins University Press, 2003.

———. *The Nature of Cities.* Baltimore: Johns Hopkins University Press, 2009.

Lister, Nina-Marie. "Sustainable Large Parks: Ecological Design or Designer Ecology?" In *Large Parks,* edited by Julia Czerniak and George Hargreaves, 35–57. New York: Princeton Architectural Press, 2007.

———. "A Systems Approach to Biodiversity Conservation Planning." *Environmental Monitoring and Assessment* 49, no. 2–3 (1998): 123–55.

Lister, Nina-Marie, and James J. Kay. "Celebrating Diversity: Adaptive Planning and Biodiversity Conservation." In *Biodiversity in Canada: Ecology, Ideas, and Action,* edited by Stephen Bocking, 189–218. Peterborough, Ont., and Orchard Park, N.Y.: Broadview Press, 2000.

Lloyd-Williams, J. J. "Re-Marking the Air Route from Ramadi to Landing Ground R." *Geographical Journal* 62, no. 5 (November 1923): 350–59.

Lodder, Christina. "Malevich, Suprematism and Aerial Photography." *History of Photography* 28, no. 1 (2004): 25–40.

Löftken, Alexander. "Luftschutz und Städtebau: Baulicher Luftschutz zur Sicherung von Stadt und Land." In *Luftschutz durch Bauen*, 7. Berlin: Deutscher Verlag, 1939.

Lokaj, Rodney. *Petrarch's Ascent of Mount Ventoux.* Rome: Edizioni dell'Ateneo, 2006.

Loth, David. *The City within a City.* New York: William Morrow, 1966.

Low, A. M. "The Future of Flying." *Airways,* December 1925, 110–13.

Luckiesh, Matthew. *Visual Illusions: Their Causes, Characteristics and Applications.* New York: D. Van Nostrand, 1922.

Lunardi, Vincent. *An Account of the First Aërial Voyage in England.* London, 1784.

Lupton, Ellen, and J Abbott Miller, eds. *The ABC's of [triangle, square, circle]: The Bauhaus and Design Theory.* New York: Princeton Architectural Press, 1991.

Lurçat, André. "Projet pour un aéroport-relais au centre de Paris." *L'Architecture d'aujourd'hui* 3, no. 2 (April 1932), 86–89.

MacLean, Alex S. *Designs on the Land: Exploring America from the Air.* London and New York: Thames and Hudson, 2003.

———. *Over: The American Landscape at the Tipping Point.* New York: Abrams, 2008.

———. *Up on the Roof: New York's Hidden Skyline Spaces.* New York: Princeton Architectural Press, 2012.

Macy, Christine, and Sarah Bonnemaison. *Architecture and Nature: Creating the American Landscape.* London and New York: Routledge, 2003.

Malewitsch, Kasimir. *Die gegenstandslose Welt.* 1927. Translated by Alexander von Riesen. Berlin: Kupferberg, 1980.

Mann, Thomas. *Deutschland und die Deutschen.* Stockholm: Bermann-Fischer Verlag, 1947.

Mantziaras, Panos. "Rudolf Schwarz and the Concept of Stadtlandschaft." *Planning Perspectives* 18, no. 2 (2003): 147–76.

Marchant, Anyda. "Aviation in Colombia, Chile and Brazil." *Contemporary Law Pamphlets.* Comparative Law Series 3, no. 1. New York: New York University School of Law, 1939.

Martin, Reinhold. "Organicism's Other." *Grey Room* 4 (Summer 2001): 34–51.

Matless, David. "Regional Surveys and Local Knowledges: The Geographical Imagination in Britain, 1918–39." *Transactions of the Institute of British Geographers* 17, no. 4 (1992): 464–80.

———. "The Uses of Cartographic Literacy: Mapping, Survey and Citizenship in Twentieth-Century Britain." In *Mappings*, edited by Denis Cosgrove, 193–212. London: Reaktion, 1999.

Matteini, Milena. *Pietro Porcinai: Architetto del giardino e del paesaggio.* Milan: Electa, 1991.

Mauch, Christof, and Thomas Zeller, eds. *The World beyond the Windshield.* Athens: Ohio University Press, 2008.

McCabe, Lida Rose. "Camouflage, War's Handmaid." *Art World* 3, no. 3 (1918): 313–18.

McDonnell, M. J., and S. T. A. Pickett, eds. *Humans as Components of Ecosystems: The Ecology of Subtle Human Effects and Populated Areas.* New York: Springer-Verlag, 1993.

McGregor, C. H. *Kansas City as an Aviation Center.* Kansas Studies of Business 13. Lawrence: School of Business, University of Kansas, 1930.

McHarg, Ian. *Design with Nature.* Garden City, N.Y.: Natural History Press, 1969.

———. "An Ecological Method for Landscape Architecture." *Landscape Architecture* 57, no. 1 (January 1967): 105–7.

———. "Ecological Planning for Evolutionary Success." In *Master Planning the Aviation Environment*, edited by Angelo J. Cerchione, Victor E. Rothe, and James Vercellino, 7–10. Tucson: University of Arizona Press, 1970.

———. "Ecology for the Evolution of Planning and Design." *Via* 1 (1968): 44–67.

———. *A Quest for Life: An Autobiography.* New York: John Wiley and Sons, 1996.

———. "Regional Landscape Planning." In *Resources, the Metropolis and the Land-Grant University,* edited by A. J. W. Scheffey, 31–37. Proceedings of the Conference on Natural Resources. Amherst: University of Massachusetts, 1963.

McKinley, Ashley C. *Applied Aerial Photography.* New York: John Wiley and Sons, 1929.

Mehrotra, Rahul, ed. *Everyday Urbanism: Margaret Crawford vs. Michael Speaks.* Ann Arbor: University of Michigan; New York: Arts Press, 2005.

Meisch, Francis. "Architecture and Air Transportation." *New Pencil Points* 24, no. 11 (November 1943): 36–69.

Meller, Helen. *Patrick Geddes: Social Evolutionist and City Planner.* London: Routledge, 1990.

Menhinick, Howard Kenneth. "Municipal Airports."

Master's thesis, Graduate School of Landscape Architecture, Harvard University, 1926.

Merleau-Ponty, Maurice. "Eye and Mind." Translated by Carleton Dallery. In *The Primacy of Perception,* edited by James M. Edie, 159–90. Chicago: Northwestern University Press, 1964.

———. *The Visible and the Invisible.* Edited by Claude Lefort. Evanston: Northwestern University Press, 1968.

Merrill, Vincent N. "The Two Arts of Camouflage and Landscape Architecture." *Landscape Architecture* 34, no. 1 (October 1943): 15–16.

Meuser, Philipp. *Vom Fliegerfeld zum Wiesenmeer: Flughafen Berlin-Tempelhof, Geschichte und Zukunft.* Berlin: Berlin Ed. , 2000.

Meyer, Elizabeth K. "The Post–Earth Day Conundrum: Translating Environmental Values into Landscape Design." In *Environmentalism in Landscape Architecture,* edited by Michel Conan, 187–244. Washington, D.C.: Dumbarton Oaks Research Library and Collection, 2000.

———. "The Public Park as Avant-Garde (Landscape) Architecture: A Comparative Interpretation of Two Parisian Parks, Parc de la Villette (1983–1990) and Parc des Buttes-Chaumont (1864–1867)." *Landscape Journal* 10, no. 1 (1991): 16–26.

Meyers, Mary E. "The Line of Grace: Principles of Road Aesthetics in the Design of the Blue Ridge Parkway." *Landscape Journal* 23, no. 2 (2004): 121–40.

———. "Power of the Picturesque: Motorists' Perceptions of the Blue Ridge Parkway." *Landscape Journal* 25, no. 1 (2006): 38–53.

Migge, Leberecht. *Die Gartenkultur des 20. Jahrhunderts.* Jena: Eugen Diederichs, 1913.

Misselwitz, Philipp, Philipp Oswalt, and Klaus Overmeyer. "Stadtentwicklung ohne Städtebau-Planerischer Alptraum oder gelobtes Land?" In *Urban Pioneers: Temporary Use and Urban Development in Berlin,* edited by Senatsverwaltung für Stadtentwicklung Berlin, 102–9. Berlin: Jovis Verlag, 2007.

Mitchell, William. *Skyways: A Book on Modern Aeronautics.* Philadelphia and London, 1930.

Moholy-Nagy, László. *Von Material zu Architektur.* Munich: A. Langen Verlag, 1929.

Morgan, S. H., and Leslie Bacon. *Models for Architectural, Town Planning, Industrial Planning, Educational, Exhibition and Display Purposes.* Tan-y-Garth, Wales: self-published, 1948.

Morshed, Adnan. "The Aesthetics of Ascension in Norman Bel Geddes's Futurama." *Journal of the Society of Architectural Historians* 63, no. 1 (2004): 74–99.

———. "The Architecture of Ascension: Aviation and the Avant-garde Imagination of the Future City." In *Center 23: Record of Activities and Research Reports,* June 2002-May 2003, edited by Center for Advanced Study in the Visual Arts, 105–8. Washington D.C.: National Gallery of Art.

———. "The Cultural Politics of Aerial Vision: Le Corbusier in Brazil (1929)." *Journal of Architectural Education* 55, no. 4 (May 2002): 201–10.

"Mosaic Maps of Cities." *American City* 27, no. 3 (1922): 253–55.

Mouffe, Chantal, *The Democratic Paradox.* London: Verso, 2000.

Mumbower, L., and J. Donoghue. "Urban Poverty Study." *Photogrammetric Engineering* 33, no. 6 (1967): 610–18.

Nadar, Félix. *Quand j'étais photographe.* Paris: Flammarion, 1899.

Nagel, Thomas. *The View from Nowhere.* New York: Oxford University Press, 1986.

Naveh, Zev, and Arthur S. Lieberman. *Landscape Ecology: Theory and Application.* New York: Springer-Verlag, 1984.

Neale, H. J. "Trees—by the Side of the Road." *Roads and Streets* 85 (February 2, 1942): 50, 52–53, 56–57.

Neutra, Richard. *Survival through Design.* New York: Oxford University Press, 1954.

———. "Terminals?—Transfer!" *Architectural Record* 68, no. 2 (1930): 99–104.

Newark, Timothy. *Camouflage.* London: Thames and Hudson, 2007.

Newton, Wesley Phillips. *The Perilous Sky: U.S. Aviation Diplomacy and Latin America 1919–1931.* Coral Gables: University of Miami Press, 1978.

Nolen, John. *Airports and Airways and Their Relation to City and Regional Planning.* New York: National Conference on City Planning, 1928.

———. "Civic Planning for Airports and Airways."

Journal of the Society of Automotive Engineers 22 (April 1928): 411–18.

———. "Under What Jurisdiction Should Public Airports Be Placed?" *City Planning* 6, no. 2 (1930): 125–27.

Norman, Nigel. "London Air Terminal." *Airways and Airports* (March 1934), 326–29.

Nuti, Lucia. "Mapping Places: Chorography and Vision in the Renaissance." In *Mappings*, edited by Denis Cosgrove, 90–108. London: Reaktion, 1999.

———. "The Perspective Plan in the Sixteenth Century: The Invention of a Representational Language." *Art Bulletin* 76, no. 1 (1994): 105–28.

———. *Ritratti di Città*. Venice: Marsilio, 1996.

Nye, David E. *American Technological Sublime*. Cambridge: MIT Press, 1994.

———. *When the Lights Went Out: A History of Blackouts in America*. Cambridge: MIT Press, 2010.

Odum, Howard Washington. "Patrick Geddes' Heritage to 'the Making of the Future.'" *Social Forces* 22, no. 3 (March 1944): 275–81.

Oertel, Robb C. *Community Airports and Airparks*. New York: Esso Aviation Products, 1945.

Oeser, Hans Ludwig. *Wunder der grossen und der kleinen Welt*. Berlin: Deutsche Buch-Gemeinschaft Berlin, 1937.

Oettermann, Stephan. *The Panorama: History of a Mass Medium*. New York: Zone, 1997.

Ogburn, William Fielding. *The Social Effects of Aviation*. Cambridge, Mass.: Riverside Press, 1946.

O'Hare Airport: A Design Potential Study. Urbana-Champaign: College of Fine and Applied Arts, 1965.

Oleksijczuk, Denise Blake. *The First Panoramas: Visions of British Imperialism*. Minnesota: University of Minnesota Press, 2011.

Olmsted, H. M. "The Airport and the Municipality." *American City* 38, no. 1 (1928): 117–19.

Onosaki, Masashi. *Airport as a Factor in Landscape Architecture*. Landscape Architecture Pamphlet no. 1. Tokyo: Japanese Landscape Architectural Society, 1928.

Orange County Great Park Corporation. *From Concept to Production: Planning for a Great Park*. Orange County Great Park Corporation Annual Report, 2010.

Ortolano, Guy. *The Two Cultures Controversy: Science,*

Literature and Cultural Politics in Postwar Britain. New York: Cambridge University Press, 2009.

Park, Robert E. "The Urban Community as a Spacial Pattern and a Moral Order." In *The Urban Community: Selected Papers from the Proceedings of the American Sociological Society*, edited by Ernest W. Burgess, 3–18. Chicago: University of Chicago Press, 1926.

Parpagliolo, Maria Teresa. "Le zone verdi nelle citta." *Domus* 10, no. 111 (1937): 33–40.

Paschal, Huston. *Defying Gravity: Contemporary Art and Flight*. Raleigh: North Carolina Museum of Art, 2003.

Pascoe, David. *Airspaces*. London: Reaktion, 2001.

Pearson, A. W. "Allied Military Model Making during World War II." *Cartography and Geographic Information Science* 29, no. 3 (2002): 227–41.

Pearson, Chris, Peter Coates, and Tim Cole, eds. *Militarized Landscapes: From Gettysburg to Salisbury Plain*. London and New York: Continuum, 2010.

Pelkonen, Eeva-Liisa. *Alvar Aalto: Architecture, Modernity and Geopolitics*. New Haven, Conn.: Yale University Press, 2009.

Pereira, Margareth da Silva. "The Time of the Capitals: Rio de Janeiro and São Paulo: Words, Actors and Plans." In *Planning Latin America's Capital Cities, 1850–1950*, edited by Arturo Almandoz, 75–108. London: Routledge, 2002.

Pérez Oyarzun, Fernando, and José Rosas Vera. "Cities within the City: Urban and Architectural Transfers in Santiago de Chile, 1840–1940." In *Planning Latin America's Capital Cities, 1850–1950*, edited by Arturo Almandoz, 109–38. London: Routledge, 2002.

Phillips, D. C. "Organicism in the Late Nineteenth and Early Twentieth Centuries." *Journal of the History of Ideas* 31, no. 3 (1970): 413–32.

Phillips, John. "The Biotic Community." *Journal of Ecology* 19, no. 1 (1931): 1–24.

Pick, Martin. "Aerial Photography." *Garden Cities and Town Planning Magazine* 10, no. 4 (1920): 71–86.

Pignatti, Terisio. "La pianta di Venezia di Jacopo de' Barbari." *Bolletino dei Musei civici veneziani* 9 (1964): 9–49.

Piper, John. "Prehistory from the Air." *Axis* 8 (1937): 3–6.

Pirath, Carl. *Aerodromes: Their Location, Operation, and Design*. London: Sir Isaac Piman and Sons, 1938.

———. *Flughäfen: Raumlage, Betrieb und Gestaltung*. Berlin: Verlag von Julius Springer, 1937.

Pisano, Dominick A., ed. *The Airplane in American Culture*. Ann Arbor: University of Michigan Press, 2003.

Poggi, Christine. *In Defiance of Painting*. New Haven, Conn., and London: Yale University Press, 1992.

Pückler-Muskau, Hermann Ludwig Heinrich Fürst von. *Tutti frutti: Aus den Papieren des Verstorbenen*. Vol. 1. Stuttgart: Hallberger'sche Verlangshandlung, 1834.

Rainey, Reuben M. "Environmental Ethics and Park Design: A Case Study of Byxbee Park." *Journal of Garden History* 14, no. 1 (1994): 171–78.

Rancourt, Judie, and Peter Teuber. *The Illustrated Guidebook to Residential Airparks*. Wayne, N.J.: Aero, 1995.

Reade, Charles C. "Aeroplanes and Town Planning." *Garden Cities and Town Planning* New Series 2, no. 12 (December 1912): 265–68.

Reagan, William T. "Shaded-Relief Maps in the German Air Force." *Photogrammetric Engineering* 11, no. 4 (1945): 278–82.

"Recent References on Camouflage." *Landscape Architecture* 32, no. 4 (July 1942): 169–72.

Reed, Harrison P. "The Development of the Terrain Model in the War." *Geographical Review* 36, no. 4 (1946): 632–52.

Reed, Lieut. Henry A. *Photography Applied to Surveying*. New York: John Wiley and Sons, 1888.

Reichsstatthalter der Stadt Hamburg, Der Architekt des Elbufers, *Bombensichere Luftschutzbauten: Erste städtebaulich-architektonische Ausrichtung*. Hamburg: Broschek, 1941.

Reit, Seymour. *Masquerade: The Amazing Camouflage Deceptions of World War II*. New York: Hawthorne, 1978.

"Relief Model of New York Region Aids County Planning." *American City* 51 (November 1936): 42.

Reps, John W. *Bird's Eye Views*. New York: Princeton Architectural Press, 1998.

———. *Views and Viewmakers of Urban America: Lithographs of Towns and Cities in the United States and Canada, Notes on the Artists and Publishers, and a Union Catalog of Their Work, 1825–1925*. Columbia: University of Missouri Press, 1984.

Ridings, Willard A. "A Model for City Planning." *Engineering News-Record* 127 (July 1941): 107–8.

Robbins, Charles Robinson. "Northern Rhodesia: An Experiment in the Classification of Land with the Use of Aerial Photographs." *Journal of Ecology* 22, no. 1 (1934): 88–105.

Robinson, Charles Mulford. "A Railroad Beautiful." *House & Garden*, no. 2 (November 1902): 564–70.

Robinson, Florence B. *Landscape Planting for Airports*. Aeronautics Bulletin 2. Urbana: University of Illinois, 1948.

Rome, Adam. *The Bulldozer in the Countryside: Suburban Sprawl and the Rise of American Environmentalism*. Cambridge: Cambridge University Press, 2001.

Root, Ralph Rodney. *Camouflage with Planting*. Chicago: Ralph Fletcher Seymour, 1942.

———. *Contourscaping*. Chicago: Ralph Fletcher Seymour, 1941.

Rorty, Richard. *Philosophy and the Mirror of Nature*. Princeton: Princeton University Press, 1979.

Sackman, Douglas Cazaux. *Orange Empire: California and the Fruits of Eden*. Berkeley and Los Angeles: University of California Press, 2005.

Saint-Amour, Paul K. "Modernist Reconnaissance." *Modernism/modernity* 10, no. 2 (2003): 349–380.

Saint-Gaudens, Homer. "Camouflage and Art." *American Magazine of Art* 10, no. 9 (July 1919): 319–22.

Sanderson, Jim, and Larry D. Harris, eds. *Landscape Ecology: A Top-Down Approach*. Boca Raton, Fla.: Lewis, 2000.

Scheffey, A. J. W., ed. *Resources, the Metropolis and the Land-Grant University*. Proceedings of the Conference on Natural Resources. Amherst: University of Massachusetts, 1963.

Schelcher, André, and A. Omer-Decugis. *Paris vu en ballon et ses environs*. Paris: Hachette and Cie., 1909.

Schiff, Stacy. *Saint-Exupéry*. London: Chatto and Windus, 1994.

Schlemmer, Tut. *The Letters and Diaries of Oskar Schlemmer*. Translated by Krishna Winston. Middleton, Conn.: Wesleyan University, 1972.

Schmal, Helga, and Tobias Selke. *Bunker-Luftschutz und Luftschutzbau in Hamburg*. Hamburg: Christians Verlag, 2001.

Schmidt, Hans. *Beiträge zur Architektur 1924–1964*. Berlin: VEB Verlag für Bauwesen, 1965.

Schmitt, Günter. *Als in Johannisthal der Motorflug begann*. Berlin: Rat d. Stadtbezirks Berlin-Treptow, 1987.

———. *Als die Oldtimer Flogen*. Berlin: Transpress, Verl. für Verkehrswesen, 1987.

Schrader, Paul. "Poetry of Ideas: The Films of Charles Eames." *Film Quarterly* 23, no. 3 (1970): 2–19.

Schreiber, Karl-Friedrich. "The History of Landscape Ecology in Europe." In *Changing Landscapes: An Ecological Perspective*, edited by I. S. Zonneveld and R. T. T. Forman, 21–35. New York: Springer-Verlag, 1990.

Schröder, Thies. *Rekombinationen: Büro Kiefer Landschaftsarchitektur*. Stuttgart: Ulmer, 2005.

Schulz, Juergen. "Jacopo de'Barbari's View of Venice: Map Making, City Views, and Moralized Geography before the Year 1500." *Art Bulletin* 60, no. 3 (September 1978): 425–74.

Schwartz, Hillel. *The Culture of the Copy: Striking Likenesses, Unreasonable Facsimiles*. New York: Zone, 1996.

Schwarzer, Mitchell. *Zoomscape: Architecture in Motion and Media*. New York: Princeton Architectural Press, 2004.

Science in War. Harmondsworth: Penguin, 1940.

Sebald, Winfried Georg. *On the Natural History of Destruction*. Translated by Anthea Bell. London: Hamish Hamilton, 2003.

Secret Report by the Police President of Hamburg (as Local Air Protection Leader) on the Heavy Air Raids on Hamburg in July/August, 1943. London: Home Office, Civil Defence Department, Intelligence Branch, 1946.

Sekula, Allan. *Photography against the Grain*. Halifax: Press of the Nova Scotia College of Art and Design, 1984.

Senate Department for Urban Development. *Tempelhof Parkland Open Landscape Planning Competition Followed by a Negotiated Procedure Invitation to Tender*. Berlin, 2010.

Senatsverwaltung für Stadtentwicklung Berlin. *Parklandschaft Tempelhof offener landschaftsplanerischer Wettbewerb mit anschliessendem Verhandlungsverfahren, Ergebnisprotokoll der Sitzung des Preisgerichts vom 11./12.06.2010*. Berlin, 2010.

———, ed. *Urban Pioneers: Temporary Use and Urban Development in Berlin*. Berlin: Jovis Verlag, 2007.

Senatsverwaltung für Stadtentwicklung und Umweltschutz Berlin, ed. *Johannisthal-Adlershof Technologie- und Wissenschaftsstadt*. Berlin: Kulturbuchverlag, 1994.

Sennett, Richard. *Flesh and Stone*. New York: Norton, 1994.

Sert, José Luis. *Can Our Cities Survive?* Cambridge: Harvard University Press, 1942.

Sheller, Mimi, and John Urry. "Introduction: Mobile Cities, Urban Mobilities." In *Mobile Technologies of the City*, edited by Sheller and Urry, 1–18. London: Routledge, 2006.

Shelmerdine, Lieut.-Colonel Sir Francis. *Airports and Airways*. London: Royal Institute of British Architects, 1937.

Shepheard, Michael, George A. Goulty, and John R. Herbert. "The Landscape of Power Stations." *Journal of the Institute of Landscape Architects* 62 (November 1963): 4–6.

Sheppard, Stephen R. J., and Petr Cizek. "The Ethics of Google Earth: Crossing Thresholds from Spatial Data to Landscape Visualization." *Journal of Environmental Management* 90, no. 6 (2009): 2102–17.

Shirer, William L. *Berlin Diary: The Journal of a Foreign Correspondent*. New York: Knopf, 1941.

Sichel, Kim. *To Fly: Contemporary Aerial Photography*. Boston: Boston University Art Gallery; Seattle: University of Washington Press, 2007.

Simo, Melanie L. *The Coalescing of Different Forces and Ideas: A History of Landscape Architecture at Harvard, 1900–1999*. Cambridge: Harvard University Graduate School of Design, 2000.

Sloane, Eric. *Camouflage Simplified*. New York: Devin-Adair, 1942.

Smith, André. "Notes on Camouflage." *Architectural Record* 17, no. 5 (November 1917): 468–77.

Smith, F. A. Cushing "Aerial Photography and the Model as Aids in Campus Design." *American Landscape Architect* 3, no. 4 (October 1930): 39–42.

Smith, H. T. U. *Aerial Photographs and their Applications*. New York: Appleton-Century, 1943.

Smith, Ken. "The Orange County Great Park: A New Park on the Site of a Former Air Base in Southern California Aims to Strike a Balance between the Needs of Humans and the Natural World." *Topos* 63 (September 2008): 78–83.

Smith, Thomas R., and Lloyd D. Black. "German Geography: War Work and Present Status." *Geographical Review* 36, no. 3 (1946): 398–408.

Smithson, Robert. "Aerial Art." *Studio International* 177, no. 910 (April 1969): 180–81.

———. "Proposal for Earthworks and Landmarks to be Built on the Fringes of the Fort Worth-Dallas Regional Air Terminal Site (1966–67)." In *Robert Smithson: The Collected Writings,* edited by Jack Flam, 354–55. Berkeley and Los Angeles: University of California Press, 1996.

Smuts, Jan Christiaan. *Holism and Evolution.* New York: Macmillan, 1926.

Snow, C. P. *The Two Cultures and the Scientific Revolution.* New York: Cambridge University Press, 1959.

Snyder, Joel. "Res ipsa loquitur." In *Things That Talk: Object Lessons from Art and Science,* edited by Lorraine Daston, 194–221. New York: Zone; Cambridge: MIT Press, 2004.

Soleri, Paolo. "The City as the Airport." In *Master Planning the Aviation Environment,* edited by Angelo J. Cerchione, Victor E. Rothe, and James Vercellino, 11–13. Tucson: University of Arizona Press, 1970.

Solomon, Solomon J. *Strategic Camouflage.* New York: Dutton, 1920.

Sontag, Susan. *On Photography.* New York: Picador, 1977.

Sørensen, Carl Theodor. *39 Haveplaner.* Copenhagen: Arkitektens Forlag, 1966.

Speer, Albert. *Erinnerungen.* 1969. Berlin: Propyläen Verlag, 1970.

Spirn, Anne Whiston "Ian McHarg, Landscape Architecture, and Environmentalism: Ideas and Methods in Context." In *Environmentalism in Landscape Architecture,* edited by Michel Conan, 97–114. Washington, D.C.: Dumbarton Oaks Trustees for Harvard University, 2000.

Spoon, Jacob John. "Landscape Design for Airports." *American Landscape Architect* 3, no. 6 (1930): 33–36.

———. "Modern Landscape Art in Germany." *American Landscape Architect* 5, no. 4 (1931): 30–33, 39.

———. "Why Not Artistic Design in Airports?" *American Landscape Architect* 3, no. 2 (1930): 31–33.

Spooner, Charles. "Use of Aerial Photographs in the Construction of Military Terrain Models." *Photogrammetric Engineering* 14, no. 4 (1948): 513–21.

Spurr, S. H. *Photogrammetry and Photo-interpretation.* New York: Ronald Press, 1960.

Stanley, Roy M., II. *To Fool a Glass Eye.* Washington, D.C.: Smithsonian Institution Press, 1998.

Starr, Kevin. *Embattled Dreams: California in War and Peace, 1940–1950.* Oxford and New York: Oxford University Press, 2002.

Starrs, Paul F. "The Navel of California and Other Oranges: Images of California and the Orange Crate." *California Geographer* 28 (1988): 1–41.

Steele, Fletcher. "Modern Landscape Architecture." In *Contemporary Landscape Architecture and its Sources,* 23–25. San Francisco: San Francisco Museum of Art, 1937.

———. "New Pioneering in Garden Design." *Landscape Architecture* 20, no. 3 (1930): 159–77.

———. "New Styles in Gardening." *House Beautiful* 65, no. 3 (March 1929), 317, 352–54.

Steichen, Edward. "American Aerial Photography at the Front." *U.S. Air Service* 1, no. 5 (June 1919): 33–39.

Stein, Gertrude. *Everybody's Autobiography.* New York: Random House, 1937.

———. *Picasso.* London: B. T. Batsford, 1938.

Steinberg, S. S. "Mapping from the Air." *Scientific Monthly* 40, no. 4 (April 1935): 363–66.

Steinitz, Carl, et al. *A Comparative Study of Resource Analysis Methods.* Cambridge: Department of Landscape Architecture Research Office, Graduate School of Design Harvard University, 1969.

Steinitz, Carl, Paul Parker, and Lawrie Jordan. "Hand-Drawn Overlays: Their History and Prospective Uses." *Landscape Architecture* 66 (September 1976): 444–55.

Stilgoe, John. "The Railroad Beautiful: Landscape Architecture and the Railroad Gardening Movement, 1867–1930." *Landscape Journal* 1, no. 2 (1982): 57–65.

Stoddart, D. R. *On Geography and Its History.* Oxford: Basil Blackwell, 1989.

Strang, Lord. "Power Production and Transmission in the Countryside." *Journal of the Royal Society of Arts* 107, no. 5043 (February 1960): 209–10.

Strohmeier, William D. "More Fun at the Airport." *Aviation* 39, no. 11 (November 1940): 38–39, 106.

Stryker, Kimberlee S. "Pietro Porcinai and the

Modern Italian Garden." *Studies in the History of Gardens and Designed Landscapes* 28, no. 2 (2008): 252–69.

Sudell, Richard. *Landscape Gardening*. London and Melbourne: Ward, Lock, 1933.

Sutton, Richard. "Ernst Herminghaus, Landscape Architect." *Nebraska History* 66, no. 4 (1985): 372–91.

Tansley, A. G. "The Use and Abuse of Vegetational Concepts and Terms." *Ecology* 16, no. 3 (1935): 284–307.

Taylor, A. D., Henry V. Hubbard, and Harold Merrill. "Committee on National Defense." *Landscape Architecture* 32, no. 1, Supplement (1942): 14–15.

Thirkettle, David. "Ground Modelling." *Journal of the Institute of Landscape Architects* 53 (February 1961): 11–15.

Till, Karen. "Neotraditional Towns and Urban Villages: The Cultural Production of a Geography of 'Otherness.'" *Environment and Planning D: Society and Space* 11, no. 6 (1993): 709–32.

Tobey, Ronald C. *Saving the Prairies: The Life Cycle of the Founding School of American Plant Ecology, 1895–1955*. Berkeley and Los Angeles: University of California Press, 1981.

Tobin, Kathleen A. "The Reduction of Urban Vulnerability: Revisiting 1950s American Suburbanization as Civil Defense." *Cold War History* 2, no. 2 (2002): 1–32.

Troll, Carl. "Fortschritte der wissenschaftlichen Luftbildforschung." *Zeitschrift der Gesellschaft für Erdkunde*, no. 7/10 (December 1943): 278–384.

———. *Landscape Ecology*. Delft: ITC-UNESCO Centre for Integrated Surveys, 1966.

———. "Landscape Ecology (Geoecology) and Biogeocenology—A Terminological Study." *Geoforum* 2, no. 4 (1971): 43–46.

———. "Luftbild und ökologische Bodenforschung." *Luftbild und Luftbildmessung* 20 (1941): 5–7.

———. "Die Pflege der Luftbildinterpretation in Deutschland." *Bildmessung und Luftbildwesen* 37, no. 4 (1969): 120–25.

———. *Tagebücher der Reisen in Bolivien 1926/1927*. Edited by Ingeborg Monheim. Stuttgart: Franz Steiner Verlag Wiesbaden Gmbh, 1985.

Trunz, Helmut. *Tempelhof: Flughafen im Herzen Berlins*. Munich: GeraMond, 2008.

Turner, Charles C. *Aerial Navigation of To-day*. London: Seeley, 1910.

Tyrwhitt, Jaqueline. "The Valley Section: Patrick Geddes' World Image." *Journal of the Town Planning Institute* 37, no. 3 (January 1951): 61–66.

Umbach, Maiken. "The Deutscher Werkbund, Globalization, and the Invention of Modern Vernaculars." In *Vernacular Modernism*, edited by Bernd Hüppauf and Maiken Umbach, 114–40. Stanford, Calif.: Stanford University Press, 2005.

Urhammer, Christian. "Neue Aufgaben des Landschaftspflegers (Betr. Luftschutz und Geländetarnung)." *Die Gartenkunst* 49, no. 4 (1936): 2–3.

Urry, John. "Aeromobilities and the Global." In *Aeromobilities*, edited by Saulo Cwerner, Sven Kesselring and Urry, 25–38. London: Routledge, 2010.

U.S. Army Corps of Engineers, *Camouflage Materials and Manufacturing Techniques, War Department Field Manual FM 5–20H*. War Department, July 1944. Washington, D.C.: U.S. Government Printing Office, 1944.

U.S. Bureau of Aeronautics. *Photo Surface Modeling, Device No. 16-B–2*. Washington, D.C.: U.S. Government Printing Office, 1944.

U.S. Department of Commerce, Aeronautics Branch. *Air Marking*. Aeronautics Bulletin 4 (July 1, 1929). Washington, D.C.: U.S. Government Printing Office, 1929.

———. *Airport Rating Regulations*. Aeronautics Bulletin 16 (January 1, 1929). Washington, D.C.: U.S. Government Printing Office, 1929.

———. *Aviation Training*. Aeronautics Bulletin 19 (August 1, 1928). Washington, D.C.: U.S. Government Printing Office, 1928.

U.S. Department of Commerce and Civil Aeronautics Administration. *Airport Landscape Planting*. Washington, D.C.: U.S. Government Printing Office, 1950.

———. *Small Airports*. Washington, D.C.: U.S. Government Printing Office, 1945.

U.S. Department of the Interior. *Environmental Impact of the Big Cypress Swamp Jetport*. 1969.

U.S. Office of Civil Defense. *Precautionary Camouflage: Planning for Low Visibility without Reliance upon Artificial Coverings*. OCD Publication 2019. Washington, D.C.: U.S. Government Printing Office, 1943.

"'Urban Agriculture ist ein heikles Stichwort': Eelco Hooftman im Gespräch mit Kaye Geipel und

Doris Kleilein." *Stadtbauwelt* 191, no. 36 (2011): 27–35.

U.S. War Department. *Blackouts*. Washington, D.C.: U.S. Office of Civilian Defense, 1941.

———. *Civilian Defense: Protective Concealment.* Washington, D.C.: United States Office of Civilian Defense, 1942.

Uttal, David H., and Lisa S. Tan, "Cognitive Mapping in Childhood." In *Cognitive Mapping: Past, Present and Future,* edited by Rob Kitchin and Scott Freudenschuh, 147–65. London: Routledge, 2000.

Vaccarino, Rossana. "The Correspondence of Time and Instability: Two Gardens." In *Roberto Burle Marx: Landscapes Reflected,* edited by Vaccarino, 41–60. New York: Princeton Architectural Press, 2000.

Valentien, Otto. "Mehr bodenständige Gartengestaltung." *Die Gartenwelt* 36, no. 16, (1932): 220–21.

Veale, S. E. *To-morrow's Airliners, Airways and Airports.* London: Pilot Press, 1945.

Vera, André. *Les jardins.* Paris: Émile-Paul, Frères, 1919.

———. *Le nouveau jardin.* Paris: Émile-Paul, Frères, 1912.

Virilio, Paul. *Bunker Archeology.* Translated by George Collins. New York: Princeton Architectural Press, 1994.

———. *The Vision Machine.* Bloomington and Indianapolis: Indiana University Press, 1994.

———. *War and Cinema: The Logistics of Perception.* Translated by Patrick Camiller. London and New York: Verso, 2009.

Voigt, Wolfgang. "From the Hippodrome to the Aerodrome, from the Air Station to the Terminal: European Airports, 1909–1945." In *Building for Air Travel,* edited by John Zukowsky, 27–49. Chicago, Munich, and New York: Prestel and Art Institute of Chicago, 1996.

Wagner, Sterling R. *The Modern Airport.* Technical Publication No. 33. *Bulletin of New York State College of Forestry at Syracuse University* 4 (June 1931).

Wagstaff, Samuel, Jr. "Talking with Tony Smith." *Artforum* 5, no. 4 (December 1966): 14–19.

Walker, Ernest E. "Camouflage Planning: Its Needs and Prospects." *American Forests* 48, no. 5 (May 1942): 208–11, 239–40.

Walker, Peter. "Other Directions in Contemporary Landscape Architecture." *SD: Space Design* 30, no. 7 (1994): 87–96.

Walsh, H. Vandervoort. "Architectural Principles Applied to Airport Design." *Aero Digest* 19 (August 1931): 35–36, 128.

Waters, Theodore. "The Roof-Dwellers of New York." *Harper's Weekly* 08/08 (August 1903), 1300.

Way, Douglas S. *Air Photo Interpretation for Land Planning.* Cambridge: Department of Landscape Architecture, Harvard University, 1968.

———. *Terrain Analysis.* Stroudsburg, Pa.: Dowden, Hutchinson and Ross, 1973.

Weilacher, Udo. *Zwischen Landschaftsarchitektur und Land Art.* Basel: Birkhäuser, 1999.

Weinhart, Martina. "The World Must Be Made Romantic." In *Wunschwelten: Neue Romantik in der Kunst der Gegenwart,* 34–44. Frankfurt: Kunsthalle Schirn Hatje Cantz, 2005.

Weir, L. H. "The Airport a Transportation Terminal." *City Planning* 6, no. 2 (April 1930): 119–20.

Weisman, Winston R. "The First Landscaped Skyscraper." *Journal of the Society of Architectural Historians* 18, no. 2 (1959): 54–59.

Welchman, John. "Here, There & Otherwise." *Artforum* 27, no. 1 (September 1988): 19.

Welter, Volker M. *Biopolis: Patrick Geddes and the City of Life.* Cambridge: MIT Press, 2002.

Wenneman, Jos H. *Municipal Airports: History, Development and Legal Aspect of Municipal Airports.* Cleveland: Flying Review, 1931.

Wertheimer, Max. "On Truth." *Social Research* 1, no. 2 (1934): 135–46.

———. "Untersuchungen zur Lehre von der Gestalt II." *Psychologische Forschung* 4 (1923): 301–50.

Whately, Thomas. *Observations on Modern Gardening.* Dublin, 1770.

Wheeler, J. B. *A Course of Instruction in the Elements of the Art and Science of War.* New York: D. Van Nostrand, 1893.

Whitbeck, Captain J. E. "Airports." *Parks & Recreation* 13, no. 3 (January-February 1930): 105–9.

White, L. Milner. "The Landscape of Industry: Factories." *Journal of the Institute of Landscape Architects* 57 (February 1962): 4–9.

Whyte, William H. *The Last Landscape.* New York: Doubleday.

Wichert, Fritz. "Luftschiffahrt und Architektur."

Frankfurter Zeitung und Handelsblatt 53, no. 80
(March 21, 1909): 1–2.

Wiepking-Jürgensmann, Heinrich Friedrich. *Die
Landschaftsfibel*. Berlin: Deutsche Buchhandlung,
1942.

Wigoder, Meir. "The 'Solar Eye' of Vision: Emergence of the Skyscraper-Viewer in the Discourse
on Heights in New York City, 1890–1920." *Journal
of the Society of Architectural Historians* 61, no. 2
(2002): 152–69.

Wilkinson, Toby C. "Falling out of an Aircraft: Aero-
visualism and the Aerial Photography of J. S. P.
Bradford." *Visual Anthropology* 21, no. 1 (2008):
18–38.

Wills, F. L. "The Work of the Aerial Camera Man."
Airways (November 1924): 99–100.

Winchester, Clarence, and F. L. Wills. *Aerial Photography*. London: Chapman and Hall, 1928.

Wirth, Theodore "The Municipal Airport—A Proper
Function of Park Administration." *Parks & Recreation* 12, no. 1 (September-October 1928): 10–14.

Wittenstein, Matthew M. "Uses and Limitations
of Aerial Photography in Urban Analysis and
Planning." *Photogrammetric Engineering* 21, no. 4
(1955): 566–78.

Wittmann, Karl W. "Flughafenbau." In *Neuzeitlicher
Verkehrsbau*, edited by Hermann Gescheit and
K[arl Otto] Wittmann, 189–95. Potsdam: Müller
and J. Kiepenheuer GmbH Verlag, 1931.

Wittmann, Konrad F. *Industrial Camouflage Manual*.
New York: Reinhold, 1942.

Wohl, Robert. *A Passion for Wings: Aviation and the
Western Imagination, 1908–1918*. New Haven,
Conn.: Yale University Press, 1994.

———. *The Spectacle of Flight: Aviation and the Western Imagination, 1920–1950*. New Haven, Conn.:
Yale University Press, 2005.

Wood, John Walter. *Airports: Some Elements of Design
and Future Development*. New York: Coward-
McCann, 1940.

Wray, James R., et al. "Photo Interpretation in Urban
Area Analysis." In *Manual of Photographic Interpretation*, edited by Robert N. Colwell, 667–716.
Washington, D.C.: American Society of Photogrammetry, 1960.

Wright, Marshall S. "The Application of Aerial
Photography to Land Use Problems." *Soil Science
Society of America Journal* 1 (1936): 357–60.

Zeller, Thomas. *Driving Germany: The Landscape of
the German Autobahn 1930–1970*. New York and
Oxford: Berghahn, 2007.

———. "Molding the Landscape of Nazi Environ-
mentalism: Alwin Seifert and the Third Reich."
In *How Green Were the Nazis?*, edited by Tim Page,
Franz-Josef Brüggemeier, Mark Cioc, and Zeller.
Athens: Ohio University Press, 2005.

Zonneveld, Isaak S. *Land Evaluation and Land(scape)
Science*. ITC Textbook of Photo-Interpretation,
vol. 7. Enschede: ITC, 1972.

———. "Land(scape) Ecology, a Science or a State of
Mind." In *Perspectives in Landscape Ecology*, edited
by S. P. Tjallingii and A. A. de Veer, 9–15. Wagen-
ingen: Pudoc: Centre for Agricultural Publishing
and Documentation, 1982.

Zueblin, Charles. "The World's First Sociological
Laboratory." *American Journal of Sociology* 4, no. 5
(1899): 577–92.

Index

layer-cake representation, 226
Leatherbarrow, David, 80
Le Bourget (Paris), 24
Le Corbusier. *See* Corbusier, Le
Lee, Willis T., 131
Lefebvre, Henri, 75–76
Léger, Fernand, 81, 157
Legrain, Pierre, 133
Lehigh Airports Competition, 33, 40; entries for, *35, 36*
Lehigh Portland Cement Company, 33
Lennar Corporation, 273
Le Nôtre, André, 42
Leopold, Luna, 72
Le Play, Frederick, 110
Lever, James, 191
Lewin, Kurt, 117
Lewis, Nelson Peter, 113–14
Lewis, Philip H., 108, 225–26, 228
LeWitt, Sol, 233
Liberty Plaza, New York International Airport, *61. See also* Idlewild International Airport (NYC)
Life magazine, on Idlewild International Airport, 289n127
Light, Jennifer, 216, 292n145, 299n7
Lilliput, 80
Lincoln (Neb.), 50
Lindbergh, Charles, 5
Linderhof Palace (Bavaria), 153, *154*
Linear City (Arturo Soria y Mata), 176
Linnard, Lawrence G., 195
Lippe+ project, 243–44
Lissitzky, El, 138
lithographic prints, 89
Lock, Max, 220
Lockheed aircraft factory (Burbank, Calif.), *181*
Löftken, Alexander, 188
Logan Airport (Boston), 70
Lohmann, Karl B., 285n24
Lombards Bridge (Lombardsbrücke, Hamburg), 165, *166*
London, 24, 28, 32, 82, 83, 107, 114, 120, 126, 146, 147, 175
Long Beach (Calif.), 84
Long Island (N.Y.), 39
Loudon, John Claudius, 185; sketches of tree plantings, *186*

Lovejoy, D., 299n157
Low, Archibald M., 24
Lowe, Thaddeus S. C., 83
Luckiesh, Matthew, 158
Lufthansa AG, 4, 6, 285n17; 1929 spring schedule and air route plan, *7*
Luiz Cezar Fernandes Garden (Brazil), 142
Lunardi, Vincent, 18, 80, 82, 114
Lüneburg Heath (Germany), 271
Lurçat, André, 24, 133
Lusikkaniemi Point (Finland), 144–45, *145*
Lustgarten (Berlin), 123
Lyon, province of, 2

MacKaye, Benton, 226
MacLean, Alex, 245
Maentwrog Hydroelectric Power Station (Wales), 203
Magdeburger Börde (Germany), 188
Mahoney, Paul, 30
Malevich, Kazimir, 1, 136, 138, 285n1
Mallet-Stevens, Robert, 133
Manáos (Brazil), 144
Manchester (England), 219
manga art, 279–80
Manhattan, 24, 111, 113, 149; Rockefeller Center, *149*
Manning, Warren, 227
Manual de urbanismo (Brunner), 130
maps and map-making. *See* cartography
Maps Live, 11, 242
Marble, Duane, 219
Marc, Franz, 156
Maria Moors Cabot Foundation for Botanical Research, 196
Marine Corps Air Station El Toro. *See* El Toro Air Station (Orange County, Calif.)
Mariscal Sucre International Airport (Quito), 249
Marseilles, bay of, 2
Mary Miss Studio, 305n53
Maschsee (Hannover), 167
Maskelyne, Jasper, 160
Massachusetts Institute of Technology, 193, 201

Masson, André, 81
Matless, David, 108
Mattern, Hermann, 51, 160, 188; landscape design for Stuttgart airport, 52
Mattery, Garrick, 82–83
Mau, Bruce, 262–64
Maumee River (Ohio), 31
Maurice Rose Army Airfield (Frankfurt), 249
McCabe, Lida Rose, 157
McClintock, Miller, 30
McGuiness, William, 179
McHarg, Ian, 72, 108, 110, 220, 223–26, 228, 234
McMillan Plan for Washington, D.C., 112, 229
mechanical objectivity, 93
mechanical photography, 232
Meigs Field (Chicago), 249
Meisch, Francis, 44
Menhinick, Howard K., 30
Merionethshire (Wales), 203
Merleau-Ponty, Maurice, 14, 92, 239
Merrill, Elmer D., 196
Merrill, Vincent N., 193–94
Messel, Oliver, 160
Messter, Oskar, 89
Metropolitan Housing Council (Chicago), 299n7
metropolitanism, 112, 226
Meydenbauer, Albrecht, 291n64
Mia Lehrer and Associates, 305n53
Miami, 39
Michael Reese Hospital (Chicago), 299n7
Middletown (Conn.), 95
Mielziner, Jo, 160
Migge, Leberecht, 27
Milan, 88
Milky Way, 232
Miller, Lee, 153; camouflaged gardens of Linderhof Palace, *154*
Minneapolis (Minn.), 29, 30; Municipal Airport, 287n33
Miralles/Tagliabue, 305n53
Miss, Mary, 303n155
Mississippi River, 198
Missouri River, 50
Mitchell, Donald G., 3
Mitchell, William, 23, 79, 85, 90, 93, 244

mobile hedges, 182
Modern Camouflage (Breckenridge), 192
Modern Gardens and the Landscape (Kassler), 138
modernity, 7, 46, 133, 134, 140, 157
Moholy-Nagy, László, 10, 75, 81, 84, 103, 160, 231–32
Monck Mason, Thomas, 83
Monier, Robert B., 218–19, 300n40
Monson, Donald, 177
Montfaucon (France), 117
Montgolfier, Étienne and Joseph, 17–18; balloon, *19*
Mont Ventoux (France), 2, 93
Morris, Robert, 233
Morshed, Adnan, 128, 129
Mount Vernon (Va.), 57, *58*
Mulder, Jacopa, 71
Mumbower, L., 219
Mumford, Lewis, 108, 209, 226
Munich, 32, 66, 68, 153, 174, 240; aerial view, *155*
Munich-Riem Airport, 249
Museum of Modern Art (Rio de Janeiro), 141
Mussolini, Benito, 177

Nadar (Gaspard-Félix Tournachon), 80, 87–88, 101
Nansen, Odd, 34; airport design by, *35*
Naples, 88
Nason, George L., 160, 195
National Airport (Washington, D.C.), 20
national identities, 10, 11, 58–59, 122, 143
nature, 2, 13, 14, 82, 128, 129, 133, 141, 144–145, 146, 201, 204, 210, 224, 231, 258, 260, 271, 275, 282; and art, 15, 139, 207; bond with, 124; and the city, 114–15; as commodity, 14, 282; and conservation movement (Germany), 270; versus culture dichotomy, 281; ideas of, 251, 252; imitation of, 158–59, 162, 180, 184–85, 187; nature's nation, 279; nonhuman, 14, 15, 209, 245, 249; primordial, 270; reconnection with, 59, 176, 188; reserves, 144, 243, 249, 265–66, 268–70, 277, 305n44;

return to, 15; and technology, 20, 73, 123, 282; transformation of, 282; "true to," 88, 92, 189; writing, 115
Nature and Landscape Park Johannisthal. *See* Johannisthal Nature and Landscape Park (Berlin)
Natur-Park Südgelände (Berlin), 249–50
neoliberal policies, 251, 252, 259, 261, 272, 281
neotraditional style, 274
Neukölln (Berlin), 251, 257
Neutra, Richard, 26–27, 39, 285n1
Newark (N.J.), 110, 171
New Deal Relief and Public Works Program, 37
New Landscape in Art and Science, The (Kepes), 201, 230
New Romanticism, 254–56, 258
Newton, Norman, 160
New Vision, The (Moholy-Nagy), 75, 231
New York City, 24, 60, 81, 99, 110, 119, 146–50, 175, 219; aerial mosaic map of, *112*; Rockefeller Center, *148, 149*
New York Civilian Camouflage Council, 198
New York Harbor, 157, 198
New York International Airport, *61*
New York Times on camouflage, 158, 197
Niagara Falls, 115, 198
Nice (France), 81
Nichols, Chester W., 193
Nolen, John, 29–30, 40–41, 43, 113, 119, 142, 147; airport design by, *41*
Norman, Nigel, 28
Northern Rhodesia, 104
North Rhine–Westphalia, 243
Nuti, Lucia, 88
Nye, David E., 147, 170

Oakland (Calif.), golf course at airport in, 39
obelisks, 34
Oberammergau (Bavaria), 153, *154*
oblique aerial photographs, 90, 108, 214–15, 290n14
observation parking, 57

Odette Monteiro Garden (Brazil), 142
Oeser, Hans Ludwig, 231
Office of Civilian Defense (OCD, U.S.), 175–76, 187, 192
Ogburn, William Fielding, 26, 44
O'Hare Airport. *See* Chicago O'Hare International Airport
O'Keeffe, Georgia, 303n145
Oldbury (England), 204, 206; landscape design for nuclear power station, *206*
Olin, Laurie, 238
Olin Partnership, 306n53
Olmsted, Frederick Law, 229, 277, 279, 294n77
Omer-Decugis, Albert, 132
Onosaki, Masashi, 27–28, 52–53, 286n27, 289n106
On Photography (Sontag), 96
open space, 5, 17, 27, 130–31
Operation Gomorrah (1943), 165
Oppenheim, Dennis, 234
Oppenheimer, Michael, 238
Orange County (Calif.), 249, 272–81
Orange County Great Park (OCGP), 14, 250, 251, 272–82, *273, 276, 279, 280*
Orange County Great Park Corporation, 306n55
Organisation Todt, 189
Oswalt, Philipp, 293n145
Our World from the Air (Gutkind), 210
Outlook Tower (Edinburgh), 108
overlay method, 226–27

Pace Associates, 299n7
Pacific Ocean, 183
Packard, Edward L., 193
Paddington Station (London), 24
Palazzo d'Italia (NYC), 148
Palo Alto Airport (Calif.), 238, *239*
Pampulha Airport (Brazil), 141
Panama, 106, 130
panoramas, 83. *See also* balloon panoramas; bird's-eye panoramas
parallactic displacement, 94
Paraná River Delta (Argentina), 81
Parc de la Villette (Paris), 262–64